JAPAN STUDIES

Studies in Japanese History and Civilization

Japanese Government Documents
(of the Meiji Era)

JAPANESE GOVERNMENT DOCUMENTS

EDITED, WITH AN INTRODUCTION
BY
W. W. McLAREN, Ph.D.

Volume 2
(Pages 250-681)

ASIATIC SOCIETY OF JAPAN
TOKYO

Reprint edition published in 1979 by

UNIVERSITY PUBLICATIONS OF AMERICA, INC.
Washington, D.C.

ISBN: 0-89093-265-4

Library of Congress Catalog Card Number: 79-65472

Manufactured in the United States of America

PREFACE.

This collection of documents illustrates a brief but highly important period of about twenty-two years (1867-1889) in the history of modern Japan. During these years there was to be seen on one hand, the destruction of the old order, and on the other, the creation of a new. In the first of these processes our interest is very limited, and ends with the clearing away of the feudal institutions of government in 1871. That the spirit of feudalism continued to animate the nation is no mere conjecture ; but the manifestations of that spirit or the means adopted to foster or destroy it can hardly be shown by presenting relevant documents. It is the second of the processes, the reconstruction of the institutions of government, which holds our attention until the climax was reached in 1889. Here again it is necessary to indicate limits upon the scope of the documents, only the organisation for central and local government having been illustrated. The executive and legislative branches of government have received about equal treatment, whereas the judicial has been almost entirely neglected ; two documents, the "Law of the Organisation of the Courts of Justice," and " Regulations for carrying out the Law of the Organisation of the Courts of Justice," contain all the information which is given on that subject.

In dealing with the legislative branch of government I have given not only the documents which provide for the organisation of the various legislative bodies, but some others which serve to display the nature of the efforts of the people to obtain representative institutions and of the Government to prevent the too precipitate fulfilment of such popular desires. In the appendix will be found a number of speeches, papers, memorials and miscellaneous documents that seemed too interesting or too useful to omit, and for which no other suitable place could be found.

For the arrangement of the documents I must accept entire responsibility. My object has been to enable the student to follow chronologically the process by which the feudal system was destroyed, the administration, whether central or local, gradually organised, and the popular element cautiously admitted to some slight power in legislation. Explanations and cross references I have added in footnotes. I likewise accept all responsibility for the views expressed in the Introduction.

With few exceptions the documents are drawn from public sources. In each case the reference is given either to the Hōrei-Zensho (Complete Collection of Laws and Ordinances) or the Meiji-Shi-Yo (Collection of Laws of Meiji), or else the number and date of issue of the law is specifically stated. As for the translations, many are copied from the files of the *Japan Weekly Mail*, others are official, and the remainder were made for me by Mr. Iwao Murata, an Instructor in Keiōgijuku. While I am not able to vouch for the absolute accuracy of any of the translations, I have no reason to suppose that any serious errors have been made in them.

It only remains to thank the officers and members of the Council of the Asiatic Society of Japan for the interest which they have displayed in the work of compiling this collection, and for the advice and direction which I have received from them and especially from the retiring President, Mr. J. C. Hall; and to express my gratitude to Dr. D. S. Spencer, of Nagoya, for compiling the index.

W. W. McLaren.

Tōkyo, April 1914.

TABLE OF CONTENTS.

INTRODUCTION

DOCUMENTS

I.—THE RESTORATION

I.—THE RESIGNATION OF THE SHOGUN

II.—THE FIRST ORGANISATION OF THE CENTRAL GOVERNMENT

III. Organisation of the Central Government, 1885-89

JAPANESE GOVERNMENT DOCUMENTS

Volume 2

4—THE ORGANISATION FOR LOCAL GOVERNMENT.

1. OFFICIALS OF THE FU AND KEN.[1]

Fu Officials.	Ken Officials.
Chiji	Chiji
Gon-chiji	Gon-chiji
Dai-sangi	Dai-sangi
Gon-daisangi	Gon-daisangi
Shō-sangi	Shō-sangi
Gon-shōsangi	Daisakwan
Tenji	Gon-daisakwan
Gon-tenji	Shō-sakwan
Daisakwan	Gon-shōsakwan
Gon-daisakwan	Shishō
Shō-sakwan	Chōjō
Gon-shōsakwan	
Shishō	
Chōjō	

H-Z., 1871, 317.

2. OFFICIALS OF THE FU AND KEN (FU-KEN-KWANSEI).

(Dec. 9, 1871.)

Official Class.	Fu.	Ken.
3rd class	Chiji	
4th ,,	Gon-chiji	Chiji
5th ,,	Sangi	Gon-chiji
6th ,,	Gon-sangi	Sangi
7th ,,		Gon-sangi
8th ,,	Tenji	Tenji
9th ,,	Gon-tenji	Gon-tenji

1. *Cf.* the officials of the Han in 1870 as presented on p. 28.

Official Class.	Fu.	Ken.
10th ,,	Dai-sakwan	Dai-sakwan
11th ,,	Gon-daisakwan	Gon-daisakwan
12th ,,	Shō-sakwan	Shō-sakwan
13th ,,	Gon-shōsakwan	Gon-shōsakwan
14th ,,	Shishō	Shishō
15th ,,	Shusshi	Shusshi

The Gon-sangi is an office which need not necessarily be created.

H-Z., 1871, 375.

3. THE KEN-CHIJI'S DESIGNATION IS CHANGED.

(Dec. 13, 1871.)

The Ken-chiji is to be called the Ken-rei.

H-Z., 1871, 377.

4. REDUCTION OF THE NUMBER OF THE KEN.

(January 1, 1872.)

The number[1] of the Ken is reduced from 302 (September 25, 1871) to 72.

H-Z., 1871, 377.

5. A LIST OF THE FU AND KEN AND THE NUMBER OF GUN INTO WHICH EACH WAS DIVIDED.

(January 1, 1872.)

Name.	Province.	Number of Gun.

THE FU:—

Tōkyō	Musashi	4
Kyōto	Yamashiro and Tamba	11
Ōsaka	Settsu	7

1 *Vide* p. 33.

Name.	Province.	Number of Gun.

THE KEN :—

Name.	Province.	Number of Gun.
Hyōgo	Settsu	5
Iruma	Musashi	13
Niibari	Hitachi and Shimōsa	9
Utsunomiya	Shimodzuke	4
Watarai	Shima, Ise and Kii	8
Shidzuoka	Suruga	7
Gifu	Mino	21
Fukushima	Iwashiro and Iwaki	6
Morioka	Rikuchū	6
Sakata	Uzen and Ugo	2
Kanazawa	Kaga	4
Aikawa	Sado	3
Hamada	Iwami	6
Fukatsu	Bitchū and Bingo	17
Myōdō	Awa and Awaji	12
Kōchi	Tosa	7
Miuma	Chikugo	10
Ōita	Bungo	8
Kumamoto	Higo	9
Miyakonojō	Hyūga and Osumi	9
Nagasaki	Hizen and Iki	5
Ashigara	Sagami and Idzu	10
Haraki	Hitachi	5
Nara	Yamato	15
Nagoya	Owari	7
Yamanashi	Kai	4
Chikuma	Shinano and Hida	7
Taira	Iwaki	10
Aomori	Mutsu and Matsumaye	4
Akita	Rikuchū and Ugo	8
Nanao	Noto and Etchu	5
Toyooka	Tamba, Tajima and Tango	16
Shikawa	Harima	16

Name.	Province.	Number of Gun.
Hiroshima	Aki and Bingo	16
Kagawa	Sanuki	11
Fukuoka	Chikuzen	15
Kokura	Buzen	8
Imari	Hizen and Tsushima	11
Yashiro	Higo	6
Mimitsu	Hyūga	5
Niigata	Echigo	2
Kisaradzu	Awa and Kadzusa	13
Gumba	Kōdzuke	11
Sakai	Kawachi and Idzumi	20
Nukada	Mikawa and Owari	9
Ōtsu	Ōmi	6
Nagano	Shinano	6
Wakamatsu	Iwashiro	4
Yamagata	Uzen	3
Tsuruga	Wakasa and Echizen	6
Shinkawa	Etchu	3
Tottori	Inaba, Hoki and Oki	18
Hōjō	Mimasaka	12
Yamaguchi	Nagato and Suwō	12
Matsuyama	Iyo	10
Kanagawa	Musashi and Sagami	7
Saitama	Musashi	3
Imba	Shimōsa	9
Tochigi	Kōdzuke and Shimodzuke	8
Anotsu	Iga and Ise	12
Hamamatsu	Totomi	12
Nagahama	Ōmi	6
Sendai	Iwaki and Rikuzen	13
Ichinoseki	Rikuzen and Rikuchū	8
Oitama	Uzen	1
Fukui	Echizen	5
Kashiwazaki	Echigo	5

Name.	Province.	Number of Gun.
Shimane	Idzumo	10
Okayama	Bizen	8
Wakayama	Kii	7
Uwajima	Iyo	4

M-S-Y., V, 93-102.

6. RANKS OF THE FU AND KEN OFFICIALS (FU-KEN-KWANTO).

(January 6, 1872.)

The Officials of the 3rd class, the Fu-chiji, are to be of *chokunin* rank ; the Officials of the 4th, 5th, 6th and 7th classes are to be of *sonin* rank ; all the other officials from the 8th to the 15th classes are to be of *hannin* rank.

H-Z., 1871, 419.

7. REGULATIONS FOR THE KEN GOVERNMENT (KEN-CHI-JŌREI).

(January 6, 1872.)

1. Chiji. Where there is a Chiji, no Gon-chiji is to be appointed.

2. Sangi. There is to be but a single Sangi.

3. Gon-sangi. There is to be but a single Gon-sangi. He is to be appointed only in cases of necessity. The duty of the Sangi is to assist the Chiji, and to act for the Chiji during his absence, or if the office is vacant.

4. Tenji. The Tenji superintends the business of all the bureaux, of which the following is a list :—the Shomu-kwa (Bureau of General Affairs); Chō-shō-kwa (Bureau of Litiga-tion); Sozei-kwa (Bureau of Taxes); Sui-tō-kwa (Bureau of Finance).

5. Gon-tenji. In the absence of or during a vacancy the Gon-tenji acts for the Tenji. The other officers of the local administration are directed and controlled by the Tenji or the Gon-tenji.

H-Z., 1871, 420.

8. The Order of the Fu and Ken (Fu-Ken-Retsujun).

(January 31, 1872.)

The Fu ; Tōkyō, Kyōto, Ōsaka.

The Ken ; Kanagawa, Hyōgo, Nagasaki, Niigata, Saitama, Iruma, Ashigara, Kisaradzu, Imba, Niibari, Haraki, Gumba, Tochigi, Utsunomiya, Nara, Sakai, Anotsu, Watarai, Nagoya, Nukada, Hamamatsu, Shidzuoka, Yamanashi, Ōtsu, Nagahama, Gifu, Chikuma, Nagano, Sendai, Fukushima, Iwasaki, Waka-matsu, Ichinoseki, Morioka, Aomori, Yamagata, Oitama, Sakata, Akita, Tsuruga, Fukui, Kanazawa, Nanao, Shinkawa, Kashiwa-zaki, Aikawa, Toyooka, Tottori, Shimane, Hamada, Shikama, Hōjō, Okayama, Kukatsu, Hiroshima, Yamaguchi, Wakayama, Myōdō, Kagawa, Matsuyama, Uwajima, Kōchi, Fukuoka, Miuma, Kokura, Ōita, Imari, Kumamoto, Yashiro, Miyakonojō, Mimitsu, Kagoshima.

H-Z., 1871, 451.

9. The Offices of the Kochō and the Fuku-Kcchō are created.

(May 15, 1872.)

The Offices of the Shōya, Nanushi, Toshiyori, etc. (local officials of the old order) are all abolished. The offices of the Kochō (Chief Magistrate or Headman of a town or village) and the Fuku-kochō (Deputy Magistrate or Headman) are created.

H-Z., 1872, 88.

10. THE TŌKYŌ METROPOLITAN POLICE OFFICE (KEISHI-CHŌ).[1]

(January 15, 1874.)

The Keishi-chō is established in Tōkyō.

H-Z., 1874, 19.

11. CONSTITUTION AND RULES FOR THE CONDUCT OF BUSINESS OF THE TŌKYŌ METROPOLITAN POLICE OFFICE.

(Feb. 7, 1874.)

CONSTITUTION.

I. Chō (Chief). The Chō presides over the general police-affairs of the city of Tōkyō, and controls the Dai-keishi and other subordinate officials. He promotes and degrades officials of the *hannin* rank and below on the recommendation of the Dai-keishi and the Shō-keishi. He may receive instructions from the Sei-in with reference to national police-affairs.

II. Dai-keishi and Gon-daikeishi. These officials control and direct the Shō-keishi and other subordinates; they assist the Chō and represent him in his absence; they participate in the consultations upon the affairs of the office.

III. Shō-keishi and Gon-shō-keishi. These officials take charge of police affairs in accordance with the orders of the Dai-keishi. They preside over the branch offices in the large wards.

IV. Other and subordinate officials are the Dai-keibu and the Gon-daikeibu, Chū-keibu and the Gon-chūkeibu, the Shō-

---

1. This office was abolished in January 1877, and its functions were absorbed by the Department of Home Affairs. To perform those functions the office of the Chief Police Inspector (Daikeishi) was erected in the Department. However in January 1881 the Metropolitan Police Office was reconstituted in Tōkyō and has continued to exist till the present. See below Document No. 50.

keibu and the Gon-shōkeibu, and the Junsa of the 1st, 2nd, 3rd and 4th classes.

RULES FOR THE CONDUCT OF BUSINESS.

I. The cardinal purpose of the Metropolitan Police is to prevent evils and secure the public peace (administrative police, gyo-sei-keisatsu).

II. The functions of the office are classified under four heads, viz., rights, health, conduct, and political affairs.

The police must protect the rights of the people, and safeguard their property.

The police must take measures to prevent the spread of disease, and protect the lives of the people.

The police must suppress immoral conduct, and purify popular habits.

The police must search out and punish those guilty of political offences.

III. The jurisdiction of the Office is confined within the limits of Tōkyō-fu.

IV. If the administrative police does not prevent the commission of offences, and some person violates the law, that offender must be sought out and arrested (judicial police, shiho-keisatsu). The officials of the administrative police may act in such arrests, in accordance with the regulations governing public procurators (kenji) and the judicial police.

H-Z., 1874, 389 *et seq.*

12. REVISION OF THE PREFECTURAL GOVERNMENT REGULATIONS.

(April 8, 1875.)

The Bureau of Education (Gwakumu-kwa) is newly created, and the provisions concerning education and educational institutions are added to the Prefectural Government Regulations (Kenchi-Jōrei).

H-Z., 1875, 583.

13. REGULATIONS CONCERNING TEMPORARY RELIEF IN THE
PERFECTURES (Kyūmin-Ichijikyūjo-kisoku).

(July 12, 1875.)

I. To those who have lost their property in consequence
of natural calamity, and are unable to feed themselves, 3 go of
rice, 6 go of wheat, or 9 go of other grain for one male per
diem, and 2 go of rice, 4 go of wheat, or 6 go of other grain
for one female per diem are to be given for fifteen days. Those
who are of good parentage are to be excluded from the benefits
herein provided.

Adult males over seventy years of age and boys under
fifteen are to be treated as in the case of women.

II. To those who have lost their houses five *yen* in cash
is to be given for each house so destroyed upon the condition
that it be paid back within a term of five years in annual
instalments.

To those who have suffered in a lesser degree, three *yen*
in cash is to be lent under the same conditions as in the
previous case. Exceptions are made, however, in the cases of
those who live in rented houses or those who occupy houses
jointly with other people.

III. To those who find it difficult to obtain agricultural
tools, money is to be lent to the amount necessary for purchasing them, but not exceeding ten *yen* for each house.

IV. In case of an epidemic, the provisions of Article I.
are to be applied for the benefit of those who cannot feed themselves, but the circumstances must be communicated to the
Department of Home Affairs.

V. In case several villages or towns have simultaneously
suffered from great calamity, food shall be supplied, and, if
necessary, huts shall be built to provide temporary shelter.

VI. Provisions, seeds, and unhulled rice are to be supplied
in case of natural calamity.

VII. Money is to be lent for the purpose of purchasing

horses or oxen to replace those destroyed by great natural calamities.

In the cases contemplated in Articles VI and VII, the circumstances must be communicated to the Home Office and advice received therefrom before and dispositon of the cases can be effected.

H-Z., 1875, 659.

14. THE FUNCTIONS OF THE KEIBU (POLICE SERGEANTS) AND THE JUNSA (POLICEMEN).

(Oct. 24, 1874.)

The Keibu take charge of police affairs in the Ken, exclusive of Tōkyō-fu, under the supervision of the Chiji, and control the Junsa.

Those who have been called Rasotsu are to be called Junsa.

H-Z., 1875, 752.

15. REVISION OF THE PREFECTURAL GOVERNMENT REGULATIONS.

(Nov. 30, 1875.)

The Kenchi-jōrei is abolished and the Fuken-shokusei and the Fuken-Jimushōtei are notified in lieu thereof.

CONSTITUTION (Fuken-Shokusei).

I. The Chiji. Where there is a Chiji there is no Gon-chiji.
II. Gon-Chiji.
III. Kami.   Where there is a Kami there need be no Gon-Kami.
IV. Gon-Kami.

These officials execute all laws and ordinances, maintain peace and protect the people, impose taxes, encourage trade, education, etc., etc. They are charged with the supervision of markets and open ports, if any such exist in the bounds of their jurisdiction, and they are held responsible for the management of these affairs.

They are to report concerning the behavior of officials of *sonin* rank ; and it is in their discretion to inquire into the deportment and efficiency of officials of *hannin* rank, and to appoint or remove them. In case of necessity they may ask for the asistance of a chindai (garrison).

V. The Sanji

VI. The Gon-sanji

In the Fu there may be both these officials, but in the Ken there is to be no Gon-sanji if there is a Sanji. These officials assist the Chiji and Kami in the management of affairs, and represent them in their absence.

The other subordinate officials are under the supervision and control of the Chiji or Kami. The functions of the Sakwan and the Shishō are divided into six bureaux (kwa), viz , General Affairs (Shomu-kwa), Trade (Kwangyō-kwa), Taxes (Sojei kwa), Public Safety (Keiho-kwa), Education (Gwakumu-kwa), and Finance (Suitō kwa).

RULES FOR THE CONDUCT OF BUSINESS (Fu-Ken-Jimushōtei).

According to the new Business Regulations (Fu-Ken-Jimushōtei), the prefectural authorities have the following powers and functions :—

To grant prizes other than those provided for regularly by law.

To grant relief other than that provided for regularly by law.

To establish or abolish government branch-offices.

To establish or abolish shrines or temples.

To employ foreigners other than those employed as teachers.

To permit the establishment or cause the suspension or abolition of banks or other corporations.

To manage the affairs concerning the bestowal or deprivation of allowances or prizes.

To grant mining rights.

To grant copy-rights.

To grant patent-rights to inventors.

To establish public schools.

To defray extraordinary expenditures, and expenditures in excess of the sums fixed in the budget.

To contrive and execute plans for the safekeeping of government funds.

To erect or improve Imperial sepulchres, shrines, government offices, official residences, and jails.

To change the terms of redemption of debts or to cancel them.

To dispose of grains, etc. received.

To receive cash or grains other than those regularly provided for by law.

To take such action as is necessary to restore taxes, miscellaneous government-funds, and certificates, etc. when they are lost or injured in consequence of robbery, fire, storm, flood, or other unavoidable causes.

To determine the sums to be collected upon lands and title-deeds.

To lessen the taxes upon lands that have decayed or suffered damage, and to exempt from taxes lands which cannot be used.

To impose, abolish, or change the rates of local taxes.

To subdivide or unite districts (cho) or villages (mura), or change their names or boundaries.

To grant certain tracts of land for the use of government offices.

To determine the location of parks and cemeteries, and to

investigate celebrated places and buildings of historical importance.

To create ports, to change the courses of rivers, and erect
embankments, roads, and bridges.

To reclaim public forests, to dispose of public lands and
buildings as well as the trees and stones found therein.

To superintend the reclamation of private forests so as to
regulate the sources of streams and prevent the outflow of
earth and sand.

To establish regulations for the local police.
(The exercise of these and a few other powers requires the
approval of the Department concerned.)

To take a census.

To make a record relating to the government and its results.

To allow shizoku to be classed among the commoners.

To inquire into the expenditures of towns.

To grant prizes and relief according to the regulations.

To grant rights for the manufacture and sale of commodities in accordance with regulations.

To use the school-funds in accordance with the regulations.

To accept contributions for schools, hospitals, etc., and
expend them.

To defray expenses the amounts of which are determined
beforehand.

To grant capitalised pensions within the regulations.

To dispose of miscellaneous articles which are not being
used.

To repair government offices, official residences, jails, etc.

To collect taxes upon land, title-deeds, etc. to the amount
determined beforehand.

To reduce the taxes upon land, or exempt from all
taxes for a time as fixed by the regulations.

To inquire into and determine the price of land, and
register title-deeds upon the sale or transfer of land.

To prolong the period for the payment of taxes, within a

period of two months, in the cases of those who have lost their dwellings by fire or flood.

To dispose of fields or moors by calling for tenders in accordance with the provisions of the regulations.

To lend public lands and embankments according to the provisions of the regulations, and upon condition that they must be returned at the request of the government authorities.

To dispose of lands reclaimed from the sea, according to the provisions of the regulations.

To accept contributions of land when it is convenient to do so.

To determine the ownership of the contributed lands according to the proper regulations.

To dispose of the lands occupied by Shintō and Buddhist priests (excepting the grounds of temples or shrines), in accordance with the regulations.

To offer certain pieces of land as sites for public, middle or primary schools.

To repair embankments, roads, and bridges to the extent of the funds provided for that purpose.

To grant permission for the dredging of rivers, the repairing of ports and harbours, and the construction of hospitals and work-houses, etc. at private expense.

To sanction the establishment of transportation agencies for the convenience of the public.

To permit the construction or modification of roads and bridges of the third class, at private expense.

To sanction the imposition of tolls upon roads and bridges, etc., in order to meet the expenses of construction.

To dispose of fallen or dead trees upon the public land in accordance with the proper regulations.

To dispose of public buildings which are no longer used in accordance with the proper regulations.

To lend public buildings and warehouses in accordance with the proper regulations.

To dispose of animals, plants, earth and stones belonging to the public lands in accordance with the proper regulations.

To construct avenues.

To hire foreigners as teachers.

(The exercise of these powers and a few others does not require the approval of the Department concerned, but it is necessary to report the case after it has been disposed of.)

H-Z., 1875, 769-777.

16. RULES FOR DISCIPLINARY PUNISHMENT OF OFFICIALS.

(Imp. Dec. No. 34, April 14, 1876.)

I. For the future all offences committed by officials in respect to their duties—the same not being private offences—shall be punished by the Chiefs of the Departments to which such officials belong.

II. The penalties shall be three in number, viz., reprimand, confiscation of pay, and dismissal from office.

III. Reprimand is the mildest form of punishment, a lecture of censure being given by the Chief of the Department.

IV. Confiscation of pay consists of deprivation of salary for a period of not less than half a month and not more than three months.

In carrying this out there shall be confiscated every month half of the salary for that month, and when the total sum has been thus collected it shall be sent in to the bureau of Finance.

V. As regards a person to be punished with dismissal, in the case of officials of *sonin* rank there shall be sent in to the Government, upon the desire of the Chief of the Department, a written statement of the circumstances, after which the said official shall be dismissed, and his certificate of rank restored to the Government.

Note. In the case of an official to be dismissed, but not

by way of punishment, the Chief of the Department shall explain the matter and cause such an official to send in his resignation and thereafter he shall be dismissed.

VI. The Chiefs of the several Departments shall inflict penalties upon their subordinates both of *sonin* and *hannin* ranks, at their own discretion.

VII. Officials of *sonin* rank in the Fu and Ken shall be punished by the Prime Minister, and *hannin* officials of the Fu, or Ken or of the Police Department by their Chiefs.

VIII. Judges (Hanji) of the fourth class and below shall be punished by the Chief of the Department of Justice. Those officials of the Fu and Ken who hold the additional office of Hanji shall punish their subordinate officials of *hannin* rank, only after having consulted with some other official of the Fu or Ken, who is of *sonin* or higher rank.

IX. When the Governor of a Fu or Ken or the Chief of the Police Office shall punish a subordinate official of *hannin* rank other than by reprimand, he shall take such steps as he deems fit for enforcing either confiscation of pay or dismissal from office, and shall at once report the same to the Minister of the Department of Justice. When Fu or Ken officials who hold the additional office of Hanji punish their subordinates of *hannin* rank by confiscation of pay or dismissal from office, they may take such steps as they think fit, and shall at once report the same to the Minister of the Department of Justice.

X. Those officials who may be guilty of intentional private offences shall, even though they may have committed those offences in their public capacity, be handed over to the judicial authorities and their Chief shall not have any power to deal with them.

J.W.M., 1876, pp. 396-97.

17. INSTRUCTIONS TO BE OBSERVED IN INFLICTING DISCIPLINARY
PUNISHMENTS.[1]

(Imp. Dec. No. 35; Apl. 14, 1876.)

I. The several Chiefs of Departments shall always superintend their subordinates, and in case any faults are committed by the latter, shall deal with them according to the rules relating to disciplinary punishments.

II. By "faults" are meant those results caused by errors, inadvertence, or negligence. The results of dilatoriness are also to be considered "faults." Those persons who by not regulating their behaviour bring discredit upon the service shall also be considered as guilty of a "fault" and shall be liable to punishment.

III. Those faults which occation evil results shall be considered grave faults, but those which occasion evil results which can be rectified, or those which do not cause evil results shall be considered as being lighter.

It is, however, left to the discretion of the Chief to determine the lightness or gravity of the fault according to the circumstances of the case.

IV. In cases where several officials of a Department unite in the commission of a fault, the responsibility for the same shall rest upon their immediate superior—in a Department with the Chief, in an Office with the Head thereof, in a bureau (police) with the Superintendent of the same, and in all minor offices with the officials charged with their supervision. The official next to the Chief and those coming after him shall be dealt with proportionately. In the cases of subordinate officials who have received the consent of their superiors to carry out some matter in accordance with their own ideas, the responsibility shall rest both with the superiors and the subordinates alike. In the cases of subordinate officials who commit faults while in the execution of matters within their duty or powers and act

---

1. This document and the preceding one relate to both the central and local government services.

according to their own ideas, their superiors are not responsible. But those subordinates who exceed their duty or powers and act according to their own ideas, shall be deemed to be guilty in a graver degree.

V. In cases of subordinate officials themselves detecting their own errors and sending in inquiries as to whether they shall or shall not tender their resignations in consequence, their Chief shall institute inquiries into the matter, and shall deal in accordance with the rules with those who are merely unintentional offenders; but those who are intentional and wilful offenders, who ought to be delivered up to the judicial authorities, shall be handed over to the latter by the Chief, either to the Minister of the Department of Justice, or else to the Kenji, or in places where no Kenji is stationed to the Hanji. Should the judicial authorities ascertain clearly that the offence was not intentionally committed, or that the offender is not liable to be punished under the Criminal Code, the offender shall be returned to the Chief of the Department, who shall then deal with him according to the rules.

VI. It is not permitted to re-employ persons who have been dismissed as a punishment, unless after the expiration of a period of two years or more.

VII. Whenever it is desired to employ at some other government Department anyone who has been previously dismissed from office—whether as a punishment or otherwise—reference must be made in each case to his former Chief, and inquiry made as to his opinion of the person to be employed.

VIII. In the case of an official being dismissed, but not as a punishment, his Chief shall explain the matter and cause him to send in his resignation. Those who do not accept these directions and refuse to send in their resignations, shall be dismissed at once.

IX. In the cases of those persons who, during their tenure of some former office, have committed faults which come to light after they have been appointed to some other office, or of those who themselves confess their errors, reference shall be made to the Chief of the Department to which they formerly belonged and punishment shall then be inflicted by their new Chief.

J.W.M., 1876, p. 397.

18. TERMS OF SERVICE OF PREFECTURAL OFFICIALS (KENKWAN-NINKI-REI).

(Imp. Notif. No. 75, July 27, 1876.)

I. The term of office of the Prefect (Kenrei) is fixed at twelve years. Every third year he must submit to an inspection with regard to the efficiency of his administration.

II. He must serve a term of three years as Assistant-Prefect, and if he demonstrates his efficiency in that term, he may be raised to the rank of Prefect. Fifty *yen* shall be added to his monthly salary, if he proves efficient for the next three years; the same shall be done again, and he shall be raised to *chokunin* rank if he proves the same during the next three years. He may continue in office after the expiration of his term.

III. The Prefect shall fix his original domicile in the prefecture in which he holds office.

IV. A pension[1] equal to ten times as much as his monthly salary shall be granted him upon his retirement after twelve years' service. The ordinary regulations for money grants shall apply to Prefects who have held other offices before their service as Prefect began, in respect of those former offices. The same applies to those who remain in office after the expiration of their term of office, and in addition they shall be

---

1. The word "pension" is obviously incorrectly used here, for the sum mentioned was not granted annually. According to this provision a Prefect upon retiring after twelve years' service received a gratuity of *yen* 2,500. See the list of salaries given in the next document.

entitled to receive a grant equal to half a month's salary per annum during their further service.

V. The Sanji has no fixed term of office; as in the case of the Prefect, he becomes a Sanji only after he has discharged efficiently the duties of his office as Gon-Sanji during a period of three years.

VI. Every third year he must submit to an inspection with regard to the efficiency of his administration. If he has been exceedingly diligent a reward equal to one month's salary shall be granted him.

VII. Every third year the Sakwan shall submit to an inspection with regard to the efficiency of his administration. If he proves to have been exceedingly diligent a reward equal to one third of a month's salary shall be granted him.

VIII. Anyone who is to be promoted to *sonin* rank, or whose salary is to be increased must come up to the capital and have his elevation proclaimed according to proper rites. It is not permissible that he should be so elevated in the place where he is to serve.

H-Z., 1876, 322.

19. CLASSES AND SALARIES OF PREFECTURAL OFFICIALS.

(Jan. 16, 1877).

Class.	Monthly Salary.	Name of Office.
4th	*Yen* 250	Fu-chiji and Kenrei.
5th	,, 200	Gon-chiji and Gon-rei.
6th	,, 100	Daishokikwan.
7th	,, 80	Shō-shokikwan.
8th	,, 60	Ittō-zoku.
9th	,, 50	Nitō-zoku.
10th	,, 45	Santō-zoku.
11th	,, 40	Shitō-zoku.

Class.	Monthly Salary.	Name of Office.
12th ... ... „	35	... Gotō-zoku.
13th ... ... „	30	... Rokutō-zoku.
14th ... ... „	25	... Shichitō-zoku.
15th ... ... „	20	... Hachitō-zoku.
16th ... ... „	15	... Kutō-zoku.
17th ... ... „	12	... Jittō zoku.

H-Z., 1877, p. 139.

20. THE CHIEF POLICE INSPECTOR (Daikeishi).[1]

(Imp. Notif. No. 7, Jan. 16, 1877.)

The Chief Police Inspector (Daikeishi) of the Home Office shall take charge of the Police Affairs of Tōkyō-Fu.

H.-Z., 1877, 141.

21. FINES (Bakkin).

(Imp. Dec. No. 13, Jan. 29, 1877.)

Anyone who violates the regulations issued by the Fu or Ken authorities is liable to a fine not exceeding *Yen* 1.50.

H-Z., 1877, 12.

22. REGULATIONS FOR THE ORGANISATION OF GUN, KU[2], CHO, AND SON. (Imp. Dec. No. 17, July 22, 1878.)

I. Fu and Ken shall be subdivided into Gun (Rural Divisions), Ku (Cities), Cho (Towns), and Son (Villages).

---

1. *Supra* p. 256, foot note.

2. " Ku," in the modern use of the term, designates a ward of a city, but in 1878 it was used both in its modern connotation and as meaning also a city except in the cases of the Fu, where it evidently referred to merely a ward.

II. The extent and names of Gun, Cho, and Son shall remain as before.

III. If a Gun is too extensive and consequently inconvenient for administration it shall be divided into several Gun.

IV. The three Fu (Tōykō, Kyōto and Ōsaka) and the five open ports (Yokohama, Kobe, Nagasaki, Niigata and Hakodate), and other densely populated centres shall be known as Ku, and in case of their size being inconveniently large each of them shall be subdivided into several Ku.

V. The Chief Official of the Gun shall be the Gun-chō, and of the Ku the Ku-chō. A number of small sized Gun may be presided over by a single Gun-chō.

VI. The Chief Official of the Cho or Son shall be the Ko-chō. A number of Cho or Son may be presided over by a single Ko-chō.

(The succeeding articles were appended by Imp. Dec. No. 14, 1880.)

VII. In islands where it is impossible to carry out the regulations here prescribed, some other system of administration may be adopted.

VIII. The boundaries and names of the existing Ku, Gun, Cho, and Son may be changed to suit the convenience of the locality, and upon the petition of the people.

IX. In the cases of the changes contemplated in Articles III, IV, VII, and VIII, the Fu-chiji or Ken-rei shall refer the matter to the Home office (Naimushō) and ask for the Government's approval. In the case of changes contemplated in the boundaries or names of the Cho or Son the consent of the Home Minister only is necessary.

H-Z., 1878, 11.

23. REGULATIONS CONCERNING THE PREFECTURAL ASSEMBLY.

(Imp. Dec. No. 18, July 22, 1878.)

CHAPTER I. GENERAL PROVISIONS.

I. The Prefectural Assembly (Fu-Ken-Kwai) shall consult upon the budget of the expenditures which are to be defrayed out of the local taxes, and upon the means of raising the local taxes.

II. The meetings of the Prefectural Assembly are of two kinds ; ordinary, which meet at stated times, and extraordinary, which are called together upon special occasions.

III. Whether at ordinary or extraordinary meetings all bills must be initiated by tl e Governor (Fu-chiji or Ken-rei).

IV. The extraordinary meetings of the Assembly shall not proceed to any business other than that for the consideration of which the meetings have been called together.

V. All matters which involve the expenditure of local funds shall be brought into the Prefectural Assembly for consideration, the resolutions of the Assembly can only be carried out after they have been approved by the Governor. If the Governor thinks it wise to veto such resolutions, he must have his veto confirmed by the Home Minister.

VI. At the opening of the ordinary meeting of the Assembly in each year a report of the local tax revenues and expenditures shall be made.

VII. At an ordinary meeting a member or several members, who intend to make a representation to the Government as to affairs which affect the prefecture, must first obtain the consent of the Chairman, and then the motion may be brought into the Assembly. When the motion has been seconded and supported by an absulote majority of the members, it shall be presented to the Home Minister through the Chairman.

VIII. The Prefectural Assembly shall consult upon matters relating to the prefecture on the request of the Governor.

IX. The Prefectural Assembly shall form its own rules of procedure, subject to the approval of the Governor.

CHAPTER II. ELECTIONS.

X. Every Gun (Division) or Ku (City or ward) shall elect five members or less according to its population.

XI. The Chairman and Vice-Chairman shall be elected from among the members of the Assembly, but the Governor must approve of their election and report the same to the Home Minister.

XII. The Chairman shall appoint a Clerk, who shall attend to miscellaneous affairs. His salary shall be paid out of the funds of the Assembly.

XIII. Male inhabitants, except as hereinafter stated, who are full twenty-five years of age, who have their original domiciles and have lived more than three years in the prefecture, and who have been paying during those years land-tax to the amount of ten *yen* or more, shall be eligible for election to the Assembly. Persons falling under the following categories are not eligible :—

1. Lunatics and idiots.

2. Persons who have been sentenced to imprisonment at hard labor for a year or for a longer term.

3. Persons who have been declared bankrupt and have not yet discharged their liabilities.

4. Officials and teachers.

XIV. Male inhabitants, except as hereinafter stated, who are full twenty-five years of age, who have their domiciles in the Gun or Ku concerned, and have been paying land-tax to the amount of five *yen* or more shall constitute the electorate.

Persons falling under categories 1, 2, 3, of the preceding Article are not qualified to vote.

XV. In order to hold an election, the Governor shall proclaim that the election meeting shall be opened in a certain month, then the Gun-chō and Ku-chō in every Gun and Ku shall determine the date of the election and shall notify the people at least fifteen days beforehand.

XVI. Voting shall take place at the Gun or Ku Office on the appointed date. The Gun-chō or Ku-chō shall preside over the election.

The voting may take place at other places than the Gun or Ku Office.

XVII. The method of casting the ballot is as follows :— the elector having received a balloting paper from the Chō of the Gun or Ku, shall write upon it his own name and age and those of the candidates for whom he wishes to vote. A plurality is sufficient to elect. In case of a tie, the older candidate shall be declared elected, and if two candidates are of the same age one shall be chosen by lot.

Voting by proxy is permitted.

XVIII. When the poll is closed the Chō shall examine into the legality of the ballots by reference to the voter's list, and into the eligibility of the persons elected by consulting the list of eligible persons.

In the case of an illegal election, or of the non-acceptance of office by an elected person, the candidate with the next greatest number of votes shall be declared to have been elected.

XIX. When the examination into the eligibility of the elected persons has been completed the Chō of the Gun or Ku shall summon the candidates elect to attend at the Gun or Ku Office, and hand to them their certificates of election, and receive receipts therefor from them.

Thereafter the Chō of the Gun or Ku shall publish the names of the successful candidates.

XX. If one and the same person has been elected by more than one Gun or Ku, he shall choose freely for which Gun or Ku he shall sit.

XXI. The term of office shall be four years, one half of the members retiring every two years. Those who shall retire in the second year of the first Assembly shall be chosen by lot.

XXII. The Chairman and Vice-Chairman shall be elected for terms of two years at every renewal of the members of the Assembly.

XXIII. In the case of the two preceding Articles, retiring members of the Assembly and the retiring Chairman and Vice-Chairman shall be eligible for re-election.

XXIV. A by-election may be held when any member of the Assembly has been disqualified by coming under any of the categories mentioned in Article XIII, or by removing his domicile, or when a vacancy has been caused by the death of a member.

Anyone who refuses to attend the meeting of the Assembly shall be struck off the list of members, and a by-election shall be held to fill his place.

Chapter III. Debates.

XXV. No debate can be begun until one half of all the members are present.

XXVI. A decision shall be arrived at by an absolute majority of the members present, and in case of a tie the Chairman shall cast the deciding vote.

XXVII. The Governor or his Deputy shall be allowed to attend the sessions of the Assembly for the purpose of explaining the objects of a bill, but he shall not have any vote in the decision of the question.

XXVIII. The public shall be admitted to the meetings of the Assembly. A session may be held behind closed doors by the request of the Governor or at the order of the Chairman.

XXIX. The members of the Assembly shall be allowed to debate a question as long as they desire. No criticism of the personal character of a member shall be permitted.

XXX. To maintain order during the sessions of the Assembly is one of the duties of the Chairman.

If any member infringes the rules of order, the Chairman shall request him to desist; if the member refuses to obey the order of the Chairman he shall be ejected; if a member resorts to violent conduct he shall be handed over to the police.

CHAPTER IV.   OPENING AND CLOSING.

XXXI. The Prefectural Assembly shall be opened in March every year. The session shall last not longer than thirty days, and shall be opened and closed by the Governor. The Governor may prolong the session if he is so requested by the Assembly, but in that event the Governor shall immediately inform the Home Minister of the fact and give reasons for his action.

XXXII. The Governor may summon an extraordinary meeting of the Assembly if the circumstances call for it. But in such a case he shall at once inform the Home Minister of his action, and give reasons therefor.

XXXIII. If the debate is such as to disturb the peace of the country, or is contrary to laws and regulations, the Governor shall suspend the meeting, and ask for instructions from the Home Minister.

XXXIV. If the debate threatens to disturb the peace of the country the Home Minister may dissolve the Assembly.

XXXV. When the Home Minister has dissolved any Assembly a new election of members shall be held.

H-Z., 1878, 12 ff.

24. CONSTITUTION AND POWERS OF THE FU AND KEN GOVERNMENTS.[1]

(Imp. Dec. No. 32, July 25, 1878.)

CONSTITUTION.

There shall be a Fu-chiji (Governor) in every Fu, and a Ken-rei (Prefect) in every Ken.

---

1. The Japanese names used in these documents for local areas and their English equivalents are as follows :—Fu, of which there three, is translated by "city"; Ken by "province," Ku by " urban division," Gun by " rural division," Cho by " urban district," and Son by " rural district." The officials are respectively the Fu-chiji (Governor), Kenrei (Prefect), Ku-chō (Urban Division Magistrate Gun chō (Rural Division Magistrate), Cho-chō (Urban District Magistrate, Son-chō (Rural District Magistrate).

I. The Governor or Prefect shall exercise full authority over all administrative matters in the district under his jurisdiction, and shall enforce the laws of the Empire and the instructions of the Government throughout the same.

II. The Governor or Prefect shall be under the general control of the Minister for Home Affairs; but in matters relating to the special business of other Departments of State, he shall receive instructions from the Ministers of those Departments.

III. The Governor or Prefect may, if he deems it necessary, institute a special system for the enforcement of the laws and the instructions of the Government, and proclaim the same throughout his City or Prefecture; in cases where he is authorised to use his own discretion as to the method of enforcing such, according to the circumstances, he may frame such regulations as he may think fit, and proclaim the same throughout his City and Prefecture; but in such cases, he shall, immediately after having issued such a proclamation, make a report of the same to the Minister of the Department concerned.

IV. If the proclamation so issued or the steps so taken by a Governor or Prefect should be deemed to be contrary to the tenor of the laws, or the instructions of the Government, or to be in excess of his power, the First Minister of State or the Minister of the Department concerned may order the same to be cancelled.

V. In dealing with matters requiring previous instruction from the Minister of a Department concerned, the Governor or Prefect shall conform to the regulations in that behalf to be found below.

VI. The Governor or Prefect is empowered to levy the local taxes, and thereout to defray the expenses of his City or Prefecture. Both estimates and definite accounts of these shall be laid before the Ministers of Home Affairs and Finance; and, in places where there is a City or Provincial Assembly, the estimates and accounts shall be submitted to that body for deliberation.

VII. The Governor or Prefect is empowered to appoint, dismiss, promote or degrade the subordinate officers of his City or Prefecture, and to assign them their duties.

VIII. The Governor or Prefect is empowered to appoint, dismiss, promote or degrade the Magistrates and clerks of Rural Divisions (Gun) and shall have the general direction and supervision of the affairs of such Divisions.

IX. In case of extraordinary occurrences (such as rebellions, riots, etc.) the Governor or Prefect is empowered to take such steps as the circumstances may demand in concert with the Commanding Officer of the nearest garrison (chindai) or branch barracks.

X. The Governor or Prefect is empowered to call meetings of the City or Provincial Assembly or to suspend its deliberations.

XI. The Governor or Prefect shall prepare bills and submit them to the Fu or Ken Assembly, and is empowered to approve or reject the decisions of that body.

SECRETARY AND ASSISTANT SECRETARY.

In a City one officer of each of these grades shall be appointed ; in a Prefecture only one of them shall be appointed. However in a Prefecture, where there is an Open Port, and the business to be transacted is considerable, one of each of these officers may, upon an application to that effect being granted, be appointed as in the case of a City.

I. The Secretaries shall assist the Governor or Prefect in the administration of the district.

II. In the absence of the Governor or Prefect or in other like cases a Secretary shall be appointed to act in his behalf.

CLERKS (1-10th CLASSES).

They shall take their orders from the Governor or Prefect, and shall severally transact the miscellaneous business of the local government.

INSPECTORS OF POLICE (1-10TH CLASSES).

They shall take their orders from the Governor or Prefect and conduct all police matters in the City or Prefecture.

MAGISTRATES OF RURAL DIVISIONS.

Gun-chō (this officer has rank corresponding to that of regular officers of the 8th class). One officer in each Rural Division (Gun).

I. The salary of the Gun-chō shall be fixed according to the circumstances of the district by the Governor or Prefect at a sum not exceeding 80 *yen* per month and shall be paid out of the local taxes.

II. The Gun-chō shall be appointed from among persons borne on the register rolls of the City or Prefecture in which the appointment is held.

III. The Gun-chō shall take his instructions from the Governors or Prefect and shall enforce the laws and instructions of the Government throughout his Division, and generally administer the affairs of the Division.

IV. In matters the management of which has been assigned to him by virtue of laws, instructions, or regulations, or has been specially entrusted to him by the Governor or Prefect, the Gun-chō shall act as he may think fit according to the circumstances, and afterwards make a report to the Governor or Prefect.

V. Should any measure adopted by the Gun-chō be deemed improper, the Governor or Prefect may order its withdrawal.

VI. The Gun-chō shall exercise supervision over the Kochō.

CLERKS OF RURAL DIVISIONS (GUN).

These officers have rank corresponding to those of regular officers of the 10-17th classes. Their number is indefinite.

The salaries[1] of clerks of Rural Divisions (Gun) shall be fixed according to the circumstances of the locality by the Governor or Prefect at a sum not exceeding 20 *yen* per month and

---

1. The salary provision was repealed by Notification No. 45, 1878.

shall be paid out of the local taxes. Their appointment, promotion, etc. shall be made by the Governor or Prefect upon the recommendation of the Gun-chō.

Magistrates and Clerks of Urban Divisions (Ku) shall stand in all respects upon the same footing as Magistrates and Clerks of Rural Divisions (Gun).

POWERS OF GOVERNORS AND PREFECTS.

In dealing with any of the following matters the Governor or Prefect must obtain the previous sanction of the Department specially concerned in each case :—

I. The appointment of a Gun-chō over a portion of, or over more than one Gun, and the establishment of an Urban Division or Divisions (Ku).[1]

II. The re-establishment of the boundaries of a Rural or Urban Division, and the incorporation into one District of outlying lands belonging to another.

III. Fixing the amount of the expenditures to be defrayed out of the National Treasury for the service of the year.

IV. The payment or receipt of Government money in cases where no precedents or regulations exist.

V. Framing rules for the custody of Government money, and the system for the transmission of the same by means of Bills of Exchange, and for depositing the same.

VI. The construction of public buildings and prisons.

VII. Granting permission for the deferred payment of taxes by persons who have sustained injury through floods or drought.

VIII. Granting permission to persons who have been rendered homeless by floods or fire to defer the payment of taxes for more than two months after the time at which the same would otherwise be payable.

IX. Changing the class of land.

---

1. Repealed by Imp. Notif. No. 38. 1881.

X. Reducing the amount of the land-tax according to change in the value of land.

XI. The appraisment of land, and fixing the amount of the tax accordingly ; provided that the fixing of the amount of the land-tax upon land gone out of cultivation, or upon waste land on the same being reclaimed, and upon newly cultivated land at the expiration of the period (during which it has been free of taxation) will constitute exceptions to this rule.

XII. The execution of public works upon rivers, harbours, roads, embankments, bridges, land-cultivation, etc., which extend beyond the limits of the City or Prefecture, or of which the expenses are to be defrayed from the National Treasury independently of the fixed annual grant.

XIII. Granting permission to defer for more than six months the repayment of money lent by the Government, or absolutely waiving repayment of the same.

XIV. Felling timber in forests belonging to the Govern-ment ; provided that this does not include cutting trees or bamboos in Government forests of the third class, to be used for embanking and repairing water-courses and roads.

XV. The sale of Government land or buildings and the timber and stones thereof.

XVI. The purchase of land for official uses.

XVII. The re-settlement of the boundaries of land granted, free of taxation, to Shintō and Buddhist temples.

XVIII. Fixing a standard of value for wines and spirits for the purpose of assessing the amount of taxes to be levied thereon.

XIX. The sale of Government forests.

XX. Prohibiting the felling of timber in forests of both Government and private property.

XXI. Determining the ownership, between Government aud private persons, of forests, or of trees or bamboos therein.

XXII. The settlement of the boundaries of mines leased to private persons.

XXIII. Allowing in favor of lessees deferred or diminished payment of, or complete relief from, the rent of mines.

XXIV. The treatment of offenders against the mining laws.

XXV. The exchange of obsolete gold or silver coins, or defaced currency.

XXVI. Matters concerning foreigners travelling in the interior.

XXVII. Matters concerning foreigners living outside the foreign settlements.

XXVIII. Leasing ground in the foreign settlements to foreigners by public auction.

XXIX. Granting permission for marriages between natives and foreigners.

XXX. Paying out the subsidies to schools otherwise than as laid down by the regulations in that behalf.

XXXI. The suppression of p ivate schools.

XXXII. Making contracts with foreigners under his official title of Governor or Prefect.

XXXIII. Contracting, under his official title, loans of money which will have to be repaid out of the treasury.

XXXIV. Granting rewards otherwise than as laid down by the regulations or precedents.

XXXV. Dealing with applications for the establishment, re-establishment, restitution, etc., of Shintō and Buddhist temples, having the effect of increasing the total number.[1]

In matters the conduct of which has been placed absolutely in the hands of Governors or Prefects by virtue of decrees, proclamations, notifications or orders, or in matters governed by regulations or precedents, Governors or Prefects are to act on their own responsibility and should not seek the previous sanction of their superior authorities. Nevertheless, where the regulation or precedent in the case cannot under the circumstances be followed, but special action is necessary, they may

---

1. Added by Imperial Notification No. 61, 1880.

apply for such sanction, the grounds for doing so being set forth in the application.

In matters which merely pass through the hands of the Governors or Prefects ministerially under the provisions of any law or regulation, such as applications for licenses for the formation of companies, for licenses to work mines, for copy-right in books, for licenses for the sale of drugs, and the like (these matters not being in the class for which previous sanction is required), Governors or Prefects should merely endorse or affix their seals to the documents relating to such matters for the purpose of certifying the facts therein stated, and forward the same to the Department concerned.

In laws or regulations to be hereafter issued, any matters contained therein for dealing with which previous sanction must be obtained shall be clearly specified.

All matters within the ordinary scope of the duties of Governors or Prefects and not enumerated in the preceding clauses, excepting those of grave importance not governable by regulation or precedent, and excepting any of an extraordinary nature, may be dealt with by the Governors or Prefects according to their own views and afterwards reported to their superior authorities.

POWERS OF URBAN AND RURAL DIVISION MAGISTRATES.

The following are the cases in which the Magistrates of the Rural or Urban Divisions may take action according to their own views, afterwards reporting the fact to the Governor or Prefect :—

I. The collection of taxes, national and local, and the treatment of defaulters.

II. The examination of persons liable to military service.

III. Dealing with the property of bankrupts.

IV. Administering the property of persons who abscond, of deceased persons, or of families whose line has become extinct.

V. The sale of trees on Government property which have fallen down or died.

VI. Cutting down trees which belong to the Government and which obstruct telegraph wires, roads, rice-fields, vegetable gardens, or watercourses.

VII. The examination of foreshores leased to private persons.

VIII. Dealing with applications to shoot, whether as a business or for sport, and for the use of air-guns.

IX. Dealing with applications for licenses to retail revenue stamps and stamped papers.

X. Administering the funds of primary schools, and such other matters as may by specially entrusted to his care by the Governor or Prefect.

DUTIES OF THE HEADMEN OF URBAN OR RURAL DISTRICTS.

I. The circulation throughout the district of all decrees and proclamations.

II. The collection of the land and other taxes and forwarding the same to the proper quarter.

III. The management of all matters connected with the census.

IV. The preliminary examination of persons liable to military service.

V. Endorsing and fixing his seal to documents relating to the pawn, mortgage or sale of land, buildings, or ships.

VI. Keeping the official register of titles to land.

VII. Giving information at the police station of cases of lost children, foundlings, sick travellers, deaths through unnatural causes, and other unusual events.

VIII. Reporting to his superiors cases of extreme distress through calamities arising from natural causes or otherwise.

IX. Reporting to his superior authorities conspicuous instances of filial piety, womanly virtue and benevolence.

X. Using his endeavors to promote the regular attendance of children at school.

XI. Keeping correct impressions of the seals used by the inhabitants of his district.

XII. Preserving safely and in good condition all official books and documents.

XIII. The expression of his views as to the advantages or disadvantages of harbours, rivers, roads, embankments, bridges, etc., the expenses of repairing or maintaining which are to be defrayed out of the National Treasury or out of the fund for local expenses of the City or Prefecture.

All business besides the above, which may be assigned to him by the Governor or Prefect or by the Divisional Magistrate, he shall attend to in accordance with the regulations or any special orders.

Moreover, he shall, notwithstanding the above provisions, have control over all such matters as the repairing, cleansing, etc., of roads, bridges, or water courses (drinking and waste) which are confined to his own district and of which the expenses are defrayed by the people of the district.

J.W.M., 1881, pp. 1137-39.

25. TERMS OF SERVICE OF PREFECTURAL OFFICIALS.[1]

(Imp. Notif. No. 35, Aug. 3, 1878.)

I. The full official term of office of the Fuchiji or Kenrei shall be twelve years. Every three years an official inspection shall be made of his method of administration, and if found

---

1. *Cf.* Document No. 18, p. 268. A further revision was made by Imperial Notification No. 16, Feb. 6, 1884, which provided that the salary of the Governor should begin at 200 *yen* a month, and that every third year it should be increased 50 *yen* a month, till the maximum, 350 a month, should be reached after nine years of service.

competent he shall be confirmed in his office until the next period of inspection.

II. The Fuchiji or Kenrei shall receive a monthly salary of 200 yen for the first three years, which shall be increàsed by 50 yen per month for each successive term that he is confirmed in his office. After nine years of office he shall be promoted to *chokunin* rank. At the end of twelve years, being the expiration of his official term, he may retain his position if he so desires, but no further increase of salary shall be allowed.

III. If after twelve years of office the Fuchiji or Kenrei wishes to retire, he shall be presented with an honorarium representing ten times the amount of his monthly salary. Shokikuan (secretaries) are not limited as to their term of office, but will be subjected to official examination every three years, when those who prove able and industrious will receive a reward of one month's salary.

IV. The subordinate officers shall undergo inspection every year, when an amount representing one-third of their monthly salary shall be awarded to the deserving.

SUPPLEMENTARY PROVISIONS.

In the case of officials now holding the post of Governor or Prefect, the number of years during which they have held office before the issue of these rules shall be reckoned. In other cases, as where a Governor or Prefect has been transferred from one City or Prefecture to another, or where an official now holding the post of Governor or Prefect has held the same post previously, but with an interval between the two terms, in reckoning his years the total number of years in which he has held the post of Governor or Prefect shall be reckoned.

In the case of officials hereafter appointed from any other post to that of Governor or Prefect, their services shall only commence to be reckoned from their appointment as such and shall be regulated according to the provisions hereof.

J.W.M., 1881, pp. 1139-40.

26. The Kochō to be Locally Elected.[1]

(Notif. No. 54, of the Naimushō, Aug. 26, 1878.)

The Kochō is hereafter to be elected by a majority of the people as near as possible in every cho and son, but the appointment must be ratified by the Fuchiji or Kenrei.

J.W.M., 1878, p. 881.

27. Amendment of the Regulations[2] for Prefectural Assemblies.

(Imp. Dec. No. 13, Apl. 4, 1879.)

XIII, category 2, is amended as follows :—

" Persons who have been sentenced to imprisonment with hard labor for a term of not less than one year, or to confinement without hard labor for a term of not less than one year, on account of some political offence.

" Seven years after the expiration of the term of imprisonment this disqualification no longer applies."

H-Z., 1879, p. 46.

28. The Abolition of the Ryūkyū Han.

(Imp. Dec. No. 14, Apl. 4. 1879.)

Ryūkyū Han is abolished, and Okinawa Ken is created in its place. The Prefectural Office is established at Shuri.

H-Z., 1879, 46.

---

1. This provision for the election of the Kochō marks the beginning of the popular government of the smaller local areas.

2. The original Regulations were promulgated in the preceding year by Imperial Decree No. 18, July 22.

29. CREATION OF TOKUSHIMA KEN.

(Imp. Notif. No. 6, March 2,1880.)

It is hereby notified that the Prefecture of Tokushima has been established with jurisdiction over the whole province of Awa.

J.W.M., 1880, p. 308.

30. AMENDMENT[1] OF THE REGULATIONS FOR PREFECTURAL ASSEMBLIES.

(Imp. Dec. No. 15, Apl. 4, 1880.)

VI. At the opening of the ordinary meeting of the Assembly every year, a financial statement for the previous year shall be made, and the Assembly shall have power to question the Governor about the various items of the statement. In case the Assembly and the Governor fail to agree about any of the items the matter shall be immediately reported to the Home Minister and the Minister of Finance.

IX. The Prefectual Assembly may deliberate upon and determine its own rules of procedure, and with the approval of the Governor put them in force. The Assembly may also inquire into the conduct of those who absent themselves from the meeting of the Assembly without forwarding a notice with proper reasons for so doing, and may declare their seats vacant.

XIII. Category 2. Those who have been sentenced to imprisonment with hard labor for a term of not less than one year, or to confinement without hard labor for a term of not less than one year, on account of some political offence.

Seven years after the expiration of the term of imprisonment this disqualification shall no longer exist.

---

1. The Regulations referred to were promulgated by Imp. Dec. No. 18, July 22, 1878. See above pp. 272-76.

XIII. Category 5. Persons whose seats in the Assembly have been declared vacant for non-attendance or any other reason, for a period of four years.

XIV. Proviso. Persons who are prescribed in the categories 1, 2, 3, and 4 of the preceding Article shall not have a right to vote at elections for the Assembly.

XXXV. When the Home Minister has ordered the dissolution of an Assembly, a new election shall be held within ninety days of such dissolution.

H-Z., 1880, 61.

31. REGULATIONS FOR CITY (FU) AND PROVINCIAL (KEN) GOVERNMENTS.

(Imp. Dec. No. 15, April 8, 1880.)

PART I.—GENERAL RULES,

I. The duties of the City and Prefectural Assemblies are to discuss and settle the estimates of expenditure to be defrayed out of the local taxes, and the means of levying the same.

II. The sessions of the City or Provincial Assemblies are either ordinary or extraordinary; those summoned at the prescribed period are ordinary, and those specially summoned are extraordinary sessions.

III. In both ordinary and extraordinary sessions all bills are sent down for consideration by the Governor or Prefect.

IV. At extraordinary sessions discussion shall be confined to the special subject for deliberation upon which the session has been summoned, and no other business may be brought forward.

V. The decisions arrived at by a City or Prefectural Assembly shall be put into operation only after being approved by the Governor or Prefect. If the Governor or Prefect does not think fit to approve the decision, he shall report the circumstances of the case to the Minister of Home Affairs for instructions.

(In the case contemplated in the preceding clause, the Governor or Prefect may, if he thinks it advisable, submit for reconsideration the bill in respect of which such decision has been arrived at; if after such reconsideration he should still think that such decision ought not to be approved, then he may submit the case to the Minister of Home Affairs for instructions as provided for in the preceding clause.[1])

VI. There shall be submitted to the City and Provincial Assemblies at the commencement of the annual ordinary session, an account of the sums actually received and expended under the head of local taxes during the previous fiscal year, and the members shall be entitled to require explanations thereupon from the Governor or Prefect; if any item in the accounts is disapproved by the Assembly, the Assembly may in the President's name present a memorial on the subject to both the Ministers of Home Affairs and Finance.

VII. If during an ordinary session two or more members wish to address the Government with regard to any matter concerning the interests of the City or Prefecture, they may by permission of the Assembly, submit the memorial for its consideration, which, if approved, may be forwarded in the President's name to the Minister of Home Affairs as the memorial of the Assembly.

VIII. It is the duty of a City or Provincial Assembly to discuss any matters referred to it for its opinion by the Governor or Prefect with regard to measures proposed to be carried out in the City or Prefecture.

IX. Every City or Provincial Assembly may make by-laws for regulating its own debates, and the same shall be operative after receiving the approval of the Governor or Prefect.

---

1. The parenthesis was added by Imp. Dec. No. 4, 1881.

Every City or Prefectural Assembly shall investigate all cases in which members have failed to comply with a summons calling them to attend a sitting without stating the grounds of their absence ; and may declare such members to have forfeited their seats.

(Should a Governor or Prefect on the one side and a City or Provicial Assembly on the other differ in their interpretion of the laws, or should disputes arise as to their respective rights, they may submit the case to, and invoke the decision of the Government. In such a case the Governor or the Prefect may suspend either the debate or the sitting of the Assembly in the meantime.[1])

PART II.—ELECTIONS.

X. The City or Prefectural Assembly shall consist of persons elected by the various Divisions, both Urban and Rural[2], in the City or Prefecture, each Division electing five or a less number of members according to its size.

XI. The members shall elect from among themselves a President and a Vice-President ; such election shall be reported to the Governor or Prefect who shall in turn report the same to the Minister of Home Affairs.

No salaries shall be paid to the President, Vice-President or members; provided that allowances, for lodging expenses during the session of the Assembly, and travelling expenses to and from to the place of meeting, shall be paid upon a scale to be fixed by the Assembly itself.

XII. Clerks shall be chosen by the President and shall conduct miscellaneous business under his direction. Their salaries shall be included under the head of expenses of the Assembly.

XIII. The only persons qualified for election as members of the City or Prefectural Assemblies are males fully 25 years old borne on the register-rolls of the City or Prefecture, having

---

1. The parenthesis was added by Imp. Dec. No. 4, 1881.
2. An Urban Division was called Ku, a Rural, Gun.

resided therein for at least three years and paying land-tax to the amount of ten *yen* or upwards per annum in respect of land situated in the City or Prefecture; provided that the following classes of persons shall not be eligible :—

1. Insane persons and idiots.

2. Persons who have undergone the punishment of penal servitude for a period of one year or more, or of imprisonment for the same period, if adjudged for a political offence ; provided that, after the lapse of a period of seven years from the termination of such punishment, the same shall no longer affect their eligibility.

3. Persons who have been bankrupt and have not yet discharged their debts.

4. Government officials and priests.

5. Persons previously declared by the Assembly to have forfeited their seats ; provided that, after the lapse of four years from the date of such declaration, the same shall no longer affect their eligibility.

XIV. The only persons entitled to vote at the election of members are males of fully 20 years of age borne on the register-rolls of the Division, and paying land-tax to the amount of 5 *yen* or upwards per annum in respect of land situated within the City or Prefecture ; provided that, persons coming under the 1st, 2nd, 3rd, and 5th classes enumerated in the preceding Article shall not be entitled to vote.

XV. When an election of members is to be held, a notice shall be issued by the Governor or Prefect appointing the month in which the election shall be held. The Divisional Magistrate shall thereupon appoint a day for the voting in each Division and shall give public notice thereof throughout the Division at least fifteen days previously.

XVI. The election in every Division shall be held at the office of the Divisional Magistrate on the day appointed; the voting papers shall be examined by the Divisional Magistrate who shall also be charged with the preservation of order on the day of election; provided that, if convenience requires, the election may be held at a place other than the office of the Divisional Magistrate.

XVII. Each voter shall inscribe his own name and address in full, and likewise the name and address of the candidates for whom he votes, upon the ballot previously issued to him by the Divisional Magistrate, and shall present the same to the last named on the day of the election. The candidate receiving the greatest number of votes shall be elected; in case the votes of two or more candidates are equal, the election shall be decided by seniority in age or by lot if their ages are equal. The voting ticket may be presented by proxy.

XVIII. When the election has closed, the Divisional Magistrate shall verify the voting papers by comparing them with the list of voters, and shall also examine whether the candidates elected are qualified according to the list of persons qualified for election. If any candidate prove ineligible under any of the rules restricting the eligibility of candidates, or if the candidate elected declines the seat, the candidate who has received the next highest number of votes shall be declared elected.

XIX. When a decision as to the eligibility of the candidates elected has been arrived at by such an examination as aforesaid, the Divisional Magistrate shall summon the members elected to his office and there hand to them a certificate of membership, the receipt of which they shall acknowledge in writing; provided that, when all members duly elected have so acknowledged their certificates of membership, the Divisional Magistrate shall publicly proclaim their names, etc., throughout the Division.

XX. In case the same person be elected in more than one Division, he may choose which one he will represent.

XXI. Members shall be elected for a term of four years; a fresh election of one half of the total number of members shall be held at intervals of two years; the members to retire at the end of the first two years of the existence of any Assembly shall be determined by lot.

XXII. The President and Vice-President shall be elected from among the members of the Assembly for a term of two years. Their election shall take place publicly upon the election of the new members every two years.

XXIII. In both of the cases contemplated by the two preceding Articles, the same persons are eligible for re-election.

XXIV. In the event of any member falling into any of the classes of persons enumerated in Article XIII., or going to reside outside of the City or Prefecture to the Assembly of which he belongs, or in the occurence of a vacancy through any other cause, a new member shall be elected in his stead.

Part III.—Rules of Debate.

XXV. Unless there is a majority of the total number of members present at a sitting, no business shall be done.

XXVI. All questions in debate shall be decided by a majority of votes. When the numbers are equal, the President shall have the casting vote.

XXVII. The Governor or Prefect may be present at the sittings of the Assembly, either personally or by deputy, for the purpose of stating the grounds of bills; but he shall not be entitled to vote in the decision thereof.

XXVIII. Strangers will be permitted to listen to the debate; provided that they may be excluded either on the demand of the Governor or Prefect or at the discretion of the President.

XXIX. Members shall have the right to give free expression to their views in debate; provided that this freedom shall not be deemed to make it permissible for a member to advert to the character of individuals whether in praise or blame.

XXX. The proceedings of the Assembly shall be conducted under the direction of the President. If any member transgresses the rules and when called upon by the President disregards his authority, the latter may order him to withdraw from the chamber. In the event of any member resorting to actual violence, the President may request the intervention of the police officers.

PART IV.—SESSIONS.

XXXI. The ordinary session of a City or Prefectural Assembly shall be opened during the month of March in each year ; its commencement and closing shall be directed by the Governor or Prefect ; the session shall not ordinarily exceed thirty days in duration, provided that the Governor or Prefect may with the consent of the Assembly prolong the session, but in such circumstances he must at once report the case to the Minister of Home Affairs.

XXXII. Whenever there is any special business to be laid before the Assembly at any time when not in ordinary session, the Governor or Prefect may summon the Assembly for an extraordinary session, provided that, if he do so, he must at once report to the Minister of Home Affairs the circumstances rendering such extraordinary session necessary.

XXXIII. If the Governor or Prefect considers that views expressed by the Assembly are dangerous to the public peace or in violation of existing rules and regulations, he shall suspend the sittings of the Assembly, and report the circumstances of the case to the Minister of Home Affairs for instructions.

XXXIV. If the Minister of Home Affairs considers that the proceedings of any Assembly are calculated to endanger the public peace or are in violation of existing rules and regulations he may, at any time whatsoever, order the dissolution of the Assembly.

XXXV. In the event of an Assembly being dissolved by the order of the Minister of Home Affairs, an election for the members of the new Assembly shall be held within ninety days of the date of such order.

J.W.M., 1881, pp. 1258-59.

32. REGULATIONS FOR CITY (KU), TOWN (CHO), AND VILLAGE
(SON) ASSEMBLIES.

(Imp. Dec. No. 18, April 8, 1880.)

I. The city, town or village assemblies shall deliberate
upon matters relating to the general interests of the locality, and
upon the means of defraying expenses incurred therein.

II. The rules of procedure in these assemblies shall be
determined in accordance with the local circumstances, but in
all cases must be approved by the Governor.

III. In case several cities, towns or villages have a joint
assembly the rules of procedure shall be determined in accordance with the local circumstances, but in all cases they must be
approved by the Governor.

IV. The Ku-chō carries into effect the resolutions of the
city assembly, and the Ko-chō those of the town or village
assemblies. If they consider these resolutions improper, they
may suspend the execution until they have asked for the Governor's advice.

V. The Ku-chō carries into effect the resolutions of a joint
assembly of several cities; and the Ko-chō, Gun-chō or Ku-
chō those of the joint assemblies of several towns or villages.
In case they consider the resolutions improper the same procedure as set forth in the preceding Article shall be followed.

VI. The Gun-chō or Ku-chō may suspend any resolution
of the Gun or Ku Assembly which he considers unlawful, until
he has asked the advice of the Governor.

VII. The Governor may delay the execution of any resolution of a city, town or village assembly if he considers it
unlawful; and may dissolve any such assembly.

VIII. In case there is need to hold a meeting of the inhabitants of towns or villages to discuss matters relating to land or
the improvement of rivers, the necessary regulations shall be
drawn up with the consent of the Governor.

IX. In the execution or the suspension of the resolutions of such a meeting as is provided for in the previous Article, the provisions of Articles IV.-VII. shall be adopted.

X. When such a meeting as is provided for in Articles III. and VIII. is held, and some persons or some cities, towns or villages do not attend, the Governor shall refer the case to the Prefectural Assembly, and be guided by its decision. When the Prefectural Assembly is not in session, and the case is urgent, the Governor shall act upon his own discretion and report his action to the Assembly at its next session.

H-Z., 1880, 72.

33. Regulations Concerning Prefectural Assemblies.[1]

(Imp. Dec. No. 49, Nov. 5, 1880.)

Chapter V.—Standing Committees.[2]

XXXVI. The Assembly shall elect from among its members a Standing Committee composed of from five to seven members.

XXXVII. The Standing Committee shall be consulted by, and give advice to, the Governor in accordance with the resolutions of the Assembly, upon the method and procedure of carrying out the works which are to be paid for out of the local taxes. In cases of urgent necessity, the Standing Committee may decide the amount to be spent upon such works, and report the same to the Assembly later.

XXXVIII. The Committee shall report the outlines of its

---

1. Added to Imp. Dec. No. 15, April 8, 1880.

2. The subsequent history of these Standing Committees forms an interesting chapter in the development of the administration of the Cities and Prefectures, but that history does not fall within our period. The Standing Committees were transformed into Councils, and as such exercised semi-official advisory powers in the administration. In the late nineties they fell into bad repute, and were finally abolished some three years ago.

resolutions to the Prefectural Assembly at the opening of its meeting. The Committee shall also receive bills to be introduced by the Governor into the Assembly, and shall give its opinion thereon at the meeting of the Assembly, whether ordinary or extraordinary.

XXXIX. The meetings of the Standing Committee shall be held at regular intervals at the Prefectural office.

XL. At the meetings of the Committee projects may be discussed which have not yet been formally drafted in a bill.

XLI. The Governor takes the chair at the meetings of the Committee. In the cases contemplated in Article XXXVIII. the Chairman shall be elected from among the members of the Committee.

XLII. The quorum of the Committee shall be one-half of the members. The decision rests with the majority. In case of a tie the Chairman has the casting vote.

XLIII. The debates at the meetings of the Standing Committee shall be recorded by the Clerk.

XLIV. The Governor may cause his chief subordinates to attend the meetings of the Committee to explain the matters up for discussion.

XLV. No stranger shall be admitted to the meetings of the Committee.

XLVI. The members of the Committee shall be elected for terms of two years, but are eligible for re-election.

XLVII. The Clerk shall be appointed by the Chairman from among the Prefectural officials.

XLVIII. The members shall receive a monthly salary of from 30 to 80 *yen*, as well as travelling expenses, the amount of which is to be decided by the Assembly.

XLIX. The salaries and travelling expenses of the members, and any other expenses incurred in connection with the Committee shall be paid out of the local taxes.

H-Z., 1880, 257.

34. Constitution and Rules for the Conduct of Business of the Board of Metropolitan Police[1].

(Imp. Dec. No. 3, January 14, 1881.)

Constitution.

The Board of Metropolitan Police administers all police affairs for the City of Tōkyō, and exercises control over the fire-brigades and prisons. The business of the Board is transacted by and divided among the following offices and branches:—

Private Secretariat, General Secretariat, two Bureaux (one charged with the conduct of affairs relating to the executive police, and the other with those of the judicial police), Chief Inspector's office, stationary police offices, office of the Chief Superintendent of fire-brigades and prisons.

Superintendent-General of Police: He will exercise supervision, subject to the control of the Minister of Home Affairs, over all police officials, will give directions to Magistrates of Divisions (Ku and Gun) and Headmen of Districts (Cho and Son) within the City, and have general control of police affairs.

With regard to the appointment and dismissal, promotion and degrading of the officials of the Board, he will make recommendations to the Minister of Home Affairs in the case of those in the second grade and will act independently in the case of those in the third grade or below.

He will take instructions directly from the Ministers of Departments in such police matters as may be respectively under their control.

In matters of state-police he is liable to receive instructions directly from any Minister of State or Privy Councillor.

Vice-Superintendent of Police: He will generally assist the Superintendent-General in the discharge of his duties. In the absence from office of the Superintendent-General he may act in his behalf.

---

1. A Board which was semi-independent of the Department of Home Affairs.

Superintendents of Police of the 1st to 5th classes: They will receive orders from the Superintendent-General and severally transact such business as is assigned to them.

Clerks of Police: They will severally attend to miscellaneous business.

The above constitute the Board. The work of the Board is done mainly through the officers and staffs referred to under the four following heads :—

1. The police force proper consists of a Chief Inspector, an Assistant-Chief Inspector, Divisional Superintendents, Inspectors, Assistant-Inspectors, and Police Inspectors.

2. The Detective Branch consists of first and second class detective police, assistant detective police, and clerks.

3. The fire-brigades are controlled by a Chief and Assistant-Chief Superintendent, Commanders of divisional brigades, Commanders of companies and Commanders of sections.

4. The Prisons are governed by a Superintendent and Assistant-Superintendent, Clerks, Chief Warders, Assistant-Chief Warders and Warders.

Rules for the Conduct of Business.

In transacting the business of the Board in matters mentioned below, the Superintendent-General shall submit his views to, and receive the sanction of, the Minister of Home Affairs or of any other Department concerned, before taking action. In all matters not here mentioned, the Superintendent-General may take independent action, provided that all responsibility for the execution of both classes of business shall rest with the Superintendent-General.

The matters in respect of which previous sanction is necessary are as follows :—

I. Sending abroad any officials under his control on business of the Board.

II. The establishment, abolition, or rearrangement of the offices and branches of the Board.

III. Framing rules for the conduct of the business of the offices and branches of the Board.

IV. Entering into or terminating engagements with foreigners in the service.

V. Introducing novel arrangements or deviating from existing rules.

J.W.M., 1881, p. 1024.

35. The Creation of Fukui Ken.

(Notif. No. 3, Feb. 7, 1881.)

It is hereby notified that a new prefecture, named Fukui Ken, has been established over the two provinces Echizen and Wakasa. Also that Sakai Ken has been abolished and will for the future be included in Ōsaka Fu.

The seat of Fukui Ken local government is to be Fukui, Echizen province.

J.W.M., 1881, p. 161.

36. Revision of the Regulations Concerning the Prefectural Assemblies.[1]

(Imp. Dec. No. 4, Feb. 14, 1881.)

V. The following clause is added :—" In the case set forth in the preceding clause the Governor may demand the reconsideration of the measure in question. If the resolution still remains inadmissable, then he shall ask for the decision of the Home Minister, as in the case of the preceding clause."

---

1. Revision of Imperial Decrees No. 18, 1878, and 15, 1880.

IX. The following clause is added :— "In case the Governor and the Assembly differ in legal opinions, or there is some dispute[1] over their relative competencies, either of them may state the case to the Government and ask for its decision. In this event the Governor may suspend the debates of the Assembly pending the decision of the Government."

XXXIII. The following clauses are added :—1. "In event of the Assembly refusing to deliberate upon bills, the Governor, having obtained permission from the Home Minister, may put the measures in force without the decision of the Assembly." 2. "In case more than half of the members of the Assembly absent themselves from the meeting, and the deliberations cannot go on, the Governor shall report the matter to the Home Minister for instructions."

XXXIV. The first clause is revised to read as follows :— "In case the Assembly acts in such a way as to disturb the peace of the State, or passes resolutions which are contradictory of laws or regulations, the Governor may at any time dissolve it." The following clause is added :—" In the case contemplated in the preceding clause, bills which have not yet been considered shall be debated by the newly elected Assembly."

XXXVII. The first clause is revised as follows :—" The Standing Committee shall be consulted by and give advice to the Governor upon the method and procedure of conducting works."

H-Z., 1881, 3.

31. REGULATIONS RELATING TO THE DETAILS OF MATTERS TO BE DEBATED IN THE PREFECTURAL ASSEMBLIES.

(Imp. Dec. No. 6, Feb. 14, 1881.)

The Prefectural Assemblies may submit the details of the matters to be debated therein to the city, town, or village

---

1. It was to settle disputes of this kind that the Board of Adjudication was established in the Central Government on Feb. 14, 1881.

assembly, or to the association for land or river improvements (suiri-dokō-kwai).

H-Z., 1881, 5.

38. REGULATIONS CONCERNING CITY, TOWN, AND VILLAGE ASSEMBLIES.[1]

(Imp. Dec. No. 7, Feb. 14, 1881.)

VIII. In case there is need to hold a meeting of the inhabitants of a certain locality who are interested in the land or river improvements, regulations necessary for such a meeting may be drawn up with the consent of the Governor.

H-Z., 1881, 5.

39. URBAN AND RURAL SECTIONS (KUBU-KWAI AND GUMBU-KWAI) IN THE ASSEMBLIES OF THE THREE FU AND KANAGAWA KEN.

(Imp. Dec. No. 8, Feb. 14, 1881.)

I. In Tōkyō-Fu, Kyōto-Fu, Ōsaka-Fu and Kanagawa Ken, the Prefectural Assemblies shall be divided into two parts ; one, the Kubu-kwai, to deliberate upon matters concerning the urban sections, the other, the Gumbu-kwai, upon matters concerning the rural sections.

II. The Assembly shall determine the matters which are to be deliberated separately by the Kubu-kwai and the Gumbu-kwai, and those which are to be considered by the whole Assembly.

III. In order to increase the number of the members of the Urban Section meeting beyond the limit set forth in Article X. of

---

1. A revision of Imp. Dec. No. 18, April 8, 1880.

the Prefectural Assembly Regulations, the Governor must first apply to and obtain the consent of the Home Minister.

IV. The quorum of the Kubu-kwai and the Gumbu-kwai shall be one half of the members.·

V. In matters which are to be deliberated upon by the whole Assembly, the members of the urban and rural sections, at a joint meeting, shall receive inquiries and make resolutions.

Such joint meetings shall not proceed to business unless one-half of the members are present[1].

VI. The limitations upon the taxes on trade (eigyō-zei) and the miscellaneous taxes (zasshu-zei) in the urban districts may be changed with the concurrence of the Government, the Governor reporting the matter to the Home Minister and the Minister of Finance, along with the appropriate resolutions of the Urban Section.

VII. Necessary expenses not provided for in the local tax regulations may be added with the consent of the Government, the Governor reporting the matter to the Home Minister and the Minister of Finance, along with the appropriate resolutions of the urban section.

VIII. Reports of the local taxes which are assessed jointly by the urban and rural authorities shall be made to the Assembly, and those which are assessed separately by the urban and rural authorities shall be reported to the respective meetings of the urban or rural sections.

H-Z., 1881, 5.

40. ADDITION TO THE KUBU-KWAI AND GUMBU-KWAI REGU-
    LATIONS.

(Imp. Dec. No. 20, March 29, 1881.)

In Prefectures other than that mentioned[2] where urban

---

1. *Cf.* the translation in the *J.W.M.*, 1881, pp. 1286-87.
2. In Imperial Decree No. 8, Feb. 14, 1881. See preceding Document.

organisations have been set up, these rules may be applied with the concurrence of the Government.

H-Z., 1881, 9.

41. CREATION OF TOTTORI KEN.

(Imp. Dec. No. 42, Sept. 12, 1881.)

It is hereby notified that a Prefecture named Tottori Ken, with control over the provinces of Inaba and Hoki has been created.

The seat of the Kencho will be at Tottori.

J.W.M., 1881, p. 1086.

42. THE OFFICE OF POLICE SERGEANT-GENERAL (KEIBU-CHŌ)

(Imp. Notif. No. 99, Nov. 26, 1881.)

The Keibu-chō (one in number) is created to manage local police affairs.

I. Subject to the instructions of the Governor, he takes charge of the general police affairs of the Prefecture.

II. In national police affairs he shall receive instructions from the Home Minister, and shall report upon all matters direct to the Home Minister.

H-Z., 1881, 340.

43. REVISION OF THE PREFECTURAL ASSEMBLY REGULATIONS.[1]

(Imp. Notif. No. 10, Feb. 14, 1882)

VII. A representation, when supported by at least two members, may be introduced and deliberated in the Assembly,

---

1. See Imp. Decrees Nos. 15 and 49, 1880.

and if adopted it shall be presented in the name of the Chairman to the Home Minister, or to the Governor, as the opinion of the Assembly.

In the case of an extraordinary session, it is possible to make representations only in connection with those matters for which the meeting was summoned.

X. The following sentence is added :—Besides the required number of members, each District or City may elect not more than ten members for the purpose of filling up the vacancies which may occur.

XIII. Category 2 is changed to read :—

1. " Those who have been sentenced to imprisonment with hard labor, or to confinement on account of some political offence, for a period of not less than one year, in accordance with the old regulations, and have not yet passed five years since the completion of the sentence."

2. " Those who have been deprived of their civil rights, or whose civil rights have been suspended, according to the new regulations ; and those who have been sentenced to harder or lighter confinement for a period of not less than one year, according to the same, and have not yet passed five years since the completion of their sentence."

Category 4 is changed to read :—

" Government officials, teachers, and military and naval men in active service."

XIV. The proviso is revised to read :—

" Those who are enumerated in the categories 1, 2, 3, &c., as well as military and naval men have no right to vote at Prefectural Assembly elections."

XXIV. When there are some members to whom some of the categories of Article XIII are applicable, or members who have changed their domicile, or when a vacancy occurs for other reasons, a new election shall be held.   If there are substitute members (koketsu-in) substitution shall be made in the order in which they were elected.   When this provision does not meet the actual need, then the provision of the preceding clause shall be followed.

XXXVI. The following clauses are added :—

" Besides the limited number of members of the Standing Committee, several substitute members may be elected, and every vacancy be filled by them, according to the order in which they have been elected."

" In the Prefectures where the Kubu-Kwai and the Gumbu-Kwai exist, the election of the additional members shall be carried out separately by the Kubu and Gumbu-kwai."

XL. The following sentence is added :—

" At the meetings held to receive and discuss questions written bills are not required."

XLI. At the meetings of the Standing Committee referred to in the preceding Article the Governor shall take the Chair, but at all other meetings the Chairman shall be appointed at every meeting from among the members.

XLVII. The Clerk of the Standing Committee shall be appointed by the Governor from among the Prefectural officials.

H-Z., 1882, 7.

44. CITY, TOWN, AND VILLAGE ASSEMBLY REGULATIONS[1].

(Imp. Dec. No. 11, Feb. 14, 1882.)

X. Proviso is to read as follows :—

" In case the Prefectural Assembly is not sitting and it is impossible to wait for its opening, the matter shall be submitted to the Standing Committee and decided, and afterwards reported to the Assembly at its next sitting."

H-Z., 1882, 8.

---

1. A revision of Imperial Decree No. 18, April 8, 1880.

45. REVISION OF THE KUBU-KWAI AND GUMBU-KWAI REGULA-
TIONS[1].

(Imp. Dec. No. 12, Feb. 14, 1882.)

VI. and VII. are expunged.

IX. In order that the kosūwari in urban districts may be converted into kaoku-zei it is necessary to obtain the sanction of the Government ; the Governor shall report the matter along with the appropriate resolution of the Kubu-Kwai to the Home Minister and the Minister of Finance.

H-Z., 1882, 8.

46. REVISION OF THE PREFECTURAL ASSEMBLY REGULATIONS[2].

(Imp. Dec. No. 68, Dec. 28, 1882.)

VI. 2nd clause to read as follows :—

" At the request of the Assembly, the Governor or his delegate shall make explanations of the financial reports."

XXXI. The Prefectural Assembly shall be opened in March once a year.   The sitting shall not last longer than thirty days.

The Governor shall perform the opening and closing ceremonies.

In Prefectures where Kubu-kwai and Gumbu-kwai exist, the sitting may be prolonged not more than one week.

XXXII. The Governor, if is necessary, may call an extra-ordinary meeting of the Assembly, not to last longer than one week, and shall report the reasons therefor to the Home Minister.

XXXIII. clause 2 is revised to read :—

" In case the Prefectural Assembly has not deliberated

---

1. A revision of Imperial Decree No. 8, Feb. 14, 1881.
2. A revision of Imperial Decrees Nos. 15 and 49 of 1880, and No. 4 of 1881

upon necessary bills, or has failed to conclude its deliberations thereon, within the period of the meeting, the Governor, with the consent of the Home Minister, may put such bills in force."

Clause 4 is as follows :—

"In the case set forth in the first clause, the Home Minister may suspend the sitting of the Assembly and the Governor may determine the amount of the local expenses and the means of defraying them, and execute his plans with the consent of the Home Minister, until the Assembly has been reopened."

XXXVII. At the request of the Governor, the Standing Committee shall advise the Governor as to the method and procedure of conducting works, and as to the use to be made of the Reserve Fund, but in conformity with the resolutions of the Assembly.

In cases of urgent need, the Standing Committee may determine the amount of the expenditures and the methods of raising the necessary funds, for carrying on public works, the expenses of which are to be paid out of the local taxes. In this case the Standing Committee shall report the matter at the next sitting of the Assembly.

H-Z., 1882, 98.

47. REGULATIONS FOR THE TERMS OF SERVICE OF PREFECTURAL OFFICIALS.[1]

(Imp. Dec. No. 9, January 4, 1884.)

Article III. of the Regulations for the Terms of Service of Prefectural Officials is repealed.

H-Z., 1884, 156.

---

1. A revision of Imp. Dec. No. 35, Aug. 1878.

48. City (Ku), Town (Cho), and Village (Son) Assembly Regulations.[1]

(Imp. Dec. No. 14, May 7, 1884.)

I. The city, town, and village assemblies are to debate upon matters which involve expenses which are to be defrayed out of the local taxes, and upon the means of raising the necessary funds.

II. The Governor shall determine the length of the sessions of such assemblies by proclamation, the numbers of members thereof, their terms of office, re-election, etc.

III. The Ku-chō convokes the city assembly, the initiaive resting with him. The Ko-chō convokes the town or village assembly, the initiative resting with him.

IV. The Ku-chō executes the resolutions of the city assembly, and the Ko-chō those of the town or village assemblies. In case such resolutions seem improper, they shall suspend the execution thereof, and ask the advice of the Governor.

V. In case the Ku-chō or Ko-chō (the Chief Magistrate of the city, town or village) regards the debates of the city assembly (or the town or village assembly) as unlawful or prejudicial to public peace, he shall suspend the debates and ask for the advice of the Governor.

VI. In case the Governor regards the debates of the city, town or village assembly as unlawful or prejudicial to the public peace, he may suspend the meeting or dissolve the assembly in question.

VII. When a city, town or village assembly has been suspended or dissolved, as provided for in the previous Article, the Ku-chō or the Ko-chō may determine the expenditures and means of raising the necessary funds, and carry out their plans with the approval of the Governor.

---

1. A new set of regulations for the assemblies in the smaller urban and rural areas.

VIII. In case a city, town or village has not elected the members of the assembly, or the members have not obeyed the summons, and consequently the assembly has not met, and in case the city, town or village assembly has not deliberated upon bills which are necessitated by law, or has failed to conclude its debates within the period of the sitting, the provisions of the preceding Article are applicable.

IX. Those eligible to exercise the franchise must be males of full twenty years, who have resided and have been paying land-taxes in the city, town or village. Those who are declared ineligible in Article XIII., clauses 1, 2, and 3, of the Regulations for Prefectural Assemblies, as well as military and naval men in active service, have no votes.

X. Those eligible for election to the assembly must be males of full twenty-five years, who have their residence and have been paying land-tax in the city, town or village. Those who are declared ineligible in Article XIII., clauses 1, 2, 3, and 4, of the Regulations for Prefectural Assemblies cannot be elected.

XI. The Ku-chō shall take the Chair at the meetings of the city assembly, and the Ko-chō at the meetings of the town or village assembly. In case of the disability of the Ku-chō or the Ko-chō to perform this function he shall nominate a member of the assembly to occupy his place.

XII. In case the Governor regards it impossible to hold meetings of the town or village assemblies within his jurisdiction, he shall ask for the advice of the Home Minister.

XIII. The Governor may call a joint meeting of several cities, towns, or villages, within a fixed area, to discuss matters of common interest.

XIV. To manage the affairs concerning land or river improvements, which cannot be dealt with in the city, town or village assemblies, or in a joint meeting of several cities, towns, or villages, the Governor may establish an association for land and river improvements (suiri-dokō-kwai) within a fixed area.

XV. The provisions contained in this regulation shall apply to the joint meetings of several cities, towns, or villages, and the meetings of the land and river improvement associations.

H-Z., 1884, 36.

49. REVISION[1] OF THE PREFECTURAL ASSEMBLY REGULATIONS.

(Im. Dec. No. 28, Dec. 8, 1884.)

XXXI. is made to read November instead of March.

H-Z., 1884, 47.

50. ORGANISATION OF THE METROPOLITAN POLICE OFFICE (KEISHI-CHŌ).[2]

(Imp. Ord. No. 42, May 4, 1886.)

The Officials of the Metropolitan Police Office are :—
1. The Chief (one).
2. First, second, third, fourth and fifth class Police Inspectors.
3. Clerks.
4. Police Sergeants.
5. Assistant Police Sergents.

The main regulations concerning the Chief are :—

I. The Chief of the Metropolitan Police Office shall be of *chokunin* rank of the first or second grade. Subject to the direction and supervision of the Home Minister, he shall preside over matters concerning police, prevention of fires, and jails.

---

1. This revision was not to come into effect till November 1885.
2. *Supra* pp. 256-57.

II. Subject to the direction of the Prime Minister, he shall take charge of the national police affairs, and he shall be subject to the direction and supervision of the Ministers of State when he deals with matters relating to their respective jurisdictions.

III. He may issue police ordinances (keisatsu-rei) relating to police affairs in Tōkyō-Fu, on the strength of his own authority, within limits not contradictory of law or ordinance.

IV. He shall exercise control over all his subordinates ; he may promote or degrade officials of *sonin* rank, referring the matter to the Home Minister, and officials of *hannin* or lower rank at his own discretion.

V. He shall direct the Chief Magistrates of the Urban and Rural Divisions, Towns, and Villages in the matters with which he is entrusted.

H-Z., 1886.

51. Organisation of the Local Government Service.

(Imp. Ord. No. 54, July 12, 1886.)

Cities and Prefectures.

I. In each City and Prefectural Government, there shall be the following officers :—
> One Governor.
> Secretaries.
> One Chief Tax-collector.
> Clerks.
> Tax-collectors.
> > Governor of Prisons.
> > Assistant-Governor of Prisons.
> > Clerks of Prisons.
> > Chief Warders of Prisons.
> > Assistant-Chief Warders of Prisons.

II. The Governor shall be of either 2nd class *choku-nin* rank, or 1st class *sonin* rank, and shall carry out statutes and instructions, and superintend the administrative and police business of the territory over which his jurisdiction extends, under the direction and control of the Minister of State for Home Affairs. Should a particular matter fall within the competency of any other Department, he shall deal with it under the direction and control of the Minister of that Department. The Governor of Tōkyō may be promoted to the 1st class *chokunin* rank.

III. The Governor shall, by virtue of his functionary powers, or by virtue of powers specially delegated to him, issue, within the limits of statutes and instructions, City or Prefectural ordinances either for the whole territory under his control or for a part of it, relating to administrative and police business.

IV. City and Prefectural ordinances shall come into force after they shall have been promulgated through the columns of the *Official Gazette*, or in other methods which may be specially established.

V. When a City or Prefectural ordinance is deemed by the Minister of State for Home Affairs, or by any other competent Minister, to be prejudicial to the public interest, or contrary to an existing law or regulation, or to overstep the limits of the legal power of the official issuing it, such ordinance may be ordered to be suspended or rescinded.

VI. The Governor shall have control over 'all the officials attached to him. He should report on the conduct of officials of *sonin* rank to the Minister of State for Home Affairs, or to any other Minister within whose competency the matter falls. The appointment and dismissal of officials of *hannin* rank shall be entirely in the competency of the Governor.

VII. The Governor shall have the power of meting out to the officials under his control disciplinary punishment, in conformity with the rules laid down by statutes or instructions. In the case of officials of *sonin* rank, the matter must be laid before the Minister of State for Home Affairs, and in the case of officials of and below *hannin* rank, the Governor shall have full power to take action into his own hands.

VIII. When military force is rendered necessary in any case of extraordinary emergency, or military defence is advisable as a precautionary measure, the Governor shall have power to request the presence of troops by sending a despatch to the Commander of the garrison (chindai) or of a detachment (bun-tai).

IX. The Governor shall determine the distribution, separation, and amalgamation of branch police offices in each urban and rural Division.

X. The Governor shall have power to enact detailed rules for the conduct of business in his office.

XI. The Governor shall have power, according to the requirements of the public business, to engage employés, but the salaries paid in his office must not exceed the amount estimated.

XII. The Governor shall have power, within the estimated amount of expenditure in his office, to reward, at the end of each year, such officials of and below *sonin* rank as may have distinguished themselves by special services. In the case of officials of *sonin* rank, the matter must be laid before the Minister of State for Home Affairs, and in the case of officials of and below *hannin* rank it will lie within the absolute power of the Governor.

XIII. The Governor shall have power, according to requirements, and within the estimated amount of salaries, to appoint an Engineer in conformity to the Regulations as to the Official Rank and Salaries of Engineers (Gijutsukan Kantō Hōkyū Rei), subject to the approval of the Minister of State for Home Affairs. Should such appointment require to be made in connection with any work the cost of which is to be defrayed from the local taxes, the engineer may be hired as an employé, after the sanction of the Minister of State for Home Affairs has been obtained.

XIV. The Secretaries shall be two in number, shall be

of or under 2nd class, *sonin* rank, shall, under the direction of the Governor, assume the position of Directors of Divisions, and shall manage the business of such Divisions.   In the case of the inability of the Governor to transact business, the senior Secretary shall represent him in his functions.

XV. The Chief Tax-collector shall be of or under 4th class, *sonin* rank, and shall have control, under the direction of the Governor, of affairs relating to the imposition and collection of taxes.

XVI. Clerks shall be of *hannin* rank, and shall engage under the direction of their superiors, in the general business o, book-keeping, etc.

XVII. Tax-collectors shall be of *hannin* rank, shall be attached to the Division of Taxation (Shuzei-bu), and shall engage, under the direction of the Chief Tax-collector, in the business allotted to them.

XVIII. Governors of prisons shall be of either 1st or 2nd class, *hannin* rank, shall superintend, under the direction of either the Governor or the Director of the Section, all business connected with prisons, and shall have control over prison clerks, warders, and other officials under them.

XIX. Assistant-Governors of prisons shall be of 3rd, 4th, 5th class, *hannin* rank, shall assist the Governors generally, and in the case of their inability to transact business shall represent them in their functions.

XX. Prison Clerks shall be of or under 6th class *hannin* rank, and shall, under direction of the Governors of prisons, engage in the business allotted to them.

XXI. Chief Warders of prisons shall be of the 5th, 6th, or 7th class, *hannin* rank, shall, under the direction of the Governors, have supervision over prisons, and shall superintend the work of the warders.

XXII. Assistant-Chief Warders shall be of or under 8th class, *hannin* rank, and shall assist the Chief Warders in discharging their duties.

XXIII. Rules relating to Prison Warders shall be established by special enactment.

XXIV. In order to distribute the business of the City or Prefectural Government among the different officials, Divisions, No. I. and No. II., each subdivided into Sections, according to the convenience of the Division, shall be established under the Directorship of the Secretaries :—

DIVISION NO. I.

1. Affairs connected with the Local Assembly, the committee dealing with engineering works (hydraulic, etc.), and the town and district committees.

2. Affairs connected with local taxes, town and district rates, and the agricultural distress and relief fund.

3. Affairs connected with foreigners.

4. Affairs connected with correspondence, and the keeping of official seals and city or prefectural seals.

5. Affairs connected with agriculture, manufactures, and commerce.

6. Affairs not falling within the sphere of other Divisions.

DIVISION No. II.

1. Affairs connected with engineering works.

2. Military affairs.

3. Affairs connected with education.

4. Affairs connected with prisons.

5. Affairs connected with sanitation.

6. Affairs connected with accounts and public bonds.

XXV. Besides these Divisions, there shall be, in each City and Prefectural Government, a Division of Taxation, which shall have control over all the business connected with the assessment and collection of taxes, and the expensrs of such collection. The establishment of Sections in each Division shall be carried out according to the basis of Article XXIV.

XXVI. In the case of temporary business, not specified in the foregoing Articles, the Governor shall have power to determine where and by whom it will be dealt with, according to the convenience of the case.

POLICE OFFICIALS.

XXVII. In each City and Prefectural Government, there shall be the following police officials :—

Chief Police Inspector.

Police Inspectors.

Police Sergeants.

XXVIII. The Chief Police Inspector shall be of the 5th, or a lower, class of *sonin* rank ; and shall superintend the following business, under the direction and control of the Governor :—

1. Supervision of all higher police business in the territory of the local government.

2. The arrangement of all business relating to police matters in such territory, and the expenses of the police force.

3. The direction of all police officials under him, and control of the whole force in case of emergency.

4. The distribution of the required police officials to all police offices and branch police offices in the district.

XXIX. Police inspectors shall be of 1st to 7th class, of *hannin* rank ; and sergeants shall be of 8th, or a lower, class of *hannin* rank. They shall superintend the police business under their special charge and have direction and control over the policemen under them, subject to the direction and control of the Chief Police Inspector.

XXX. In each City and Prefectural Government there shall be established Police Headquarters, forming a separate Division in the City or Prefectural Government, in addition to those mentioned in Article XXIV. This Division shall be under the Directorship of the Chief Police Inspector, and the business mentioned in Article XXVII shall be transacted by establishing therein various Sections.

XXXI. In each urban or rural division of a City or Prefecture there shall be established a police office ; and attached to each police office there shall be branch police offices. The former shall be under the charge of a police inspector, and the latter either under an inspector or a sergeant according to convenience. These shall have control over the higher administrative and judicial policing of the district under their charge, and shall superintend the carrying out of statutes and instructions. The business under their charge may be specified as follows :—

1. Affairs connected with trades, market-places, companies, manufactories, weights and measures, temples, religious associations, preaching, and worship.

2. Affairs connected with theatrical establishments, places of amusement, places for sport, resting places, decorations, festivals, funerals, gambling, lotteries, and other matters relating to public conduct.

3. Affairs connected with shipping, embankments, riverbanks, roads, bridges, fords, railways, telegraphs, parks, vehicles, horses, buildings of all kinds, fields and forests, fishing and hunting, and the collection of sea-weed.

4. Affairs connected with injuries to human life, crowding of people, quarrels, fire-arms, gunpowder, explosives, spontaneously combustible substances, swords, floods, fires, ship-wrecks, articles lost and found, and substances which have been buried in the earth.

5. Affairs connected wlth contagious diseases, and their prevention, disinfection, and inspection, vaccination, liquors, food, drinking water, medical treatment, medicines, live stock, butchery establishments, graveyards, cremation yards, and all other matters relating to sanitation.

6. Affairs connected with the detection and apprehension of criminals of all kinds, the collection of evidence and the transmission of the latter to public prosecutors.

7. Affairs connected with deserters, lunatics, lost children, and persons under police supervision.

8. Affairs connected with political associations, political meetings, newspapers, magazines, books, and other matters relating to publication.

XXXII. Each police official shall discharge his duty by virtue of functional powers, or by the orders of his superiors, or at the request of the Director of the Division of police, the chief tax-collector, the chief of the town or district office, the head-man or other executive official, or, in matters connected with judicial policing, by the order of a public prosecutor.

XXXIII. In any and every case, when an executive or judicial official submits a request on his own responsibility, police officials will be obliged to comply with such request.

XXXIV. When correspondence between one local government and another is necessary in connection with a police matter, it should pass through the Governor. But in cases where promptitude is required, the correspondence may be addressed directly to the chief police inspector, or to the chief police official of the locality in which action is to be taken.

XXXV. Rules relating to policemen will be specially enacted.

XXXVI. Business relating to policing and prisons under the government of the city of Tōkyō, shall be dealt with according to Imperial ordinance[1] No. 42, relating to the Organization of the Metropolitan Police, and accordingly such business does not come under the scope of any of the Articles of the present ordinance.

Rural and Urban Divisions.

XXXVII. In each or several rural Divisions there shall be a Chief of the District Office ; and in each urban Division, there shall be a Chief of the Municipal Office. In both there shall be several clerks.

XXXVIII. The Chief of the District or Municipal Office shall be of or under the 4th class, *sonin* rank ; and Clerks shall be of or under 4th class, *hannin* rank.

---

1. *Supra* pp. 312 ff.

XXXIX. The Chief of the District or Municipal Office shall carry out statutes and instructions in the district under him, and superintend the executive business of the district, according to the direction and under the control of the Governor.

XL. In cases the power to deal with which is delegated to him by statutes or instructions, or by the special order of the Governor, the Chief of the District or Municipal Office shall have power to act according to convenience,. and shall afterwards report his action to the Governor.

XLI. The Chief of a District or Municipal Office shall have control over the headmen under him, in executive affairs; and in the case of district affairs, he shall superintend them.

XLII. The Chief of a District or Municipal Office shall report to the Governor on the appointment and dismissal of clerks.

XLIII. The Chief of a District or Municipal Office shall have power to issue notifications applying to the district under him, on matters for which the power is delegated to him by statutes or instructions or by the Governor.

XLIV. The chief of a District or Municipal Office shall have power to request a police official to effect the carrying out of administrative measures in the district.

XLV. The clerks of a District or Municipal Office shall engage in general business, according to the orders of the chief of such office.

INSULAR LOCALITIES.

XLVI. In the Prefectures of Nagasaki and Kagoshima, and in other Cities and Prefectures to be determined, there shall be appointed a Director of Islands, who shall have power to manage the executive affairs of the locality ; and in the case of matters for which the power is delegated to him by the Governor, he shall have authority to act according to the requirements of the case.

XLVII. Directors of Islands shall be under 3rd class, *sonin* rank.

J.W.M., 1886, July 31, pp. 114-15.

52. REGULATIONS FOR LOCAL OFFICIALS[1] (CHIHOKWAN-KWANSEI).

(Imp. Ord. No. 55, July 12, 1886.)

The Local Officials in the Prefectures are :—

The Governor (Chiji), the Secretary (Shokikwan), the Tax-Inspector (Shūzei-chō), Clerks (Zoku), the Taxing Officers (Shūzeizoku), the Prison Governor (Tengoku), Assistant Prison Governor (Fuku-Tengoku), Prison Clerks (Shoki), Jailors (Kanshu), Chief Jailor (Kanshu-shō).

The main regulations for the Governor are :—

I. The Governor shall be of *chokunin* rank of the second class, or of *sonin* rank of the first class. He shall be subject to the direction and control of the Home Minister ; the Ministers of the Departments of State shall direct and supervise his actions, each of them so far as it lies within his jurisdiction to do so. In this way the Governor shall preside over the administration and the police affairs of the Prefecture. The Governor of Tōkyō-Fu may be promoted to *chokunin* rank of the first class.

II. As regards the administration and the police affairs of his Prefecture the Governor may issue prefectural ordinances (fuken-rei), within limits not contradictory of laws and ordinances, upon the strength of his legal authority, and by special enactment for the whole or a part of the Prefecture concerned.

III. Prefectural ordinances shall be put into effect after they have been published in the *Official Gazette*, or in compliance with other regulations specially enacted.

IV. In case the Home Minister or other Minister of State

---

1. *Cf.* the translation in the *J.W.M.*, 1886, July 31, p. 114.

shall consider a prefectural ordinance to be contradictory to the public interest or the provisions of laws or ordinances, or to be *ultra vires*, he may annul it or suspend its execution.

V. The Governor shall exercise control over all his subordinate officials ; he may promote or degrade officials of *sonin* rank, with the consent of the Home Minister or the Minister of the Department concerned, and officials of *hannin* rank or below upon his own discretion.

VI. The Governor may reprove his subordinates in accordance with laws or ordinances ; in case of officials of *sonin* rank the matter shall be reported to the Home Minister, but in the case of *hannin* rank or below no report need be made.

VII. In emergencies the Governor may ask the Commandant of the chindai or its branch barracks for the despatch of soldiers, if the force of arms is necessary to preserve the peace.

The Local Officials of the Division (Gun) and City (Ku) are :—

I. The Chief Magistrate of a Division (Gun) is the Gun-chō, of a City (Ku) the Ku-chō ; there are also several clerks.

II. The Gun-chō and the Ku-chō shall be of *sonin* rank of the fourth class or lower, and the clerks of *hannin* rank of the third class or lower.

III. The Gun-chō and Ku-chō shall execute laws and ordinances and be entrusted with the administration of the Division or City concerned.

IV. The Gun-chō and the Ku-chō shall have charge of all matters specially entrusted to them by laws and ordinances or by the Governor, and shall report the cases to the Governor after execution.

V. The Gun-chō shall direct all the Magistrates of the towns and villages within his jurisdiction as regards administrative affairs and control them in general public affairs.

VI. The Gun-chō and the Ku-chō shall consult the Governor in the appointment or dismissal of the Divisional or City clerks.

VII. The Gun-chō and the Ku-chō shall announce to the public all matters entrusted to them by laws and ordinances or by the Governor.

VIII. The Gun-chō or the Ku-chō may cause the police officers to carry out their administrative measures within their respective jurisdictions.

IX. Subject to the instructions of the Gun-chō and the Ku-chō the Divisional or City clerks shall have charge of miscellaneous affairs.

The Local Officer in an Island :—

I. In Nagasaki, Kagoshima, and other Prefectures to be designated hereafter, a Governor of an Island (Tōshi) may be appointed in order to take charge of administrative affairs, and he shall deal with all matters entrusted to him by the Governor.

II. The Tōshi shall be of *sonin* rank of the third class.

H-Z., 1886.

53. INSTRUCTIONS ADDRESSED TO THE GOVERNORS OF CITIES
    AND PREFECTURES.

(By the Minister President of State, September 28, 1887.)

Since the Restoration, affairs of state, connected with our home administration as well as our foreign policy, have become infinitely diversified in character and perplexingly vast in amount. But the one fixed purpose for which all these affairs have been carried out on a fixed line of policy has unswervingly been to strengthen the vitality of the nation, to assert our national rights, to promote the happiness of the people, and to lay a permanent basis to work upon, thereby bequeathing to posterity a line of policy to be forever pursued. Such is in fact the aim which His Majesty the Emperor has even to this day with gracious anxiety (for the good of Empire) caused his officials, central as

well as local, to keep their minds upon, so as never to deviate
therefrom.

Now the proclamation of an Imperial Rescript in April,
1875 (8th year of Meiji), announcing the gradual formation of
constitutional government; the establishment of the Senate[1] and
of the Court of Revision[2] in the same year ; the inauguration of
local assemblies in 1879 (12th year of Meiji) ; the proclamation
of the Imperial Rescript of October of 1881 (14th year of Meiji),
declaring the opening of a Deliberative Assembly in 1890
(23rd year of Meiji), and in December of 1885 (18th year of
Meiji) the organization of the different Departments, which was
thoroughly established,—these measures have all of them been
the outcome of a fixed policy on the part of the Government,
the object kept in view having been the attainment of the
ultimate completion of the whole work by a gradual process.

Now that His Majesty's judgment has become ripened after
years of thought, has become strengthened more than ever, and
now that the work of the Restoration is so near its completion that
" only a cart-load of earth," so to speak, is needed to give the
last finish to the hills we have been building up, should any
of the people in the country, not clearly understanding His Imperial Majesty's views, be led astray into erroneous ideas by
doubts or misgivings, no small injury will be inflicted upon the
great work in hand. We hereby inform you, in respectful
obedience to the gracious will of His Imperial Majesty, of a
general view of the policy of the country, both as to internal and
external affairs, and point out to you the course of administration to be pursued.

Firstly,—the fundamental principles of our constitutional
system of government shall be based upon the historical traditions of the country and the principles that have been handed
down by the Imperial Ancestors, modified by careful consideration of the actual circumstances of the times ; respect shall be
paid to the rights of the subject and extension be given to the

1. The Genro-in. 2. Daishin-in.

power of public representation. These things, it must be observed, are gracious gifts which His Imperial Majesty is pleased to grant to his subjects upon His own judgment and condescension. These points may without difficulty or elucidation be understood, if one but glances at the dignified and majestic character of our national polity since the days of the first Imperial Ancestor, and of the Imperial Rescripts of April, 1875 (8th year of Meiji) and of October, 1881 (14th year of Meiji).

In foreign countries the course each nation pursues is different from that pursued by others, owing to the historical peculiarities of each nation. Opinions are consequently divided according to the different schools of thinkers, and these opinions are as yet far from being unified. Different scholars maintain different theories, and each advocating his own ideas by copious arguments they do not seem to come to any agreement. They have each of them more or fewer reasons for the support of their positions, which are plausible enough to effect an agitating influence upon the general public. It cannot but follow from such a state of things that men holding opinions more or less coinciding with each others' should gradually form themselves into a combination, and should be in perpetual conflict with those differing from them. Such is indeed what is very frequently observed in other countries. Yet in this country the upholding of the divine emblems of the Imperial Ancestors in a position permanent and inviolable, the maintenance of the dignity of the Imperial Family, while on the other hand the granting to subjects the right of representation, are matters of the most significant importance in their bearing upon the national polity and upon the great aims of the Imperial Ancestor. With regard to this matter, therefore, neither the one nor the other of His Majesty's subjects has the slightest shadow of right to attempt an intrusion. Should any of them either before or after the proclamation of the Constitution offer any objection to the determination of it according to His Majesty's own personal judgment, he should be looked upon as having overstepped the limits of freedom of speech, and that of holding public meetings and of petition ; and should any individual, under pretext of such objection, instigate or persuade others to plan insurrection, such necessary measures as expediency may require should be adopted for the maintenance of the public peace.

Secondly,—Administrative affairs ought to advance hand in hand with the march of social improvement. Since the Restoration the condition of society has been greatly changed with the downfall of the feudal system, and the mode of living and all sorts ct undertakings have assumed an entirely new phase and are now in a career of striking progress. Now, in this transition from the old to the new order of things, we inevitably find many forces in a stationary and unprogressive state, while other elements and antagonistic tendencies may be found perpetually conflicting with each other, and thereby preventing a happy harmonisation of social life. It is the Government's purpose to superintend these social forces, to protect deserving ones, and to point out the direction in which they ought to be conducted so as to secure the gradual and complete results of progress. It is owing to these circumstances that embarrassments and difficulties of an extraordinary nature are encountered in the field of administrative affairs. This is, indeed, unavoidable in the existing state of things.

Under these circumstances, those engaged in the work of administration ought to make stability and permanence their object, and disregarding all immediate results should foster in concert with the people the spirit of enterprise, industry, and perseverance. They ought, further, to make it their aim to promote the happiness and prosperity of the people and to enable them to prove to the eyes of the world their capacity to be a perfectly independent, unrestrained, and inviolate nation, thus bequeathing to our posterity the honour of being the subjects of a permanent and mighty Empire. To this end ought we to direct our aims, and to this end should we march in a straight line, carrying out to good effect all sorts of administrative affairs concerning education, industries, engineering works, economy, local self-goverument and the like. Such is the fixed plan of His Majesty's Government, originally designed and arranged by the anxious efforts of the lately deceased Ministers of State, in pursuance of His Majesty's profound ideas, and which has been left by them to us, holding us responsible to accomplish its completion. If at this juncture enterprise in the provinces should suffer relaxation on account of any excitement of the popular mind caused by occasional political agitation, and were the scheme of administration planned during these past twenty years, to be left to take care of itself, what would become of the future of our nation! You, whose duty it is to directly care for the welfare of the people, ought to spare no pains to promote their good.

The country being at present in the full career of progress, multifarious affairs, domestic as well as foreign, demand our attention. Particularly, for the existence and defence of the country, military and naval affairs ought not for a moment to be left neglected. Glancing at the general aspect of affairs in the outer world, and considering the permanent policy of this country, it cannot but be noticed that we, His Majesty's subjects, have a heavy burden to bear and have to endeavour with all preserverance and endurance to maintain the dignity of the country in the present and for the future. It is, therefore, the earnest desire of the Government that the people prove their loyalty and patriotism by faithfully discharging the two duties of paying taxes and of performing the military service; while on the other hand the Government shall strive after strictness, integrity and accuracy in expenditure, avoiding all superfluities and aiming at usefulness; and shall husband the resources of the country, and keep them available for every emergent demand. You should bear these points in mind, and should not fail to guide the people in the proper direction. You should also endeavour with every care not to injure the fostering of the resources of the people.

Thirdly :—Since the late Iwakura was sent abroad as Ambassador in 1871 (4th year of Meiji), Treaty Revision has always remained our unmovably fixed object, and opportunities have frequently been taken advantage of for the purpose of obtaining the result aimed at. Recently, conferences have been held by delegates appointed by our Government and by those of all the Treaty Powers, but before a conclusion had been arrived at, our Government had to announce the adjournment of the proceedings. This step was made necessary by the unfortunate circumstance that there were points in the views of the parties concerned that could not be brought to a solution. The revision of the treaties has important bearings both at home and abroad and the Government has to act with caution and prudence, so as to avoid, for the sake of the future of the country, all errors which it might not be in the power of the nation to repair. We shall pursue a fixed and unmovable line of policy for the purpose of revising the existing treaties containing an extraterritoriality clause, and of newly establishing on a footing of equality, friendly relations with the Treaty Powers, with a view to promote our mutual benefit. But for the attainment of the purpose in question, we must rely upon the improvement and perfection of our internal administration and of the laws of the country. Such is the step we have been forced to adopt from a careful consideration of expendiency in the peculiar situation in which the country is placed. As to the opinion that diplomatic affairs should be submitted to the public deliberation of the people, it must be observed that no such course is followed in any constitutional monarchy. The supreme powers connected with military and foreign affairs are exculsively in the hands of sovereigns, and excepting in certain cases no such affairs are submitted to the public deliberation of the people. Were the power of declaring war and of concluding peace and treaties to be delegated to the public, where it must be asked would be the supreme power of the Sovereign? For these reasons, the proposition above alluded to must be rejected according to our future constitution. This is also a point which you shall bear in mind in guiding the course to be followed by the people.

Besides what has thus far been set forth the Government will not fail to carry out by degrees, in accordance with the Imperial Rescripts, all measures necessary for the establishment of the constitution. Our object is to see every department of business conducted in good order and honestly so that the machinery of administration may be kept free from relaxation of effort and from corruption. We trust that you will, in obedience to the gracious wishes of His Imperial Majesty, endeavour not to deviate from the course already settled, and that, discharging your obligations to share the responsibility, and by the consistency of your conduct, you will not neglect to secure the honour of having contributed to the completion of the great work of the Restoration.

J.W.M., 1887, Oct. 8, pp. 352-53.

54. LOCAL CONTRIBUTIONS AND EXPENDITURES.

(Imp. Ord, No. 56, November 4, 1887.)

I. Money, grain, or other articles contributed towards objects the expense of which would otherwise be defrayed out of the local taxes, should be applied solely to the purposes named by the contributors under the decision of the local assembly concerned.

II. Expenditures coming under the heading of miscellaneous in connection with the local administration should be submitted to the consideration of the assembly concerned in the same way as the estimates of the other outlays.

III. The present regulations shall come into force from and after the 21st fiscal pear of Meiji.

J.W.M., 1887, Nov. 19, p. 496.

55. The Creation of Nara Ken.

(Imp. Ord. No. 59, Nov. 4, 1887.)

Nara Ken is to be established. The Kencho is to be at Nara. The extent of the jurisdiction is the province of Yamato. *J.W.M.*, 1887, Nov. 19, p. 496.

56. Organisation of the Government of Cities (Shi).[1]

(Law No. 1, April 14, 1888.)

Title I.—General Provisions.

Chapter 1.—Of Cities and their Circumscriptions.

I. The present law shall apply to every town separated from the gun and declared a city.

II. A city shall be considered a juristic person, and shall administer by itself its own affairs subject to the supreme control of the Government.

III. The boundaries of a city shall remain as they are, so long as no alteration thereof is made in conformity with the provisions of the present law.

IV. In case of any alteration of the boundaries of a city, or of the incorporation of a town or village with a city, or of the detachment of a part of a city, Article IV. of the Organisation of Towns and Villages shall apply.

V. Disputes concerning the boundaries of a city shall be decided by the Fu or Ken Council. Against the decision of the latter an action may be brought in the Administrative Court.

Chapter 2.—Of the City Residents (Shisumin) and of their Rights and Duties.

VI. All those who have their residence in a city shall be called the " residents" of the city.

All the residents of a city shall be entitled on the one hand

---

1. This law is commonly referred to as the Municipal Code.

to the common use of its establishments as well as its property, and on the other shall be subject to the duty of sharing the common burden of such city in accordance with the provisions of this law ; the provision of this Article, however, shall not prejudice any rights or duties founded on the civil law.

VII. Every independent male person being a subject of the Empire and in the enjoyment of his civil rights, shall be a citizen (*komin*) of a city, provided he has fulfilled the following conditions for the preceding two years:—1. That he has been a resident of such city.   2. That he has contributed toward; the common burden of such city.   3. That he has paid national land tax of two or more *yen* or other direct national taxes in such city.   Persons who have received alms from any public sources within the last two years shall be excepted.   The term of two years fixed in this Article may be dispensed with in particular cases, according to circumstances, by a decision of the city assembly.

An independent person, in the sense of this law, shall mean a person who has completed his twenty-fifth year, and has a household, provided, however, that he is not deprived of the right of freely disposing of and administering his property.

VIII. Every citizen shall be entitled on the one hand to the right of taking part in the city elections, and of eligibility for any honorary office in the city assembly or administration, and shall be bound on the other by the obligation of assuming such honorary office.

No citizen may refuse to accept any such office or resign the same during the term of the office, except when one of the following reasons shall exist :—

1. Inability to discharge his official duties on account of disease or illness.

2. Necessity of frequently absenting himself from the city on account of occupation.

3. Being sixty years old or more.

4. Engagement in the government service whereby he is unable to discharge his official duties in the city.

5. That he was an official of the city without salary for four years and that four years have not elapsed since, or that he was a member or the city assembly for six years and that six years have not elapsed since.

6. Any other valid ground of excuse recognized as such by the city assembly.

Any citizen who, without being sustained by any of the above enumerated reasons, refuses to accept any honorary office, or resigns it during the term of the office, or when the office is one of no definite duration of term does not fulfil his duties therein for a period of at least three years, or any honorary officer who actually evades the duties of any such office, may, by a decision of the city assembly, be subjected to suspension of citizenship for from three to six years, together with an additional levy, during the same period, or from one-eighth to one-quarter more than his ordinary share of contribution to the city expenditure.

Against the aforementioned decision of the city assembly a complaint may be made to the Fu or Ken Council, and against the decision of the latter an action may be brought in the Administative Court.

IX. A citizen shall lose his citizenship when he loses any of the necessary conditions prescribed in Article VII.

The citizenship shall be suspended during bankruptcy proceedings, during the pending of a judical enquiry or judicial detention when such enquiry or detention is on account of a supposed crime or delict which if proven shall involve the loss or suspension of civil rights, or during execution on account of a failure in payment of a tax.

Persons in actual military or naval service may not take part in the public affairs of a city.

Loss or suspension of citizenship shall also entail the loss of an office that is dependent thereon.

CHAPTER 3.—OF THE CITY LAWS.

X. Every city may issue by-laws for regulating such affairs of the city and such rights and duties of its residents, as to which the present law contains no express provision or gives authority for treating differently.

Every city may issue regulations for any of its establishments.

By-laws and regulations may not be in conflict with laws and ordinances, and shall be published according to the customary modes of the locality for notifying official documents.

TITLE II.—OF THE CITY ASSEMBLIES.

CHAPTER I.—OF THE CONSTITUTION AND ELECTIONS.

XI. The members of a city assembly shall be elected by the electors of the city from amongst the eligible citizens. The city assembly shall consist, in proportion to the population, of thirty members, in a city of less than fifty thousand souls, and of thirty-six, in one which has fifty thousand or more souls.

In a city with more than a hundred thousand souls, three members shall be added for every fifty thousand souls in excess; in one with more than two hundred thousand souls, the same number shall be added for every ten thousand in excess, and the highest number in one city shall be limited to sixty.

The number of members in a city assembly, however, may be changed by a city by-law, provided that it does not exceed the maximum.

XII. All citizens shall have the suffrage, excepting those whose citizenship is suspended (Article VIII. 3, Article IX. 2), or those who are in actual military or naval service.

Every Japanese subject in the enjoyment of his civil rights, and paying any direct city taxes, the amount of which exceeds that which is paid by one of the three citizens who pay the largest amount of such taxes in the city, shall also have the suffrage in that city, although he may lack in the qualifications enumerated in Article VII., unless there exists some reason which would cause a suspension of citizenship or unless he is in actual military or naval service.

Companies established in accordance with law and other juristic persons shall also have the suffrage under the same conditions as described in the preceding paragraph.

XIII. The electors shall be divided into three classes.

The first class shall consist of those electors who pay the highest sums of direct city taxes, the total of which amounts to one-third of the whole amount of direct city taxes paid by all the electors.

The second class shall consist, after excluding those belonging to the first class, of those electors who pay the highest sums of direct city taxes, the total of which amounts to one third of the whole amount of such taxes paid by all the electors. The remaining electors shall compose the third class.

An elector, the amount of whose taxes may fall into two classes, shall belong to the higher class. Should there be two or more persons that pay the same amount of taxes, and they come between two classes, that one or those, as the case may be, whose residence in the city has been the longest, shall be included in the higher class. When the matter cannot be decided by length of residence it shall be decided by seniority of age, and in case of infeasibility of the latter, by lot drawn by the Shichō.

Every class shall elect for itself one-third of the members from amongst the eligible citizens, irrespective of the classes.

XIV. In an extensive or thickly populated city electoral districts may be formed by a city by-law for all the classes or specially for the second or third one.

The number and extent of electoral districts, as well as the number of members to be elected by each district, shall be determined by a city by-law, but shall be based as much as possible upon the number of electors.

The district to which an elector belongs shall be determined by his place of residence, and in the absence of such residence, by the place wherein is situated the object on which he is taxed ; and in case he is taxed upon several distinct objects situated in several different districts, then the place wherein the objects on which he is taxed the most shall be decisive.

When electoral districts are formed, the clases shall be formed separately in each district.

Eligibility shall not be confined to persons belonging to the same district.

XV. All citizens having the suffrage (Article XII. 1) are eligible to membership.

The following persons, however, may not become members of a city assembly :—

1. Goverment officials attached to respective Fu or Ken authorities.

2. Salaried city officials.

3. Public prosecutors and police officers and forces.

4. Shintō or Buddhist priests and ministers of all other creeds.

5. Teachers of elementary schools.

As to other kinds of Government officials, the permission of the chief of the office to which they belong is required for becoming members.

Persons, not being recognized advocates, that make it their business to transact business for others in law courts or other public offices are ineligible.

A father and his son or brothers may not be members of a city assembly at one and the same time. In case such persons have been elected, the one who has polled the largest number of votes shall be declared elected, and in case of a tie, then the senior in age shall be declared elected. When they have been elected at different periods, the one last elected may not become a member.

A person having the relationship of father or son, or brother, to a member of a city council, shall for the time being, be disabled from becoming a member of the assembly of the same city. When a person having the same relationship to a member of a city assembly accepts the appointment of a member of the council of that city, such member of the city assembly shall have to retire from his membership.

XVI. Membership of a city assembly is honorary. The term of membership is six years and every three years one half of the members elected by each class shall be renewed. When the number of members is not divisible into two equal parts, the greater half shall be renewed first. The members who shall have to retire first shall be determined by lot.

Outgoing members are re-eligible.

XVII. Vacancies occurring between ordinary elections shall be supplied by substitutionary elections held at the same time that the ordinary elections are held. When, however, such vacancies amount to one-third or more of the whole number of members, or when it is deemed necessary by the city assembly, by the city council or by the Fu or Ken Chiji, an election for substitutional members shall be held, without awaiting the ordinary election.

A substitutional member shall retain his membership up to the end of the term of the membership of him whom he has replaced.

Ordinary and substitutionary elections shall be held by the same class and the same district by and from which the members to he replaced have been elected.

XVIII. Sixty days previous to an election the Shichō shall make out an original register of electors, describing their qualifications, and out of the orginal register shall draw up lists of electors. When the city is divided into two or more electoral districts original registers and lists shall be separately made out for each district.

The lists shall be exhibited for the public inspection of interested persons, for seven days, at the Shichō's office, or in other suitable public places in the locality. When any interested person wishes to make a complaint about the lists, he may do so during the above mentioned period to the Shichō. The Shichō in accordance with the decision of the city assembly (Article XXXV., 1) shall revise the lists, if it is necessary, ten days before the election and make them the final lists. No person whose name is not on the final lists may take part in the election.

The final lists made out according to this Article shall also be used in case a new election is necessary on account of refusal to serve as member by any one that has been elected, or in case an election is void or declared null.

XIX. When an election is to be held the Shichō shall issue a notification seven days before the election day, stating the time and place and the number of members to be elected by each class and from each district.

The election of the third class shall be held before that of the second and the first classes, and that of the second class before that of the first class.

XX. Election officers shall consist of either two or four persons, as honorary officers, chosen for the purpose by the Shichō from among the electors, and of the Shichō or his deputy, as Chairman, who shall open and close the election meeting, and shall keep order in the polling station. When two or more electoral districts are formed, there shall be such election officers for each district.

XXI. No one but the electors may enter the polling station during the election hours. Electors may not consult together or make suggestions to one another in that room.

XXII. The elections shall be made by ballots on which shall be inscribed the names of those for whom the vote is cast, and, after having been safeguarded in a folded paper (fūsin), shall be handed to the Chairman by the electors themselves; the names of the electors shall not be inscribed.

When the electors hand in their ballots. they shall orally give their full names and places of residence, and the Chairman, after having referred such names and places to the lists shall put the ballots unopened into a ballot-box. The ballot-box may not be opened until the polling is closed.

XXIII. A ballot containing a greater or smaller number of names than the one required shall not be void on that account. In the first case, the redundant names shall be rejected in order beginning with the one at the bottom.

The following ballots shall be void :—

1. Those containing no name at all or those containing any illegible names, so far as those names are concerned.

2. Those by which the persons voted for cannot be identified, so far as those persons are concerned.

3. Those containing the names of persons who are not eligible, so far as those names are concerned.

4, Those mentioning any matter other than the desiginat-ion of the persons voted for.

The question whether any particular votes shall or shall not be received and also the question as to the validity or nullity of a vote shall be provisionally decided by the officers, and in case of an equality of votes, they shall be decided by the Chairman.

XXIV. Voting shall be done in person; votes by proxy are not allowed.

Electors entitled to the suffrage by virtue of Article XII., 2, may vote by proxy and in case any of them is not an independent male or is a company or some other juristic person, then the voting must be by proxy. Such proxy must be a Japanese subject, being an independent male person, and in the enjoyment of civil rights. One and the same person, however, may not be a proxy for more than one person, and every proxy must show his authority of proxy to the election officers.

XXV. Those obtaining the greatest number of valid votes shall be declared elected. In case of a tie, seniority of age shall determine, and when it cannot be so determined, it shall be determined by lot drawn by the Chairman.

Where more than one substitutional member is elected (Article XVII), the one who obtains the largest number of votes shall be the one to take the place of that replaced member whose remaining term of membership is the longest. In case of a tie the order shall be determined by lot.

XXVI. Election officers shall keep minutes of an election which shall contain the details of the election operations. These minutes having been read aloud at the end of the election shall be signed by the election officers and attached to the lists of electors.

The ballots cast shall be attached to the minutes and preserved until the completion of the election.

XXVII. When an election is over the Chairman shall give to the persons elected notice of their election. Persons who decline such election shall notify the Shichō within five days at the latest from time of notice of such election.

Any one who has been elected for more than one electoral district or by more than one class of electors, shall notify the Shichō within the same period, which election he will accept. Should he give no notice, he shall be considered as having declined all, and shall be dealt with in accordance with Article VIII.

XXVIII. When an elector wishes to make any complaint as to the validity of the election proceedings, he shall do so to the Shichō within seven days from the time of the election (Article XXXV., 1).

When an election is over the Shichō shall make a report thereof of the Fu or Ken Chiji, and should the Chiji entertain any objection to the validity of the election based upon serious grounds, he may, irrespective of any complaint, submit the case to the decision of the Fu or Ken Council, and it shall be disposed of in accordance with such decision.

When there has been any essential irregularity in election proceedings, such election shall be declared altogether null and void, and when any person who has been elected is found to be without qualifications his election shall be void. In either of these cases a new election shall be held.

XXIX. When a person declared elected is afterwards discovered to be without the requisite qualifications or has subsequently lost them, his election shall become void. The question whether such qualifications are wanting or not shall be decided by the city assembly.

CHAPTER 2.—OF COMPETENCY AND BUSINESS.

XXX. The assembly of a city shall represent the city and decide on all subjects relating to the city affairs in conformity with the provisions of this law, and also on those matters which have already been entrusted to its management or which may hereafter be so entrusted by laws or Imperial ordinances.

XXXI. The matters that are to be decided by a city assembly are principally as follows :—

1. The making and altering of city by-laws and regulations.

2. Affairs the expenses of which are to be defrayed out of the city revenues, with the exception of those mentioned in Artcle LXXIV.

3. The determining of the budget of the city as well as the approving of an outlay not included in the budget or of one exceeding the estimate.

4. The giving discharge to the annual accounts of the receipts and expenditure.

5. The determining of the modes of imposing and of collecting duties for use (shiyoryo), fees, city taxes, and services in person or in kind, so far as not determined by-laws or Imperial ordinances.

6. Alienation, purchase, exchange, or mortgage of the immovable property of the city.

7. Matters relating to the disposition of the stock property.

8. The incurring of a new liability or the relinquishment of an acquired right, so far as it has not already been determined by the budget.

9. The determining of the modes of management of the city property and establishments.

10. Requisition of security from city officials, as well as determination of its amount.

11. Entering in to a law-suit or in to an arbitration concerning the city.

XXXII. The city assembly shall elect the city officials within its competency by virtue of laws or Imperial ordinances.

XXXIII. The city assembly shall be competent to examine papers and accounts relating to the city affairs and to demand reports from the Shichō, in order to ascertain whether the management of affairs, the execution of the decisions of the assembly, and the collection and the application of the revenue are properly carried out.

The city assembly may present to the superintending authority memorials on matters concerning the public interest of the city.

XXXIV. The city assembly shall present its views on any subject when such views are asked for by the government authorities.

XXXV. The city assembly shall also decide all complaints brought before it relating to the question as to whether or not any particular person possesses the right of a resident or of a citizen in the city or the qualifications of the elector or for eligibility, as to the correctness or incorrectness of electoral lists or of the formation of the electoral classes, as to the right of voting by proxy (Article XII. 2), and also as to the validity of any election of the members of the assembly (Article XXVIII.)

Against any such decision of the city assembly, a complaint may be made to the Fu or Ken Council, and against the decision of the latter, an action may be brought in the Administrative Court.

With regard to the matters mentioned in this Article the Shichō also may enter a complaint or bring an action.

No complaint or action shall have a suspensive effect. No new election, however, may be held before there is a final decision.

XXXVI. No member of a city assembly may bind himself by the direction or request of any of his constituents.

XXXVII. The city assembly shall annually elect for the year from amongst its own members at the beginning of each calendar year a President and Vice-President.

XXXVIII. When the matter of any question before the city assembly relates personally to the President himself, or to his parents, his brothers, his wife, or his children, the President shall be deemed as prevented from taking the chair, and the Vice-President shall act in his place.

When both the President and Vice-President are prevented from presiding, the senior member in point of age shall act as president.

XXXIX. The members of a city council may be present in the city assembly and give explanations on matters under consideration in the assembly.

XL. The city assembly shall be convoked by its President whenever there is any necessity for its meeting. It shall also be convoked when it is demanded by a fourth or more of its members, by the Shichō, or by the city council. The notification of convocation and the subjects to be deliberated upon, shall be announced at least three days beforehand, except when the case demands urgency. The city assembly may, by its decision, fix beforehand its regular days of meeting.

The above provisions shall also apply to the invitation of members of the city council to the meetings of the city assembly.

XLI. The quorum of a city assembly shall be two-thirds of the members. An exception to this shall be where the members have been convoked a second time in regard to one and the same subject, and yet the requisite number of members has not appeared.

XLII. The decision of the city assembly shall be determined by a majority of votes. In case of an equality of votes, the matter shall be debated and voted upon a second time. Should the votes still be equally divided the President shall decide.

XLIII. No member may participate in deciding a question in the city assembly, on a matter personally concerning himself, his parents, his brothers, his wife, or his children.

In a case where it happens that the assembly is unable to obtain a quorum, on account of the exclusion of several members in the above manner, the Fu or Ken Council shall decide upon the matter in question for the city assembly.

XLIV. The election of the city officials to be elected by the city assembly, shall be made by secret ballot separately and severally for every such official, and whoever obtains more than half of the numbers of valid votes shall be declared elected. In case no one obtains such requisite number of votes, a new ballot shall be taken for the two individuals among them that have obtained the highest number of votes ; and when three or more persons obtain the highest, but an equal number of such votes, a new ballot of two of them determined by lot drawn by the President, shall be taken. When in either of these cases, neither of the two obtains a majority of votes, it shall be decided by lot. As to other details, Articles XXII., XXIII., and XXIV., 1, shall apply.

For the election mentioned in this Article, an election by nomination may be substituted upon the decision of the city assembly.

XLV. The sittings of city assemblies shall be public, but strangers may be excluded when it is deemed desirable by the President.

XLVI. The President shall allot assembly works to the members, shall superintend meetings and elections, shall open, adjourn, and close the sitting and keep order in the assembly chamber. He may cause any stranger who openly signifies his assent or dissent, or who is in any way disorderly to retire from the chamber.

XLVII. The city assembly shall cause its clerks to keep minutes wherein shall be recorded the decisions, the results of elections held therein, and the names of the members present.

Such minutes shall be read aloud at the end of the sitting, and shall be signed by the president and at least two of the members present.

The decisions of the city assembly shall be reported to the Shichō together with a copy or the original of the minutes.

The clerks of the city assembly shall be appointed by it.

XLVIII. The city assembly shall provide itself with business regulations ; such regulations may contain provisions for penalties, not exceeding two *yen*, to be inflicted upon members who may infringe the same.

TITLE III.—OF THE CITY ADMINISTRATION.

CHAPTER I.—OF THE CONSTITUTION AND APPOINTMENT OF THE CITY COUNCIL AND OFFICIALS.

XLIX. There shall be a council in every city that shall consist of the following members :—

    1. A Shichō (Mayor).
    2. Assistants; three in Tōkyō, two in Kyōto and Ōsaka, and one in all other cities.
    3. Honorary councilmen, twelve in Tōkyō, nine in Kyōto and Ōsaka, and six in all other cities.

The number of assistants and of honorary councilmen, may be varied by city by-laws.

L. The Shichō shall be a salaried official, and his term of office shall be six years. For the Shichō, the Minister of State for Home Affairs shall cause the city assembly to propose three candidates, of whom he shall make his representations to His Majesty the Emperor, and ask his pleasure in regard to the selection of one of them. If he is unable to obtain the Imperial approval of any of them, he shall cause the assembly to make another proposal of candidates. If he is still unable to obtain the Imperial approval, he shall, until he causes the city assembly to make a further proposal of candidates and obtain the Imperial approval of one of them, either appoint a deputy *pro tempore*, or despatch a government official at the expense of the city for discharging the Shichō's duties.

LI. The assistants and the honorary councilmen shall be elected by the city assembly. The election shall be carried on in conformity with Article XLIV, with this exception, that in case of a tie, the selection shall be made by the Fu or Ken Council and not by lot.

LII. The assistants shall be salaried officials and their term of office shall be six years.

The elections of assistants shall be approved by the Fu or Ken Chiji, and when such approval is withheld with regard to any assistant, a new election shall be held. When this second election does not receive approval, the Fu or Ken Chiji may himself either appoint a deputy assistant *pro tempore*, or despatch at the expense of the city a government official for discharging the duty of the assistant, until a new election receives approval.

LIII. It is not essential that the Shichō or the assistants be citizens of the city, but they shall be entitled to citizenship when they are appointed to the office.

LIV. The honorary councilmen shall be elected from amongst those citizens of the city that are thirty years old or over, possessing the suffrage. Their term of office shall be four years, but they shall remain in office even after the completion of their terms, until their successors enter upon the office.

One-half of the honorary councilmen shall be renewed every two years. When their number is indivisible into two equal parts, the greater half shall be renewed first. The councilmen to go out of office first shall be determined by lot. Any outgoing councilmen are re-eligible.

When any vacancy occurs among the honorary councilmen in the meantime, an election for a substitutional councilman for the remainder of the term shall at once be held.

LV. The offices of the Shichō, the assistants, and of the other members of the council are incompatible with the offices mentioned in the second paragraph of Article XV; and the persons mentioned in the fourth paragraph of the same Article may not be elected honorary councilmen,

Persons having the relationship to each other of father and son or of brother may not both be members of the council at one and the same, and when any one bearing such relationship to a member is made Shichō such member shall have to resign his membership. As to what remains Article XV. paragraph 5 shall apply.

The Shichō and any assistant may resign office by giving notice to that effect, three months beforehand ; but by so doing all claim to pension shall be lost to them.

LVI. Neither the Shichō nor any assistant may hold a salaried office of any other kind, or become a director of a joint stock company, or hold any important position therein ; and with regard to other kinds of commercial or industrial occupations, neither of them may carry one on without having received permission from the Fu or Ken Chiji.

LVII. The city council shall decide upon the validity or invalidity of the election of the honorary councilmen.

When it is discovered that a person already elected did not possess the requisite qualifications, or when he has lost them after he has entered upon office, his election shall become void. The question as to such qualifications shall be decided by the city council. Against such decision a complaint may be made to the Fu or Ken Council, and against the decision of the latter an action may be brought in the Administrative Court. As to what remains the last paragraph of Article XXXV. shall apply.

LVIII. There shall be a treasurer in every city, who shall be appointed by the city assembly on the proposal of the city council.

The treasurer may not at one and the same time be also a member of the city council.

The appointment of the treasurer requires the approval of the Fu or Ken Chiji. As to what remains, Articles LI, LII, LIII, LV, and LXXVI shall apply.

The treasurer shall furnish security.

LIX. There shall be clerks and other necessary supplementary employés and servants in every city, to whom suitable salaries shall be given. The number of such persons shall be determined by a decision of the city assembly, and their appointment shall be made by the city council.

LX. A city may be by a decision of the council divided for convenience of administration into several districts, each having a Kuchō and a deputy. The Kuchō and his deputy shall be honorary officials, except in Tōkyō, Kyōto, and Ōsaka, where they may be made salaried officials.

The Kuchō and his deputy shall be elected by the city assembly from amongst the citizens belonging to that particular district or to neighbouring ones, and who possess the suffrage. When there is a separate assembly for such district (Article CXIII), the Kuchō and the deputy shall be elected by that assembly, except in Tōkyō, Kyōto, and Ōsaka where they shall be appointed by the city council.

In Tōkyō, Kyōto, and Ōsaka, there may be appointed supplementary employés and servants for a district in conformity with the preceding Article.

LXI. A city may, upon a decision of the city assembly, institute temporary or permanent committees. Their functions shall be honorary.

Committees may either be composed of members of the council, or of those of the assembly, or of members of both of these and citizens having the suffrage ; a member of the council shall be chairman of any such committee.

The members of a committee taken from amongst the members of the assembly, shall be elected by the assembly, and those taken from amongst the citizens, by the council; the remainder shall be appointed by the Shichō.

With regard to the composition of permanent committees special provisions may be made by city by-laws.

LXII. The Kuchō and the members of a committee may, by a decision of the city assembly, be allowed remuneration suitable to their trouble, besides compensation for the actual expenses needed for the discharge of their duties.

LXIII. The city officials may be re-elected upon the completion of their term of office.

The city officials and servants may be discharged at any time unless there exist special provisions or a contract to the contrary.

CHAPTER 2.—OF THE COMPETENCY AND BUSINESS OF THE
CITY COUNCIL AND OFFICIALS.

LXIV. The city council shall be the local authority of the city and shall carry on the administration thereof. The principal affairs to be undertaken by the city council are as follows:—

1. The preparation of subjects for deliberation in the city assembly, and the execution of the decisions of the assembly. When it appears that any decision of the assembly exceeds its competency, or is in conflict with laws or ordinances, or is prejudicial to the public good, the council shall, upon their own judgment or by instruction of the superintending authority, suspend the execution of such decision, explaining the reason therefor, and cause the matter to be discussed a second time. If the assembly does not change its decision, the council shall apply for the ruling of the Fu or Ken Council. When the suspension is on account of a decision of the assembly exceeding its competency or on account of conflict with laws or Imperial ordinances, an action may be brought in the Administrative Court against the ruling of the Fu or Ken Council.

2. The management of the establishment of the city, and superintendence of the management of such establishments when there are special managers thereof.

3. The administration of the city revenue, the ordering of receipts and of payments fixed in the budget or by special decision of the assembly, and the superintendence of the management of the treasury and accounts.

4. Looking after the rights of the city and the administration of its property.

5. Superintendence over the city officials and servants, and exercising disciplinary authority over them, the Shichō excepted. Disciplinary penalties shall consist of reprimands and of fines not exceeding ten *yen*.

6. The custody of all papers and documents.

7. Representation of the city as against outsiders, especi-

ally in lawsuits, or in arbitrations, and communications with other authorities or private individuals, in the name of the city.

8. Imposing and collecting duties for use, fees, city taxes, as well as services in person or in kind, in accordance with laws or Imperial ordinances or with decisions of the city assembly.

9. The carrying out of all other affairs entrusted to the council by laws and ordinances, or by the instructions of the superior authority.

LXV. The quorum of the city council shall consist of the chairman or his deputy and of one third of the whole number of honorary councilmen.

A decision of the council shall be determined by a majority of votes, and in case of an equality of votes the chairman shall decide.

Matters decided upon shall be recorded in the minute book.

When it appears that any decision of the council exceeds its competency, or is in conflict with law or ordinances, or is prejudicial to the public good, the Shichō shall, upon his own judgment, or by instruction of the superintending authorities, suspend the execution of the decision, explaining the reason therefor, and shall apply for the ruling of the Fu or Ken Council. When the suspension is on account of a decision exceeding its competency or on account of conflict with laws or Imperial ordinances, an action may be brought in the Administrative Court against the ruling of the Fu or Ken Council.

LXVI. The provision described in Article XLIII. shall also apply to the city council. When the council is unable to obtain a quorum on account of this provision, the city assembly shall decide for the council.

LXVII. The Shichō shall direct and superintend all the administrative affairs of the city and shall do his best for prompt despatch of business.

The Shichō shall convoke the meetings of the council and shall be the chairman thereof. When the Shichō is prevented from taking the chair by any cause, his place shall be taken by his deputy.

The Shichō shall prepare the subjects of deliberation for the council, shall execute its decisions, and shall hold and sign correspondence in the name of the council.

LXVIII. When any question which belongs to the competency of the council requires an urgent settlement, so that there is no time for convoking a meeting of the council, the Shichō may decide and settle it upon his own judgment, and make a report thereon at the next sitting of the council.

LXIX. The members of the council shall assist in the business of the Shichō, and shall act for and represent him when he is prevented from discharging his duties from any cause.

The Shichō may with the consent of the city assembly, entrust the members of the council with the administration of some particular branch of the city administration. In such cases honorary councilmen may receive remuneration suitable to their trouble, besides compensation for the actual expenses needed for the discharge of duties.

Special duties, if any, of the assistants and of the honorary councilmen and the order in which members shall act for and represent the Shichō, shall be regulated by a city by-law. In the absence of such regulations, the Shichō shall be represented by the members of the council, in the order which shall be determined by Fu or Ken Chiji.

LXX. The treasurer shall manage the receipts and expenditure and the accounts of the city.

LXXI. The clerks shall be subordinate to the Shichō and shall discharge the office business allotted to them.

LXXII. The Kuchō and his deputy (Article LX) shall, as the organ of the council, receive and carry out its orders and directions, and assist in the execution of the administrative affairs of the city relating to the district.

LXXIII. Committees (Article LXI) shall be subordinate to the council and shall either take charge of some special branches of the city administration or some establishments of the city, or take charge of any affairs temporarily entrusted to them.

The Shichō may sit and take the chair at any time, with full right of voting in the meetings of the committees. With regard to the competency of a permanent committee, special provisions may be made by a city by-law.

LXXIV. The Shichō shall also discharge the following duties in conformity with laws and ordinances :—

    1. Where there is no special office established for discharging the duties of the local police ; (1) duties incumbent upon him as an auxiliary officer of the judicial police, and (2) duties of local police affairs incumbent upon him by virtue of laws or ordinances.

    2. The business of a wreck office.

    3. The administrative affairs of the Fu or Ken, and those in general of the Central Government, relating to the locality, in so far as no special officials are appointed for the affairs.

Any of the affairs mentioned in the preceding three headings may, by permission of the superintending authority, be entrusted to another member of the council.

Expenses requisite for the conduct of the affairs mentioned in this Article shall be borne by the city.

CHAPTER 3.—OF SALARIES AND ALLOWANCES.

LXV. Honorary functionaries may only receive compensation for the actual expenses needed for the discharge of their duties, unless there are special provisions prescribed in this law.

The amount of compensations and of remunerations where they are allowed shall be determined by the city assembly.

LXXVI. The amount of salary to be paid to the Shichō, to the assistants, and to other salaried officials as well as to servants, shall be fixed by the decision of the city assembly.

The fixing of the salary of the Shichō requires the approval of the Minisier of State for Home Affairs. When he sees reason for not giving such approval, he may fix the amount himself.

The fixing of the salaries of assistants requires the approval of the Fu or Ken Chiji. When he sees reason for not giving such approval, he shall cause it to be fixed by the Fu or Ken Council.

The amount of salary to be paid to the Shichō, to the assistants, and to other paid officials, may be regulated by a city by-law.

LXXVII. Provision may be made by a city bye-law for pensions to be given to the Shichō and other salaried officials.

LXXVIII. Disputes about the salaries and pensions of paid officials and about the allowances mentioned in Art. LXXV. shall be decided by the Fu or Ken Council on application of the interested party. Against such decision an action may be brought in the Administrative Court.

LXXIX. When anyone in receipt of a pension obtains an appointment in government service or in a fu, gun, city, town, or village, or in any public corporation, whereby he becomes the recipient of a salary, such pension shall be suspended while he receives such salary ; and when he becomes entitled to a new pension, the amount of which is equal to or greater than that of the former one, his right to the latter shall become extinct.

LXXX. Salaries, pensions, remuneration, and compensations shall be a burden upon the city.

TITLE IV.—OF MANAGEMENT OF CITY PROPERTY.

CHAPTER I.—OF CITY PROPERTY AND CITY TAXES.

LXXXI. The city is bound to keep and maintain as "Stock Property" its immovable property, its capitalized money, its stored-up grain, &c.

Extraordinary receipts of money or grain shall be added to the property, excepting donations or the like given for some special purposes.

LXXXII. The city property shall be managed and made use of for the common benefit of the city, excepting where there exists any special title founded on the civil law.

LXXXIII. Where residents of a city are entitled by any old custom to the direct use of lands or other objects belonging to the city, such custom shall not be altered except upon a decision of the city assembly.

LXXXIV. Admission to the use of any land or other object belonging to the city, may be made, by a city by-law, dependent upon the payment of an annual duty for use (shiyoryo) or of an entrance fee or of both of them. Any enjoyment of special rights by virtue of the civil law shall not come under this rule.

LXXXV. Persons entitled to the use of any such land or object (Articles LXXXIII. and LXXXIV.) shall have to bear the necessary expenses required for the land or the object in use, in proportion to their share in the use.

LXXXVI. The city assembly may, in case it is necessary for the common good of the city, withdraw or restrict any right of use (Articles LXXXIII. and LXXXIV.) excepting where such rights rest on the civil law.

LXXXVII. All the selling or letting of the city property as well as all contracts for buildings and purveyances shall be made by way of public competition. A deviation is only permissible in cases of special urgency, or when the cost would be out of proportion to the advantages to be derived therefrom, or when special approval is obtained from the city assembly.

LXXXVIII. The city is bound to bear its own necessary expenditure as well as those which are already imposed upon it by laws or ordinances or which may be imposed in future by laws or Imperial ordinances.

When the revenue arising from the property, duties for use fees (Article LXXXIX), fines, penalties, and other kinds of income belonging to a city by virtue of laws or Imperial ordinances does not cover the expenditure of the city, it may impose and collect city taxes (Article XC) and services in person or in kind (Article CI).

LXXXIX. The city may impose and collect duties or the use of its property and establishments and fees for anything done specially for the benefit of some individuals.

XC. As city taxes may be imposed :—

1. Additional percentages upon national and Fu or Ken taxes.
2. Special direct or indirect taxes.

Additional percentages shall be imposed as a rule to direct national, Fu or Ken taxes on the whole extent of the city, and at a uniform rate. Special taxes may be imposed only when, besides the additional percentages, some further tax is required by a city.

XCI. So far as no express provisions are prescribed in this law, minute regulations relating to duties for use and fees (Article LXXXIX), special taxes (Article IX. par. 1, heading 2), and Ku, Cho, or Son rates hitherto existing, shall be provided for by a city by-law. In such by-law the imposition of a penalty not exceeding one *yen* and ninety-five *sen* may be provided.

The imposition and collection of these penalties shall be the duty of the council. Against an imposition of such penalty an action may be brought in a court of law, within fourteen days from the time when sentence of penalty is served.

XCII. All those who shall sojourn in a city for a period of three months or over, shall be liable to the payment of city taxes, and that liability shall commence from the beginning of such sojourn.

XCIII. Persons who nave no residence in a city and who do not sojourn therein for a period of three months, but own lands or houses in the city or carry on some trade therein (excepting pedlars and hawkers), shall be subjected to the city tax imposed with respect to those lands, houses, trades, and incomes derived therefrom. The case shall be the same with regard to juristic persons, the government postal, telegraph, and railway services excepted.

XCIV. When additional percentages are imposed on income taxes, or city income taxes are specially levied in and for the city, the amount of income derived by persons subjected to such taxes, from lands, houses, or trades (pedlars and hawkers excepted) owned or carried on without the city, shall be deducted from the aggregate amount of their incomes.

XCV. When a person possessing residences or places of sojourn in several cities, towns or villages is subjected to the city taxes mentioned in the preceding Article, the amount of his income that arises from other sources than lands, homes, or trades, shall be divided into equal parts, according to the number of cities, towns, or villages, and only one part thereof may be made subject to such taxes in one place.

XCVI. Incomes mentioned in Article III. of the Income Tax Regulations shall be exempted from city taxes.

XCVII. The following shall be exempted from city taxes :—

1. Grounds, establishments, and buildings used for direct public purposes and belonging to the state, to a fu, ken, gun, city, town, or village, and other public corporations.

2. Shintō and Buddhist temples, government or public schools and hospitals ; grounds, esblishments, buildings, devoted to scientific, artistic, or charitable purposes.

3. Forests and waste lands belonging to the state, except in cases where any work is undertaken benefitting such forests or lands, and when, to cover the expense incurred for such work, assessments are made thereon by permission of the Minister of State for Home Affairs and of the Minister of State for Finance.

Newly cultivated or reclaimed lands may be exempted from city taxes for a certain length of time by a city by-law.

XCVIII. Other objects besides those mentioned in the preceding two Articles, that are to be exempted from city taxes, shall be determined by special laws or Imperial ordinances. With regard to city taxes to be imposed on members of the Imperial family, they shall remain as they are at present until they are regulated by futher laws or Imperial ordinances.

XCIX. When in the city there is an establishment which may solely benefit some particular individuals, expenses of its repairs or maintenance shall be borne by such interested individuals.

When an establishment is kept up for the sole benefit of a particular district in a city, the expenses of its repairs and maintenance shall be borne by those that are resident or sojourning in the district or that own lands or houses or carry on a trade therein (excepting pedlars and hawkers). Should there be property owned by that district, the income derived therefrom shall be applied first to the defraying of the expenses.

C. City taxes shall be imposed in monthly apportionment from the beginning of the month following the one in which the liability for them arises, to the end of the month in which it ceases.

When in the course of a financial year, any one becomes free from liability to payment of taxes or such liability undergoes a change, notification thereof shall be made by him to the Shichō. Up to the end of the month in which such notification is given the same taxes may be levied as in the past.

CI. For public works of a city, or for the maintenance of the public peace and order, services in person or in kind may be imposed on the tax payers. No personal service of a scientific or professional nature may be imposed.

Except in urgent cases, services in person or in kind shall be imposed in proportion to the amount of direct city taxes, and their money value shall be estimated beforehand.

Individuals liable to personal service may perform the same, either in their own persons or by suitable substitutes, at their own convenience, and excepting in cases of urgent necessity they may compound them by a payment of their money value.

CII. When any person does not pay in due time his duty for use or fees (Article XCVIII.), his city taxes (Article XC.), the money value for service (Article CI.), duties for use or entrance fees in regard to the common property of the city (Article LXXXIV), or any other city dues, the city council shall call upon him to pay and in case he still fails to do so he shall be dealt with in accordance with the regulations for the treatment of non-payers of national taxes.   For sending such call a fee may be exacted by virtue of a city by-law.

In regard to persons in extreme need, the city council may, at its discretion, grant a delay of payment of dues, so long as such delay does not extend beyond the period of the current financial year.   When it does extend beyond such period the decision of the city assembly must be taken.

With regard to the collection of arrears, to the prescriptions and to the privileges of priority, the provisions concerning national taxes shall apply.

CIII. Additional percentages on land taxes shall be imposed on the payers of the land taxes.   Other city taxes imposed on lands may be imposed either on the owners or the occupiers thereof.

CIV. Complaints in regard to imposition of city taxes shall be brought before the council within three months from the time of service of the writ of imposition ; when this period elapses without any complaint, all right to demand reduction, exemption, or refunding of taxes for the current financial year, shall be lost.

CV. Complaints concerning the imposition of city taxes and the right to the use of an establishment or of common property of a city, or of the benefits arising therefrom, shall be decided by the city council, excepting when the disputed right in question is founded on civil law.

Against the above decision a complant may be made to the Fu or Ken Council, and against the decision of the latter an action may be brought in the Administrative Court.

The complaints or actions mentioned in this Article shall have no suspending effect.

CVI. The raising of loans in a city shall be limited to cases when it is for the repayment of the principal of an old loan or when an entraordinary outlay is required on account of an act of nature or of a calamity, or such like, or of some matter of permanent benefit to the city, and yet no augmentation of the ordinary revenue can be made without inflicting an excessive burden on the residents.

When the raising of a loan is decided upon by a city assembly it shall also predetermine the mode of raising it, the rate of interest to be paid and the method of repayment. The first instalment of such repayment shall be made within three years, and there shall be a fixed proportion of annual instalment of repayment, so that the whole shall be paid off within thirty years from the raising thereof.

Temporay loans necessary for meeting outlays, the estimates for which are contained in the budget, shall not come under the restrictions of this Article, provided such loans are repaid out of the income of the current financial year ; for such cases, no decision of the city assembly is required.

CHAPTER 2.—OF THE ESTIMATES AND ACCOUNTS OF THE REVENUE AND EXPENDITURE OF THE CITY.

CVII. The city council estimating, as far as possible, the probable amount of revenue and of expenditure of the city for the next financial year, shall make a draft of the budget for the year two months in advance. The financial year shall be the same as that of the state.

The Minister of State for Home Affairs may fix the form of such budget by a departmental ordinance.

CVIII. The draft of the budget shall be submitted to the deliberation of the city assembly before the beginning of the financial year, and when it is finally settled, it shall be reported to the Fu or Ken Chiji, and the important points therein shall be notified to the public, according to the customary mode of publication of official documents in the locality.

When the draft of a budget is introduced into the city assembly, it shall be accompanied by a report of the city council on the general transactions of the city, and by an inventory of the city property.

CIX. Expenditures not contained in the budget or that

exceed the estimates in the budget, can be defrayed only upon approval of the assembly.

In every budget there may be provided the "contingencies fund " (yobihi) for meeting any unexpected expenditures and it may be applied by the council without previous approval of the assembly to expenses not mentioned in the budget, or to those exceeding the budget estimates. Such funds, however, may not be applied to any expenses expressly negatived by the assembly.

CX. When a budget is determined by the assembly a copy thereof shall be transmitted by the Shichō to the treasurer of the city. When in a budget there is any matter requiring the authorisation of the superintending authority or of the council (Articles CXXI-CXXIII.), such authorisation shall be obtained beforehand.

The treasurer may make no payment without an order of the council (Article LXIV. heading 3) or of the superintending authority, and even when he receives such an order from the council, he may make no payment which is not provided for in the budget or when such order is not in accordance with the provisions of the preceding Article.

The treasurer shall be responsible for all payments made by him in contravention of the preceding paragraph.

CXI. The treasury of the city shall be examined monthly on a fixed day, and a special examination shall be made at least once a year. The monthly examination shall be made by the Shichō or his deputy, and the special by the Shichō or his deputy with the assistance of one or more members of the assembly chosen for the purpose by election by the members of the assembly.

CXII. The annual accounts shall be made up within three months from the end of the financial year, and shall together with papers and documents be presented by the treasurer to the council, who after examining the same shall submit it with its own observations thereon, to the approval of the Assembly. The decision of the assembly shall be reported by the Shichō to the Fu or Ken Chiji.

Audit of accounts shall be considered a case of hindrance for the members of the council in the sense of Articles XXXVIII and XLIII.

TITLE V.—OF THE ADMINISTRATION OF DISTRICTS POSSESSING SEPARATE PROPERTY.

CXIII. When a district in a city possesses any separate property or establishment of its own, and bears the expenses entailed by it (Article XCIX), the city assembly may issue a by-law and institute a ku assembly for affairs relating to the aforesaid property or establishment. In such case the provisions for the city assembly shall apply to such ku assembly.

CXIV. The administration of the affairs mentioned in the preceding Article shall be carried on by the city council in conformity with the provisions for city administration, but with a separate treasury and account.

TITLE VI.—OF THE SUPERINTENDENCE OF THE ADMINISTRATION OF CITIES.

CXV. The administration of the cities shall be superintended by the Fu and Ken Chiji in the first instance and by the Minister of State for Home Affairs in the second, with the reservation of cases, where the coöperation of the Fu or Ken Council is required by virtue of law.

CXVI. Excepting in cases where it is provided otherwise in this law, a complaint against any measure or decision, relating to the administrative affairs of a city, taken or made by the Fu or Ken Chiji or by the Fu or Ken Council, may by brought before the Minister of State for Home Affairs.

Complaints relating to the administrative affairs of a city, shall be presented, together with reasons justifying the same, within fourteen days from the day on which the decree of the decision has been served or otherwise notified, except in cases where some special limitation of time is prescribed in this law. Actions to be brought by virtue of this law in the Administrative Court against any Fu or Ken Chiji or the Fu or Ken

Council shall be limited to twenty-one days from the day on which the decision has been served or otherwise notified.

In all cases where a decision is given in the Administrative Court, no complaint touching the same matter may be laid before the Minister of State for Home Affairs.

When complaint is laid or an action is brought in regard to a measure or to a decision, the execution of the same shall be suspended, except where there are special provisions in this law to the contrary, or where such suspension shall be deemed by the competent authority prejudicial to the common good of the city.

CXVII. The superintending authorities shall look after the administration of the city, to see that it does not infringe any law or ordinance, or that there is no irregularity or delay in the transaction of its business. To this end the superintending authorities may demand reports on any administrative affairs, and the production of papers and documents relating to budgets and accounts, and the like; they may also examine the state of affairs and the treasury by visiting the actual spot.

CXVIII. When a city does not include in its budget an expenditure burdened upon it by law or Imperial ordinance, or that has been ordered by the competent authorities, or when it does not approve or actually supply funds for an extraordinary expenditure, the Fu or Ken Chiji may, upon statement of his reason for so doing, embody the amount of such expenditure in the budget or order payment of the same.

Against a measure taken by the Fu or Ken Chiji in pursuance of the preceding paragraph, an action may be brought in the Administrative Court by the city.

CXIX. When a city assembly or city council does not render a decision npon any matter which it ought to decide, the Fu or Ken Council shall do so in its stead.

CXX. The Minister of State for Home Affairs may dissolve the city assembly. When the city assembly is dissolved, it shall be simultaneously ordered that a new election shall be held within three months. Until the newly elected assembly meets all matters to be decided by the city assembly shall be decided by the Fu or Ken Council in its stead.

CXXI. The decision of the city assembly relating to the following matters requires the approval of the Minister of State for Home Affairs :—

    1. Issuing or altering by-laws.

    2. The alienation, mortgaging, exchanging, or any significant alterations of objects valuable from a scientific or historical point of view.

With regard to matters mentioned under the first heading, approval shall be given only after an Imperial decsion is previously obtained in the matter.

CXXII. A decision of the city assembly, relating to the following matters, requires the approval of the Minister of State for Home Affairs and of the Minister of State for Finance :—

    1. The raising of new loans or the increasing of loans ; or when it is necessary to deviate from the provisions of Article CVI., par. 2. Loans, the terms of the repayment of which is within three years, shall not come under the limitation of this Article.

    2. Introducing a new city special tax, duty for use or a fee, or raising the amount thereof, or any other essential alteration of the same.

    3. Imposition of additional percentages exceeding one-seventh of the land tax, or fifty per cent. of other direct national taxes.

    4. Imposition of additional percentages on indirect national taxes.

    5. Determining the sum of expenditure toward which a certain proportional subsidy is given by the Government, in accordance with laws or Imperial ordinances.

CXXIII. A decision of the city assembly relating to the following matters requires the approval of the Fu or Ken Council :—

    1. The making or altering of regulations relating to the establishments of the city.

    2. Measures to be taken with regard to stock property (Article LXXXI).

3. Alienation or mortgage of immovable city property.

4. Charges in regard to the use of lands by individual residents (Article LXXXVI).

5. Giving security of any kind for another.

6. Entailing, for the next five years or more, upon the residents of the city, a new burden that does not arise from any obligation founded on laws or Imperial ordinances.

7. Imposition of additional percentages on national taxes or on Fu or Ken taxes otherwise than at uniform rates (Article XC, par. 2).

8. Imposition of expenses upon certain particular individuals, or particular district, in accordance with Article XCIX.

9. Imposition of services in person or in kind otherwise than at the rates prescribed in Article CI.

CXXIV. The Fu or Ken Chiji may exercise disciplinary authority over the Shichō, the assistants, the other members of the city council, the members of the committees, the Kochō, and other city officials. The penalty for such disciplinary measure shall consist of a reprimand, or of a fine not exceeding twenty-five *yen*.

Until a special disciplinary law for city officials is issued the disciplinary regulations for goverment civil officials shall be applied with the following modifications :—

1. Against a disciplinary measure taken by the city council (Article LXIV. par. 2, head. 5) a complaint may be laid before the Fu or Ken Chiji, and against the decision of the latter, an action may be brought in the Administrative Court.

2. Against a disciplinary measure taken by the Fu or Ken Chiji an action may be brought in the Administrative Court.

3. Any city official mentioned in the first paragraph of this Article who repeatedly or grossly violates his duty, or who is guilty of immoral or dishonorable conduct, or whose means are in a disorderly condition beyond the circumstances of his position, or who is unable to carry on his official business, may be dismissed from the service by a disciplinary sentence. Officials who may be discharged at

any time shall not be subjected to a disciplinary sentence (Article LXIII).

All those who are dismissed shall lose their claim to the pension, excepting in cases of incapacity without any fault on their part.

4. Examinations in disciplinary proceedings (par. 3) shall be undertaken by the Fu or Ken Chiji, and the sentence to be passed shall be decided on by the Fu or Ken Council. Against the decision of the latter an action may be brought in the Administrative Court. A decision involving the dismissal of the Shichō shall not be executed until after it has been first submitted to His Majesty the Emperor.

The superintending authority may order suspension from official duty of an official or stoppage of his salary before disciplinary sentence is finally passed.

CXXV. When any city official or servant has to indemnify the city on account of negligence of duty on his part or of exceeding his competency the matter shall be decided by the Fu or Ken Council. Against such decision an action may be brought in the Administrative Court within seven days from the day on which the decision is served, or otherwise notified. When such action is instituted the Fu or Ken Council may temporarily attach the property of the party bringing the action.

TITLE VII.—SUPPLEMENTARY PROVISIONS.

CXXVI. This law shall come into force from the first day of April, 1889, in the localities designated by the Minister of State for Home Affairs according to the local circumstances on the representation of the Fu or Ken Chiji.

CXXVII. Until the Fu or Ken Council and the Administrative Court are instituted, the official duties of the Fu or Ken Council shall be performed by the Fu or Ken Chiji, and those of the Administrative Court by the Cabinet.

CXXVIII. For the first elections, the official duties of the city council and the city assembly shall be executed by, and the matters left to city by-laws to be determined shall be determined by the Fu or Ken Chiji or other officials designated by them.

CXXIX. With regard to Shintō and Buddhist temple-associations and to all others of a religious nature, this law shall not apply, and existing provisions of law and local customs shall be left in their present state.

CXXX. The term " population " made use of in this law, shall always mean the number of souls according to the latest official enumeration thereof, with the exception of persons in actual military or naval service.

CXXXI. The classification of existing taxes into direct and indirect taxes in the sense of this law shall be notified by the Minister of State for Home Affairs and the Minister of State for Finance.

CXXXII. Imperial Ordinance No. 130, October, 1876, *i.e.* —Regulations for Public Works and for the Management of the Communal Property and Public Loans of Ku, Cho, or Son ; the fourth clause of Imperial Ordinance No. 17, July, 1878, *i.e.* The Law of the Organisation of Gun, Ku, Cho, and Son ; Imperial Ordinance No. 14, May, 1884, *i.e.*—The Law of the Ku, Cho, and Son Assemblies ; Imperial Ordinance No. 15, May, 1884 ; Imperial Ordinance No. 23, July, 1884 ; Imperial Ordinance No. 25, August, 1885 ; and all other provisions of law or ordinances which are in conflict with this law shall be abrogated from the day on which the same shall come into force.

CXXXIII. The execution of this law is entrusted to the Minister of State for Home Affairs, who shall issue the ordinances and instructions necessary for the purpose.

J.W.M., 1888, Aug. 11, pp. 133-38.

57. ORGANISATION[1] OF THE GOVERNMENT OF TOWNS (CHO) AND VILLAGES (SON).

(Law No. 1, April 14, 1888.)

TITLE I.—GENERAL PROVISIONS.

CHAPTER I.—OF TOWNS AND VILLAGES AND THEIR CIRCUMSCRIPTIONS.

I. This law shall apply to all towns and villages, excepting those where the Law for the Organization of Cities applies.

II. A town or village shall be considered a juristic person, and shall administer by itself its own affairs, subject to the supreme control of the Government.

III. The boundaries of a town or village shall remain as they are, so long as no alteration thereof is made in conformity with the provisions of the present law.

IV. When it is necessary to abolish or create a town or village, or amalgamate several of them into one or divide one into several, the Fu or Ken Council shall decide it, after consulting with the interested city, town or village assembly, and the Gun Council, and shall receive the approval of the Minister of State for Home Affairs.

When an alteration of the boundaries of a town or village is necessary, the Gun Council shall decide it, after consulting with the interested town or village assemblies and land-owners. When, however, several Gun or the boundaries of a city are concerned in such alteration, it shall be decided by the Fu or Ken Council.

When a town or village does not possess the capacity of fulfilling the obligations made incumbent upon it by laws, or when it is necessary for the public interest, several towns or villages may be amalgamated into one, or their boundaries may be altered, regardless of the objections of the interested parties.

When on account of a measure taken in accordance with

---

1. This law is commonly referred to as the Town and Village Code.

this Article, an arrangement with regard to town or village property is required it shall also be decided upon.

V. A dispute between any towns or villages about their boundaries shall be decided by the Gun Council. When, however, such towns or villages belong to more than one Gun severally and separately, or when, the boundaries of a city are concerned, the dispute shall be decided by the Fu or Ken Council. Against the decision of the Gun Council a complaint may be laid before the Fu or Ken Council, and against the decision of the latter an action may be brought in the Administrative Court.

CHAPTER 2.—OF THE TOWN OR VILLAGE RESIDENTS (CHO-SON-JUMIN) AND OF THEIR RIGHTS AND DUTIES.

VI. All those who have their residence in a town or village shall be called the "residents" of the town or village.

All the residents of a town or village shall be entitled on the one hand to the common uses of its establishments as well as its property, and on the other shall be subject to the duty of sharing the common burden of such town or village in accordance with the provisions of this law ; the provision of this Article, however, shall not prejudice any rights or duties founded on the civil law.

VII. Every independent male person being a subject of the Empire and in the enjoyment of his civil rights, shall be a citizen (*komin*) of a town or village, provided he has fulfilled the following conditions for the preceding two years :—(1) that he has been a resident of such town or village, (2) that he has contributed towards the common burdens of such town or village, (3) that he has paid national land tax of two or more *yen* in other direct national taxes in such town or village. Persons who have received alms from any public sources within the last two years shall be excepted. The term of two years fixed in this Article, may be dispensed with in particular cases, according to circumstances, by a decision of the town or village assembly.

An independent person, in the sense of this law, shall mean a person who has completed his twenty-fifth year, having a household; provided, however, that he is not deprived of the right of freely disposing of and administering his property.

VIII. Every citizen shall be entitled on the one hand to the right of taking part in the town or village elections, and of eligibility for any honorary office in the town or village assembly or administration; and shall be bound on the other by the obligation of assuming such honorary offices.

No citizen may refuse to accept any such office or resign the same during the term of the office, except when one of the following reasons shall exist:—

1. Inability to discharge his official duties on account of disease or illness,

2. Necessity of constantly or frequently absenting himself from the town or village on account of occupation.

3. Being sixty years old or more.

4. Engagement in the government service whereby he is unable to discharge his official duties in the town or village.

5. That he was an official of the town or village without salary for four years and that four years have not elapsed since, or that he was a member of the town or village assembly for six years and that six years have not yet elapsed since.

6. Any other valid ground of excuse recognized as such by the town and village assembly.

Any citizen who, without being sustained by any of the above enumerated reasons, refuses to accept any honorary office, or resigns it during the term of the office, or, when the office is one of no definite duration of term, shall not fulfil his duties therein for a period of at least three years, or any honorary officer who actually evades the duties of any such office, may, by a decision of the town or village assembly, be subjected to suspension of citizenship, for from three to six years, together with an additional levy, during the same period, of from one-eighth to one-quarter more than his ordinary share of contribution to the town or village expenditure.

Against the aforementioned decision of the town or village assembly a complaint may be made to the Gun Council, against the decision of the Gun Council to the Fu or Ken Council, and against the decision of the latter an action may be brought in the Administrative Court.

IX. A citizen shall lose his citizenship when he loses any of the necessary conditions prescribed in Article VII.

The citizenship shall be suspended during bankruptcy proceedings, during the pending of a judicial enquiry or judicial detention when such enquiry or detention is on account of a supposed crime or delict which if proven shall involve the loss or suspension of civil rights, or during execution on account of a failure in payment of a tax.

Persons in actual military or naval service may not take part in the public affairs of a town or village.

Loss or suspension of citizenship shall also entail the loss of an office that is dependent thereon.

CHAPTER 3.—OF THE TOWN OR VILLAGE BY-LAWS.

X. Every town or village may issue by-laws for regulating such affairs of the town or village and such rights and duties of its residents, as to which the present law contains no express provision or gives authority for treating differently.

Every town or village may issue regulations for any of its establishments.

By-laws and regulations may not be in conflict with laws and ordinances, and shall be published according to the customary modes of the locality for notifying official documents.

TITLE II.—OF THE TOWN OR VILLAGE ASSEMBLIES.

CHAPTER I.—OF THE CONSTITUTION AND ELECTIONS.

XI. The members of a town or village assembly shall

be elected by the electors of the town or village from amongst the eligible citizens. Their number shall be as follows, in proportion to the population of the town or village ; such number, however, may be changed by town or village by-laws :—

    a. A town or village with a population of less than 1,500, 8 members.

    b. A town or village with a population of 1,500 or more, and less than 5,000, 12 members.

    c. A town or village with a population of 5,000 or more, and less than 10,000, 18 members.

    d. A town or village with a population of 10,000 or more and less than 20,000, 24 members.

    e. A town or village with a population of 20,000 or more, 30 members.

XII. All citizens of a town or village (Article VII) shall have the suffrage, excepting those whose citizenship is suspended (Article VIII. 3, Article IX. 2) or those who are in actual military or naval service.

Every Japanese subject in the enjoyment of his civil rights, and paying any direct town or village taxes, the amount of which exceeds that which is paid by one of the three citizens who pay the largest amount of such taxes in the town or village, shall also have the suffrage in that town or village, although he may lack in the qualifications enumerated in Article VII. unless there exists any reason which would cause a suspension of citizenship or unless he is in actual military or naval service.

Companies established in accordance with law and other juristic persons shall also have the suffrage under the same conditions as described in the preceding paragraph.

XIII. The electors shall be divided into two classes.

The first class shall consist of those electors who pay the highest sums of direct town or village taxes, the total of which amounts to one-half of the whole amount of direct town or village taxes paid by all the electors. The remaining electors shall form the second class.

An elector, the amount of whose taxes may fall into two classes, shall belong to the first class. Should there be two or more persons that pay the same amount of taxes, and that come between two classes, that one or those, as the case may be, whose residence in the town or village has been the longest shall be included in the first class. When the matter cannot be decided by length of residence it shall be decided by seniority of age, and, in case of infeasibility of the latter, by lot drawn by the Chochō or Sonchō.

Each class shall elect for itself one-half of the members from amongst the eligible citizens, irrespective of the classes.

XIV. In a town or village where the application of the system prescribed by the preceding article is found inconvenient owing to any peculiar circumstance, a different system may be provided by a town or village by-law.

XV. All citizens having the suffrage (Article XII. 1) are eligible for membership.

The following persons may not become members of assembly :—

1. Government officials attached to respective Fu or Ken authorities.
2. Salaried officials.
3. Public prosecutors and police officers and forces.
4. Shintō or Buddhist priests and ministers of all other creeds.
5. Teachers of elementary schools.

As to other kinds of government officials, the permission of the chief of the office to which they belong is required for becoming members.

Persons, not being recognized advocates, who make it their business to transact business for others in law courts or other public offices, are ineligible.

A father and his son or brothers may not be members of a town or village assembly at one and the same time. In case such persons have been so elected, the one who has polled the largest number of votes shall be declared elected, and in case of a tie, then the senior in age shall be declared elected. When they have been elected at different periods, the one last elected may not become a member.

A person having the relationship of father or son, or of brother to the Chochō or Sonchō or the assistant shall for the time being be disabled from becoming a member of the assembly of the same. When a person having the same relationship to a member of a town or village assembly is elected Chochō or Sonchō or assistant and the election obtains approval, such member of the assembly shall have to retire from his membership.

XVI. Membership of a town or village assembly is honorary. The term of membership is six years and every three years one-half of the members elected by each class shall be renewed. When the number of members is not divisible into two equal parts, the greater half shall be renewed first. The members who shall have to retire first shall be determined by lot.

Outgoing members are re-eligible.

XVII. Vacancies occurring between ordinary elections shall be supplied by the substitutionary elections held at the same time that the ordinary elections are held. When, however, such vacancies amount to one-third or more of the whole number of members, or when it is deemed necessary by the town or village assembly, by the Chochō or Sonchō or by the Gunchō, an election for substitutional members shall be held, without awaiting the ordinary election.

A substitutional member shall retain his membership during the unexpired term of him whom he has replaced.

Ordinary and substitutionary elections shall be held by the same class by and from which the members to be replaced have been elected.

XVIII. Sixty days previous to an election the Chochō or Sonchō shall make out an original register of electors, describing their qualifications, and out of the original register shall draw up lists of electors.

The lists shall be exhibited for the public inspection of interested persons, for seven days, at the Chocho or Soncho or in other suitable public place in the locality. When any interested person wishes to make a complaint about the lists, he may do so during the above-mentioned period, to the Chocho or Sonchō. The Chochō or Sonchō in accordance with the decision of the assembly (Article XXXVII. 1) shall revise the lists, if it is necessary, ten days before the election and make them the final lists. No person whose name is not on the final lists may take part in the election.

The final lists made out according to this Article shall also be used in case a new election is necessary on account of refusal to serve as member by any one that has been elected, or in case an election is void or declared null.

XIX. When an election is to be held the Chochō or Sonchō shall issue a notification seven days before the election day, stating the time and place and the number of members to be elected by each class.

The election of the second class shall be held before that of the first class.

XX. Election officers shall consist of either two or four persons, as honorary officers, chosen for the purpose by the Chochō or Sonchō from the electors, and of the Chochō or Sonchō or his deputy, as Chairman, who shall open and close the election meeting, and shall keep order in the polling station.

XXI. No one but the electors may enter the polling station during the election hours. Electors may not consult together or make suggestions to one another in that room.

XXII. The elections shall be made by ballots on which shall be inscribed the names of those for whom the vote is cast, and, after having been safe-guarded in a folded paper (fūsin), shall be handed to the Chairman by the electors themselves; the names of the electors shall not be inscribed.

When the electors hand in their ballots, they shall orally give their full names and places of residence ; and the Chairman, after having referred such names and places to the lists shall put the ballots unopened into a ballot-box. The ballot-box may not be opened until the polling is closed.

XXIII. A ballot containing a greater or smaller number of names than the one reqnired, shall not be void on that account. In the first case, the redundant names shall be rejected in order beginning with the one at the bottom.

The following ballots shall be void :—

1. Those containing no name at all or those containing any illegible names, so far as those names are concerned.

2. Those by which the persons voted for cannot be identified, so far as those persons are concerned.

3. Those containing the names of persons who are not eligible, so far as those names are concerned.

4. Those mentioning any matter other than the designation of the persons voted for.

The question whether any particular votes shall or shall not be received and also the question as to the validity or nullity of a vote, shall be provisionally decided by the election officers, and in case of an equality of votes, they shall be decided by the Chairman.

XXIV. Voting shall be done in person ; votes by proxy are not allowed.

Electors entitled to suffrage by virtue of Article XII. par. 2, may vote by proxy and in case any of them is not an independent male or is a company or some other juristic person, then the voting must be by proxy. Such proxy must be a Japanese subject, being an independent male person, and in the enjoyment of civil rights. One and the same person, however, may not be a proxy for more than one person, and every proxy must show his authority of proxy to the election officers.

XXV. In an extensive or thickly populated town or village, branch polling stations with definite circumscriptions may be provided by the decision of the town or village assembly ; such branch stations may be provided for the second class only.

The election officers of a branch station shall consist of a deputy of the Chochō or Sonchō, appointed by him, as Chairman, and of either two or four assessors appointed in accordance with Article XX.

The ballot-boxes of the branch stations shall be brought unopened to the head station, and the votes contained therein shall be counted together with other votes.

The polling at the branch stations, shall be held at one and the same time as at the head station. As to the proceedings and maintenance of order, the provisions for the head station shall apply.

XXVI. Those obtaining the greatest number of valid votes shall be declared elected. In case of a tie, seniority of age shall determine, and when it cannot be determined, it shall be determined by lot drawn by the Chairman.

Where more than one substitutional member is elected (Article XVI), the one who obtains the largest number of votes shall be the one to take the place of that replaced member whose remaining term of membership is the longest. In case of a tie, the order shall be determined by lot.

XXVII. Election officers shall keep minutes of an election which shall contain the details of the election operations. These minutes having been read aloud at the end of the election shall be signed by the election officers and attached to the lists of electors.

The ballots cast shall be attached to the minutes and preserved until the completion of the elections.

XXVIII. When an election is over the Chairman shall give to the persons elected notice of their election. Persons who decline such election shall notify the Chochō or Sonchō within five days at the latest from time of notice of such election.

Any one who has been elected by both classses of electors, shall notify the Chochō or Sonchō within the same period which election he will accept. Should he give no notice, he shall be considered as having declined all, and shall be dealt with in accordance with Article VIII.

XXIX. When an elector wishes to make any complaint as to the validity of the election proceedings, he shall do so to the Chochō or Sonchō within seven days from the time of the election (Article XXXVII. par. 1).

When an election is over the Chochō or Sonchō shall make a report thereof to the Gunchō, and should the Gunchō entertain any objection to the validity of the election, based upon serious grounds, he may, irrespective of any complaint, submit the case to the decision of the Gun Council, and it shall be disposed of in accordance with such decision.

When there has been any essential irregularity in election proceedings, such election shall be declared altogether null and void, and when any person who has been elected is found to be without requisite qualifications, his election shall be void. In either of these cases a new election shall be held.

XXX. When a person declared elected is afterwards discovered to be without the requisite qualifications, or has subsequently lost them, his election shall become void. The question whether such qualifications are wanting or not shall be decided by the town or village assembly.

XXXI. In a small town or village, the town or village assembly may be, by a town or village by-law, decided upon by the Gun Council substituted by a general meeting of all citizens having the suffrage.

CHAPTER II.—OF COMPETENCY AND BUSINESS.

XXXII. The assembly of a town or village shall represent the town or village, and decide on all subjects relating to the town or village affairs, in conformity with the provisions of this law, and also on those matters which have already been entrusted to its management or which may hereafter be so entrusted by laws or Imperial ordinances.

XXXIII. The matters that are to be decided by a town or village assembly, are principally as follows:—

1. The making and altering of town or village by-laws and regulations.

2. Affairs, the expenses of which are to be defrayed out of the town or village revenues, with the exception of those mentioned in Article LXIX.

3. The determining of the budget of the town or village, as well as the approving of an outlay not included in the budget or of one exceeding the estimate.

4. The giving discharge to the annual accounts of the receipts and expenditure.

5. The determining of the modes of imposing and of collecting duties for use (shiyoryo), fees, town or village taxes, and services in person or in kind, so far as not determined by laws or Imperial ordinances.

6. Alienation, purchase, exchange, or mortgage of the immovable property of the town or village.

7. Matters relating to the disposition of the stock property.

8. The incurring of a new liability or the relinquishment of an acquired right, so far as it has not already been determined by the budget.

9. The determining of the modes of management of the town or village property and establishments.

10. Requisition of security from town or village officials, as well as determination of its amount.

11. Entering in a law-suit or in an arbitration concerning any town or village.

XXXIV. The town or village assembly shall elect the town or village officials within its competency by virtue of laws or Imperial ordinances.

XXXV. The town or village assembly shall be competent to examine papers and accounts relating to the town or village affairs and to demand reports from the Chochō or Sonchō in order to ascertain whether the management of affairs, the execution of the decisions of the assembly, and the collection and application of the revenue, are properly carried out.

The town or village assembly may present to the superintending authority memorials on matters concerning the public interest of the town or village.

XXXVI. The town or village assembly shall present its

views on any subject when such views are asked for by the government authorities.

XXXVII. The town or village assembly shall also decide all complaints brought before it relating to the question as to whether or not any particular person possesses the right of a resident or of a citizen in the town or village or the qualifications of an elector or for eligibility, as to the correctness or incorrectness of electoral lists or of the formation of the electoral classes, as to the right of voting by proxy (Article XII., par 2), and also as to the validity of any election of the members of the assembly (Article XXIX).

In a town or village where no town or village assembly is instituted the complaints about questions whether or not any person possesses the rights of a resident or of a citizen in the town or village or about the qualification of an elector shall be decided by the Chochō or Sonchō.

Against any such decision of the town or village assembly or the Chocho or Sonchō, a complaint may be made to the Gun Council, against the decision of the Gun Council to the Fu or Ken Council, and against the decision of the latter an action may be brought in the Administrative Court.

With regard to the matters mentioned in this Article the Chochō or Sonchō also may enter a complaint or bring an action.

No complaint or action shall have a suspensive effect. No new election, however, may be held before there is a final decision.

XXXVIII. No member of a town or village assembly may bind himself by the direction or request of any of his constituents.

XXXIX. A Chochō or Sonchō shall be the president of the town or village assembly, and when he is prevented from so doing, the town or village assistant acting as his deputy shall take his place.

XL. When the matter of any question before the town or village assembly relates personally to the president himself, or to his parents, his brothers, his wife, or his children, the president shall be deemed as prevented from taking the chair, and his deputy shall act in his place.

When both the president and the deputy are prevented from presiding, the senior member in point of age shall act as president.

XLI. The Chochō or Sonchō and the assistant may be present in the town or village assembly and give explanations on matters under consideration in the assembly.

XLII. The town or village assembly shall be convoked by its president whenever there is any necessity for its meeting. It shall also be convoked when it is demanded by a fourth or more of its members. The notification of convocation and the subjects to be deliberated upon shall be announced at least three days beforehand, except when the case demands urgency. The town or village assembly may, by its decision, fix beforehand its regular days of meeting.

XLIII. The quorum of a town or village assembly shall be two-thirds of the members. An exception to this shall be where the members have been convoked a second time in regard to one and the same subject, and yet the requisite number of members has not appeared.

XLIV. The decision of the town or village assembly shall be determined by a majority of votes. In ease of an equality of votes, the matter shall be debated and voted upon a second time. Should the votes still be equally divided the president shall decide.

XLV. No member may participate in deciding a question in the town or village assembly, on a matter personally concerning himself, his parents, his brothers, his wife, or his children.

In a case where it happens that the assembly is unable to obtain a quorum, on account of the exclusion of several members in the above manner, the Gun Council shall decide upon the matter in question for the town or village assambly.

XLVI. The election of the town or village officials to be elected by the town or village assembly shall be made by secret ballot separately and severally for every such official, and whoever obtains more than half of the number of valid votes shall be declared elected. In case no one obtains such requisite number of votes, a new ballot shall be taken for the two individuals among them that have obtained the highest number of votes ; and when three or more persons obtain the highest, but an equal number of votes, two of them determined by lot drawn by the president, shall be taken. When in either of these cases, neither of the two obtains a majority of votes, it shall be decided by lot. As to what remains, Articles XXII. XXIII. and XXIV., I, shall apply.

For the election mentioned in this Article, an election by nomination may be substituted upon the decision of the town or village assembly.

XLVII. The sittings of town or village assemblies shall be public, but strangers may be excluded when it is deemed desirable by the president.

XLVIII. The president shall allot assembly works to the members, shall superintend meetings, and elections, shall open, adjourn, and close the sitting and keep order in the assembly chamber. He may cause any stranger who openly signifies his assent or dissent, or who is in any way disorderly, to retire from the chamber.

XLIX. The town or village assembly shall cause its clerks to keep minutes wherein shall be recorded the decisions, the results of elections held therein, and the names of the members present. Such minutes shall be read aloud at the end of the sitting and shall be signed by the president and at least two of the members present.

The clerks of the town or village assembly shall be appointed by the president.

L. The town or village assembly shall provide itself with business regulations ; such regulations may contain provisions for penalties, not exceeding two *yen*, to be inflicted upon members who may infringe the same.

LI. Articles XXXII. to XLIX. shall also apply to the general meeting of a town or of a village.

TITLE III.—OF THE ADMINISTRATION OF TOWNS AND VILLAGES.

CHAPTER I.—OF THE CONSTITUTION AND APPOINTMENT OF TOWN OR VILLAGE OFFICIALS.

LII. There shall be a Chochō or Sonchō and an assistant for every town or village. The number of assistants, however, may be changed by a town or village by-law.

LIII. The Chochō or Sonchō and assistants, shall be elected by the town or village assembly from amongst the citizens of the town or village having the suffrage and being thirty years old or more.

The offices of the Chochō or Sonchō and the assistants shall be incompatible with the offices mentioned in Article XV. 2.

Persons related to each other as ather and son or as brothers may not be at the same time the Chochō or Sonchō and assistants. When any persons having such relationship with the Chochō or Sonchō is elected assistant, such election shall be annulled, and on the other hand, when any person having similar relationship to an assistant, is elected Chochō or Sonchō and such election is approved, the so related assistant shall resign his office.

LIV. The term of office of the Chochō or Sonchō and of assistants shall be four years.

The election shall be made in accordance with Article XLVI, with this exception, that in case of a tie, the selection shall be made by the Gun Council and not by lot.

LV. The office of the Chochō or Sonchō and of assistants is honorary, with the exception of the paid Chochō or Sonchō and assistants mentioned in Article LVI.

The Chochō or Sonchō may receive remuneration suitable to their trouble besides compensation for the actual expenses needed for the discharge of their duties. It shall also be the same when an assistant is entrusted with a particular branch of administrative affairs (Article LXX., 2).

LVI. The Chochō or Sonchō may be made a paid official by a town or village by-law, in case it is desirable according to the circumstances of such town or village, and in a large town one assistant may be made a paid official.

Paid Chochō or Sonchō and assistants, shall not be restricted to citizens of towns or village, but they will be entitled to the citizenship in the town or village when they are elected and their election is approved.

LVII. Paid Chochō or Sonchō and assistants may resign office by giving notice three months beforehand, in which case, however. they shall cease to be entitled to any pension.

LVIII. Neither the paid Chochō or Sonchō nor any paid assistant may hold a salaried office of any other kind, or become a director of a joint stock company, or hold any important position therein ; and with regard to other kinds of commercial or industrial occupations, neither of them may carry one on without having received permission from the Gunchō.

LIX. The election of Chochō or Sonchō and of assistants requires the approval of the Fu or Ken Chiji.

LX. When the Fu or Ken Chiji does not give the approval mentioned in the preceding Article, he shall first consult the Fu or Ken Council, and when the Fu or Ken Council disagrees with him and he still deems it necessary not to give it he may withhold it on his own responsibility.

When the Chochō or Sonchō or the town or village assembly has any ground of dissatisfaction against the disapproval of the Fu or Ken Chiji, they may represent the case to the Minister of State for Home Affairs and request his approval.

LXI. When the election of a Chochō or Sonchō and of an assistant is not approved, a new election shall be held.

If the second election does not also obtain the approval, the superintending authority having the right of approval shall either appoint a deputy *pro tempore*, or despatch a government official at the expense of the town or village for discharging the duties of the Chochō or Sonchō and the assistant.

LXII. There shall be a treasurer in every town or village who shall be appointed by the town or village assembly on the proposal of the Chochō or Sonchō.

The treasurer shall be a paid official, and his term of office shall be four years.

The treasurer may not at one and the same time be the Chochō or Sonchō or the Assistant. As to what remains Article LVI., 2, Articles LVII. and LXXVI. shall apply.

The appointment of treasurer requires the approval of the Gunchō. When he does not give approval, he shall first consult with the Gun Council, and when the Gun Council disagrees with him and he still deems it necessary not to give his approval, he may withhold it on his own responsibility. As to what remains Article LXI. shall apply.

When the Chochō or Sonchō or the town or village assembly has any ground of dissatisfaction against the disapproval of the Gunchō they may represent the case to the Fu or Ken Chiji and request his approval.

In a town or village where the amount of the receipt and expenditure is small the Chochō or Sonchō may be made by permission of the Gun-cho to discharge *ex officio* the duty of the treasurer.

LXIII. There shall be clerks and other necessary supplementary employes and servants in every town or village, to whom suitable salaries shall be given. The number of such persons shall be determined by a decision of the town or village assembly. The duty of the clerk, however, may be entrusted to the Chochō or Sonchō by giving a suitable allowance.

The supplementary employés of a town or village shall be

appointed by the town or village assembly on the proposal of the Chochō or Sonchō, and the servants by the Chochō or Sonchō himself.

LXIV. A town or village may be by a decision of the assembly divided for convenience of administration into several districts, each having a Kuchō and a deputy. The Kuchō and his deputy shall be honorary officials.

The Kuchō and his deputy shall be elected by the assembly from amongst the citizens belonging to that town or village, and who possess the suffrage. When there is a separate assembly for such district (Article CXIV.), the Kuchō and his deputy shall be elected by that assembly.

LXV. A town or village may, upon a decision of the town or village assembly, institute temporary or permanent committees. Their functions shall be honorary.

Committees shall be elected from amongst the members of the assembly, or citizens having the suffrage, and the Chochō or Sonchō or the assistant acting as his deputy shall be the chariman of any such commitiee.

With regard to the composition of permanent committees, special provisions may be made by town or village by-laws.

LXVI. The Kuchō and the members of a committee may, by a decision of the town or village assembly, be allowed remuneration suitable to their trouble, beside compensation for he actual expenses needed for the discharge of their duties.

LXVII. The town or village officials may be re-elected upon the completion of their term of office.

The town or village officials and servants may be discharged at any time unless there exist special provisions or a contract to the contrary.

CHAPTER II.—OF THE COMPETENCY AND BUSINESS OF THE TOWN OR VILLAGE OFFICIALS.

LXVIII. The Chochō or Sonchō shall be the local authority of the town or village and shall carry on the administration thereof.

The principal affairs to be undertaken by the Chochō or Sonchō are as follows :—

1. The preparation of subjects for deliberation in the town or village assembly, and the execution of the decision of the assembly. When it appears that any decision of the assembly exceeds its competency, or is in conflict with laws, or ordinances, or is prejudicial to the public good, the Chochō or Sonchō shall, upon his own judgment or by instruction of the superintending authority, suspend the execution of such decision, explaining the reason therefor, and cause the matter to be discussed a second time. If the assembly does not change its decision, the Chochō or Sonchō shall apply for the ruling of the Gun Council. When the suspension is on account of a decision of the assembly exceeding its competency or on account of conflict with laws or Imperial ordinances, an action may be brought in the Administrative Court against the ruling of the Fu or Ken Council.

2. The management of the establishments of the town or village, and superintendence of the management of such establishments when there are special managers thereof.

3. The administration of the town or village revenue, the ordering of receipts and of payments fixed in the budget or by special decision of the assembly, and the superintendence of the management of the treasury and accounts.

4. Looking after the rights of the town or village and the administration of its property.

5. Superintendence over the town or village officials and servants, and exercising disciplinary authority over them. Disciplinary penalties shall consist of reprimands and of fines not exceeding five *yen*.

6. The custody of all papers and documents.

7. Representation of the town or village as against outsiders, especially in lawsuits, or in arbitrations, and communications with other authorities or private individuals, in the name of the town or village.

8. Imposing and collecting duties for use, fees, town or village taxes, as well as services in person or in kind, in accordance with laws or Imperial ordinances or with decisions of the town or village assembly.

9. The carrying out of all other affairs entrusted to the Chochō or Sonchō by laws and ordinances, or by the instruction of the superior authority.

LXIX. The Chochō or Sonchō shall also discharge the following duties in conformity with laws and ordinances:—

1. Where there is no special office established for discharging the duties of the local police; (1) duties incumbent upon him as an auxiliary officer of the judicial police, and (2) duties in local affairs incumbent upon him by virtue of laws or ordinances.

2. The business of a wreck office.

3. The administrative affairs of the Fu or Ken, and those in general of the Central Government, relating to the locality, in so far an no special officials are appointed for those affairs.

Any of the affairs mentioned in the preceding three headings may, by permission of the superintending authority, by entrusted to the assistant.

Expenses requisite for the conduct of the affairs mentioned in this Article shall be borne by the town or village.

LXX. The assistant of a town or village shall assist in the business of the Chochō or Sonchō.

The Chochō or Sonchō may with the consent of the town or villge assembly, entrust the assistant with the administration of some particular branch of the town or village administration.

The assistant shall act for the Chochō or Sonchō when he is prevented from discharging his duty, and in case there are several assistants the one having precedence shall do so.

LXXI. The treasurer shall manage the receipts and expenditures and the accounts of the town or village.

LXXII. The clerks shall be subordinate to the Chochō or Sonchō and shall discharge the office business allotted to them.

LXXIII. The Kuchō and his deputy shall, as the organ of the Chochō or Sonchō, receive and carry on his orders and directions, and assist in the execution of the administrative affairs of the town or village relating to the district.

LXXIV. Committees (Article LXV.) shall be subordinate to the Chochō or Sonchō and shall either take charge of some special branches of the town or village administration or some establishments of the town or village, or take charge of any affairs temporarily entrusted to them.

The chairman of a committee shall have the right of voting in its decision. When an assistant is chairman, the Chochō or Sonchō may sit and take the chair at any time, with full right of voting in the meetings of the committees.

With regard to the competency of a permanent committee special provisions may be made by a town or village by-law.

Chapter 3.—Of Salaries and Allowances

LXXV. Honorary functionaries may only receive compensation for the actual expenses needed for the discharge of their duties, unless there are special provisions prescribed in this law.

The amount of compensations, of remunerations, and of allowances (Article LXIII. 1), where they are allowed, shall be determined by the town or village assembly.

LXXVI. The amount of salary to be paid to the Chochō or Sonchō, to the paid assistants, and· to other salaried officials as well as to servants, shall be fixed by the decision of the town or village assembly.

The fixing of the salaries of Chochō or Sonchō and assistants requires the approval of the Gunchō. When he sees reason for not giving such approval he shall cause it to be fixed by the Gun Council.

LXXVII. Provision may be made by a town or village by-law for pensions to be given to the salaried officials.

LXXVIII. Disputes about the salaries and pensions of paid officials and about the allowances mentioned in Article LXXVI. shall be decided by the Gun Council on application of the interested party. Against such decision a complaint may be made to the Fu or Ken Council, and against the decision of the latter an action may be brought in the Administrative Court.

LXXIX. When anyone in recipt of a pension obtains an appointment in government service or in a fu, ken, gun, city, town, or village, or in any public corporation, whereby he becomes the recipient of a salary, such pension shall be suspended while he receives such salary ; and when he becomes entitled to a new pension, the amount of which is equal to or greater than that of the former one, his right to the latter shall become extinct.

LXXX. Salaries, pensions, remunerations, and compensations shall be a burden upon the town or village.

TITLE IV.—OF MANAGEMENT OF TOWN OR VILLAGE PROPERTY.

CHAPTER I.—OF TOWN OR VILLAGE PROPERTY
AND TOWN OR VILLAGE TAXES.

LXXXI. The town or village is bound to keep and maintain as "stock property" its immovable property, its capitalized money, its stored-up grain, etc.

Extraordinary receipts of money or grain shall be added to the stock property, excepting donations or the like given for some special purposes.

LXXXII. The town or village property shall be managed and made use of for the common benefit of the town or village, excepting where there exists any special title founded on the civil law.

LXXXIII. Where residents of a town or village are entitled by any old custom to the direct use of lands or other objects belonging to the town or village, such custom shall not be altered except upon a decision of the town or village assembly.

LXXXIV. Admission to the use of any land or other object belonging to the town or village, may be made, by a town or village by-law, dependent upon the payment of an annual duty for use (shiyoryo) or of an entrance fee or of both of them. Any enjoyment of special rights by virtue of the civil law shall not come under this rule.

LXXXV. Persons entitled to the use of any such land or object (Articles LXXXIII. and LXXXIV.) shall have to bear the necesary expenses required for the land or the object in use, in proportion to their share in the use.

LXXXVI. The town of village assembly may, in case it is necessary for the common good of the town or village, withdraw or restrict any right of use (Articles LXXXIII. and LXXXIV), excepting where such rights rest on the civil law.

LXXXVII. All the selling or letting of the town or village property as well as all contracts for buildings and purveyances, shall be made by way of public competion. A deviation is only permissible in cases of special urgency, or when the cost would be out of proportion to the advantages to be derived therefrom, or when special approval is obtained from the town or village assembly.

LXXXVIII. The town or village is bound to bear its own necessary expenditures as well as those which are already imposed upon it by laws or Imperial ordinances.

When the revenue arising from the property, duties for use, fees (Article LXXXIX), fines, penalties, and other kinds of income belonging to a town or village by virtue of laws or Imperial ordinances does not cover the expenditure of the town or village, it may impose and collect town or village taxes (Article XC.) and services in person or in kind (Article CI).

LXXXIX. The town or village may impose and collect duties for the use of its property and establishments and fees for anything done specially for the benefit of some individuals.

XC. As town or village taxes may be imposed :—

1. Additional percentages upon national and fu or ken taxes.
2. Special direct or indirect taxes.

Additional percentages shall be imposed as a rule to direct national, fu or ken taxes on the whole extent of the town or village, and at a uniform rate. Special taxes may be imposed only when, besides the additional percentages, some further tax is required by a town or village.

XCI. So far as no express provisions are prescribed in the

law, minute regulations relating to duties for use and fees
(Article LXXXIX), special taxes (Article XC, 1, heading 2),
and ku, cho, or son rates hitherto existing, shall be provided for
by a town or village by-law. In such by-law the imposition of
a penalty not exceeding one *yen* and ninety-five *sen* may be
provided.

The imposition and collection of these penalties shall be
the duty of the Chochō or Sonchō. Against an imposition of
such penalty an action may be brought in a court of Law,
within fourteen days from the time when sentence of penalty is
served.

XCII. All those who shall sojourn in a town or village
for a period of three months or over, shall be liable to the
payment of town or village taxes, and that liability shall commence from the beginning of such sojourn.

XCIII. Persons who have no residence in a town or
village and who do not sojourn therein for a period of three
months, but own lands or houses in the town or village or
carry on some trade therein (excepting pedlars and hawkers),
shall be subjected to the town or village taxes imposed with
respect to those lands, houses, trades, and incomes derived
therefrom. The case shall be the same with regard to juristic
persons, the government postal, telegraph, and railway services
excepted.

XCIV. When additional precentages are imposed on
income taxes, or town or village income taxes are specially
levied in and for the town or village, the amount of income
derived by persons subjected to such taxes, from lands, houses,
or trades (pedlars and hawkers excepted) owned or carried on
without the town or village, shall be deducted from the
aggregate amount of their incomes.

XCV. When a person possessing residences or places of
sojourn in several cities, town, or villages, is subjected to the
town or village taxes mentioned in the preceding Article, the
amount of his income that arises from other sources than lands,

houses, or trades shall be divided into equal parts, according to the number or cities, towns, or villages, and only one part thereof may be made subject to such taxes in one place.

XCVI. Incomes mentioned in Article III of the Income Tax Regulations shall be exempted from town or village tax.

XCVII. The following shall be exempted from town and village taxes :—

> 1. Grounds, establishments, and buildings used for direct public purposes and belonging to the state, to a fu, ken, gun, city, town, or village, and other public corporations.
>
> 2. Shintō and Buddhist temples, government or public schools and hospitals ; grounds, establishments, and buildings, devoted to scientific, artistic, or charitable purposes.
>
> 3. Forests and waste lands belonging to the state, except in cases where any work is undertaken benefiting such forests or lands, and when, to cover the expense incurred for such work, assessments are made thereon by permission of the Minister of State for Home Affairs and of the Minister of State for Finance.

Newly cultivated or reclaimed lands may be exempted from town or village taxes a certain.length of time by a town or village by-law.

XCVIII. Other objects besides those mentioned in the two preceding Articles, that are to be exempted from town or village taxes, shall be determined by special laws or Imperial ordinances. With regard to town or village taxes to be imposed on members of the Imperial family, they shall remain as they are at present until they are regulated by further laws or Imperial ordinances.

XCIX. When in the town or village there in an establishment which may solely benefit same particular individuals, expenses of its repairs or maintenance shall be borne by such interested individuals.

When an establishment is kept up for the sole benefit of a particular district in a town or village the expenses of its repairs and maintenance shall be borne by those that are resident or sojourning in the district or that own lands or houses or carry on a trade therein (excepting pedlars and hawkers). Should there be property owned by that district, the income derived therefrom shall be applied first to the defraying of the expenses.

C. Town or village taxes shall be imposed in monthly apportionment from the beginning of the month following the one in which the liability for them arises, to the end of the month in which it ceases.

When in the course of a financial year, anyone becomes free from liability to payment of taxes or such liability undergoes a change, notification thereof shall be made by him to the Chochō or Sonchō. Up to the end of the month in which such notification is given the same taxes may by levied as in the past.

CI. For the public works of a town or village, or for the maintenance of the public peace and order, services in person or in kind may be imposed on tax-payers. No personal service of of a scientific or professional nature may be imposed.

Except in urgent cases, services in person or in kind shall be imposed in proportion to the amount of direct town or village taxes, and their money value shall be estimated beforehand.

Individuals liable to personal service may perform the same, either in their own persons or by suitable substitutes, at their own convenience, and excepting in cases of urgent necessity they may compound them by a payment of their money value.

CII. When any person does not pay in due time his duty for use or fees (Article LXXXIX), his town or village taxes (Article XC.), the money value for services (Article CI.), duties for use or entrance fees in regard to the common property of the town or village (Article LXXXIV), or any other town or village dues, the Chochō or Sonchō shall call upon him to pay, and in case he still fails to do so he shall be dealt with in accordance with the regulations for the treatment of non-payers of national taxes. For sending such call, a fee may be exacted, by virtue of a town or village by-law.

In regard to persons in extreme need, the Chochō or Sonchō may, at his discretion, grant a delay of payment of dues, out not to extend beyond the period of the current financial year. When it does extend beyond such period, the decision of the own or village assembly must be taken.

With regard to the collection of arrears, to the prescriptions and to the privileges of priority, the provisions concerning national taxes shall apply.

CIII. Additional percentages on land taxes shall be imposed on the payers of the land taxes. Other town or village taxes imposed on lands may be imposed either on the owners or the occupiers thereof.

CIV. Complaints in regard to imposition of town or village taxes, shall be brought before the Chochō or Sonchō within three months from the time of service of the writ of imposition; when this period elapses without any complaint, all right to demand reduction, exemption, or refunding of taxes, for the current financial year, shall be lost.

CV. Complaints concerning the imposition of town or village taxes and the right to the use of an establishment or of the common property of a town or village or the benefits arising therefrom, shall be decided by the Chochō or Sonchō, excepting when the disputed right in question is founded on civil law.

Against the above decision a compaint may be made to the Gun Council, against the decision of the Gun Council to the Fu or Ken Council, and against the decision of the latter an action may be brought in the Administrative Court.

The complaints or actions mentioned in this Article shall have no suspending effect.

CVI. The raising of loans in a town or village shall be limited to cases when it is for the repayment of the principal of an old loan or when an entraordinary outlay is required on account of an act of nature or of a calamity, or such like, or of some matter of permanent benefit to the town or village, and yet no augmentation of the ordinary revenue can be made without inflicting an excessive burden on the residents.

When the raising of a loan is decided upon by a town or village assembly it shall also predetermine the mode of raising it, the rate of interest to be paid, and the method of repayment. The first instalment of such repayment shall be made within three years, and there shall be a fixed proportion of annual instalment of repayment, so that the whole shall be paid off within thirty years from the raising thereof.

Temporary loans necessary for meeting outlays, the estimates for which are contained in the budget, shall not come under the restrictions of this article, provided such loans are repaid out of the income of the current financial year.

CHAPTER 2.—OF THE ESTIMATES AND ACCOUNTS OF THE REVENUE AND EXPENDITURE OF THE TOWN OR VILLAGE.

CVII. The Chochō or Sonchō estimating, as far as possible, amount of revenue and of expenditure of the town or village, for the next financial year, shall make a draft of the budget for the year, two months in advance. The financial year shall be the same as that of the state.

The Minister of State for Home Affairs may fix the form of such budget by a departmental ordinance.

CVIII. The draft of the budget shall be submitted to the deliberation of the town or village assembly before the beginning of the financial year, and when it is finally settled, it shall be reported to the Gunchō, and the important points therein shall be notified to the public, according to the customary mode of publication of official documents in the locality.

When the draft of a budget is introduced into the town or village assembly, it shall be accompanied by a report of the

Chochō or Sonchō on the general transactions of the town or village, and an inventory of the town or village property.

CIX. Expenditures not contained in the budget or that exceed the estimates in the budget, can be met only upon approval of the assembly.

In every budget there may be provided the " contingencies fund" (yobihi) for meeting any unexpected expenditures and it may be applied by the Chochō or Sonchō without previous approval of the assembly, to expenses not mentioned in the budget, or to those exceeding the budget estimates. Such funds, however, may not be applied to any expenses expressly negatived by the assembly.

CX. When the budget is determined by the assembly a copy thereof shall be transmitted by the Chochō or Sonchō to the treasurer of the town or village. When in the budget there is any matter requiring the authorization of the superintending authority or of the Council (Article CXXV-CXXVII), such authorisation shall be obtained beforehand.

The treasurer may make no payment without an order of the Chochō or Sonchō (Article LXVIII., 2, heading 3) or of the superintending authority, and even when he receives such an order from the Chochō or Sonchō he may make no payment which is not provided for in the budget or when such order is not in accordance with the provisions of the preceding Article.

The treasurer shall be responsible for all payments made by him in contravention of the preceding paragraph.

CXI. The treasury of the town or village shall be examined monthly on a fixed day, and a special examination shall be made at least once a year. The monthly examination shall be make by the Chochō or his deputy, and the special by the Chochō or Sonchō or his deputy with the assistance of one or more members of the assembly chosen for the purpose by election by the members of the assembly.

CXII. The annual accounts shall be made up within three months from the end of the financial year, and shall together with papers and documents, be presented by the treasurer to the Chochō or Sonchō, who after examining the same, shall submit them with his own observations thereon, to the approval of the assembly. In the case of Article LXIII., 5, they shall be brought in to the town or village assembly by the Chochō or Sonchō himself in a similar way. The decision of the assembly shall be reported by the Chochō or Sonchō to the Gunchō.

CXIII. Audit of accounts shall be considered a case of hindrance for the President and his Deputy in the sense of Article XL.

TITLE V.—OF THE ADMINISTRATION OF DISTRICTS POSSESSING SEPARATE PROPERTY.

CXIV. When a district in a town or village (Article LXIV) or a part of a town or village or a town or village amalgamated with another (Article IV) which is made a district by maintaining its old circumscription possesses any separate property or establishment of its own, and bears the expenses entailed by it (Article XCIX.) the Gun Council after consulting with the town or village assembly, may issue a by-law and institute a ku assembly or a general meeting of the district for affairs relating to the aforesaid property or establishment. In such case, the provisions for the town or village assembly shall apply to such ku assembly.

CXV. The administration of the affairs mentioned in the preceding Article shall be carried on by the Chochō or Sonchō in conformity with the provisions for town or village administrations, but with a separate treasury and account.

TITLE VI.—TOWN OR VILLAGE UNIONS.

CXVI. Several towns or villages may, by mutual agreement, and with the permission of the superintending authority, form a union for carrying on, in common, affairs which are common to them.

When a town or a village not possessing the capacity of fulfilling the obligations incumbent upon it by law, is unable to come to any agreement of amalgamation with other towns and villages (Article IV), or such amalgamation is inexpedient owing to circumstances, a formation of a union of several towns or villages may be forced upon them by decision of the Gun Council.

CXVII. When an agreement for union is made between several towns or villages (Article CXVI, 1) the constitution of the union assembly, the organisation of the administration, and the modes of providing means for the expenditure shall also be decided by them.

In the case of the second paragraph of the preceding Article, the modes of contribution to the expenditure of the union and other necessary matters shall be decided by mutual agreement of the interested towns or villages. Should they be unable to arrive at an agreement, the Gun Council shall decide.

CXVIII. Unions of towns or village may not be dissolved without the permission of a superintending authority.

TITLE VII.—OF THE SUPERINTENDENCE OF THE ADMINISTRATION OF THE TOWN OR VILLAGE.

CXIX. The administration of the towns and villages shall be superintented by the Gunchō in the first instance, by the Fu and Ken Chiji in the second, and by the Minister of State for Home Affaias in the third, with the reservation of cases, where the cooperation of the Gun Council or the Fu or Ken Council is required by virtue of law.

CXX. Excepting in cases where it is provided otherwise in this law, a complaint against any measure or decision, relating to the administrative affairs of a town or village, taken or made by the Gunchō or the Gun Council may be laid before the Fu or Ken Chiji or the Fu or Ken Council, and against the decision of the latter a complaint may be laid before the Minister of State for Home Affairs.

Complaints relating to the administrative affairs of a town or village shall be presented, together with reasons justifying the same, within fourteen days from the day on which the decree or decision has been served or otherwise notified, except in cases where some special limitation of time is prescribed in this law.

Actions to be brought by virtue of this law in the Administrative Court against any decision of the Fu or Ken Chiji or the Fu or Ken Council shall be limited to twenty one days from the day on which the decision has been served or otherwise notified.

In all cases where an action is given in the Administrative Court, no complaint touching the same matter may be laid before the Minister of State for Home Affairs.

When a complaint is laid or an action is brought in regard to a measure or to a decision, the execution of the same shall be suspended, except where there are special provisions in this law to the contrary, or where such suspension shall be deemed by the competent authority prejudical to the common good of the town or village.

CXXI. The superintending authorities shall look after the administration of the town or village to see that it does not infringe any law or ordinance, or that there is no irregularity or delay in the transaction of its business. To this end the superintending authorities may demand reports on any administrative affairs, and the production of papers and documents relating to budgets and accounts, and the like ; they may also examine the state of affairs and the treasury by visiting the actual spot.

CXXII. When a town or village or a town or village union does not include in its budget an expenditure burdened upon it by law or Imperial ordinance, or that has been ordered by the competent authorities, or when it does not approve an extraordinary expenditure, or actually fulfil its budget obligation, the Gunchō may, upon statement of his reason for so doing, embody the amount of such expenditure in the budget or order an extraordinary payment.

Against a measure taken by the Gunchō in pursuance of the preceding paragraph a complaint may be made to the Fu or Ken Council, and against the decision of the latter, an action may be brought in the Administrative Court by the town or village or town or village union.

CXXIII. When a town or village assembly does not render a decision upon any matter which it ought to decide, the Gun Council shall do so in its stead.

CXXIV. The Minister of State for Home Affairs may dissolve the town or village assembly. When the town or village assembly is dissolved, it shall be simultaneously ordered that a new election shall be held within three months. Until the newly elected assembly meets, all matters shall be decided by the Gun Council in its stead.

CXXV. The decision of the town or village assembly relating to the following matters, requires the approval of the Minister of State for Home Affairs :—

    1. Issuing or altering by-laws.
    2. The alienation, mortgaging, exchanging, or any significant alterations of objects valuable from a scientific, artistic, or historical point of view.

With regard to matters mentioned under the first heading, in a town or village with 10,000 or more souls, approval shall be given only after an Imperial decision is previously obtained in the matter.

CXXVI. A decision of the town or village assembly, relating to the following matters, requires the approval of the Minister of State for Home Affairs and of the Minister of State for Finance :—

    1. The raising of new loans or the increasing of loans ; or when it is necessary to deviate from the provisions of Article CVI. 2. Loans, the terms of the repayment of which is within three years, shall not come under the limitation of this Article.

2. Introducing a new town or village special tax, duty for use, or fee, or raising the amount thereof, or any other essential alteration of the same.

3. Imposition of additional percentages exceeding one-seventh of the land tax, or fifty per cent. of other direct national taxes.

4. Imposition of additional percentages on indirect national taxes.

5. Determining the sum of expenditure toward which a certain proportional subsidy is given by the Government, in accordance with laws or Imperial ordinances.

CXXVII. A decision of the town or village assembly relating to the following matters requires the approval of the Gun Council :—

1. The making or altering of regulations relating to the establishments of the town or village.

2. Measures to be taken with regard to stock property (Article LXXXI).

3. Alienation or mortgage of immovable town or village property.

4. Changes in regard to the use of lands by individual residents (Article LXXXVI).

5. Giving security of any kind for another.

6. Entailing, for the next five years or more, upon the residents of the town or village, a new burden that does not arise from any obligation founded on laws or Imperial ordinances.

7. Imposition of additional percentages on national taxes or on Fu or Ken taxes otherwise than at uniform rates (Article XC. 2).

8. Imposition of expenses upon certain particular individuals, or particular districts, in accordance with Article XCIX.

9. Imposition of services in person or in kind otherwise than at the rates prescribed in Article CI.

CXXVIII. The Fu or Ken Chiji or the Gunchō may exercise disciplinary authority over the Chochō or Sonchō, the assistants, the members of the committees, upon the Kuchō, and other town or village officials. The penalty for such disciplinary measure shall consist of a reprimand, or of a fine not exceeding ten *yen* in case of the Gunchō and twenty-five *yen* in case of the Fu or Ken Chiji.

Until a special disciplinary law for town or village officials is issued, the disciplinary regulations for government civil officials shall be applied with the following modifications :—

1. Against a disciplinary measure taken by the Chochō or Sonchō (Article LXVIII. 2, heading 5) a complaint may be laid before the Gunchō, against the decision of the Gunchō to the Fu or Ken Chiji, and against the decision of the latter an action may be brought in the Administrative Court.

2. Against a disciplinary measure taken by the Gunchō a complaint may be made to the Fu or Ken Chiji, and against the decision or measure made or taken by the latter an action may be brought in the Administrative Court.

3. Any town or village official mentioned in the first paragraph of this Article who repeatedly or grossly violates his duty, or who is guilty of immoral or dishonorable conduct, or whose means are in a disorderly condition beyond the circumstances of his position, or who is unable to carry on his official business, may be dismissed from service by a disciplinary sentence. Officials who may be discharged at any time shall not be subjected to a disciplinary sentence (Article LXVII).

All those who are dismissed shall lose their claim to the pension, excepting in cases of incapacity without any fault on their part.

4. Examinations in disciplinary proceedings (of heading 3) shall be undertaken by the Gunchō and the sentence to be passed shall be decided upon by the Gun Council. Against such decision a complaint may be made to the Fu or Ken Council and against the decision of the latter an action may be brought in the Administrative Court.

The superintending authority may order suspension from official duty of an official or stoppage of his salary, before disciplinary sentence is finally passed.

CXXIX. When any town or village official or servant has to indemnify the town or village on account of negligence of duty on his part or of exceeding his competency the matter shall be decided by the Gun Council. Against such decision, a complaint may be made to the Fu or Ken Council within seven days from the day on which the decision is served, or otherwise notified and against the decision of the latter an action may be brought in the Administrative Court. When such complaint is made the Gun Council may temporarily attach the property of the party bringing the action.

Title VIII.—Supplementary Provisions.

CXXX. Until the Gun Council, the Fu or Ken Council, and the Administrative Court are instituted, the official duties of the Gun Council shall be performed by the Gunchō, those of the Fu or Ken Council by the Fu or Ken Chiji, and those of the Administrative Court by the Cabinet.

CXXXI. For the first elections, the official duties of the Chochō or Sonchō and the town or village assembly shall be executed by, and the matters left to town or village by-laws to be determined, shall be determined by the Gunchō or other officials designated by them.

CXXXII. This law shall not apply to Hokkaido and Okinawa ken, and to other islands to be designated by Imperial ordinances, for which places the organization shall be determined by Imperial ordinances.

CXXXIII. Besides the preceding Article, in localities where special circumstances exist, certain provisions of this law may be suspended by an Imperial ordinances, upon representation of the town or village assembly, of the Chochō or Sonchō or of the Gun Council.

CXXXIV. With regard to Shintō and Buddhist temple associations and to all others of a religious nature, this law shall not apply, and the existing provisions of law and local customs shall be left in their present state.

CXXXV. The term " population " made use of in this law, shall always mean the number of souls according to the latest official enumeration thereof, with the exception of persons in actual military or naval service.

CXXXVI. The classification of existing taxes into direct and indirect taxes in the sense of this law shall be notified by the Minister of State for Home Affairs and the Minister of State for Finance.

CXXXVII. This law shall come into force from the first day of April, 1889, by the direction of the Minister of State for Home Affairs according to the local circumstances on the representation of the Fu or Ken Chiji.

CXXXVIII. Imperial Ordinance No. 130, October, 1876, *i.e.* Regulations for Public Works and for the Management of the Communal Property and Public Loans of Ku, Cho, or Son; Article VI. and the additional clause of Article IX. of Imperial Ordinance No. 17, July, 1878, *i.e.* the law of the Organization of Gun, Ku, Cho, and Son; Imperial Ordinance No. 14, May, 1884, *i.e.* The Law of the Ku, Cho, and Son Assemblies; Imperial Ordinance No. 15, May, 1884; Imperial Ordinance No. 23, July, 1884; Imperial Ordinance No. 25, August, 1885; and all other provisions of law or ordinances which are in conflict with this law shall be abrogated from the day on which the same shall come into force.

CXXXIX. The execution of this law is entrusted to the Minister of State for Home Affairs, who shall issue the ordinances and instructions necessary for the purpose.

J.W.M., 1888, Sept. 15, pp. 252-57.

58. System of Government[1] for the Three Fu.

(Law No. 12, March 22, 1889.)

I. Neither Shichō nor Assistants shall be appointed in Tōkyō shi, Kyōto shi, nor Ōsaka shi; the functions of the

---

1. To understand this law it is necessary to keep in mind the distinction between a Fu and a Shi, which may be fairly explained by reference to its French analogue, the Prefecture of the Seine and the City of Paris. The two executive officials in Tōkyō were the Governor of Tōkyō-fu and the Chief of the Metropoli-

Shichō shall be exercised by the Chiji, and those of the Assistants by Secretaries.

II. The city councils of Tōkyō shi, Kyōto shi, and Ōsaka shi, shall consist of the Chiji, Secretaries, and honorary (unofficial) members.

III. No treasurer, clerk, or other subordinate officials shall be appointed in the abovementioned shi, their duties being discharged by officials of the Fu Office.

IV. The ku hitherto existing in the abovementioned shi shall be retained, and the city council shall elect to each ku a Kuchō and several salaried clerks.

NOTE.—The number of clerks shall be specially determined by the city council.

V. No Deputy Kuchō shall be appointed in the abovementioned shi, and in the event of the Kuchō being incapable of discharging his duties his chief clerk shall represent him in his functions.

VI. The Chiji of any of the abovementioned shi may cause a Kuchō to assist him in business relating to the administration of suburban or urban districts, and in the business of the Treasurers connected with the ku of the said Kuchō.

VII. Should the amalgamation or separation of the ku in any of the abovementioned shi be necessary, an Imperial ordinance relating thereto shall be issued.

VIII. Each ku in the abovementioned shi shall be an election district for the election of members for the city assembly.

J.W.M., 1889, April 13, p. 357.

---

tan Police. In Kyōto and Ōsaka the Governor of the Fu was the executive official. This anomaly in the government of the the Fu was criticised as a reactionary measure in 1889, and formed the subject of an agitation, which has not yet ceased; for complete local self-government, or at least to the same extent as it is enjoyed by other cities, has not yet been granted to the Fu-cities.

59. LIST OF CITY GOVERNMENTS.

(Home Office Notification No. 1, February 2, 1889.)

The following is a list of the places at which, under Article CXXVI of the City Organisation Law,[1] promulgated in 1888, city organisations will be established.

Place	Population	Under jurisdiction of Municipality
Tōkyō	1,121,883	Tōkyō
Kyōto	245,675	Kyōto
Ōsaka	361,694	Ōsaka
Sakaye	44,015	Ōsaka Prefecture.
Yokohama	89,545	Kanagawa
Kobe	80,446	Hiogo
Himeji	22,677	Hiogo
Nagasaki	38,229	Nagasaki
Niigata	46,778	Niigata
Mito...	19,810	Ibaraki
Tsu ...	15,884	Mie
Nagoya	131,492	Aichi
Shidzuoka	36,838	Shidzuoka
Sendai	61,709	Miyagi
Morioka	30,166	Iwate
Hirosaki	28,170	Aomori
Yamagata	26,971	Yamagata
Yonesawa	29,203	Yamagata
Akita	29,223	Akita
Fukui	37,376	Fukui
Kanazawa	97,653	Ishikawa
Toyama	53,556	Toyama
Takaoka	17,974	Toyama
Matsuye	33,381	Shimane
Okayama	32,989	Okayama
Hiroshima	81,914	Hiroshima

1. See p. 365.

Akamagaseki	...	30,825	Yamaguchi
Wakayama	...	54,868	Wakayama
Tokushima	...	57,456	Tokushima
Takamatsu	...	37,698	Kagawa
Matsuyama	...	29,487	Ehime
Kōchi	... ...	30,987	Kōchi
Fukuoka ...	...	42,617	Fukuoka
Kurume ...	...	20,907	Fukuoka
Kumamoto	...	44,384	Kumamoto
Kagoshima	...	45,097	Kagoshima

J.W.M., 1889, February 9, p. 132.

60. REGULATIONS FOR FU AND KEN ASSEMBLY ELECTIONS (FUKENKWAI-GIIN-KISOKU).

(Law No. 6, Feb. 23, 1889.)

I. The Headman of a town (cho) or village (son) shall, on or before September 15th in every year, examine the register of the voters under the jurisdiction of the town or village office, and shall forward to the District (Gun) Magistrate a copy of the same by October 1st.

In the register there shall be inscribed the voters' full names, addresses, dates of birth, and the amounts of taxes and the places where they are paid.

II. The District Magistrate shall examine the voters' lists presented by the Headmen of the towns and villages, and shall draw up a list of all the voters in the jurisdiction of the District Office, by October 15th.

III. The Mayor (Shichō) shall on or before September 15th in each year prepare an election register, and draw up the voters' list by October 15th.

The matters to be written in the district list shall be the same as those prescribed by clause 2 of Article I.

IV. In determining the age and term of years mentioned in Article XIII of the Prefectural Assembly Regulations (Fuken-kwai-kisoku)[1] the date of compiling the voters' list shall be used as the day from which all calculations shall be made. Only those taxes which have been paid during a period of more than one full year, and paid continuously for that period, shall be counted. However, if during the interval property has been inherited, the taxes paid by the original owners shall also be counted in the sum paid by the person who has inherited the property.

V. Electors who are paying taxes in places other than the city, town or village in which they reside shall furnish to the Mayor of the city or the Headman of the town or village in which they reside information as to the amount of such taxes and a certificate of the same from the Mayor or Headman of the city or the town or village in which the taxes are paid.

Taxes not reported in accordance with the terms of the preceding clause shall not be counted in determining his qualifications either for voting or sitting as a member of the assembly.

VI. The Mayor of a çity or the Magistrate of a district shall, during fifteen days from October 20th, expose the copies of the voters list in the district or city office. The same shall be done in the town or village offices upon the request of some of the persons concerned.

VII. During the period referred to in the preceding Article all omissions or errors in the voters' list shall be pointed out by the persons concerned.

VIII. In the contingency provided for in the preceding Article the Mayor or the Magistrate of the district shall examine into and decide the matter within ten days, and shall immediately act accordingly, notifying all changes made under the premises throughout the district or city, and even in the towns or villages where the persons concerned reside.

IX. In cases contemplated in the preceding Article the

---

1. Imp. Dec. No. 18, 1878. *Supra* pp. 272 ff.

Mayor or the Magistrate of the district shall have power to summon and examine the persons concerned, if a thorough investigation of the case requires such action.

X. If the person concerned is dissatisfied with the decision of the Mayor or the Magistrate of the district he may institute a suit in the Court of First Instance within seven days of the publication of the said decision.

XI. In case of a suit provided for in the preceding Article the Court shall hear the case immediately.

XII. Against the judgment of a Court of First Instance in a suit such as is provided for in the preceding Article an appeal may be made to the Court of Cassation, but not to the Court of Appeal.

XIII. The voters' list shall be finally determined on November 15th, and shall stand without further revision during the year. However, any changes which are necessitated by the findings of a Court shall be made within twenty-four hours and notified throughout the city or district, and even in the town or village in which the person concerned resides.

Moreover, the Mayor or the Magistrate of a district may at any time remove form the list the names of any persons who have lost their qualifications.

The finally revised voters' list shall be used during the year in case substitutional elections have to be held.

XIV. Elections shall be held in February or March, except when the assembly has been dissolved and a new election has been ordered, or when substitutional elections have to be held.

The Governor, with the consent of the Minister of Home Affairs and the Assembly, may order an election at a time other than that stipulated in the preceding Article, if the circumstances of the Prefecture require such a change.

XV. When an election is to be held, the Governor shall announce, at least a month beforehand, throughout his jurisdiction, the date, hours, and place at which the election shall be held, and the number of members to be elected.

The time for polling shall be not less than four nor more than ten hours.

XVI. When the announcement provided for in the preceding Article has been issued, the Mayor or the Magistrate of the district shall cause all the matters mentioned in the said Article to be notified throughout his jurisdiction.

XVII. The Mayor or the Magistrate of a district shall appoint five scrutineers from among the electors of his jurisdiction, and shall request them to be present at the place where the election meeting is to be held on the day appointed for the meeting.

In case it is necessary to hold sub-election meetings, the scrutineers shall, in accordance with the preceding clause, be chosen from among the electors belonging to the sub-election districts.

The scrutineers provided for in the foregoing clauses, shall not be allowed, without proper reasons being given, to decline to act; but in case one of them is absent at the time of the opening of the election meeting, the highest tax-payer among the electors present shall act for him provisionally.

XVIII. The Mayor or the Magistrate of the district shall preside and exersise control over the election meeting. In event of the disability of the abovementioned officials the deputy-clerk (dairishoki) shall take his place.

A clerk of election shall be appointed by the Mayor or the Magistrate of a district from among the city or district clerks.

XIX. The electors may vote at any time between the opening and closing of the ballot-box.

XX. Every place at which an election meeting is held shall be furnished with a ballot-box, a record of election and writing materials.

The ballot-box shall be opened in the presence of the electors in order to show that it contains nothing.

XXI. Ballots shall be furnished at the place where the election meeting is held. The form of the ballot shall be determined by the Governor and shall be uniform throughout the jurisdiction. Ballots shall be delivered to the electors by the chairman of the election meeting or the clerk.

In case substitute members are to be elected in addition to ordinary members, the ballots shall be divided into two categories,—A and B,—the former being used for ordinary, the latter for substitute members.

XXII. The electors shall vote in person; proxies shall not be allowed.

XXIII. The electors shall write on the ballots the names of the persons for whom they wish to vote along with their own names, and shall affix their seals thereto. In addition their addresses, ranks or orders of merit, and other signs of respect, may be inscribed on the ballots.

XXIV. When an elector casts his vote the chairman of election shall identify him as a person whose name is on the voters' list, shall affix his seal on the ballot and shall cause the elector himself to put his ballot in the box.

XXV. In case of the illiteracy of the elector, the chairman shall cause the clerk to write on his behalf, read the name thus written, and show the ballot to the scrutineers, whereupon the elector shall affix his seal and cast his ballot.

XXVI. No one shall be allowed to enter the polling place except the electors and the officials conducting the election.

XXVII. No one shall be allowed to vote except those whose names are on the voters' list, or who possess a written judgment from a Court declaring that their names should be on the voters' list.

XXVIII. At the polling place no one shall be allowed to speak for the purpose of influencing others, nor to create a disturbance.

XXIX. If some one causes a disturbance at a polling place the chairman shall warn him, and if he does not desist, the chairman shall order him to leave the room. Such a one may, however, be called in later for the purpose of casting his vote.

The chairman may ask for the assistance of the police to maintain order during the election meeting.

XXX. In case a ballot is inserted into the box by a person who is not entitled to vote, or by one who impersonates a voter the chairman shall remove such a ballot from the box.

XXXI. When the time to close the ballot-box has come, the chairman shall order the clerk to close the outer door of the room, and shall then ask whether there are any persons in the room who have not yet voted ; if there be any such he shall cause them to vote immediately and thereafter close the box.

XXXII. Two books of record shall be furnished at every polling place and shall be in charge of two clerks.

XXXIII. Ten minutes after closing the ballot-box the chairman shall open the box in the presence of the scrutineers and take out the ballots. He shall then unseal and examine them and cause the clerks to read the names both of the voters and the persons voted for. The clerks in charge of the records shall inscribe therein the number of votes received by each candidate.

XXXIV. The electors may witness the examination of the ballots.

XXXV. When all the ballots have been examined the chairman shall cause the clerks to record the total number of votes obtained by each candidate, and to read the figures aloud.

XXXVI. The functions of the clerks, such as counting the votes, etc., shall be performed in the presence of the chairman and the scrutineers.

XXXVII. When all the votes have been recorded the chairman shall examine into the eligibility of the candidates, beginning with the candidate who has received the greatest number of votes. If two or more candidates have received an equal number of votes, the chairman shall declare him elected who in senior in point of age, or if their ages be equal, the decision shall be reached by casting lots.

If the facts necessary to conclude an election cannot be obtained at once, such delay as may be required to secure the facts shall be allowed.

In cases of elections in sub-election districts the formalities to be observed are prescribed in Article L.

If the candidate who has obtained the highest number of votes is not eligible to sit in the assembly, the person who has obtained the next highest number of votes shall be declared elected. In such a contingency the Mayor or the Magistrate of the district shall, in addition to the name of the successful candidate, notify throughout his jurisdiction the reasons therefor.

In the event of a successful candidate having his domicile in some other city or district, the case shall be decided in accordance with Article XLI.

XXXVIII. The ballots which have been examined shall be gathered up and the package containing them shall be signed by the chairman, the scrutineers and the clerk.

The ballots referred to in the preceding clause shall be preserved in the city or district office for a year, together with the other documents relating to the election. When a suit or a complaint has been instituted in connection with an election, they shall be kept until judgement has been delivered in the matter.

XXXIX. The following matters shall be written in the election record :—

1. The date and hour of the opening of the election meeting.
2. The names of the chairman and the clerks.
3. The names and addresses of the scrutineers.
4. The details of the meeting provided for in the proviso to Article XXVII.
5. The details of the measures provided for in Article XXX.
6. The time of closing the ballot-box.
7. The number of votes obtained by each of the successful candidates.
8. The names and addresses of the successful candidates,

and also the reasons why an election could not be decided at once, if such was the case.

9. The time of closing an election meeting.

10. Any other matters which the chairman shall deem necessary. In case the settlement of an election has to be postponed, the result when announced shall also be recorded.

XL. The election record shall be sealed and signed by the chairman, the scrutineers and the clerks.

XLI. In case a successful candidate has his domicile in some other city or district, the Mayor or the Magistrate of the district shall refer the matter to the corresponding official in the said city or district, and request a certificate of the candidates eligibility. If the successful candidate should not be eligible to sit in the assembly clause 5 of Article XXXVII shall be applied.

XLII. The following ballots shall be considered as " spoiled " :—

1. Ballots cast by those whose names are not on the voters' list, except in cases where a written judgement of a Court was produced.

2. Ballots other than those legally issued by the Governor.

3. Blank ballots.

4. Illegible ballots.

5. Ballots which contain other matters than those legally prescribed.

6. If a ballot is partly legible it shall be counted to the extent that it is legible.

7. If a ballot contains the names of several candidates, one or more of whom are ineligible to sit in the assembly, it shall be counted to the extent of the eligible candidates.

XLIII. A ballot which contains a lesser number of names than that required shall not be considered " spoiled "; neither shall a ballot which contains a greater number of names than is required. In the latter case the names of the candidates in excess shall be struck off beginning with the end of the list, regardless of the provisions of clauses 6 and 7 of the preceding Article.

If the name of a person is repeated on a ballot it shall not be counted more than once.

XLIV. If the names and addresses of the candidates voted for are incorrectly written, or are written in *kana*, the ballots shall not be considered as "spoiled," provided that it is clearly understood for whom the voter wished to vote.

XLV. All questions as to the validity of the ballots shall be decided by the chairman, after consulation with the scrutineers. No protest against the chairman's decision shall be allowed at the polling place.

XLVI. In case a city or district is extensive, or contains islands, and in consequence it would be a great inconvenience to the voters to come to one central polling place, sub-election districts may be may be created by direction of the Governor, or with his approval.

Although it is not necessary to make a separate voters' list for each sub-election district, the district to which each voter belongs shall be denoted on the list, and the area of each sub-election district and the place at which polling shall take place, shall be notified throughout the jurisdiction.

XLVII. The sub-election meeting shall be opened at the same time as the principal meeting, and the duration of the polling shall be the same in both. The procedure at sub-election meetings shall be similar to that at a principal election meeting. The Governor may, however, permit an election in an island or in some very distant place to be held on a date different from that of the principal election meeting, and at the same time order that the ballot-box used at such a time be returned to the principal election meeting place by the date of polling at the principal election meeting.

XLVIII. Each sub-election meeting shall be presided over by a city or district clerk of high rank. Such a clerk shall be appointed by the Mayor or the Magistrate of a district, or by the Headman of the town or village concerned.

XLIX. When the ballot-box used at a sub-election meeting has been closed, it shall be sealed and be sent to the principal election meeting place being accompanied by the chairman and a clerk. If any of the scrutineers or the electors wish to attend also they may do so.

L. When sub-election district meetings are held, the chairman of the principal election meeting concerned shall, after the closing of the ballot-box, wait for the arrival of the ballot-boxes of the sub-election meetings, and upon their arrival count all the ballots cast in accordance with the provisions of Article XXXIII, and decide upon the persons who have been elected.

LI. When the successful candidates have been determined, the Mayor or the Magistrate of the district shall immediately notify them of their election.

Within five days after such notification has been sent out the succesful candidates shall declare their intention to serve in the posts to which they have been elected. If no such declaration has been made within ten days it shall be understood that they have declined to serve.

If a successful candidate declines to serve, the Mayor or the Magistrate of the district shall declare elected the candidate who has received the next highest number of votes.

LII. The results of an election shall be notified to the Governor by the Mayor or the Magistrate of the district.

LIII. The full names and addresses of the successful candidates shall be notified by the Governor throughout his jurisdiction.

LIV. In case substitute members are to be elected in accordance clause 2 of Article X. of the Fukenkwai-kisoku[1], such elections shall be held on the same day as the election for ordinary members.

LV. In event of a candidate being elected both as an ordinary and a substitute member of the assembly, he shall be considered an ordinary member, and the candidate with the

---

1. See Imp. Dec. No. 18, 1878. *Supra* pp. 272 ff.

next highest number of votes shall be declared elected as a substitute member.

LVI. Persons concerned who are dissatisfied with the conduct of an election may request the Governor to void the election at any time during ten days after the publication of the names of the successful candidates. Those who are dissatisfied with the decision of the Governor in such an event may bring suit in the Court of Appeal. The decision of the Court shall be final.

LVII. If after the results of an election have been announced, a candidate be found to be ineligible to sit in the assembly, the Governor shall void his election and shall declare the candidate with the next highest number of votes to be elected. In such an event the circumstances of the case shall be published throughout the jurisdiction.

LVIII. It is permissable to cancel an election and hold another one only when the election was held in the contravention of the Election Regulations ; and moreover only when such contravention was flagrant.

In such an event the Governor shall first inform the Home Minister and obtain his approval, and shall publish the fact throughout his jurisdiction.

LIX. Voters guilty of false declarations with regard to their qualifications shall be liable to a fine of from two to twenty *yen.* A candidate for election who has similarly been guilty of false declarations as to his qualifications shall be liable to a fine of from ten to one hundred *yen.*

LX. Anyone who has given or promised to give money, directly or in directly, in order to obtain votes or enable others to obtain them, or who has hindered others from voting shall be liable to a fine of from five to fifty *yen.* The same liability shall hold good in the case of the recipient of bribes.

Persons referred to in the preceding clause shall be dealt with in accordance with the provisions of Article 234[1] of the Criminal Code.

---

1. See foot note on p. 186.

LXI. Anyone entering the polling place carrying arms or lethal weapons shall be liable to a fine of from two to twenty *yen*.

LXII. Anyone guilty of committing an act of violence against an elector, in order to obtain his vote or enable others to obtain it, or to prevent him from voting for another candidate, shall be liable to minor imprisonment for not less than fifteen days nor more than three months, and also to a fine of from two to twenty *yen*.

LXIII. Anyone who has committed an act of violence against an elector, or who has menaced an elector on the way to the poll or at any other time for the purpose of hindering from voting, or who has committed an act of violence againstt he election officers or scrutineers or who has caused a disturbance in the polling place, or who has detained, broken, or taken by force the ballot-box, shall be liable to minor imprisonment for not less than two months nor more than one year, and also to a fine of from five to fifty *yen*.

LXIV. Anyone who has assembled a mob and is guilty of any of the offences mentioned in the preceding Article shall be liable to major imprisonment for not less than six months nor more than two years. Those who have come together to form the mob, knowing the circumstances, shall be liable to minor imprisonment for not less than one nor more than six months.

LXV. In case a successfull candidate is guilty of any of the offences mentioned in Articles LIX-LXIV his election shall be voided.

LXVI. Anyone who is guilty of impresonation or false declaration of his qualifications shall be liable to a fine of from two to twenty *yen*.

LXVII. Charges against persons guilty of offences at elections must be preferred within a period of six months after the date of the election.

LXVIII. Articles XV, XVII, XVIII, and XIX of the Fukenkwai-kisoku and those in contradiction of the present law are hereby abrogated.

Supplementary Rules.

For the 22nd year of Meiji (1889) the Governor shall order the preparation of the voters' list irrespective of the time fixed for the purpose in the present regulations.

In Prefectures where the election of members is necessary before the preparation of the voters' list mentioned in the preceding clause, the old list shall be used, but in other cases the present regulations shall apply.

H.-Z., 1889.

61. Appointment of Local Officials.

(Imp. Ord. No. 9, 1890.)

I. Any person who holds or has held for five years an office of or above the fifth class, *hannin* rank, :may without examination be appointed Gunchō or Kuchō on being passed by a Chief of the Committee for the examingtion of Gunchō or Kuchō.

II. Persons thus appointed after being passed by a Chief of the Committee for examination of Gunchō or Kuchō, must be again passed by a Chief of the Committee if they wish to be appointed to a similar post in another part of the empire.

III. Gunchō or Kuchō who have been appointed by a Chief of Committee as above cannot be promoted to a higher office without passing the Higher Civil Service Examination.

J. W. M., 1890, Feb. 22, p. 185.

62. Instructions[1] to Local Goverment Officials.

(Issued by the Home Office and printed by permission by the *Nichi Nichi Shimbun.*)

The period for putting into practice the provisions of the

---

1. Count Yamagata, in his capacity of Minister of Home Affairs, issued to the Local Governments throughout the Empire on the 25 December, 1889, the instructions of which the above is a translation.

Constitution is now at hand, and the advent of that great political event is awaited impatiently. At the same time the people,
engrossed in politics, are forming associations and developing
agitation, as is inevitable, while the situation is farther accentuat-
ed by difficulties attending the country's foreign relations. At
such a season the unique duty of all officials is to discharge
their functions with the utmost faithfulness to the Imperial will ;
to unite earnestly in averting troubles, in aiding the consummation of constitutional government, and in bringing about a good
result. I venture, therefore, to entreat you all to join me in
performing your difficult offices to the utmost of your ability.
Upon you, each in his own sphere, have devolved the arduous
functions of local government, and your task is to determine the
best way of performing them. Before everything, what you
have to consider is that the people may be directed into the
route most conducive to their interests, and that you yourselves
may follow the path of duty without error, favour, or affection.
The executive power is of the Imperial prerogative, and those
delegated to wield it should stand aloof from political parties,
and be guided solely by considerations of the general good in
the discharge of their duties. Of whatever further improvements education, the development of the country's resources,
and the growth of enterprise in the interior may be capable, the
progress made within the past twenty years is sufficient to inspire
confidence. Should that progress be now interrupted or disturbed by political excitement, a retrogressive movement will
ensue. This again is a point to be carefully watched, to the
end that the people may be led forward in the path of prosperity.
It does not follow that local interests are necessarily associated
with national interests. The interests of the people of each
locality must be specially consulted without reference to general
politics. The inhabitants of any one hamlet are concerned in
promoting the interests of their hamlet ; the inhabitants of any
one district, in promoting the interests of their district ; the
inhabitants of any one prefecture, in promoting the interests of

their prefecture. If you keep this in view in performing your functions, the interests of the whole country will be duly promoted. But if, on the contrary, forgetting their hamlet, their district, or their prefecture, the people become engrossed in the politics of the Central Government, and engage in party discussions connected with elections or political meetings, the effects will make themselves felt even among the lower orders, evil feelings will be nurtured, violence will be encouraged, localities which ought to be devoted to educational purposes will become arenas of strife and clamour, and the growth of household prosperity and national wealth will be checked. The history of other countries shows that no season is fraught with greater danger or demands greater caution then a season of political change, and that at such a season nothing is to be more carefully guarded against than the error of confusing the functions of central administration and local government. To bring local government into conformity with these abstract principles is undoubtedly a matter of great difficulty, but it is to be hoped that each of you, carefully directing attention to them, will select and follow the proper course. Ease and smoothness of administration, friendliness towards the people, absence of estrangement between the upper and lower orders, amicable conduct of all matters lying outside the pale of law and regulation—these are the points to be aimed at. Multiplication of processes, procrastination and delay, causing the people to spend their time fruitlessly—these are the points to be specially guarded against. Let simplicity and the correction of irksome usages be the guiding principles of office. Economy should be the prime object of local finance. Luxury and display, where the material resources of the country are still only partially developed, have the effect of poisoning the sources of wealth. Officials directly concerned in popular government must be pure of life, must eschew mercenary conduct and ostentation. Every degenerate step in local affairs estranges men's hearts and helps to bring about a position from which it is difficult to emerge. The time is near when results will make themselves visible, but in the meanwhile the question of local administration causes me much concern. I have, therefore, briefly set forth the principles by which you should be guided, in accordance with the Imperial will, and I trust that each of you will closely follow them.

J.W.M., 1890, Jan. 4, pp. 4-5.

63. Penalties applicable in the Election of members of City, Town, and Village Assemblies.

(Law No. 39, May 29, 1890.)

I. Any person who shall procure his enrollment in the list of electors by misrepresenting essential matters relating to his qualifications for voting, shall be punished by the imposition of a fine of not less than 2 *yen* and not more than 20 *yen*.

Any person who has been placed on the list of electors by virtue of his concealing essential matters relating to his qualification for voting, shall be punished by the imposition of a fine of not less than 3 *yen* and not more than 30 *yen*.

II. Any person who shall give or promise to give money, goods, notes, or public or private office to an elector, with the intention of obtaining a vote or of procuring a vote on behalf of another, or of restraining any one from voting for another, shall be punished by the imposition of a fine of not less than 3 *yen* and not more than 30 *yen*.

Any person so accepting any gift or promise shall be liable to similar punishment.

III. Any person who shall offer wine or food to electors in the neighbourhood of a polling booth or on the road by which electors must go or return, or who shall furnish horses, carts, or other means of conveyance to carry electors to or from the polling booth, with the purpose mentioned in the foregoing Article, shall be punished as in Article II.

Persons who shall accept such aid or interest as mentioned in the foregoing paragraph, shall be liable to similar punishment.

IV. Any person who shall pay or promise to pay the expense of any horse, cart, journey or hotel incurred by an elector in going to or returning from the polling booth, with the purpose mentioned in Article II. shall be liable to punishment as provided in Article II.

Any person who shall accept such promise or payment shall be liable to similar punishment.

V. Any person who shall accomplish the purpose mentioned in Article II. by conduct such as noted in Articles II. III. and IV. shall be liable to punishment as provided for in Article 234 of the Penal Code.[1]

VI. Any person who shall conduct himself violently towards an elector with the purpose mentioned in Article II. shall be punished by minor imprisonment for not less than fifteen days and not more than three months, and by a fine of not less than 2 *yen* and not more than 20 *yen*.

VII. Any person who shall use threats to or shall abduct an elector, or molest him while walking, or shall by fraudulent means interfere with the exercise of an elector's just rights, shall be punished as provided for in Article VI.

VIII. Any person who shall accomplish the purpose mentioned in Article II. by such conduct as is mentioned in Articles VI. and VII. shall be punished with imprisonment of not less than two months and not more than two years, and by a fine of not less than 5 *yen* and not more than 50 *yen*.

IX. Any person who shall collect a crowd for the purpose of threatening an elector, disturbing the proceedings at a polling booth, or detaining, breaking open, or seizing by force a ballot box, shall be punished with minor imprisonment of not less than two months and out more than two years, and by a fine of not less than 5 *yen* and not more than 50 *yen*.

Any person who shall knowingly form one of a crowd of

---

1. Cf. p. 186, foot note.

persons gathered as above described, shall be punished with minor imprisonment of not less than fifteen days and not more than two months, and by a fine of not less than 2 *yen* and not more than 20 *ycn*.

X. Any person who shall offer violence to an election official (*Senkyo Kakari*) or to an official connected with an election, or shall cause a disturbance at a polling booth, or shall detain, break open, or seize by force a ballot box at the time of an election, shall be punished with minor imprisonment for not less than three months and not more than three years, and by a fine of not less than 10 *yen* and not more than 100 *yen*.

XI. Any person who shall by gathering a crowd commit an offence such as mentioned in Article X. shall be punished with minor imprisonment for not less than two years and not more than five years, and by a fine of not less than *yen* 20 and not more than 200 *yen*.

Any person who shall knowingly form one of a crowd gathered as above shall be punished with minor imprisonment for not less than fifteen days and not more than five months and by a fine of not less than 4 *yen* and not more than 40 *yen*.

XII. Any person offending as described in Articles IX. X. XI. who shall be at the time in possession of arms or lethal weapons shall undergo punishment one degree heavier than hereinbefore provided.

XIII. Any persons who shall take part in a procession or crowd, shall burn torches, ring bells, beat drums, sound trumpets or horns, or carry flags or other emblems, or conduct themselves in a manner similar thereto with the purpose of exciting the public during election proceedings in any Gun or municipality where a polling booth is, and shall fail to obey the police when ordered to desist, shall be punished with imprisonment for not less than fifteen days and not more than two months, and by a fine of not less than 3 *yen* and not more than 30 *yen*.

XIV. Any person who shall circulate a rumour to the effect that another who possesses the requisite qualification for a candidate, cannot stand as a candidate, or is unwilling to accept election, shall be punished with a fine of not less than 3 *yen* and not more than 30 *yen*.

XV. Any person who shall enter a polling booth, while in the possession of arms or other lethal weapons, shall be punished by a fine of not less than 3 *yen* and not more than 30 *yen*.

XVI. Any person who shall post up a placard or similar object with the purpose mentioned in Article II. shall be punished with a fine of not less than 2 *yen* and not more than 20 *yen*.

XVII. Any person who shall vote by fraudulently using the name of another or who, not being qualified to do so, shall vote, shall be punished by a fine of not less than 3 *yen* and not more than 30 *yen*.

XVIII. In the event of an elected candidate being punished under Articles II. to XVI. the election shall be null and void.

XIX. Offences which are specially provided for in the Penal Code, in addition to those hereinbefore referred to, shall be visited with the major degree of punishment applicable to them.

XX. In the case of offences under this law prescription shall be held to apply after a period of six months has elapsed.

XXI. This law shall be applicable to the election of members of assemblies opened and held under the Regulaticns as to Municipality, Town, and Village Organisations as well as to Law No. 11. 1889, except in the case of elections to municipality, town, and village assemblies.

J.W.M., 1890, June 14, p. 610.

III.—MISCELLANEOUS DOCUMENTS.

1.—AGITATION FOR REPRESENTATIVE INSTITUTIONS.

I. MEMORIAL ON THE ESTABLISHMENT OF A REPRESENTATIVE ASSEMBLY.

(Jan. 17, 1874.)

The opinions contained in the memorial hereto annexed which we have the honor to address to you having constantly been held by us, and some of us during our term of cffice having repeatedly memorialised you on the same subject, an understanding was come to that after the special embassy despatched to the allied powers in Europe and America should have observed the practical working of such institutions, steps should be taken after due consideration of the circumstances. But although several months have elapsed since the return of the embassy to this country, we do not learn that any measures have been adopted. Of late the popular mind has been agitated, and mutual distrust has sprung up between the governors and the governed, and a state of things has arrived in which it cannot be denied that there are signs of destruction and ruin being ready to break forth at any moment. The cause of this we regret profoundly to say is the suppression of the general opinion of the empire as ascertained by public discussion.

We trust that you will give these remarks due consideration.

(Signed)   SOYEJIMA TANEOMI,
Samurai of Saga-ken.

GŌTŌ SHŌJIRŌ,
Samurai of Tōkyō-fu.

ITAGAKI TAISUKE,
Samurai of Kōchi-ken.

ETŌ SHIMPEI,
Samurai of Saga-ken.

MITSUOKA HACHIRŌ,

YURI KIMMASA,
Samurai of Tsuruga-ken.

KOMURO NOBUO,
Samurai of Miōdō-ken.

OKAMOTO KENSABURŌ,
Samurai of Kōchi-ken.

FURUSAWA URŌ,
Samurai of Kōchi-ken.

MEMORIAL.[1]

When we humbly reflect upon the quarter in which

1. It is impossible to print all the memorials which were sent in to the government between 1874 and 1881, petitioning for the establishment of a National Assembly. In the first nine months of 1880 no less than thirty petitions were received by the Genro-in, of which twenty-three were forwarded to the Council of State for consideration. The examples which I have included will suffice to convey a fair impression of the arguments which were current at the different stages of the agitation. The expression of the public mind on the subject was not by any means confined to petitions and memorials, but after 1877 found its way into the press to an extent which is surprising. The *Choya* was the foremost of the champions of the cause, the *Nichi Nichi* of the opponents. In 1875 an Assembly was said to be necessary in order to determine whether or not there should be war against Korea, in 1880, in order to induce the foreign powers to revise the treaties. All through the period it was reiterated that a Representative Assembly would improve the administration, reduce the expenditures of the Government, decrease the burden of taxation, etc., and, moreover, was it not a natural right of the people to be represented in the government? As opposed to the agitation, the *Nichi Nichi* pointed out that it would be wiser to be content with the Assembly of Local Governors for the present. As a general thing it advocated patience and slow action, though upon occasions it stigmatised sharply the motives of the agitators.

No attempt is made to represent by documents the activities of the political parties which flourished after 1881. There is no lack of such materials, party platforms, statements of principles, etc., but the history of political parties of this period has already been published in the Transactions of this Society (Vol. XIX, Part III).

the governing power lies, we find that it lies not with the Crown (the Imperial House) on the one hand, nor with the people on the other, but with the officials alone. We do not deny that the officials respect the Crown, and yet the Crown is gradually losing its prestige, nor do we deny that they protect the people, and yet the manifold decrees of the government appear in the morning and are changed in the evening, the administration is conducted in an arbitrary manner, rewards and punishments are prompted by partiality, the channel by which the people should communicate with the government is blocked up and they cannot state their grievances. Is it to be hoped that the empire can be perfectly ruled in this manner ? An infant knows that it cannot be done. We fear, therefore, that if a reform is not effected the state will be ruined. Unable to resist the promptings of our patriotic feelings, we have sought to devise a means of rescuing it from this danger, and we find it to consist in developing public discussion in the empire. The means of developing public discussion is the establishment of a council-chamber chosen by the people. Then a limit will be placed to the power of the officials, and both governors and governed will obtain peace and prosperity. We ask leave then to make some remarks on this subject.

The people whose duty it is to pay taxes to the government possesses the right of sharing in their government's affairs and of approving or condemning. This being a principle universally acknowledged it is not necessary to waste words in discussing it. We therefore humbly pray that the officials will not resist this great truth. Those who just now oppose the establishment of a council-chamber chosen by the people say : " Our people are wanting in culture and intelligence, and have not yet advanced into the region of enlightenment. It is too early yet to establish a council-chamber elected by the people." If it really be as they say, then the way to give to the people culture and intelligence and to cause them to advance swiftly into the region of enlightenment is to establish a council-chamber chosen by the people. For in order to give our people culture and intelligence and to cause them to advance into the region of enlightenment, they must in the first place be induced to protect their rights, to respect and value themselves, and be inspired by a spirit of sympathy with the griefs and joys of the empire, which can only be done by giving them a voice in its concerns. It has never happened that under such circumstances the people have been content to remain in a backward condition or have been satisfied with want of culture and intelligence. To expect that they shall acquire culture and intelligence by themselves and advance by themselves into regions of enlightenment is like " waiting a hundred years for the water to clear." The worst argument they put forward is that to establish a council-chamber at once would be simply to assemble all the blockheads in the empire. What shocking self-conceit and arrogant contempt for the people this indicates ! No doubt there are among the officials men who surpass others in intelligence and ingenuity, but how do they know that society does not contain men who sur-pass them in intelligence and knowledge? Whence it may be inferred that the people of the empire are not to be treated with such arrogant contempt. If again they deserve to be treated with arrogant contempt, are the officials themselves not a part of the nation, in which case they also are wanting in intelligence and culture ? Between the arbitrary decisions of a few officials and the general opinion of the people, as ascertained by public discussion, where is the balance of wisdom or stupidity? We believe that the intelligence of the officials must have made progress as compared with what it was previous to the Restora-tion, for the intelligence and knowledge of human beings increase in proportion as they are exercised. Therefore to establish a council-chamber chosen by the people would promote the culture and intelligence of the people and cause them to advance rapidly into the region of enlightenment. The duty of a government and the object which it ought to promote in the fulfillment of that duty is to enable the people to make progress.

Consequently in uncivilised ages, when manners were barbarous and people fierce, turbulent and unaccustomed to obey, it was of course the duty of the government to teach them to obey, but our country is now no longer uncivilised, and the tractableness of our people is already excessive. The object which our government ought therefore to promote is by the establishment of a council-chamber chosen by the people to arouse in them a spirit of enterprise, and to enable them to comprehend the duty of participating in the burdens of the empire and sharing in the direction of its affairs, and then the people of the whole country will be of one mind.

How is the government to be made strong? It is by the people of the empire becoming of one mind. We will not prove this by quoting ancient historical facts. We will show it by the change in our government of October last. How great was the peril! What is the reason of our government standing isolated? How many of the people of the empire rejoiced at or grieved over the change in the government of October last? Not only was there neither grief nor joy on account of it, but eight or nine out of every ten in the empire were utterly ignorant that it had taken place, and they were only surprised at the disbanding of the troops. The establishment of a council-chamber chosen by the people will create community of feeling between the government and the people, and they will mutually unite into one body. Then and only then will the country become strong.

We have now proved our position by universal principles, by the actual political state of our country, by the duty of a government and by the change which occurred in our government last October. Our belief in the justice of our views is strengthened, and we are firmly of the opinion that the only way to develop and maintain the destinies of the empire is to establish a council-chamber chosen by the people and to develop public discussion among them. We will not here enlarge upon the manner in which the idea is to be wrought out, as that would occupy too much space.

We are informed that the present officials, under the pretence of being conservative, are generally averse to progress, and they nickname those who advocate reforms as "rash progressives," and oppose their opinions with the two words "too early." We ask leave to make an explanation here.

In the first place we do not comprehend the phrase "rash progression." If by rash progression is meant measures which are heedlessly initiated, then it is a council-chamber chosen by the people that will remedy this heedlessness. Do you mean by "rash progression" the want of harmony between the different branches of the administration, and the postponement of urgent matters to the less urgent in a period of reform, so that the measures carried out are wanting in unity of plan? The cause of this is the want of a fixed law in the country, and the fact that the officials proceed according to the bent of their own inclinations. The existence of these two things proves the necessity for establishing a council-chamber chosen by the people. Progress is the most beautiful thing in the world, and is the law of all things moral and physical. Men actuated by principle cannot condemn this word progress, but their condemnation must be intended for the word "rash," but the word "rash" has no connection with a council-chamber chosen by the people.

We are not only unable to comprehend what the words "too early" have to do with a council-chamber elected by the people, but our opinion is directly the opposite of what this phrase expresses. For if a council-chamber chosen by the people were established to-day, we may fairly suppose that it would not be expected to be in complete working order until many months or years had elapsed. We are only afraid therefore of a single day's delay in establishing it, and therefore we say that we hold the exact opposite of this opinion.

Another argument of the officials is that the council-chambers now existing in European and American states were not formed in a day, but were only brought into their present state by gradual progress, and therefore we cannot to-day copy them suddenly. But gradual progress has not been the case with council-chambers only ; all branches of knowledge and science and art are subject to the same conditions. The reason why foreigners have perfected this only after the lapse of centuries, is that no examples existed previously and these had to be discovered by actual experience. If we can select examples from them and adopt their contrivances, why should we not be successful in working them out? If we are to delay the using of steam machinery until we have discovered the principles of steam for ourselves, or to wait till we have discovered the principles of electricity before we construct an electric telegraph, our government will be unable to set to work.

Our object in seeking to prove that a council-chamber elected by the people ought to-day to be established in our country, and that the degree of progress amongst the people of this country is sufficient for the establishment of such a council-chamber, is not to prevent the officials from making use of various pretexts for opposing it, but we are animated by the desire that by establishing such a council-chamber public discussion in the empire may be established, the spirit of the empire be roused to activity, the affection between governors and governed be made greater, sovereign and subject be brought to love each other, our imperial country be maintained and its destinies be developed, and prosperity and peace be assured to all. We shall esteem ourselves fortunate if you will adopt our suggestions.

OPINION OF THE SA-IN.

(Jan. 23, 1874.)

With respect to the memorial presented by Soyejima, a Samurai of Saga-ken and seven others, upon the subject of the establishment of a council-chamber chosen by the people, the principle is an excellent one, and this college having received sanction to a similar proposal made by itself, has drafted a set of regulations. The suggestion, therefore, will be adopted.[1] At the same time, in view of the instructions issued last year to the Fu and Ken, with respect to Local Assemblies, and the fact that the Home Office has just been constituted, we recommend to the Council of State (Sei-in) that the Home Office shall be called upon to give its opinion, and that after the Local Assemblies shall have been opened, the question of a council-chamber chosen by the people shall then be taken up.

J.W.M., 1874, Jan. 31, pp. 81-83.

2. OBJECTIONS TO THE ESTABLISHMENT OF A DELIBERATIVE ASSEMBLY CHOSEN BY THE PEOPLE.

(January 26, 1874.)

To His Excellency SOYEJIMA (SHOSEI.)
      ,,   ,,   GŌTŌ   ,,
      ,,   ,,   ITAGAKI   ,,
      ,,   ,,   YETŌ   ,,

Gentlemen,—I have read your Memorial published in No. 206 of the *Nisshin Shinjishi* advocating the establishment of a deliberative assembly chosen by the people, and my esteem and affection for you has been suddenly increased by observing your deep dissatisfaction with the present condition of affairs, and the warmth of your patriotic feelings. At the same I cannot avoid entertaining some scruples with respect to the immediate establishment of a deliberative assembly in our present stage of progress towards civilization. I would therefore beg to draw your Excellencies' attention to my humble opinions as stated

1. The Sa-in was never a body of any influence, therefore its adoption of the plea contained in this memorial may have been sincere. At any rate, no action was taken by the Sei-in at the time, except to issue regulations for the Chiho-kwan-kwaigi, an assembly of the high local government officials, concerning which something is said in other parts of these documents.

below, and I trust that without taking account of my inferiority, you will favor me with your observations upon them.

With respect,

KATO HIROYUKI.[1]

In the original memorial, there occurs this passage: "Unable to resist the promptings of our patriotic feelings, we have sought to desire a means of rescuing it from this danger, and we find it to consist in developing public discussion by the empire," etc.

Now the developing of public discussion by the empire is the very thing which all thinking men most earnestly hope for. There is no surer foundation for the peace and prosperity of the commonwealth than this. But here one difficulty occurs to me. What is this difficulty? It is that public opinion is not invariably just and enlightened. Even in the civilised and enlightened states of Europe this sometimes happens. How can it avoid being so in our own imperfectly civilised country?

The object for which a deliberative assembly is created is no doubt the establishment of such constitutional laws as shall place the national peace and prosperity on a firm basis. Now in establishing a constitution and laws, it is necessary to observe minutely the stage of the country and of public feeling, and to choose such a constitution and laws as are suited to them. The reason is that if that be not done, the result will be like putting a round lid on a square pot, and the constitution and laws cannot be said to place peace and prosperity on a sure foundation. It is only wise men who are capable of choosing what is suitable to the present state of things and to the present state of feeling in this country. European scholars say: "What is wanted in a deliberative assembly is wide views; what is wanted in a judicial body is justice." Now it is easy for public opinion to be just, but hard for it to have wide views. This is an evil common

---

1. A learned student of Chinese knowledge, who for many years was President of the Daigaku.

to the present and former times. What is the cause of it? Is
it not the large proportion among the people of ignorant and
unlearned persons? An Englishman has said "There is no
country in Europe except England where the laws and the constitution are adapted to the wants of the country. The laws
and the constitution of other countries are on paper and nothing
more." This is a piece of national boasting and it is unnecessary to show that it is an exaggeration, but nevertheless there is
some truth in it. The reason is not far to seek. The parliament
of England contains a large proportion of wise men, and it is
therefore competent to initiate laws and constitutional measures
well suited to the wants of the country, but the deliberative
assemblies of other countries are unable to compass this. And
yet it is proposed to submit the affairs of the empire for discussion to our imperfectly civilised people and to apply the opinions
obtained in this way toward the framing of laws and a constitution. It is to be feared that this would be like climbing trees to
catch fish.

Fredrick II, a former King of Prussia was a prince of rare
merit, and at a time when a despotic form of government was
everywhere established and was approved of by a majority of
the most talented writers of the day, he was alone in maintaining
the inexpediency of an absolute form of government and argued
in favour of the extension of popular rights. It was a saying of
his that the prince is only the first magistrate of the nation and
that he has no right to exercise absolute sway over the people.
Posterity has called him the father of reform in Europe on account of the reforms which he introduced into the laws and the
constitution, and the restrictions he placed on the royal prerogative, but even he did not establish a deliberative assembly chosen
by the people, but retained in his own hands the powers of
government and exercised absolute authority. It is probable,
however, that in reality it was not because he was desirous of
using the powers of government in a despotic way that he did
so, but simply because he saw that the Prussian people at that

time were not sufficiently civilized, and that their views were not yet advanced enough to admit of their being entrusted with a share of the government.

Again at the present moment Russia has not yet been able to establish a sure deliberative assembly chosen by the people. The reason is that the views of the people are not advanced enough to make it possible to give them a share in the government. And yet it is expected that what is found impossible in Russia can be carried out in Japan. This is hard to believe. It is no doubt true that our nation is gradually moving towards enlightenment, but the peasant and merchant class are still what they have always been. They rest satisfied in their stupidity and ignorance, and it has not yet been found possible to rouse in them the spirit of activity. The soldier class alone is far in advance of them, but still how few there are in it who understand the principles of things? If, for example, one puts to them such a questions as "What is a government? What are subjects? What right has a government to levy taxes? On what does the right of a government to exact military service depend?" or other simple questions of a like kind, it will be found that not more than one or two out of ten can give an intelligent answer. Is this not a lamentable state of things? I fear that if, regardless of these facts, we proceed to establish in a sweeping way a deliberative assembly chosen by the people, the only fruit of such public discussion will be foolish ideas not worth consideration. Still if it is nothing more than foolish ideas it does not so much matter. But it is impossible to prevent great evils to the commonwealth resulting from such a course. For when a people whose intelligence is insufficiently developed is put in possession of the rights of free citizens, they do not know how to exercise them duly, and hence they fall into license, and so the danger of ultimately injuring the public peace and prosperity is incurred. Ought we not to dread such a result? The learned men of Europe of the present day are united in the opinion that while for a civilised country a deliberative assembly chosen by the people is a necessity, for an imperfectly civilised people it is a source of mischief. I make the following extract from a short treatise on Government published by one of these writers named Wildermann (*sic*), a German, which will show that my statements are not founded on mere conjecture. [Extract omitted.]

In the original memorial this passage is found :—" The way to give our people culture and intelligence and to cause them to advance swiftly into the region of enlightenment is to establish a deliberative assembly chosen by the people." But I have shown above the mischief which would result from the hasty establishment of a deliberative assembly chosen by the people. Where would be the opportunity of awaiting the advantages of civilization ?

Again this passage is found in the memorial. " The worst argument they put forward is that to establish a deliberative assembly at once would be to assemble all the blockheads of the Empire. What shocking self-conceit and arrogant contempt for the people this indicates." There is some little truth in this. Even among the statesmen of the present day it is impossible but that there should be some who are only imperfectly enlightened. But judging from what I have been able to see and hear, outside of the present government, not more than a few tens of men can be fonnd of distinguished ability. A few tens among 30,000,000 is hardly enough to raise the average level of the popular intelligence. They are certainly not enough to entitle us to describe them as a civilised nation. And even if we suppose that the government is not self-conceited and arrogant, they still find it necessary to entrust to themselves the business of the Empire for a time.

The memorial says that " The duty of a government and the object which it ought to promote in the fulfilment of that duty is to enable the people to make progress," etc. This is very true. Our country is not exactly barbarous but yet its civilisation is far from perfect and the people are too prone to submissiveness.   This is greatly to be lamented,   But if the government wishes to excite in the people the spirit of activity and to teach them to take a share in the conduct of the business of the empire, this object is not to be obtained simply by the establishment of a deliberative assembly.   The only method of obtaining it is by the establishing of schools and thus nourishing the nation's intellect.   The self-reliant and active character of the Prussian nation at the present day which has at last raised it to the position of the most powerful nation in Europe, has not been due to the establishment of a deliverative assembly, but to the fact that since the time of Fredrick II, the Prussian Government has devoted itself to the cultivation of the people's minds.

The memorial again says,—"How is a government to be made strong?   It is by the people of the empire becoming of one mind," etc.   This is incontrovertible.   Nevertheless this advantage will hardly be gained by the sudden creation of a deliberative assembly.   The only plan open to us is by turning our attention without loss of time to nourishing the intelligence of the nation and thus to render our country sufficiently civilised to admit of the establishment of a deliberative assembly.

The original memorial has this passage—"We have now proved our position by universal principles, by the actual political state of the country," etc.

Now reform is a good thing in itself.   But if it is desired to introduce reforms suddenly, it is impossible not to fall into the evil of rash progress.   There is nothing like steadily nourishing the intelligence and acting as far as possible in a gradual way.

The memorial then speaks of "rash progression," etc. I do not object to the statement that a deliberative assembly chosen by the people would deal with affairs in a wisely conservative way, but what I assert is that the abrupt establishment of a deliberative assembly cannot avoid the reproach of being a rashly progressive measure. The reasons of this I have sufficiently pointed out above.

I hope I have made tolerably clear wherein I agree and wherein I differ from the memorial.

P.S. Such are in a general way the humble opinions to which I would draw your attention. I shall think myself fortunate if you will kindly favor me with your observations. This memorial is probably the germ of a deliberative assembly chosen by the people to be established at some time in the future, and no one would be better pleased at such a result than myself, in spite of the objections I have thought it my duty to urge against it.

In short it is my conviction that although for a time it is necessary that the government should exercise absolute authority, yet the great principle must not be forgotten that the government is made for the people, not the people for the govermnent, and that it is needful to raise our country to the rank of a civilised nation by following implicitly the policy of Frederick in restricting the powers of the government, extending as far as possible the private rights of the people, encouraging liberty of speech, and promoting education.

Your memorial suggests one more remark. What do you think of the plan, which has already been carried out in one or two ken, of having for a time in the Fu and Ken assemblies constituted by choice from the samurai and the upper and middle classes of the common people, and which should discuss the internal affairs of their own Fu and Ken? The adoption or rejection of their decisions should, however, be entrusted for a time to the Chiji or Kenrei. I am yet unable to from any opinion as to whether it will be attended with the success which is hoped for from it, or whether it may not do more harm than good.

I hope, gentlemen, that you or the public will favor me with your observations on the statement of my views.

J.W.M., 1874, Feb. 14, pp. 121-123.

3. REPLY OF SOYEJIMA, GŌTŌ AND ITAGAKI TO KATO's ARGU-
MENT AGAINST REPRESENTATIVE GOVERNMENT IN JAPAN.[1]

(February 20, 1874.)

We have carefully perused and re-perused the memor-
andum lately published by you, Mr. Kato, setting forth your
doubts as to the advisability of establishing a deliberative assembly chosen by the people, and we can see that you have
applied yourself to the subject with great care and industry. It
may truly be called a generous present. We should be acting
in opposition to your own wishes if we left it unanswered, and
we therefore put forward a summary of our views.

You make the following extract from a German writer :—
"In discussing the forming of a government it is in the
first place necessary to show clearly the degree of progress
which the country has made and its actual condition, etc." This
is what Europeans call the superiority in knowledge of the 19th
over the 18th century. Our advocacy of the establishment of
such a council-chamber is based upon the imperative necessities
of the actual condition of our country, and we say that we are
speaking of the 19th century.

The establishment of the reformed government which we
have at this moment came entirely from below. In the commencement it was the low-class samurai (somo) and ronins who
raised the cry and roused the clansmen who in turn roused the
chiefs of the clans. With unity of purpose and combined action
they placed the young Emperor at their head, and thus
overturned the administration of the Tokugawa family. In
forming a (new) constitution, the Imperial Oath[2] was promulgated, according to which all measures were to be decided by
equitable discussion. In particular, all the clans were made to
send up councillors, who were to take a share in the general

---

1. It is interesting to note that during the interval between the presentation
of the original memorial and this reply, one of the original signatories, Etō
Shimpei, headed a rebellion in Saga Ken against the Government.

2. *Supra* p. 8.

business of the empire. By this means the grand achievements of the surrender to the throne of the territories and retainers of the daimyō, the formation of the administration of the fu, han and ken, and the conversion of han into ken were performed. All these measures were based upon the collective judgement of the lower (class subjects of the Emperor), and decided by the general opinion of the empire, while the Imperial Court reaped the fruits. It was for this reason that vast and wide-reaching as these measures were, their execution was easy and swift. After the conversion of the han into ken the appointment of the public councillors (Kōginin)[1] was discontinued, and the state of things which followed was not free from the abuses of a bureaucracy. The form of government which has of late prevailed resembles most what is called in English an "oligarchy," and its abuses require to be remedied. To prove the advantages of an absolute monarchy, you quote ancient facts from the reign of the Prussian King Frederick II, which are not applicable to the urgent affairs of our country. Mr. Mill somewhere says that this can be seen from the crises in history like the reigns of Charlemange, Peter the Great, or the English William III.

"It would be absurd to construct institutions for the mere purpose of taking advantage of such possibilities; specially as men of this calibre, in any distinguished position, do not require despotic power to enable them to exert great influence."

Frederick II was no doubt of the same style as Charlemange, Peter the Great and William III. The wisdom and the divine valour of His Majesty the Tennō will certainly some day deprive Frederick II and the others of the exclusive enjoyment in Europe of brilliant fame, but His Majesty's years are as yet few, and in face of the urgency of present affairs, it is only by means of a council-chamber elected by the people that our country can be preserved and upraised. The idea of establishing such a council-chamber chosen by the people is simply reviving and completing the system by which council-

1. *Supra* p. 26.

lors (kōshi)[1] were sent up from each clan, and giving full effect to the meaning of the Imperial oath. To leave the actual state of our conntry out of the question, and to quote ancient facts from the reign of Frederick II seems to be simply carrying on the error of the 18th century writers on politics. Before Frederick II succeeded to the throne he was a pupil of the Frenchman Voltaire, who in fact was the leader of the reformers of the 18th century, and whose views were so widely spread, that in a moment nearly all the sovereigns and statesmen of Europe became reformers. Even the Pope became a reformed Pope. From this may be seen the cause of the reformation of the government of those days. You say we want to do what is impossible, namely, to carry out in Japan what has not yet been done in Russia. Since the extraordinary advent of Peter the Russian government has had a succession of great and war-like Emperors and wise and enlightened statesmen, by whose hands it has been guided, and the sovereigns and their ministers being in accordance with the political condition of the country, the national policy has taken a natural shape. If you will carefully examine the causes which have certainly formed the Russian government, you will undersrand why it is deficient in a council-chamber elected by the people. We do not, however, desire to give force to our views by unnecessarily discussing the advantages and defects of othe constitutions of other countries. Mr. Mill has also discussed this subject, but we will not go out of our way to quote him. But if it depeneded on the degree of advancement and civilization of the people, the Russians would have to give way before the Greeks. But the Russians do not have a council-chamber elected by the people, because they do not feel the want of it, while it is simply the political condition of the Greeks that has caused them to rely on its benefits.

You say that the condition of the people of this whole country is such that it is not advisable to establish a council-chamber. But we reply that if such is actually the condition of

---

1. *Supra* p. 21.

our whole people a council-chamber must absolutely be established. You also say that the extreme submissiveness of our people is caused by the low degree of their civilisation. You have reversed cause and effect. The cause of the low degree of civilisation is this extreme submissiveness, and this extreme submissiveness is the result of our hitherto existing institutions. Mr. Mill says :—" Improvement in human affairs is wholly the work of the uncontented characters ; " and again :—" If there be a people whose submissiveness is so excessive that it leaves everything to its government, it is the same as caring nothing about such things, and accepting the results when agreeable as visitations of nature. How could such a people be expected to make progress and to desire to raise their civilisation." If we desire to advance the position of the whole of the people we must get them to abandon that excessive submisssion, and make them recover their original spirit of enterprise ; and the way to accomplish this is by correcting the errors of hitherto existing institutions, and that may henceforth conduce to our people's progress.

Mr. Mill says " that a savage people require a despotic government, a people of slaves require a government of guidance, but for a people who have risen above these conditions the only suitable form of government is the representative. To determine the form of government most suited to any people, we must be able, among the defects and shortcomings which belong to that people, to distinguish those that are the immediate impediment to progress ; to discover what it is, which stops the way.

" And the form of government which is most effectual for carrying the people through the next stage of progress, will still be very improper for them, if it does this in such a manner as to obstruct, or positively unfit them, for the step next beyond. The Egyptian hierarchy, and the paternal despotism of China, were suitable at the time, but they were brought to a permanent halt by the want of mental liberty and individuality, which want was the fault of their institutions.

" In all states of human improvement ever yet attained, the nature and degree of authority exercised over individuals, the distribution of power, and the conditions of command and obedience, are the most powerful of the influences which make them what they are. Therefore that which most affects the progress of the people is the government. They may be stopped short at any point in their progress, by defective adaptation of their government to that particular stage of advancement. And the one indispensible merit of a government, in favor of which it may be forgiven almost any amount of demerit compatible with progress, is that it causes the people to advance to the next stage."

Besides, if the general condition of the people be left stationary their patriotism will not be able to develop to its normal degree.

Mr. Mill again says :—" Wherever the sphere of action of human beings is circumscribed, their sentiments are narrowed and dwarfed in the same proportion. The food of feeling is action ; even domestic affection lives upon good offices. Let a man have nothing to do for his country, and he will not care for it. It has been said of old, that in a despotism there·is but one patriot, the despot himself. This completely expresses the evil effects of subjection to a master."

We have already demonstrated that the present state of the country demands urgently the establishment of a council-chamber, and the fact that our people are in a stage when they do not require a government of guidance. Seeing that our people were able not long ago to establish the reformed government why should they be unable to-day to establish a council-chamber ? Mr. Mill says :—" There are three things necessary in the condition of a people. Firstly, the people for whom the form of government is intended must be willing to accept it ; or at least not so unwilling as to insist on opposing it. Secondly, the people must be able to do what is necessary to preserve this form of government. Thirdly, the people must be able to do what is necessary for the form of government to fulfill its purposes. If anyone who argues in favor of a particular form of government requires that the people fulfill the first and second of these requirements, and that they also fulfill the third in a greater or less degree, no one can object to his argument."

Now if this council-chamber be established, we do not propose that the franchise should at once be made universal. We would only give it in the first instance to the samurai and the richer farmers and merchants, for it is they who produced the leaders of the revolution of 1868. Since we sent in our memorial to the Sa-in, a number of letters have appeared criticising it in the newspapers, but not one of them has condemned the idea of establishing a council-chamber, and they have confined themselves to personal attacks upon us. From this it may be justly inferred that the nation already fulfills the three conditions referred to above. If therefore we collect these tendencies and give them shape, what is now scattered will become concentrated, and their power, when put into motion, of co-operating usefully with the government will be more than anyone can pretend to conceive beforehand. At the beginning of the restoration, there were many opponents of it in the empire, who argued that though it sounded plausible, it never could be carried out. But when the movement once began, the opinion of these people was proved to be wrong by the result. This shows how difficult it is to prove anything by mere words. Why should we therefore hesitate in the present case?

You say that you fear the establishment of such a council-chamber, because it would be a focus of stupid views. But this is by no means certain. The persons who shall be selected to serve as councillors[1] will be men from the towns and country districts, and therefore how can anyone know beforehand that it will not be the focus of wisdom and intelligence? Human nature is such that any man who occupies a public position is certain to become conscious of his own deficiencies, and to give

---

1. Members of the proposed council-chamber.

way in silence to those of greater wisdom than himself. This is
the case with the English and French councillors, who for the
most part follow the leaders of the party to which they belong.
We cannot help thinking, therefore, that your fear of its becoming the focus of stupid views is owing to your not having
considered sufficiently these points.

You say that we ought to put aside the question of a
council-chamber and devote our efforts mainly to the education
of the people. To advocate education for the people is undoubtedly the part of the philanthropist. But why do you say
nothing about the education of the mental power of the people ?
We will therefore quote Mr. Mill against you for your benefit,
and to prove our principle that the way to promote the knowledge
and intelligence of the people, and to accelerate their progress
in enlightenment is by establishing a council-chamber elected by
the people.

" It is not sufficiently considered how little there is in most
men's ordinary life to give them largeness of the sentiments.
Their work is a routine, consisting of the contrivances which
they are habituated to use for meeting their daily wants. Consequently neither the thing done nor the process of doing it
develops the mental powers in the way of conceptions or sentiments. If instructive books are within their reach, there is no
stimulus to read them, and in most cases the individual has no
access to any person of cultivation much superior to his own.
Giving him something to do for the public supplies, in a measure,
all these deficiencies. If circumstances allow the amount of
public duty assigned to him to be considerable, it makes him
an educated man. In ancient times the intelligence of the citizens
of Athens was superior to that of other peoples simply because
they were able to develop largely their mental powers.

" Among the foremost benefits of free government is that
education of the intelligence and the sentiments, which is carried
down to the very lowest ranks of the people when they are
enabled to take part in national concerns. There are those who

doubt whether the result of the people taking a part in their national affairs can be so great. Yet unless the cultivation of the intelligence and sentiments of the people is to be an empty vision, this is the road by which it must come. If there is any-one who disputes the position that it can only come by this road, I beg him to read the great work of the famous Frenchman M. de Tocqueville :—' It has been said with reference to the edu-cation of the people that books and discourses are alone not education. Human affairs are like a sum in arithmetic, not an empty theory, and therefore action can only be learnt by action. This saying ought to be repeated again and again. A child learns to write its name only by practice and is a man taught to use his mental powers and guide his conduct merely by pre-cepts? What can be learned in schools is important but not all important. The main element in the education of human beings is their constant employment. The private money-getting of almost everyone seldom brings his faculties into play, while its exclusive pursuit tends to fasten his attention and his interest upon himself alone, making him indifferent to public affairs and ends by plunging him into selfishness and cowardice. Balance these tendencies by contrary ones, that is, let the people take a part in public business, and in the degree to which he takes a part in public affairs, in that degree his thoughts and feelings will be drawn out of this narrow circle. He then becomes acquainted with varied business, and increases his mental powers ; he learns that besides his own personal interests there are interests common to the whole country, and that the general happiness is not his happiness alone, and that it depends partly on his exertions. The desideratum of a general diffusion of intelligence among the people can only be attained by extending the right of criticising public and national affairs to the people.' "

You say that such a council-chamber cannot escape the reproach of " heedless advancement," on the ground of its sudden establishment. But if you will attentively read these extracts and at the same time consider the state of the empire, you will see that it is not so.

If you had not done the favor to express your doubts, how could we have been able to go so deeply into the matter? For this favor we are really indebted to you. You know by heart all matters European and American. Much aid is always to be derived in national reforms and advancement from the efforts of learned men, and we expect much more from you than these doubts.

(Signed)   SOYEJIMA TANEOMI.
GŌTŌ SHŌJIRŌ.
ITAGAKI TAISUKE.

J. W. M., 1874, April 25, pp. 325-327.

4. A REACTIONARY MEMORIAL.

(Presented to His Majesty the Tennō, October 1874, by Samurai of Kōchi Ken).

It is our humble opinion that the present condition of the empire is becoming daily more pressing, and monthly more and more urgent. The people are filled with suspicion, and no longer know what direction to take, whilst spirited samurai fear that the way of peaceful government of the empire has been departed from and that it will be years before things again attain a settled condition. We have been long in the enjoyment of the Imperial favors, and if at present we stood idly by, and neglected to set forth our genuine grief for the present state of our country, we should be unworthy of being called true servants of Your Majesty. But we are poor and without the means of providing travelling expenses, and we are therefore unable to take a long journey away from our native village. So that our anxious thoughts are wasted to no purpose. We have, however, humbly observed that Your Majesty dispensing in your great wisdom an enlightened policy to the nation, has established a Deliberative Assembly, and sending forth the Imperial mandate to the four quarters of the Empire, has called upon all even the lowest classes of the cities, to state, without fear of giving offence, whatever views they may entertain. If we were now to remain silent, we should not only be thwarting the intention, which Your Majesty has condescended to make known, of putting aside your own ideas and ascertaining the desires of the people, but might never perhaps have another similar opportunity. In spite of our own meanness, therefore, we humbly beg to lay before Your Majesty this paper in which we have discussed each matter in a separate paragraph.

I. It is a just principle that in establishing the laws and institutions of any country, the feelings and customs of its inhabitants should be conformed to. In this Empire there are Imperial institutions. Europe and America have institutions of their own, and the same is true in respect to other parts of the world. In this empire the fundamental relations of lord and vassals, of parent and child, are established firm and unchangeable as a mountain. In China, the transfer of the Empire from Giō to Shu is praised as a noble and magnanimous act, but it resulted afterwards in the exile of To and the punishment of Bu. It is impossible to enumerate all the occasions on which these names were envoked in after-times as a justification of regicide and parracide. France is described to us as an enlightened, wealthy, civilised, and warlike country, but their king was made prisoner by the Prussians, and we have not heard that even one Frenchman died a sacrifice to patriotism and high principle. But is it not enlightenment and civilisation where lord and vassal, parent and child, husband and wife, each observe faithfully their relative duties; where governors and governed live amicably together ; where there are no starving paupers in the streets, or robbers on the moors, and where people are slow to private quarrel, but zealous to combat in the cause of their country ? How can we first suppress courtesy and shamefacedness, and then account it enlightenment and civilisation ? For these reasons if we honor and maintain our Imperial form of government, and follow the precepts of the sages, it will necessarily become manifest whether a comparison is favorable to them or to us. But if we want only to imitate the customs of European countries, it is impossible to say that this evil may not lead to the insidious introduction of what is known to them as a republic.

II. The Court regulations for ceremonies and dresses were instituted by our ancestors, and have been observed by a long line of Emperors. They should not be altered without good reason. If there are some which are inconvenient, and which ought to be altered, this should not be done without first announcing the change at the tombs of the Emperors' ancestors and publishing it to the people. But now this is not done. Everything has been changed in imitation of European dress and ceremonies with the sole exception that the Shintō officials are allowed to retain the old forms of ceremony. The result is that not only are the people wholly unused to European forms of ceremony, but even officials, although at the public offices they imitate the European practice, adhere to the old customs when at home. In Japan, it has always been the custom to salute in squatting posture, but they consider it polite to stand. The Shintō officials alone are made to follow the old customs. Does this mean that in paying honors to our ancestors they are to worship in squatting posture but that towards other officials or towards the foreigners they are to adopt a standing position? And are officials to stand at audiences, or when they meet foreigners, but to worship in a squatting posture when paying their respects at the tombs of their ancestors? If this is really to be the case, we at any rate cannot see the fitness of such an arrangement; matters of ceremony should not be dealt with in such an off-hand manner. We pray that the regulations of our ancestors be at once reverted to.

III. Lately schools have been established in every parish, whether urban or rural, to which children of all classes are admitted. In addition to this, a large number of students have been sent to European countries, and caused to investigate their learning. At no time in history has learning been so flourishing. In education, however, the chief attention is directed to European studies, and the doctrines of the Chinese sages seem on the point of being discarded. It appears to us that the doctrines of the Chinese sages accord well in many points with the Shintō religion, and about 1600 years have now elapsed during which they have been held in high esteem by an unbroken succession of Emperors. Would it not be an error to do away entirely with them? Education should consist, first of all, in the study of our native writings by which we learn the superiority of our national constitutions over those of all foreign nations, and next in acquiring a knowledge of the doctrines of the (Chinese) sages, by which we learn the virtues of loyalty, filial piety, benevolence, and justice. After that the pupil should be taught to read European books, by which his understanding may be more and more enlarged. Any other course will end in exalting them and in thinking meanly of others and must speedily result in causing us to fall into the snares of an evil religion. Even now the religion of Jesus is flourishing in the metropolis, and there is danger of it spreading over the empire. Now the religion of Jesus is one which shows its respect for heaven by misrepresenting heaven, and whose mode of teaching men is to lead them astray. It is a religion which has the evil result of causing men to make naught of their lords and parents. If it is not now strictly prohibited, it threatens to raise its hopes even to the Imperial throne. Is not this a truly alarming state of things? We have humbly observed that the fact of the Imperial line having remained unbroken from the first foundation of the Empire until now is due to the Imperial glory being shed abroad throughout the land, and the people enjoying the blessing of Imperial favor, to the hearty observance of the respective duties of lord and vassal, and to a just distinction being maintained between high and low. But the students of western learning call those bigots who respect the religion of our empire, and ridicule as students of a far-fetched philosophy those who read Chinese books. But what do we mean by "bigot"? Is it not a person who holds fast to one thing and is incapable of progress, and would not we call it a far-fetched philosophy when a man is ignorant of the good and bad qualities of things that are before his eyes, and starts off in pursuit of that which is high and distant? Is not the bigotry of the students of western learning of the worst kind, for they do nothing but assert the fitness of the customs of foreign countries distant 10,000 *ri*, and are ignorant of the reverence due to the gods, and of the utility of the doctrines of the sages.

We pray that Your Majesty will encourage the true learning, and prohibit evil doctrines, thereby maintaining sternly the right system of education.

IV. There are at present many matters with which the State has to deal, but among them none is more pressing than to stir up the spirit of the samurai, and to calm the minds of the people. The reason why our empire has never been exposed to insult since its foundation is that the original high spirit of the samurai has been preserved. If it had not been preserved, how should we ever have been able to confront all the great continents on equal terms? In spite of this, however, the samurai have been relieved of their proper office and a system introduced which brings them to the same level as all classes of subjects. This is a name and not a reality. The samurai devotes his powers to the acquirement of learning and the art of war, and turns his attention to matters of State, and although it is desired to deprive him of the one thing in which his *forte* lies, and to convert him all at once into a peasant, it is impossible to do so, nor is it possible for him to become an artisan or merchant, however much this may be wished for. He only gives himself up to indolent habits, and consumes to no purpose the allowance issued to him. If a danger arises to our country, of what service will he be in defending it? Under the feudal system a standard of learning and accomplishments was set up, which the samurai were required to attain, but in spite of this some of them gave way to indolence. Now that there is no such control, all, without distinction of rank, prize luxury and rival each other in adopting new things ; they love what is strange, and great and small alike look to foreign countries as their model in all things. No matter what merits a Japanese thing may have they despise and disregard it. What an unnatural state of things is this !

We hope that the samurai may be at once restored to their ordinary functions, that their high spirit may be encouraged, that frugality may be earnestly practised, and that morals may be rendered pure. If these things are not attended to, all our efforts after progress towards enlightenment and civilisation will be vain.

V. In all our reforms of our government there is none in which foreign institutions have not been imitated. We ought certainly to have adopted those inventions in which foreigners excel, viz., fire-arms, ships of war and fortifications, and to have guarded our coast vigilantly by means of them. But since the revolution we have not heard of one great gun having been cast or a single fort having been erected. It is perhaps the plan of our statesmen to conduct our relations with foreign countries in accordance with foreign international law. They think that in our commerce with foreigners sincerity and justice should be the rule. They say that we have already entered into friendly relations with foreigners and if we treat them with sincerity and justice they can certainly have no pretence for invading us. These are not our views. We believe that it is our servile attitude towards foreigners that has hitherto prevented them from attacking us. If in our relations with them we took our stand on our warlike prestige they would certainly become enraged and attack us, even though we committed no breach of faith. We may see that this is so if we observe from what causes they go to war with each other. Their wars are not always owing to unavoidable causes; they often proceed from a conflict of interests, or from a rivalry in power and prestige. Ever since 1853 foreignners have despised and mocked us for our servility and have not scrupled to use their military prestige to bring pressure upon us. They have tricked us by their international law and deluded us by their false religion. The spirit they have shown toward us is greatly to be detested. Their international law and good faith and justice are certainly not to be relied on. Why therefore does our government not adopt those things in which they excel and use them for the vigilant defence of our coasts? Large sums of money are now being spent on railways and stone houses. In our opinion if these sums were to be expended on the erection of works for the defence of our own coast this object might easily be attained. We hope Your Majesty will not be led away by these erroneous ideas. It is right, however, to adopt whatever things foreigners excel in.

VI. We have heard a rumor that a difference has arisen between Japan and China, and that we are about to send an expedition against that country. If this be true it is a matter affecting the security and very existence of this empire. For weak though we may think China to be the extent of her armies is several tens of times greater than those of this country. If it is desired to strike a blow against China it will be necessary to raise an army of several hundred thousand men. And even should we attack China with an army of this size, we cannot be absolutely certain to gain the victory. We may win battle after battle and yet we could never capture the Emperor, or reduce the country to submission, while on the other hand if our armies were routed, we should be unable to send reinforcements. This would involve keeping an army on foot several years without disbanding it, and would exhaust the resources of the country. It would then become necessary to levy contributions on the property of the subject. At present the people have not yet found rest from ever changing enactments, and if in addition heavy contributions were exacted from them they would certainly learn to hate the government. Who can estimate beforehand the magnitude of the evil consequences which would follow if at such a time a man of facts but devoid of principle should come forward as their leader?

In ancient times Toyotomi Hideyoshi wielded the military power of the empire with unexampled ability. He sent Kato Kiomasa and other valiant generals with an army of 160,000 brave samurai on an expedition against Korea. There they had several engagements with an auxiliary force from China, but although they were victorious none of our troops could ever get west of the O-rioku-kō (Arinare). At last after seven years, during which time the army was never disbanded, Hideyoshi died and the troops returned to Japan. In the end we were unable to retain possession of a foot of Korean soil. And this was not owing to the want of skill on the part of our generals, or to cowardice in our troops. They labored under the disadvantage of fighting in a foreign country and were overpowered by numbers. Your Majesty is gifted with great discernment and will not require to ask scholars to tell you whether our present generals are more or less effective than those of Hideyoshi's time. To attack China suddenly with a small army would be a very dangerous step. But your servants are still unacquainted with the circumstances of the case. If our differences with China has arisen from unavoidable causes and it is necessary to send an expedition to deal out to her a just punishment, full of loyal impulse and righteous indignation, we shall of course do our best to make the Imperial glory shine out brightly beyond the seas. And if they take the initiative and invade Japan, it will be the time for us to spare no effort and even to lay down our lives in gratitude for our country. If we are unsuccessful what better can we demand than to die for Japan? Before attacking others, however, we should examine whether our own defences are sufficient. An unsuccessful attack upon an enemy will bring down upon us an attack from them, and if we are unable then to defend ourselves ruin is unavoidable. He who wishes to attack another ought to look watchfully to his own defences. At the present time our forts are dismantled, our stores are exhausted, we are unprovided with warlike engines, our coasts are unprotected with forts and our frontiers with barriers. How then can the country be defended? There is an old saying " In safety do not forget danger ; in a settled state of things do not forget disorder." These things should be the subject of everyday investigation. But they are neglected and nobody examines into them. We cannot imagine what can be the reason of this. There are even some who take delight in troubled times and place their trust in the chances of fortune. Such men tell us that if with a mighty army we assailed the cowards of China they would be crushed like withered twigs, and would without doubt make their submission. Their sub- mission having been received we would return home with an indemnity and not only gain great glory for the empire in the eyes of foreigners but also add to its resources. We are afraid that the members of the government are pleased with talk of this kind and that it may even mislead Your Majesty so as to render unavoidable a course which is possibly avoidable. We are confident that Your Majesty's wisdom is not ignorant of the utter groundlessness of such statements, but the talk in the streets is noisy and unceasing, and we have found it incumbent on us to speak out.

We beseech Your Majesty to consider what we have said, and we beg humbly to lay before You the above remarks. It is said in the Shoo-king :—" A country will stand if ruled after the method of a well-governed country ; if things are managed as in a country of disorder it will surely fall." In the reforms which have been introduced since the revolution, has the method been in accordance with that of a well-governed country? Or have things been managed as in a country of disorder ? If the former had been the case the people would not be distressed and full of apprehension as they now are, nor would the men of public spirit be lamenting the long unsettled state of the empire. If the latter has been our practice let it be at once reformed, and let us return to the institutions of our ancestors.   What need have we to imitate the customs of foreign countries 10,000 *ri* away?

Unable to contain this genuine outpouring of our stupid loyalty and zealous anxiety we have thus dared to offend against Your Majesty, and in deep humility we await the punishment of the axe for our presumption.

J.W.M., 1874, Nov. 7, pp. 914-16.

5. MEMORIAL ADVOCATING THE ESTABLISHMENT OF A REPRE-
SENTATIVE ASSEMBLY.

(Presented to the Emperor, June, 1877, by the Risshisha.)[1]

With greatest reverence we present to His Majesty the Emperor this, our most humble memorial.

Shortly after Your accession to the throne, the daimyō yielded up their territorial rights, their provinces being placed under a central government.   The feudal system was thus entirely abolished and the whole country united under one Emperor.   Laws were re-enacted; the army, navy, and system of police were established; schools were instituted; the postal system regulated; railways and telegraphs inaugurated.

The rapidity with which this country has advanced in civilisation is unparalleled in the history of the world; so powerful has the nation apparently become, that it may seem to many as though little remains to place it on a level with European and American powers.   But in reality our position is far otherwise.   Internal strife, and disaffection among the agricultural classes and the samurai keep the country in a state of constant uneasiness, while we cannot claim to exercise an external influence equal to foreign powers.   Neither the Government nor the people are freed from anxiety for a single day.

1. "The Society of Free Thinkers," a political association organised in Kōchi Ken by Itagaki Taisuke.

It is our opinion that all these evils arise from the fact that Your Majesty's ministers exercise a power solely despotic, the administration being carried on entirely without reference to the opinion of the nation.

We will not recount the various events that have taken place in other countries in ancient times that bear out our opinion, but will merely refer to what has passed in Your own land since Your Majesty favoured us by taking the reins of government.

The cause of the downfall of the *Bakufu*[1] is solely attributable to the tyranny of ministers and to their oppressing the people, instead of considering their wishes. Zealous patriots arose in all parts of the country to overthrow the *Bakufu*. In vain did it fulminate laws and mete out inhuman punishments in order to crush these patriotic spirits. They had yet to learn that tyranny and oppression cannot be relied on for safety as a support ; that the united will of a nation cannot be overcome, but will achieve its aim in the end. Thus the power of the *Bakufu* naturally waned, and was at last utterly overthrown by the efforts of the patriots it had relentlessly persecuted.

When Your Majesty came to the throne, the han were still powerful, and the foundations of the government were not firmly laid. But Your Majesty took an oath before the Gods that you would administer the government in accordance with the just will of the nation. In order to ascertain the popular feeling as to the best means to be pursued to put the affairs of the country in order, representatives of the various han were summoned to Tōkyō, and after due deliberation, it was decided that the daimyō should return to the throne the domains which they had held for hundreds of years. This decision was duly carried into effect and the former lords of the han were appointed governors (Chiji) of the provinces which, up to that time, they had been in the habit of governing independently.

1. The name ordinarily used in referring to the Shōgunate.

Your Majesty's Government, not regarding this step as sufficient to consolidate its power, divided the country into fu, han and ken, thus centralizing the power of the administration in the capital, by abolishing the Chiji of the han, and replacing them by Governors of ken. This is the first step we took towards civilisation.

Why did these changes take place? Because the will of a people will have its own way, as surely as water runs down hill. It becomes irresistible. The people have never spoken harshly of the measures which converted han into ken, or which gave heimin equal rights with samurai, because they accord with the national sense of right. It is clear, then, that the oath of the Emperor should be strictly observed, and a representative assembly established in order that the people may have a voice in the affairs of the nation, and that they may aid the ministry in promoting the welfare of their country.

The time has passed for talking about the change of han into ken and of the rights of heimin and samurai. The opportunity for establishing a limited form of government on solid foundations has arrived, and the exercise of the soundest judgement is required to secure that most precious fruit of civilisation, a representative assembly; yet the several members of the administration do not appear to be endowed with sufficient perception to see their opportunity : on the contrary they seem to have resolved to act despotically, and with wilful perversion, to do only what shall please themselves, regardless of the wishes of the nation.

Despotism and oppression were the sins of the administration of the *Bakufu*. Its overthrow can only be regarded as a just punishment for its disrespect toward the Emperor, and its oppressive treatment of the people.

Alas! the present government is following the same course. Laws have been enforced, taxes imposed, the collection of the land-tax reformed, wars declared against foreign countries, portions of the empire exchanged ; solely at the caprice of several officials, without allowing public opinion to have a voice in the matter. The sacred oath taken by the Emperor on his accession to the throne has been altogether set aside.

So great is the distance that separates the government from the people, that the latter look up to it as astronomers look up to the heavens, with the greatest uncertainty. The sky seems continually obscured by threatening clouds whose constant and terrible lightenings and thunders strike terror, if not despair, to the minds of the beholders, who tremble lest they may never see the bright beams of the sun again.

The outbreaks that have recently taken place have arisen from various causes. Those who have misunderstood the intention of the poll-tax; those who have suffered by the reform of the land-tax; those who insisted on an invasion of Korea; those who favoured a return to the feudal system; those who wished the dismissal of certain officials surrounding the Imperial throne; all these have fomented disturbances. If any one, who in the future may write the history of the first ten years of Meiji, shall say that wars ceased not for a day, and that the country was brought to the very verge of ruin, he will fairly well describe the actual condition of affairs.

The duty of a government is to preserve peace in a country; not to interfere with the happiness of the people, and to hinder them from enjoying their primary rights and privileges. With these the Omnipotent has endowed men as surely as he given them bodies and souls, and if a government, relying on its power, endeavours to prevent their full exercise, there is no reason why a people should remain passive under such oppression.

If we look into the condition of various Asiatic nations, we see that although their territory is extensive and their land fertile, the government is tyrannical and the people slavish. The latter have no control over their rights, and are separated from their rulers by a great gulf. The wants of the people do not influence the actions of the government, and so, becoming slavish, they cease to take any interest in the well-being of their country. In such a case a government cannot become upright nor a people advanced in civilisation.

Since Your Majesty's accession to the Imperial power, though great reforms have taken place, and wonderful improvements have been made, yet the nation is continually plunged into civil war, and the outside world treats us with contempt. Such evils are brought about by the government not paying attention to the will of the people.

First among the prevailing evils, and the one which causes us the greatest anxiety, is the action of the Cabinet in imposing its own oppressive measures without in any way respecting the will of Your Imperial Majesty.

On the 14th of March, 1868 (1st year of Meiji), Your Majesty in the presence of the daimyō and kuge swore before the Gods five oaths.[1] First, that the government should be administered in a liberal manner, and that the will of the nation should be consulted as to the management of its affairs. Secondly, that both the higher and the lower (meaning the government and the people) were to be united in the administration. Thirdly, that your Majesty would consider the rights of the samurai and the people. Fourthly, that old and useless customs should be abolished, and that the action of the government should be progressive. Fifthly, that the wisdom of the world should be adopted to promote the dignity of the Emperor.

Again, on the 14th of April,[2] 1875 (8th year of Meiji), Your Majesty decreed as follows, with regard to the establishment separately of the legislative, executive and judicial bodies, and the institution of a liberal form of government :—

" According to Our oath we do hereby establish the *Genro-In* as the fountain-head of law giving. We create the *Daishin-In* to give strength to upright judicial procedure. We likewise summon the local officials in order to take their opinions on matters affecting the public welfare, and so by degrees to

1. *Supra* p. 8.
2. *Supra* pp. 41-42.

build up a well founded political structure for the welfare of our
country, and we are desirous that each and everyone of you
should partake in its benefits."

When Your Majesty subscribed to these oaths the people
were put into a great state of joy, and on the issue of the above
edict could not sufficiently praise Your Majesty's benevolence,
looking confidently for the fulfilment of the several pledges.
But it seems that Your Majesty's Ministers did not choose to
act in accordance with the Imperial will, as before a month had
elapsed they ignored it utterly.   It is true that a meeting of the
Governors of the Provinces did once take place,[1] but in the
following year Your Majesty's journey to the North was made
the excuse for not summoning them to the capital, which
ought to have been done.

Moreover, when the first convocation did take place,
sufficient time was not allowed to discuss all the questions put
before the assembly.   Can it be said, therefore, that public
opinion was allowed any expression, or that the people were in
any way benefitted ?

With regard to the Genro-In, its powers were curtailed
and its mode of administration changed at the whim of the
Cabinet, so that it became essentially the same as the Sa-In.[2]
The Daishin-In met with the same fate directly after its establishment, and was put under the control of the Judicial Department.   Thus were the powers of institutions that were intended
to act as legislative and judicial bodies, rendered void by the
arbitrary will of Your Majesty's counsellors.   If the Imperial
will be treated thus, what hope is there that people will be
permitted a voice in the government, and be allowed to unite
with the official class in the administration of national affairs.

Some time ago, the ex-Sangi Soyejima Taneomi[3] urged the

---

1. In 1875.

2. This was an institution which was abolished when the Genro-In was
created. *Supra* pp. 35 and 42.

3. *Supra* pp. 426-433.

establishment of a representative assembly and the people generally agreed with his views, the lowest classes even expressing
a wish to see such an assembly established. But the Ministry
disapproved of the idea, saying that it was too early, and that the
people were too ignorant. They speak as though they are the
only men in the country who know anything, and that all the rest
are fools. Yet if they show no desire to do anything for the promotion of the welfare of the people, they are no better than the
Ministry of the *Bakufu* whose place they have taken. If this state of
things is allowed to continue, when shall we get on to the real road
to progress, and when will old and evil customs be abolished?

Those who have held the actual power in the government
since the Restoration are composed solely of men from Satsuma,
Chōshiu, Tosa and Hizen, and to serve their own interests they
all play into each other's hands. Although the Ministry limits
its choice of members to the four provinces referred to, surely
no one will say that these alone produce men of sense. Is this
acting in accordance with the oath of your Imperial Majesty?
Is this uniting the best intellect of the nation in an endeavour to
promote the dignity of the Emperor?

Your Majesty's Ministers have acted directly contrary to
Your Majesty's will, which is that the people shall have a voice
in matters of national administration. They have enacted such
laws as the press and libel laws, in order, by the former, to
stifle all expression of public opinion, and by the latter to ensnare
the people in a most obnoxious manner. Those who dare to
express an opinion on the government, or who, from their
position, might naturally be supposed to concern themselves in
the affairs of the nation, are continually under the suspicion of
the government, and are not unfrequently arrested. Imprisonment has been made the vile means of silencing all expression of
public opinion, and Your Majesty's subjects are thus kept in a
constant state of alarm.

The second evil is that the management of this government is conducted in a random and confused manner.

As we have previously stated, the Administration is in the hands of a few despotic officials who act without reference to the opinion or welfare of the nation. This is proof of the bad form of the government which causes all this disorder. All the positions, from the Daijōdaijin to the heads of the various Departments, are filled by men who formerly possessed influence in their various ken, and who received their appointments during the confusion of the civil war. They go about from one department to another, and pretend to be perfectly acquainted with the affairs of each, but in reality they know little, if anything, about them. Witness the length of time they take to execute the simplest duties. The lower class of officials, in imitation of their superiors, treat all public matters in a similar spirit, as though they alone were personally interested in them, and in this way is the government constantly chopping and changing. The officials have probably no special aims. They are men of about equal ability, but one says " go cast," the other insists on going west, and hence a state of constant confusion. The Prime Minister can with difficulty hold his own. The legislative body may be called In or Kioku ; its nature remains unchanged ; it is absolutely powerless. As for the executive Departments, when Governors memorialize the central government it is very partial in its decisions, approving on the part of one Governor what it would reject if coming from another Governor. As for the Judicial Department, although it is supposed to have been founded, its workings are far from satisfactory. For instance, the question of a mere collision between two vessels connot be decided until after several Departments have been consulted, and though it is cognizant of maladministration in certain ken, it takes no steps to have the evil corrected. Such facts as corrupt officials receiving the assistance of the chiefs of their Departments in carrying out their evil practices are not unknown. The Cabinet Ministers have all their own way. When they wish anything carried out in the several Departments under their control, they bring it before the Cabinet which they themselves form, and give it their own approval. When a measure is enforced which may benefit one Department, but is unsuitable to another, it is subject to constant alterations. Thus, notifications are always being altered and withdrawn directly after their issue, to the great misguiding of the people. Indeed, the fickleness of the government is so well-known that when a measure is passed, the people say, " Well, it may probably remain in force thirty days, " so that the constant issue of notifications causes unending confusion. No sooner have the people become used to the working of some new regulation than it is changed, and though the lower officials must understand how extremely prejudicial all this is to the welfare of the people, yet they are compelled to obey the orders of their superiors without daring to utter a word of protest. All this causes the people to dislike the government.

Such important measures as the enactment of laws and the imposition of taxes are carried out by the government without due consideration, for the reason that there is no system in its administration. At the time of the Restoration, the officials were appointed for a term of four years only,[1] but the regulation was merely a nominal one, never having been carried into effect

In order to advance the public welfare, public opinion must be allowed expression, and such liberty will be the foundation of our prosperity. Be its ministers ever so wise, it is natural for a government to become despotic. With a country in such a condition as ours, how much more likely is such a state of things to come about.

The third evil is that the power of the country has been too largely concentrated in the central government. Officials who recognised perpetually the evils of feudalism, have gathered to the capital all the powers that were originally in the hands of the daimyō. This power is far greater than it should be, and it seems as though the government was endeavouring to make itself as despotic as possible.

1. *Supra* p. 10, Article IX.

With the view of facilitating the administration of government, governors were appointed to the various ken with entire powers of jurisdiction over the people placed in their charge. But we find that the actual powers of these governors are limited to the collecting of taxes. No road, bridge or public building can be constructed without first obtaining the approval of the central government. Thus we find the time of all local officials principally occupied in writing letters and attaching seals to documents for transmission to the central government. Their time being thus frittered away, what time have they to give to the consideration of petitions and memorials sent in to them by the people? Every fraction of the taxes has to be sent to the Ōkurashō,[1] while the Naimushō[2] must always be consulted before the most trivial matter can be carried out. Then the continual receipt of notifications from the government, and the constant changing of edicts are sources of no slight amount of vexation. While, therefore, the expenditure of the local offices is strictly limited, they are called upon to perform an unlimited amount of work.

The establishing of schools and the promotion of agricultural industries are no doubt necessary and excellent, but when the ideas are carried out to an extravagant extent at the expense of the people, the only effect is to create a great deal of ill-will.

The country has been divided up into ken, and various offices has been established in connection therewith, but they are so frequently changed, one office being divided into two or three, or several being amalgamanted, that the greatest inconvenience is occasioned. The government is, in fact, always endeavouring to decrease the little power possessed by the local authorities, and to concentrate it wholly in its own hands.

Last year the government issued a regulation specifying the term of service of the local officials, and placing in their

1. The Department of Finance.
2. The Departmeut of Home Affairs.

hands a certain amount of responsibility in their discharge of the affairs of the ken. The authority granted them is, however, far from being sufficient, and in order to check the power of the central government, far more freedom of action must be permitted to the local officials.

The government, in order to prove to the people that its administration is a just one toward them, should encourage the idea of popular government and show, at the same time, that it can be influenced by public opinion. But the action of the present government is the reverse of this, for regardless of such considerations, it seeks only to accumulate the power in its own hands. The dwellers in the cities are rendered bankrupt, and the people in the country are brought to utter poverty. These are the bad results of despotic rule.

The fourth evil is that the military system will never be placed on a proper open footing, until the mode of recruiting the army is made to agree with the form of government.

General conscription and poll-taxes are not matters with which a despotic government should meddle. They can only be imposed by limited forms of government. Reforms can be more readily enforced by despotism, yet our government, despotic as it is, cannot carry out and support measures of reform. In the conducting of a limited form of administration the people unite with the government in the management of the affairs of the country, and peace is, therefore, more likely to be preserved under such a rule than under despotism. The people under limited forms of government pay taxes in order to secure to themselves the happiness that arises from a sense of protection by the government. They hold themselves responsible for the defence of the country and are willing to shed their blood in its cause. This proves that they understand the meaning of self-government.

But under a despotic rule the case is a very different one. The rulers possess absolute power while the people are in a condition very grievous to be borne. Whatever little money they may possess is wrung from them by taxation. Worse than that, they may be called upon at any time to give their blood. Surely such treatment of its people by a government cannot be pleasing in the eyes of the Gods who govern all. The people under this absolute rule have no responsible existence. The government does what it likes, and enlists troops on the plea of necessary defence of the Emperor. The system of general conscription can never work well unless it accords with the form of government.

Let us show how the military system at present in force was first brought about. After the Restoration the military and civil duties of the samurai were abolished, and a proclamation was issued to the effect that the samurai and heimin should unite in forming an army for the defence of the nation. Regulations[1] were published relative to the enlistment of young men throughout the country regardless of class, for the formation of regular forces. Now we do not hold that this system is bad, but we maintain that it is not suited to the present time, or, in other words, to the present form of government. Since the above regulations were enforced, large barracks have been built, officers dressed out in showy uniforms, the troops furnished with arms of the latest improved pattern, and everything done in splendid form. Yet we see on the occasion of a rebellion breaking out in Kiushiu, the Imperial army finds itself very hard pressed in the engagements in Higo.[2] Not only the whole of the regular army and reserves have to be sent down, but, finding they cannot suppress the insurrection, police forces are armed and despatched to the seat of war, together with large numbers of samurai of various ken. Now police were not intended to be used as soldiers in the field.

The condition of our country may be compared to that of a house ruled over by an obstinate and avaricious steward, who

---

1. *Supra* pp. 17-18.

2. Many of the engagements of the Satsuma rebellion were fought in the province of Higo.

allows the family a sufficiency of neither food nor clothing, and who even goes so far as to sieze their possessions, beating and ill-treating them if they dare to murmur, causing to all the greatest distress. With matters going on in this way, a fire breaks out in an adjoining house which quickly spreads to the dwelling of the steward. The family say, " Well, we have been existing without a sufficiency of food or clothing, and have been despoiled of everything we once possessed. What is the good of our making any efforts to save our own property when it has been taken away from us ? " And they run out of the house, saying, " We are lucky as long as we escape with our lives," and they take no pains to extinguish the flames.

Such an excellent institution—that is, excellent in the eyes of the government—as a poll-tax cannot be introduced in such countries as Japan. The people now consider it a cruel imposit-ion. Like the conscription it is only suited to a constitutional form of government, and such is the government that Japan requires. For were a popular government to be introduced, the people would get rid of their miserably slavish customs and ideas, and feeling that they were to some extent responsible for the administration of their country's affairs, they would interest themselves therein, and become happier. They would not then deem their blood too precious to be spent in their country's cause, a feeling of patriotism that is sadly wanting at the present time.

We are of the opinion that the first step toward the formation of a limited form of government was taken when the duties of the samurai were abolished. This was done principally in the interests of the people. Unless it was the intention of forming a limited government, the object of abolishing the duties of the samurai is not apparent.

Under present circumstances the general conscription is useless, and the enormous sums spent in maintaining these forces produce fruitless results. The necessity of sending to the seat of war policemen, who are only enrolled to aid in keeping civil order in peaceful times, does not arise from indolence of commanders, nor want of discipline among the troops, but because the people have no idea of their responsiblility in the affairs of the nation and because nothing is done to acquaint them with their duty. The using of policemen as troops, serviceable as they may be to the government in the present emergency, will not, we fear, prove a good thing in the end. Moreover, it is a mighty wrong that the people should have to supply the means for carrying on war and be compelled to sacrifice their lives on behalf of a government in which they have no part or voice.

The fifth evil is the mismanagement of the finances of the nation.

This is an evil from which all nations have for a long time had to suffer. In any country which has not a limited form of government, the public are, as far as possibie, kept in ignorance of the state of the exchequer. Since Your Majesty came to the throne large sums have been expended in wars, public works, and the like. We are well aware, as we see by the dismissal of officials whose services are no longer required, that all unnecessary expeneses have been done away with. Accounts of expenditure are also kept. This is all well and good, but the government departments have had branch offices in certain banking establishments, to which portions of the public money have been entrusted. This has been done without first examining the financial conditions of such establishments. But there comes a day when the suspicions of the government being aroused, it desires to withdraw its deposits. Then it is discovered that though the bank may sell off every thing it owns, the proceeds will not suffice to pay back one-tenth of the government money entrusted to it charge. In consequence of this, the government issued certain laws (concerning the depositories of national funds) which were acted upon by all the fu and ken, and which by their action brought ruin to many a banking house. The consequences were felt in all quarters and the free circulation of the currency was affected.

The taxes of the fu and ken are collected and sent directly to the Ōkurashō.   This causes great scarcity of money in the country and cripples its powers of production.   The government shows great activity in promoting schemes for agricultural industries, in opening up Yezo, and in establishing manufactures, but the officials appointed to take charge of such matters utterly mismanage whatever is entrusted to their care, and interfere with the just rights of the farmers and merchants.   Hundreds of thousands of *yen* are spent in assisting certain companies, or in forming new ones, but such benevolent acts of the government are confined to certain persons or associations, and in no way exercise any benefit for the public good.

The chiefs of the various departments have full powers to increase or decrease the allowance for their annual expenditure, as they can also increase or decrease the duties of their respective officers.   The amount of work, therefore, done by any department depends on the amount of its allowances, instead of the expenditure being in proportion to the work actually done. The taxes represent the fruits of the people's labour, won with great sweat and toil.   The government has taxed the people enormously, but we do not see that the revenue is economically used.   We see, certainly, estimates of what is apportioned each year to the several departments, but we are not shown how it is expended.   Reserve funds and surpluses from the annual allowances are spoken of from time to time, but their existence is very doubtful indeed.

On coming into the capital from the country one is struck with the vast difference there is between the wealth of the former and the wretched poverty of the latter.   It seems as though all money had collected in the capital and ceased to circulate in the country.   The nation is greatly troubled on account of this, but it is only because the government keeps everything secret from the people.   Although it shows them tables of expenditure, it never lets them see the real accounts, as to how such expenditure is conducted.

With whom does Your Imperial Majesty consult with
reference to the manner in which the expenses of war, cost of
public works, the foreign and native loans, and such like, shall
be met? If the people get no return in increased happiness for
the taxes they pay, there must be some great mismanagement of
the finances.

The sixth is the present system of collecting the land-taxes,
which constitutes an oppression too great to be borne by the
people.

It is the duty of a government to watch over the people, to
govern the country with a view solely to their welfare, and to
enable it to do this it is necessary that taxes should be levied.
Should the government rightly perform its duties, the people
will readily acknowledge their obligations. A proper administration can only be secured through the adoption of constitutional government, and when this takes place many existent evils
will be done away. But under a despotic government the
people are kept, as it were, slaves. It imposes taxes at will. It
boasts of its benevolence, but in reality the people are stripped
of their rights and properties, and no heed is paid to their
complaints. Owing to feudal influences, the method of collecting taxes has differed in nearly every province, and the issue
of the edict providing for a general reform of the land taxes,
by which all the land in the country was to be taxed equally,
caused great joy among Your Majesty's subjects. But the officials in their haste to carry this into effect caused a vast amount
of inconvenience to the farmers, who were compelled to leave
the cultivation of their lands, and set to work to survey the
ground, prepare maps, do this thing and that thing, while the
officials insisted on the taxes being paid before the value of the
land was properly settled and apportioned. Thus the good
intentions of Your Majesty in issuing this proclamation have
been entirely frustrated by the conduct of your Majesty's
officials.

The government introduces many reforms which are good

in themselves, but are totally unsuited to its present despotic form, and which result in much evil instead of the good they are intended to produce. When they saw the Imperial decree of the 4th January, 1877, the people's suspicious were again aroused. People pay taxes in order to promote their own happiness, and if they feel secure of this they pay willingly ; but how does the government propose to collect taxes before the value of the land has been settled? The Imperial degree is a good one in intention, but not in practice, for the government can at its pleasure increase or decrease the taxation. The farming class, who are the most peaceable of men, could not see the necessity of all this haste in the change of method of collecting the land tax, and pressed beyond endurance, rose in arms against the government, deeming it better that the old mode should exist rather than that they should be put to such hardships as the speedy reform involved. Surely this was not the wish of Your Imperial Majesty.

The seventh evil is the method pursued by the government in equalizing the rights of the samurai and the common people.

The samurai of Japan form a class that has existed since the middle ages. They were controlled by feudal lords, and their spirit of patriotism, though confined to their own provinces, was noble. They possessed great virtues. They hated the idea of disgrace, they were faithful to their lords, and they interested themselves in the administration of the affairs of their respective han. The lord of a province and his chief advisers were restrained from acts of oppression by the watchfulness of the samurai of the han, who could compel their feudal lord to transfer his duties to another member of his House, or enforce the resignation of an official. Since Your Majesty took the power of the administration into Your hands, the feudal system has been abolished, and the samurai are no longer required. But the samurai still retained their rank and a certain portion of their rights, in consideration of their being superior to the common people in education and knowledge. Steps should therefore be taken to render the people, by education, the equals of the samurai, so that they may be able to take the same interest in the affairs of their country, and advance in happiness. This is the will of Your Imperial Majesty.

But not only are the people prevented from taking any part in the government, but the effort is made to bring the samurai down to the same slavish level as the lower classes. No matter how cruel or deceptive the edicts of their rulers may be, they are expected to make no remonstrance. A great mistake has been made in endeavouring to lower the samurai to the level of the common people. Encouragement should have been given to the latter to raise themselves to the level of the samurai. Instead of this the government has acted in a directly contrary manner. Great consideration should be given to this question. The samurai have always taken part in the administration of affairs of their various han since the commencement of feudal times ; their minds have thus been familiarized with political matters, and they are not content to be deprived of all their prerogatives. Although their services may be no longer requir- ed their minds remain unchanged. It is owing to this that nearly all the insurrections that have taken place since the Res- toration have been caused by the samurai. To raise a rebellion is undoubtedly wrong, but that the samurai should be driven to do so is certainly due to some mismanagement on the part of the government.

A wise man once said that as long as a man has plenty to do he is not likely to commit evil, but idleness is certain to lead to crime. The real cause of the samurai of Saga, Kumamoto, Hagi and Satsuma taking up arms against the government is that they had nothing to do but brood over their grievances. This country cannot be coerced into tranquillity by means of oppression until the race of samurai has died out of the land. The government may exult over its conquests, but the country is weakened every time that it achieves a victory over its own people.

This is the present condition of Japan. Public opinion is in no way consulted. Efforts are made to hold both the samurai and the heimin in absolute slavery. They are granted no political rights. They have no control over their own welfare. What does His Majesty suppose is the cause of all this misery ?

The eighth evil is the mismanagement of foreign affairs.

As Japan has not a constitutional form of government, the people cannot enjoy peace and happiness. Neither does a country so governed obtain its just rights from nations with whom it may be in intercourse. For such errors the people hold a government responsible. There have been four mistakes committed with regard to foreign affairs—the Formosan expedition ; the Korean affair ; the cession of Sagahlien ; and the revision of the treaties ; with all of these the honour of our country is intimately concerned, as well as the happiness of the nation. Our people know that Korea is a country with which Japan has had intercourse from the most ancient times. Suddenly the intercourse was broken off, and when we sent an envoy thither he was befooled, and all his proposals rejected. Not only were the Koreans insulting, but they threatened hostile resistance. It was proposed to send a second envoy to remonstrate against the treatment of the former one, but the government suddenly changed its views, and nothing further was done. The people when they learned this became enraged, and their feelings found vent in the rebellion of the samurai of Saga. No sooner was this suppressed than sudden orders were issued for a hostile expendition against Formosa. The reason for the government's undertaking this was perfectly incomprehensible to the people. What kind of race are the Formosans? They are under no King or Emperor, but are ruled by some savage chiefs. They are cannibals and such a set of savages are not worthy of being spoken of. Korea is different. It has an established government with whom we have been on terms of friendly intercourse from times long past How comes it that our government asked no explanation for a national insult from a country like Korea with an established government, and yet sent a hostile expedition against such a barbarous island as Formosa? The reason assigned was that the Formosans had been guilty of murdering some shipwrecked sailors from Loo-Choo. Now the nationality of the Loo-Chooans has not yet been settled, as it remains undecided whether they are subjects of Japan or China. The nationality of the Formosans was also not known, as it was uncertain whether the whole or only a part of the island of Formosa belonged to China. The expense of these expeditions was immense, but on that point we will say no more here.

We will take it for granted that Loo-Choo was supposed to be under the dominion of Japan, and that for this reason we sent the expedition to Formosa, giving rise to trouble between us and China. In order that the country might suffer no disgrace, the people took up the cause in a most zealous spirit, but the government sent an envoy to China and on payment by the Chinese government of the indemnity of five hundred thousand taels, all the troops were withdrawn from Formesa and sent back to Japan. Our forces therefore neither succeeded in acquiring Formosa, nor in proving that the sovereignty over the Loo-Choo Islands pertains to Japan and to Japan alone.

An indemnity of five hundred thousand taels, and nothing else, is not sufficient to make thirty millions of our countrymen believe that the government had accomplished any great object, or to make it clear to the eyes of the world that to obtain this was the object of the expedition.

The Kokua affair took place shortly after. Before it was certainly ascertained whether the act of firing upon the Japanese vessel of war was committed by order of the Korean government, or only by some one opposed to the government, an envoy was despatched, demanding an immediate explanation. Now it is wholly inexplicable to us why the government did not demand an explanation when the Koreans openly insulted our envoy and treated Japan with contempt, when it is so ready to demand

reparation for a shot fired against a vessel of war, not by order
of the government, but by the governor of some fort. In which
was the honour of the country most concerned? Yet the
government took no notice of the former case, while it was
greatly exercised over the latter. An ambassador was sent, the
main object of his mission being identical with that of the first
envoy, the renewing of friendly and commercial intercourse.
The people are perplexed to know why what was deemed wrong
in the first instance should be thought right two years later.

But this is not all. It is natural to every one to resist any
claims that may be made on his property, and no one who had
been improperly deprived of one portion of his property would
of his own free will receive for it another portion. We will
proceed to expose the mismanagement of the government in the
Sagahlien question.

For a long time past Japan has neglected to give proper
attention to the protection of the Northern portion of her dominion. In the time of the *Bakufu*, even the children knew that
Sagahlien and the Kuriles belonged to Japan. But the Russians
have come down below the fiftieth degree to hunt, and have
commenced to devour our country.

After the Restoration, when the Kaitakushi was established
enormous sums of money were spent in opening up the northern
islands, promoting education, establishing agricultural industries
and farming institutions, founding and laying out schools and
towns. The nation looked forward to the portion of Sagahlien
which had been occupied by the Russians again becoming the
property of Japan. Instead of this the whole island has been
taken from us. What good then has the Kaitakushi done, and
what benefit have we gained from all the money spent on a place
which a treaty has taken from us?

Loo-Choo constitutes a Japanese han. Our troops are
garrisoned there, the post office and a branch of the Naimushō
have been established there; but both the king and people of
Loo-Choo are endeavouring to free themselves from the authority

of Japan. China is endeavouring to do the same with Loo-Choo as Russia has done with Sagalien. If China succeeds, our territory will gradually decrease, aad with it our power.

Let us turn to the question of the revision of foreign treaties. When the appointed time had arrived, ambassadors, with a large number of subordinate officials, numbering in all about one hundred, were sent to the various treaty powers, and returned without having accomplished any object but the spending of a vast amount of money. This caused foreigners to regard us with contempt. The Japanese people, in their rage, say that all this arose from the action of an irresponsible government.

The above eight evils that we have mentioned all arise from the despotic rule of a government, which, refusing to consult the public welfare in carrying out its administration, becomes confused. This is very clear, and cannot be denied. Hence it arises that the government and the people are continually opposed, and there is no single day when universal peace prevails.

Since the commencement of the Kiushiu rebellion, the whole of the naval and military forces have been sent to the South, the treasury is exhausted, and the government is putting forth all its power to keep back the insurgents. Now, although the government should put down the rebellion, what will it benefit the people ? Nothing at all. More than that ; when it has suppressed this rebellion, it is likely to turn all its power against objects of its hate. Examples of this have not been wanting in ancient and modern times. Under such circumstances all men of intelligence, all those who stand up for the rights and liberties of the people, would be looked upon as its enemies, and measures be taken against them accordingly. Thus the government would become the same as the Tokugawa administration previous to its final dissolution.

When the *Bakufu* interfered with the rights of the people, the latter grew more and more determined, and though one might fall in his endeavour to oppose the government others arose, and so after much blood had been shed, the present administration was established.

If a betto in riding a horse pulls too hard upon the bit, in order to escape from the pain the animal will commence to kick and bite. Does not this apply to the treament of mankind ?

Suppose that the nation were to bring forward the five oaths of Your Imperial Majesty, and Your Majesty's decrees for the establishment of a constitutional form of government, and demand the government to give an explanation why it had not acted in accordance therewith, how could they answer, or what excuse would avail Your Majesty before the gods ?

Suppose that at the present time a foreign power were to declare war against the country, what could Your Majesty do ? It is such considerations that cause us the deepest anxiety.

By this, our memorial, Your Imperial Majesty will be able to judge which of the acts of Your Majesty and of Your Majesty's Ministers are right and which are wrong. The ministry acts as though it were not in the least degree responsible for any acts done in Your Majesty's name. Should ruin fall upon our country in consequence of such acts the members of the ministry can only be degraded, while all the blame will be imputed to Your Majesty, and the people will be called upon to undergo terrible hardships.

Nothing could more tend to the wellbeing of the country than for Your Majesty to put an end to all despotic and oppressive measures, and to consult public opinion in the conduct of the government. To this end a representative assembly should be established, so that the government may become constitutional in form. The people would then become more interested and zealous in looking after the affairs of the country ; public opinion will find expression, and despotism and confusion cease. The nation would advance in civilization; wealth would accumulate in the country ; troubles from within and contempt from without would cease, and the happiness of Your Imperial Majesty and of Your Majesty's subject will be secured.

Your Imperial Majesty's oaths at the time of your ascent to the throne, and the Imperial edict of the 14th April, 1874, prove that it is the wish of Your Majesty that the people should have a voice in the administration, and that a constitutional form of government should be established. The people rejoice greatly at learning that such is your Imperial Majesty's wish.

We hope that Your Imperial Majesty will not be led astray by the words of others, but approve of this our memorial, in acting in accrdance with which happiness may be secured to Japan.

(Signed)   KATAOKA KENKICHI,
Representative of the Risshisha,
Kōchi ken (Tosa).

J.W.M., 1877, July 7, pp. 572-76.

6. MEMORIAL ADVOCATING THE ESTABLISHMENT OF A NATIONAL ASSEMBLY.

(Addressed to the Daijōdaijin, February, 1880.)

We have the honor to present to your Excellency the following memorial :—

We consider that in a great many respects the management of a country is like the regulation of water. It is impossible altogether to restrain the force of a running stream, and therefore those who are acquainted with hydraulics learn how to humor and direct the force of the current so as to avoid damage. When a flood occurs the surface of the adjoining land is submerged. The same happens to the administration of a country. When the pent-up excitement of a nation breaks forth, no force can restrain the people from accomplishing their desires ; they must be allowed to attain their ends in order to

---

1. The Memorial was signed on behalf of the Local Assembly of Miyagi Ken by Messrs. Masuda, Endo, Akiyama, Minegishi, Chiba, Atami, etc.

avoid disastrous consequences. This submission to the will of the people is, we consider, the proper way to control their actions.

We have ascertained, as the result of a careful investigation, that the people of Japan have developed a spirit of independence, and now thoroughly appreciate the respective rights of the monarch and the general mass of the community. The result of the knowledge is an increasing demand for the establishment of a constituent assembly, vesting legislative power in the people, and it is now very apparent that the movement will never cease until the required object is achieved.

We respectively submit that, until legislative powers are lodged in the hands of the people through their representatives, the judicature cannot be placed on a thoroughly satisfactory footing ; and if this be the case with the judicature with how much more force does it apply to the executive? When the people are properly represented in the government, and the judicature and the executive are in a satisfactory condition, then the wealth and prosperity of a nation increases. Every nation in Europe enjoys the advantages of what is termed " constitutional government."

His Imperial Majesty, the great and gracious Emperor who now rules over us with the assistance of your Excellency's wisdom and experience, leaves nothing to be desired in conducting the administration of the country, and yet dissatisfaction is prevalent at home, while abroad we suffer by reason of the exaction of foreigners. How is this to be explained? Is it not because no proper feeling of harmony has been established between the governors and the governed?

The prosperity of a country is inseparable from the prosperity of its inhabitants ; the government and people should therefore act in unison. Can it be right that the government should alone be charged with all affairs that pertain to the welfare of the State?

It is indisputable that the most urgently pressing measure is the establishment of a constituent assembly, so that the people

shall take part in legislative functions. Thus the three great
bodies which go to build up prosperous communities would be
working in harmony, and the welfare of the empire advanced
as that of a single individual.

It is within our memory when the Emperor, when He
first ascended the Imperial Throne, made solemn oath[1] before
Heaven that "the will of the people shall be ascertained and the
administration of the empire carried on conformably to their
wishes." Seven years afterwards His Imperial Majesty issued
an edict[2] that "constitutional government shall be gradually
introduced." His Majesty's virtues are indeed great and his
wisdom profound. Is there any other means of ascertaining
the will of the people and introducing constitutional government,
except by the establishment of a national assembly?

At the time we referred to, His Majesty evidently desired
to grant political rights to the people, but they treated the matter
with an indifference born of ignorance, and although the ex-
Privy Councillor Gotō Shōjirō and others presented a memorial[3]
on the subject, there were many among the public who expressed a conviction that the country was not ripe for such a radical
innovation. Thus the matter has been put off till the present day.

The circumstances of the Empire are, however, very different now to those of the 7th year of Meiji. Not only do the
people no longer think that the establishment of a constituent
assembly would be premature, but societies and leagues have
been formed throughout the length and breadth of the land, in
order to secure the boon. Who therefore can now affirm that
the people are now indifferent, or that they cannot be entrusted
with the participation in legislative functions?

Troubles and disturbances often take place in a country
from unexpected causes, and if those members of the political
societies who are desirous for a national assembly should find

1. *Supra* p. 8.
2. *Supra* pp. 41-42.
3. *Supra* pp. 440-45.

their hopes frustrated, it is to be feared that they will rise in insurrection and refuse to be pacified.

Again, if your Excellency, taking advantage of your exalted position and acknowledged popularity, despises the current of public opinion, and does not seek a suitable outlet for its violence, future history in speaking of your Excellency will say that you " occupied the position of Prime Minister, but did not enforce the Imperial edict, nor allow the people to succeed in their reasonable desires, nor carry on the administration of the empire so as to meet with the approbation of the public. On the contrary the people were dissatisfied, and foreigners [1] still maintained their haughty disregard for the independence of the nation." How could Your Excellency's admirers rid you of this blame? The subject has caused us much perplexity and embarrassment.

Your Excellency is well aware of all the circumstances, and will doubtless take the necessary steps to carry out the desired reforms with due care and prudence. We feel assured of this from the establishment of local and other subordinate assemblies in the cities and prefectures with the view of educating the people to the proper use of their political rights when entrusted into their hands.

But what course is to be adopted if the people are not content with the existing assemblies? We are anxious to avoid any statements which might prove unpalatable, but it is undeniable that the clamour of the public, and more especially the inhabitants of our prefecture, for a constituent assembly, is now that of a hungry man for food. This is why we have addressed a memorial to your Excellency on the subject, as we have no intention of forcing the question upon you by a conspiracy or the assemblage of multitudes of people. We do so simply because we consider it our duty, having regard to the present state of the Empire. We

1. Foreigners resident in Japan enjoyed extra-territorial privileges, *i.e.* they lived under the laws of their respective countries as administered by Consular Courts.

have not considered ourselves in this matter, but only our be-
loved country, and if, in the fullness of our feelings, we have
exceeded the bounds of politeness, we pray your Excellency to
excuse our offence and regard only the meaning and spirit of
our memorial.

J.W.M., 1880, February 28, pp. 280-81.

7. DRAFT OF A CONSTITUTION.[1]

(Compiled for Private Circulation.)

Most people are at present agreed on the vital necessity of
some reforms in our system of government, but it is very doubtful whether if the moment for making those reforms were at
hand, many would be found ready to say what fashion of constitution is best calculated to preserve the integrity of Japan and
extend her influence. Probably the subject has occupied the
attention of not a few, and some perhaps have committed their
thoughts to writing, only however to lock the documents in
their desks and keep them from the public ken ; but we question
whether they have done more than examine certain portions of
the matter, not going so far as to map out a complete scheme.
The reticence hitherto observed upon this subject is we pre-
sume, attributable to a consciousness of its great importance,

---

1. This document is said to have been circulated widely among the members
of the political societies and clubs during 1881 ; what influence it exerted it is impossible to to estimate   A comparison of this draft with the constitution as promulgated in 1889 will serve to reveal an immense difference between the ideas
here presented and those adopted by the government. It is interesting, however, to
note that the Rescript fixing the date for the convening of the National Assembly
was issued on October 12, 1881, also that from internal evidence the Rescript was
issued under stress, to relieve a situation that had become dangerous to the continued existence of the government.   It was in the second half of the year
1881 that Ōkuma, the Minister of Finance, risked and (lost) his official position,
by memorialising the Throne with a view to the early establishment of a parliament (in 1883).

seeing that any error in the polity of a country affects the welfare of the people at large. The compilers of this scheme, too, are very sensible to the responsibility of the task they have undertaken, yet since nothing definite has been formulated, and since popular opinion is still in a condition to consider the subject dispassionately, the present seems to them an excellent occasion to propose something which may serve as a basis for candid discussion and help to direct people's thoughts into the proper channel. Regardless therefore of any charge of presumption that may be brought against them, they have prepared this document for circulation among their friends, to the end that the latter may correct what they think faulty, and supplement what they deem deficient, thus elaborating finally some fairly complete scheme for a national constitution, to the great benefit not of its compilers alone but of every man in Japan.

The Imperial Functions.

I. The Emperor will govern the country by means of Ministers, a Senate and a National Assembly.

II. The Emperor's right to rule is divine and must never be called in question, but the duties of government will devolve upon his Ministers.

III. All matters relating to the national debt and legislation, in general, will be discussed and settled by the Senate and the National Assembly, and having received the Imperial sanctional will become law.

IV. The governing power belongs to the Emperor; the duties of government will be carried on by the Ministers in conformity with the laws.

V. The Judicial Power belongs to the Emperor; the duties of the Judiciary, civil and penal alike, will be carried on by the law officers in conformity with the laws.

VI. The Imperial functions will include the issue of proclamations, organisation of the army and navy, settlement of questions concerning external relations, the making of treaties, appointments to office, conferring rank and rewards for military service, the issue of coins, the disposal of rebels, the convocation and prorogation of the National Assembly and Senate, the dissolution of the former body by a message to the Senate, and the submission to these two assemblies of questions connected with the customs duties at the open ports.

VII. The Emperor will clothe the Privy Council with authority to carry on the whole government.

VIII. The Privy Council will be composed of the Ministers of Departments and the Imperial Adviser.

IX. The affairs of State, both internal and external, will be conducted by the whole Privy Council in session, matters which are solely within the competence of any particular Minister being excepted.

X. There will be a President of the Privy Council, by whom all measures that have received the Imperial sanction and all proclamations will be signed.

XI. In the event of the Privy Council failing to come to a decision, the President will be competent to settle the question and afterwards submit it for Imperial approval.

XII. The President of the Privy Council will be chosen in accordance with the will of the Emperor and of the people, and the other members of the Privy Council will be appointed by him.

XIII. Members of the Privy Council will be either members of the Senate or of the National Assembly.

XIV. The estimates of the National revenue and expenditures must be passed by the Privy Council.

XV. Bills sent down by the Privy Council will first be discussed by the National Assembly and afterwards submitted to the Senate.

XVI. The yearly estimates of the total revenue and expenditure, as well as all matters of importance, having reference to the internal or external affairs of State, will be made known by the Privy Council to the Senate and National Assembly.

XVII. Should it happen that the two Assemblies refuse to endorse the acts of the Privy Council, the members of the latter will resign, or the National Assembly will be dissolved by the Emperor.

THE SENATE.[1]

XVIII. All matters having reference to the national revenue and expenditure, taxation, the national debt and laws in general, will be discussed and passed by the National Assembly and Senate.

XIX. The Senate will consist of the Chamber of Nobles and House of Representatives.

XX. The members of the Chamber of Nobles will be Princes of the Blood, Nobles, persons who have held high office of State or men of learning. They will be selected and appointed by the Emperor, and will be members for life unless disqualified by their own fault. Their number will not exceed two-thirds of the whole Senate.

XXI. The members of the House of Representatives will be chosen by the people, two from every electoral division. Their term of membership will be four years.

XXII Every Prefecture will constitute an electoral district. The persons qualified to vote for members of the National Assembly in each electoral district will choose two hundred electors, who will subsequently select two of their number to be members of the Senate.

XXIII. All Japanese who are males of thirty years and upwards, without distinction of class, shall be eligible for election to the Senate. But Governors of Cities, Prefects,

---

1. The use of this word is most confusing ; the fault may lie in the translation. If the term National Assembly be used in its stead, and made to include the House of Peers and the House of Representives, the existing confusion will be greatly reduced, and anyone familiar with the structure of governmental institutions will have no great difficulty in understanding the scheme here outlined.

Magistrates of Urban and Rural Divisions, and officials whose duties are connected with the election of members, will not be eligible for election.

The following will also be ineligible for election, viz. :— persons who have committed any serious crime and who have not yet expiated their offence ; bankrupts who have not yet discharged their debts ; idiots and insane persons ; persons not residing in Japan ; priests, judges and assistant judges.

XXIV. Although the Chamber of Nobles is not an elective body, its members must be Japanese by birth and residents of the country, while Princes of the Blood must be twenty-five, and all others thirty years of age in order to be eligible.

XXV. With the exception of Ministers and Vice-Ministers of Departments, the Imperial Adviser, Officers of the Household, Chiefs of Bureaux, and Field Officers of the Army and Navy who are unattached, all officials on becoming members of either the Chamber of Nobles or the House of Representatives must resign their offices ; while members, on the other hand, will be required to withdraw their names if they accept any official appointment during their period of membership.

XXVI. Members of the Senate will receive from the Treasury a yearly salary of not less than three thousand *yen.*

XXVII. Senators may not be arrested during session or for a period of thirty days before or after, unless they have committed some serious crime ; and they shall be responsible to the Senate only for the speeches they deliver or the opinions they advocate during the session, unless they themselves make those opinions the subject of a public appeal.

XXVIII. Whenever the National Assembly passes a vote of censure on any official for treasonable conduct or other miscarriage of duty, the Senate in session shall investigate the matter, and if two-thirds or more of the members present pronounce the accused guilty, he shall be deprived of office by the Emperor's authority, after which he shall be tried and punished by the courts of law.

XXIX. The Senate shall be convoked or prorogued by Imperial authority at the same time as the National Assembly.

XXX. The Senate will choose a new President and Vice-President every four years who shall be appointed by the Emperor's command.

XXXI. Questions that come before the Senate shall be decided by a majority of the members present. Should opinion be equally divided the President shall have the casting vote.

XXXII. The Senate will decide upon its own rules of procedure by a vote of not less than one half of its total membership, and these rules having received the Imperial sanction shall become law.

XXXIII. Among those rules of procedure the Senate will embody clauses providing suitable penalties, which will be within the competence of the Senate to inflict upon persons infringing the rules.

XXXIV. Debates shall be open to the public, but this privilege may be interdicted by the rules of procedure or on exceptional occasions.

XXXV. One-fifth of the whole number of the Senate shall constitute a quorum.

XXXVI. The Senate may take a recess at convenient times, but that recess must not exceed ten days unless by agreement with the National Assembly.

XXXVII. The Senate shall cause minutes of its proceedings to be kept and published from time to time, matters which it is inexpedient to make public being of course excepted.

XXXVIII. Bills that have passed the Senate and have not yet been discussed by the National Assembly, as well as those that have come up from the latter and been amended by the former, shall be submitted finally to the National Assembly and after they have passed that body the President's of both the National Assembly and the Senate shall submit them for Imperial approval.

THE NATIONAL ASSEMBLY.

XXXIX. The National Assembly, in conjunction with the Senate, will be charged with the conduct of all affairs relating to the national revenue and expenditure, taxation, the national debt and the laws of the empire.

XL. The members of the National Assembly will be publicly chosen by the votes of all persons throughout the Empire possessing the franchise, and their term of service will be four years.

XLI. For the purpose of returning members to the National Assembly each province shall constitute an electoral division; or the province shall be divided into several urban divisions, and each section of eighty thousand men shall constitute an electoral division with the power of returning one member; in the case of an urban division containing less than eighty thousand the right of returning one member shall still be conferred, but when the number of inhabitants is less than forty thousand, the division shall not be represented. In the case of a province, however, the right of returning one member shall be conferred, provided the number of inhabitants shall be twenty thousand or upwards.

XLII. Towns containing twenty thousand inhabitants or upwards shall constitute one electoral district. Those with more than twenty and less than forty thousand shall elect one member; those with more than forty and less than eighty thousand inhabitants shall return two members; and those with more than eighty thousand, shall return one additional member for every additional sixty thousand inhabitants.

XLIII. The following persons shall be qualified to vote for candidates for the National Assembly :—residents of rural divisions or districts possessing land on which a land-tax of five *yen per annum* is levied, or persons residing in houses of their own valued at two hundred *yen* or upwards, or who have lived for at least two months in rented houses valued at four hundred *yen* or upwards ; provided that all such electors shall be males of twenty-one years at least.

The following shall be ineligible for the franchise, viz :— Persons undergoing punishment for crime, persons who have undergone punishment for crime and are still under police supervision, bankrupts whose debts have not been discharged, idiots and insane persons, persons not residing in Japan, judges, Governors and Prefects, and persons officially connected with the conduct of elections, and priests.

XLIV. All males of the Japanese nation of twenty-five years or upwards, without reference to the division in which they reside, shall be eligible for election to the National Assembly, but Governors, Prefects, Magistrates of urban or rural divisions, and persons officially connected with the conduct of elections shall not be eligible to represent the divisions in which their duties lie.

Other causes constituting ineligibility shall be the same as those enumerated in Article XLIII.

XLV. With the exception of Ministers, Vice-Ministers, Officers of the Imperial Household, and Chiefs of Bureaux, all officials who may be returned as members of the National Assembly shall immediately resign their appointments, and conversely members of the Assembly shall cease to be such on appointment to any official position.

XLVI. Vacancies in the National Assembly shall be filled as soon as possible after they occur.

XLVII. Members of the National Assemby shall receive a salary of at least three thousand *yen per annum* from the Treasury.

XLVIII. Members of the National Assembly may not be arrested during the session, nor for a period of thirty days before and after, unless they have committed some serious crime ; and they shall be responsible only to the National Assembly for the speeches they deliver or the opinions the advocate during the session, unless they themselves make those speeches or opinions the subject of a public appeal.

XLIX. It shall be within the competence of the National Assembly to pass a vote of censure upon any official guilty of treasonable conduct or other dereliction of duty.

L. The drafting of all bills having reference to taxation shall be confined to the National Assembly or the Privy Council ; and should such bills be amended by the Senate, they shall be submitted to the National Assembly for re-deliberation, when a majority of two-thirds of the members shall be sufficient to pass the bill, whether the Senate's amendments be accepted or rejected, after which the President of the Assembly shall immediately submit the bill for the Imperial sanction.

LI. The National Assembly shall hold one regular session each year, and may further be extraordinarily convened on special occasions.

LII. After the dissolution of the National Assembly, according to the form prescribed in Article VI., the election of new members shall take place with sufficient expedition to render possible the meeting of the new Assembly within ninety days of its dissolution.

LIII. The National Assembly will elect a President and Vice-President from among its members, and those officials shall be afterwards appointed by the Emperor.

LIV. Questions that come before the National Assembly shall be decided by a majority of the members in session. Should opinions be equally divided the President shall have a casting vote.

LV. The National Asssembly will decide on its own rules of procedure by the vote of not less than one-half of its total number of members, and these rules, having received Imperial sanction, will become law.

LVI. Among these rules of procedure the National Assembly will embody clauses providing suitable penalties, which it will be within the competence of the Assembly to inflict upon members infringing its rules.

LVII. Members whose elections have been proved to have

been compassed by unlawful means shall be deprived of their seats by the authority of the Assembly.

LVIII. It shall be within the competence of the Assembly to deprive of his seat any member who may have been guilty of unbecoming conduct during the session, but such deprivation must be voted by at least two-thirds of the whole Assembly.

LIX. Debates in the National Assembly shall be open to the public, but this privilege may be interdicted by the rules of procedure or on special occasions.

LX. One-fifth of the whole number of the Assemby shall constitute a quorum.

LXI. The National Assembly may take a recess at convenient times, but that recess must not exceed ten days unless by agreement with the Senate.

LXII. The National Assembly shall cause minutes of its proceedings to be kept, and published from time to time, matters which it is inexpedient to make public being excepted.

LXIII. Bills that have passed the National Assembly and have not yet been discussed by the Senate, as well as those that have been sent down by the latter and amended by the former, shall be finally submitted to the Senate, and after that body has passed them, the Presidents of both the National Assembly and the Senate shall submit them for Imperial sanction.

THE JUDICIARY.

LXIV. The Codes of Law shall be administered by the officers of justice at fixed places, duly selected, in conformity with the law, neither shall it be legal to open any independent court for the purpose of conducting independent judicial proceedings.

LXV. The officers of justice shall receive their appointments from the Emperor and shall hold office for life, unless disqualified by the commission of some offence.

LXVI. Judicial investigations and all proceedings in the Courts of Law shall be conducted publicly, otherwise such investigations and proceedings shall be null and void. The Courts shall be closed only for the trial of cases which, if made public, would tend to injure morality.

LXVII. All persons arraigned on criminal charges shall have the services of an advocate, otherwise the trial shall be null and void.

LXVIII. Persons guilty of offences against military or naval law shall be tried by the military or naval courts.

PERSONAL PRIVILEGE.

LXIX. Every Japanese citizen may be free to embrace any religion he or she may please, provided the religion be not prejudicial to the welfare of the realm.

LXX. Every Japanese citizen shall be free to express or publish his opinion on any subject, unless by so doing he prejudices public or private interests.

LXXI. Japanese citizens, not carrying arms and behaving in an orderly fashion, shall be free to hold public meetings whenever they please, or to address petitions to the government on any grievance they desire to have redressed.

LXXII. A Japanese citizen may not be arbitrarily deprived of his property. Should his possessions be required by the State for the public weal, suitable compensation shall be provided by the government.

LXXIII. Japanese citizens unless they are in active rebellion, or in the absence of a legal warrant duly issued by the proper authorities, may not be arrested, or their houses entered and searched, or their chattles, documents, etc. carried off.

LXXIV. Japanese citizens must be brought to trial within forty-eight hours of their arrest. They may not be detained pending examination after that period except on the authority of a fresh warrant duly issued.

LXXV. Japanese citizens when arraigned on criminal charges may be released on finding bail in suitable amounts with competent sureties. The privilege may, however, be withheld in cases where the carriage of justice would be endangered thereby.

LXXVI. Torture shall never be adopted to extract confession from an accused person in Japan.

LXXVII. All Japanese persons, without distinction of rank or social position, shall enjoy the same privileges before the law.

LXXVIII. Laws may not have a retrospective action. This will not however prevent the enactment of laws to deal with special offences.

REVISION OF THE CONSTITUTION.

LXXIX. The laws of the Constitution may be amended or repealed by a vote of not less than two-thirds of the total members of the Senate and National Assembly subject to the Imperial sanction. Articles relating to the Imperial functions may not however be discussed with a view to revision except under the written authority of the Emperor himself.

J.W.M., 1881, Sept. 10, pp. 1052-53.

2.—PUBLIC MEETINGS AND ASSOCIATIONS.

1. REGULATIONS FOR PUBLIC MEETINGS AND ASSOCIATIONS.

(Imp. Dec. No. 12, April 5, 1880.)

I. Whosoever intends to assemble the public in order to lecture, or deliberate, upon any matter referring to politics must, three days before the meeting, in the name of the convener, president or director of the gathering, obtain sanction from the police authorities in whose jurisdiction the meeting is to be held ; the subjects of the lectures or deliberators, the names and addresses of the lecturers or deliberators, the names and addresses of the lecturers or debaters, the site and date of the meeting must be notified to the police authorities.

II. Any one organising an association for the purpose of lecturing or deliberating upon political matters shall previously inform the police authorities concerned as to its name, rules, and place of meeting, together with the list of its members, and obtain the sanction of the police. In case the rules be revised or the membership be changed the same shall be notified to the police. To any inquiries made by the police at the time of the information being forwarded to them, explanations shall be given in regard to all matters whatsoever relating to the organisation of the association.

III. In regard to any meeting in which the subjects of the lectures or debates, the number of lecturers or debaters, the place and date of which is fixed, information thereof shall be forwarded to and sanction obtained from the police authorities three days before the opening of the meeting; similar information need not be sent in for regular meetings, held by the association thereafter. But Article I. shall be conformed with when any change is made in the conditions detailed above.

IV. The police authorities concerned shall not give their sanction, in case the meeting or association is, through any of the information furnished as prescribed in Articles I., II., or III., deemed injurious to the public peace.

V. The police authorities shall send officials in uniform to the place of meeting. Such officers shall examine the warrant of official sanction and exercise control over the meeting.

VI. The police officers shall dissolve the meeting when the warrant of official sanction is not produced on demand ; when the lecturers or deliberators go beyond the subjects mentioned in the information ; when the discourses are found to have any tendency to lure or tempt people into crimes or delicts, or may be deemed prejudicial to public tranquillity; or when those who, from their positions are prohibited from attending such meetings, do not obey the police when ordered to leave.

VII. All military and naval men now on active service or in the first or second reserves, police officers, teachers and students of government, public, or private schools, agricultural or technological apprentices, must not attend any meeting where politics form the subject of address or deliberation. Neither may they become members of any political association.

VIII. No political association, intending to lecture or deliberate upon politics, may advertise its lectures or debates, persuade people to enter its ranks by despatching commissioners or issuing circulars, or combine and communicate with other similar societies.

IX. Open-air lectures or debates on political subjects are prohibited.

X. If a meeting shall be held without the permission mentioned in Article I. being first obtained, the convener shall be liable to a fine of not more than twenty nor less than two *yen*, or to minor imprisonment for not more than three months nor less than eleven days. The person who lent the place of meeting, the president, the general managers, lecturers and debaters shall severally be liable to a fine of not more than twenty and not less than two *yen*, and every breach of Article III. shall be punished in like manner.

XI. In case the information has not been forwarded punctually to the police authorities concerned, in accordance with Article II., as to the rules of the association and the list of its members, or as to any revisal of the said rules or changes in the membership ; or in case no answers have been made to the questions of the police authorities, the president of the said association shall be liable to a fine of not more than twenty nor less than two *yen*. In case the rules or list of members of the association have been falsely stated, or untrue answers have been given to the questions asked by the police authorities, the president of the said association shall be liable to minor imprisonment of not more than three months nor less than eleven days, in addition to the fine mentioned above.

XII. When, in defiance of the provisions of Article V., the police officials are refused admission, the convener, president, director and general managers shall severally be liable to a fine of not more than fifty nor less than five *yen*, or to minor imprisonment for not more than one year nor less than one month. Similar sentences will be pronounced upon any one who has made no answer or has answered falsely when the name of a speaker has been asked.

Any one who has infringed the provisions of this Article twice shall be liable to a fine of not more than one hundred and not less than ten *yen*, or to minor imprisonment for not more than two years nor less than two months.

XIII. When the persons assembled at any meeting are ordered by the police officials in attendance to disperse, every one refusing to do so shall be liable to a fine of not more than twenty nor less than two *yen*, or to minor imprisonment for not more than six months nor less than eleven days.

XIV. For any breach of Article VII., the convener and president of the meeting, or the president and general manager of the society, will be severally liable to a fine of not more than twenty nor less than two *yen*, or to minor imprisonment for not more than three months nor less than eleven days. If the offence is considered a grave one the society may be suppressed ; and if anyone, in defiance of Article VIII., shall enter into the membership of a society or attend a meeting, he shall be liable to a fine of not more than twenty nor less than two *yen*.

. XV. For every breach of Article VIII., the convener and president of a meeting and the president and general managers of a society shall severally be liable to a fine of not more than fifty nor less than five *yen*, or to minor imprisonment for not more than one year nor less than one month. In addition, the society shall be suppressed, and every one implicated in a breach of the said Article will be liable to similar punishment to that hereinbefore mentioned. Any person who shall compel another to join a society, or who has been previously convicted of a breach of Article VIII., shall be liable to a fine of not more than one hundred nor less than ten *yen*, or to minor imprisonment for not more than two years nor less than two months. The president and directors shall also be prohibited from forming or joining any other similar society for a period of not more than five years nor less than one year.

XVI. These Regulations do not apply to any public meetings inaugurated by law.

J. W. M., 1882, June 10, pp. 712-13.

2. Regulations for Public Meetings and Associations.

(Imp. Dec. No. 27, June 3, 1882.)

I. (The same).

II. Anyone organising an association for the purpose of lecturing or deliberating on political subjects, no matter under what name, shall previously inform the police authorities concerned of the name, rules and site, and shall furnish a list of the names of its members. Any change proposed to be made in the rules, or increase or decrease of the members shall, in like manner be notified. To the inquiries made by the police authorities at the time of the information being forwarded to them, explanations shall be given with regard to all matters whatsoever referring to the organisation of the society.

In case an association such as is referred to in the preceding clause, or any other affiliation, intends to hold a meeting in order to lecture or deliberate on politics, the course provided in Article I. shall be followed.

III. (The same).

IV. The police authorities shall not give their sanction, or shall withdraw it after it is granted, in case the meeting or association is, through the information furnished as prescribed in Articles I., II., and III., deemed injurious to the public peace.

V. (Clause 1 the same, clause 2 added).

The police officers shall have their choice of seats, and information shall be furnished to them on any subject into which they choose to inquire.

VI. (A second paragraph is added).

Should the authorities order the dissolution of any assembly under the preceding clause, the local Prefect or Governor (or in Tōkyō, the Chief of the Metropolitan Police) may prohibit the orators of that meeting from lecturing, or publicly discussing politics in that jurisdiction, for a period not longer than one year. Further the association may be dissolved if necessary. And again, the Home Minister can, if he deem it expedient, prohibit the lecturer from delivering public discourses anywhere throughout the country, for a period not exceeding one year.

VII. (The same).

VIII. No political association for the purpose of lecturing or deliberating on politics, may advertise a summary of the discourses, excite the public by sending out commissioners or circulars, or correspond and join together with other similar societies.

IX. (The same).

X. (The same).

XI. In case the information is, in defiance of the second clause of Article II., not forwarded to the police authorities, nor explanations given of the matters referred to, the president of the association shall be punished by a fine of not more than twenty nor less than two *yen*. When perjured evidence or untrue information is given, in addition to the fine above mentioned, minor imprisonment for a period of not more than three months nor less than eleven days may be ordered.

XII. When in defiance of the provisions of Article V., the police officials are refused admission, or the seats required for them are not supplied, the convener, president, director, and general managers shall be severally liable to a fine of not more than fifty nor less than five *yen*, or minor imprisonment for not more than one year nor less than one month. Similar sentences may be pronounced against those who have not answered questions from the police officials, or have given false explanations. A fine of not more than one hundred nor less than ten *yen*, or minor imprisonment for not more than two years nor less than two months, will be imposed in such cases on any one who has infringed this Article twice.

XIII. (The same).

XIV. (The same).

XV. (The same).

XVI. The police officials may, when they dcem it necessary for the maintenance of the public peace, attend scientific or any other public meetings. Should they be refused admission the objectors are liable to be punished according to the provisions of Article XII.

Should political subjects be introduced into a scientific meeting the offenders shall be liable under the provisions of Article X.

XVII. When, in the case described in the preceding Article, the proceedings are deemed injurious to the public peace, the offenders will be punished in accordance with the provisions of Article VI.

XVIII. When the Minister of Home Affairs deems any meeting or association prejudicial to the public peace, he may permanently suspend it. In case his order is not complied with, or the association or meeting continues secretly in existence, the offenders shall be liable severally to a fine of not more than one hundred nor less than ten *yen*, or to minor imprisonment for not more than two years nor less than two months.

XIX. (The same as Article XVI. in the original).

J.W.M. 1882, June 10, pp. 712-13.

3. PEACE PRESERVATION REGULATIONS[1] (HOAN-JOREI).

(Imp. Rescript, Dec. 25, 1887.)

I. Secret societies and secret assemblies are hereby forbidden, and every person joining a secret society or taking part in a secret assembly, shall be liable to be punished by minor confinement for a period of not less than one month and not more than two years, together with a fine of from ten *yen* to one hundred *yen*, and every person acting as ringleader or instigator of such society or assembly shall be liable to penalties one degree heavier than the above.

In order to the better carrying out of this Article, as well as to the enforcement of the provisions of Article VIII.[2] of the Assemblies Regulations having reference to the distribution of circulars, the Minister of State for Home Affairs is hereby authorised to enact suitable regulations, and any person violating them shall be liable to the abovementioned penalties.

II. It shall be competent for the police, without preliminary reference to a higher authority, to put a stop to open air meetings or assemblies, whenever they deem such a course necessary. And any person disobeying the injunction of the police, or inciting others to disobey, or any person willingly attending such meeting or assembly in spite of such injunction, or any person

---

1. The *Nichi Nichi Shimbun* commenting editorially upon the ordinance remarked that it had been made necessary by the foolish policy of the Government in suppressing public discussion, and thereby driving into dangerous and secret channels feelings and ideas which if uttered publicly, would be comparatively harmless. The *Jiji Shimpo* and many others of the Tōkyō papers openly approved of the measure, those which objected said nothing. The *Japan Mail* regarded the law as an unfortunate incident not to be taken as an expression of the Cabinet's policy. It generally approved of the measure so far as it would operate to repress " everything savoring of secret conspiracy and covert combination to disturb good order." The actual result of the immediate enforcement of the law was the driving out of Tōkyō of some three hundred suspects, the best known of whom were Ozaki Yukio, the Editor of the *Choya Shimbun*, Hoshi Toru, the Editor of the *Koron Shimpo*, Shimamoto Chūdo, Nakashima Nobuyuki, and Hayashi Yuzo.

2. *Supra* p. 497.

assisting to bring about such meeting or assembly, shall be liable to minor confinement for a period of not less than three months and not more than three years, together with a fine of from ten to one hundred *yen*. And any person acting as a follower of the above, shall be liable to a fine of from two to ten *yen*. And any person carrying arms, or causing arms to be carried, at such meetings or assemblies, shall be liable to penalties two degrees heavier than the above.

III. Any person who plots disturbance, or who instigates it, or who publishes books or pictures designed to disturb public tranquillity, or any person who prints such books or pictures, shall, in addition to the penalties prescribed by the Criminal Code and by the Publication Regulations, be liable to confiscation of all such publications as well as of all plant used in their preparation and issue. Ignorance of the import of such publications shall not constitute a valid plea for exemption from the penalties imposed by this Article.

IV. Any person residing or sojourning within a distance of three *ri* ($7\frac{1}{2}$ miles) radius around the Imperial Palace or around an Imperial place of resort, who plots or incites disturbance, or who is judged to be scheming something detrimental to public tranquillity, may be ordered by the police, or local authorities, with the sanction of the Minister of State for Home Affairs, to leave the said district within a fixed number of days or hours. And anyone who, being thus ordered to depart, fails to comply within the appointed time, or who, after departure, is again guilty of any of the aforesaid offences, shall be liable to a penalty of from one to three years' minor confinement, and further, to police surveillance for a period not exceeding five years, such surveillance to be exercised within the district of the offender's original registration.

V. In the event of peace and good order in any district being imperilled by popular excitement, or preparations pointing to disturbances, or by secret plotting, it shall be competent for the Cabinet to proclaim that district, and to order that the following provisions, either wholly or in part, shall be applied within it for a fixed period :—

1. All public meetings, whether in the open air or otherwise, under whatsoever pretext they may be held, shall be illegal, unless they have been previously sanctioned by the police authorities.

2. The publication of all newspapers and printed matter shall be illegal without a preliminary examination by the police authorities.

3. It shall be illegal to use, carry, or trade in guns, pistols, gunpowder, sword-canes, and so forth, without special permission from the local authorities.

4. The comings and goings of travellers shall be submitted to surveillance, and a special passport system shall be put in force.

5. Any person guilty of an offence against these Regulations shall be liable to minor confinement for a period of from one to two years, together with a fine of from five to two hundred *yen*. And anyone guilty of an offence against the Criminal Code as well as against these special Regulations, shall be further liable to the penalties prescribed by that Code.

VI. This Ordinance shall take effect from the day of its promulgation.

J.W.M., 1887, Dec. 31, p. 643.

4. PUBLIC MEETING REGULATIONS (REVISED).

(Law No. 31, Dec. 14, 1889.)

VII. Military and naval officers and men in active service or those of the first or second reserves, police officers, teachers and students of government, public, or private schools, as well as the agricultural and technological apprentices shall not be allowed to attend or enter any meeting or association the purpose of which is to discuss political matters or lecture thereon.

J.W.M., 1889, Dec. 21, p. 577.

5. Government Officials and Public Speaking.

(Cabinet Instruction, January 24, 1889.)

Government officers may, from and after this date, deliver addresses or lay statements[1] before the public on political or scientific matters even though not lying within their own functions.

NOTE.—The above privilege shall be exercised subject to the supervision of superiors, and shall not apply to those officials whose competence is otherwise defined by laws or regulations.

J.W.M., 1889, February 2, p. 106.

3.—THE ASSEMBLY OF THE LOCAL GOVERNMENT OFFICIALS (CHIHOKWAN-KWAIGI)[2]

1. Constitution and Rules for the Chihokwan-kwaigi.

(Imp. Dec. No. 58, May 2, 1874.)

It is hereby notified that the Constitution and Rules contained in the accompanying book have been ordained for the assembly of all the local jurisdictions which is now to be convened. The time of meeting will be notified hereafter.

(Signed) SANJO SANEYOSHI.

---

1. The order forbidding the practice was issued by the government in 1875, but it attracted no attention, because the general view then held was that the affairs of government were under the control of the Emperor, and were administered by officials who were responsible to the Emperor. In 1879 public speaking by officials was again strictly interdicted. The revocation of the order in 1889 was evidently intended to give the government the power of acquainting the people with their policy, since that policy was sure to be discussed in Parliament in the following year.

2. The meetings of this assembly which created the greatest interest in the country were held in 1875 and 1878. At the former Kido presided, at the latter Ito. The history of this institution has already been discussed at length in the Introduction.

IMPERIAL MESSAGE TO THE MEMBERS.

In accordance with the meaning of the Oath taken by Me at the commencement of my reign and as a gradual development of its policy, I am convening an assembly of representatives of the whole nation so as by the help of public discussion to ordain laws, thus opening up the way of harmony between governors and governed and of the accomplishment of national desires, and I trust by ensuring to each subject throughout the nation an opportunity of peacefully pursuing his vocation to awaken them to a sense of the importance of matters of state.

I have therefore issued this constitution of a deliberative assembly providing for the convening of the chief officials of the different local jurisdictions and for their meeting and deliberating as the representatives of the people.

Observe it well ye members of the assembly !

CONSTITUTION.

I. The assembly is of the chief officials of all the local jurisdictions assembled for deliberation. It will under ordinary circumstances be opened once a year. Extraordinary meetings may be called by Imperial decree giving notice of the date of such meeting beforehand. If the chief official is unable to attend he should be represented by the official next in rank.

II. At meetings of the assembly the chiefs of the great Departments of State or their representatives may be present to give their opinions, but they may not be included in the number of those who decide for or against the expediency of a measure.

III. At the opening and closing of the meeting the Emperor will be present in person with the Daijin and will conduct the ceremonies.

IV. The Emperor in consulting the opinion of the assembly may either send a draft measure, or he may send a commissioner fully to explain his views.

V. All bills are to be laid before the assembly by the

President, and when a decision for or against has been made it is to be reported to the Emperor who will himself decide whether or not it is to be put into execution.

NOTE.—It is important that this clause should be acted upon in conjunction with clauses X. and XI.

VI. The main object of the assembly is exhaustive discussion, weighing the practical expediency or inexpediency of measures. The members are expected to consider them in all their bearings fairly and honestly, and without factious opposition.

VII. The decision of the matter under discussion is with the majority of those of the same opinion. Where the numbers are equal the President decides.

VIII. At the meetings of the assembly every member may maintain his views fully and minutely, nor shall he be called to account even though he touch forbidden matters.

IX. If when the Crown consults the assembly on a measure their discussion of it proves unsuitable to the times, the bill may be withdrawn by an Imperial decree. This rule does not apply to other bills.

X. The general bills brought forward by the Crown affecting local interests, taxation, etc. will be laid before the assembly for its decision which in turn will be reported to the Emperor, and he will himself decide whether or not they shall be put into execution.

XI. When the assembly decides in favor of any measure brought forward by a member, it should be laid before the Emperor who will decide whether or not it shall be adopted.

XII. The President will of course be appointed from among the members, but until a good plan of doing so has been decided upon, the selection will be made by the Emperor himself.

XIII. The duties of the President are to enforce the observation of the rules of the assembly, to control the members, to cause discussion with respect to bills proceeding from the Crown and others, to consider fully the purport of the arguments adduced by members and to give a decision in the case of equal numbers on both sides. At meetings of the assembly, however, he will not be allowed to express his own opinions.

PREFACE TO THE RULES OF THE ASSEMBLY.

By "greater assembly" in the rules of the assembly is meant the ordinary meeting of the members at which a number of subjects may be discussed in order one after the other.

By "lesser assembly" is meant "committee meeting" which differs from the ordinary meeting. For instance, after a measure has been approved by the "greater assembly," when it is desired to discuss minutely such matters as the provisions of the bill or the working of the clauses, a special meeting is opened at which the President vacates the chair and takes his seat along with the other members, and takes part in the debate. At meetings of this kind only the subsidiary provisions of a measure can be decided, and no other subjects of discussion must be introduced. On these occasions the Chief Chairman acts as President. A "lesser assembly" may consist either of all the members present, in which case it is called a "general lesser assembly" (committee of the whole house), or a number of the members may be specially commissioned to deliberate on a question, in which case it is called a "select lesser assembly" (select committee). Whether the question is referred to a general lesser assembly or to a select lesser assembly will be decided at the time according to its importance.

RULES OF THE ASSEMBLY.

I. The Chief Chairman. His duty is in the absence of the President to supply his place, and to preside over meetings of the "lesser assembly." In other respects his duties are the same as those of the other Chairman.

II. Chairmen. They have the right of managing all the business of the assembly under the direction of the President, and they examine all memorials and petitions to ascertain whether or not they should be laid before the assembly.

III. Secretaries. The secretaries attend to all the records of the assembly.

IV. Assistant Secretaries. The Assistant Secretaries assist the Secretaries in the keeping of the records.

V. Treasurer. The Treasurer manages the expenditures in connection with the assembly.

VI. Assistant Treasurers. The Assistant Treasurers shall assist the Treasurer in managing the expenditure connected with the Assembly.

The above six officials are of *sonin* rank, and are appointed by the Crown on the nomination of the President ; those of *hannin* rank are appointed by the President at his own discretion.

VII. The members are sixty-three in number. The Chiji of the three Fu, and the Kenrei of the various local jurisdictions, while retaining the full authority of their proper offices, are all to be considered as the representatives of the entire nation when they attend the assembly.

VIII. For the sake of convenience in making investigations, the members shall be previously divided into sections as the President shall think fit.

IX. The arrangement of the seats in the assembly shall be previously decided by lot, and each chair shall be numbered. At every sitting members shall occupy their own chairs. When the President makes his appearance in the assembly-hall the members and secretaries shall salute him by standing up. The arrangements of the assembly-hall as well as other arrangements for the day are to be superintended by the Chairmen and the Secretaries.

X. The hours of the sittings shall be from 9 o'clock in the forenoon till 4 in the afternoon, but the sittings may be either extended or curtailed when convenient by the President.

During the session the members shall attend daily and shall investigate matters relating to the deliberations of the assembly. In regulating the times of meeting the President should consider the amount of business on hand.

XI. The first meeting (the first reading of a bill). The President explains the principle of the bill on which the assembly is consulted by the Crown, and distributes copies of it among them, thus enabling them to make themselves acquainted with its purport. The members all stand up to listen, and when they have retired from the assembly carefully read and consider the bill.

XII. The second meeting (the second reading). Each member having stated in writing his views respecting the bill which has been previously been put into his hands, reads his paper aloud, or he may deliver his opinion *viva voce*, and in either way discuss the matter freely.

If two or more speakers rise at the same time, they shall speak in the order of the number of their seats. Whilst one member is speaking, the others shall listen in silence, and allow him to be heard over the whole hall.

XIII. The third meeting (the third reading). Each member having reflected on the discussion of the previous meeting marks in red ink upon the bill the word " for " or " against," and on this day hands it to the President, who ascertains on which side the majority rests, and thus decides for or against the bill. He then causes a draft decision to be drawn up by the secretaries and communicates it to the members. Any further amendments he shall refer to the " lesser assembly " and when a clean copy is made he shall lay it before the Emperor.

The members shall attach their seals to the original in token of the fact that they have perused it.

XIV. In cases where a bill brought forward by the Crown is such that it is necessary to discuss its details, and it is impossible to answer simply " for ' or " against," the President will explain this clearly at the first meeting, whereupon the members will, after retiring, maturely consider them and prepare drafts setting forth their views, which will be referred to a number of competent members. These members will prepare a draft embodying the views of the majority of the same opinion. **This** draft will then be laid before a " lesser assembly " and be fully discussed. At the second meeting the suitable provisions are finally determined, amendments made and a reply framed.

XV. When any member wishes to bring in a bill, he furnishes a copy of it to the President, and when the President considers it fit to be laid before the assembly for discussion, he puts it to the meeting and the mover of the bill shall answer such questions as may be put to him respecting the bill.

When a member wishes to bring forward any matter for discussion he must announce the general purport of it at least six days previously.

XVI. The President shall open the discussion of all matters brought forward for consideration by members by causing the secretary to read the bill aloud. If at this time the proposer of the bill wishes in person further to explain it to the assembly so as to make them thoroughly comprehend its purport, he may do so after the secretary has finished the reading, the President's leave having been obtained.

XVII. In the case of important matters where the sense of the bill cannot be gathered by simply hearing it once read by the secretary, copies should be distributed to the members before the meeting.

XVIII. In cases where the provisons of a bill seem on the whole worthy of being adopted, but it has been decided to amend parts which have not been thoroughly considered, the President will consult the members again as to the character of such amendments, and learn all their opinions fully. He shall then direct the secretary or some members chosen for the purpose to prepare a draft of these amendments which should be discussed in the " lesser assembly."

XIX. When memorials or petitions are presented through local authorities, they are to be laid before a Chairman who shall examine whether or not they ought to be brought for. ward for discussion. If his decision is favorable, he lays them before the President, who submits them for consideration to the assembly. If his decision is unfavorable they are returned.

XX. In the case of urgent business a decision should be come to even though lamps are lit and the sitting be protracted till midnight, and in such cases a "second meeting" need not be waited for.

XXI. At a "greater assembly" if member A wishes to make an inquiry of member B, he must do so in presence of the President, and when B has addressed his reply to the President, A shall not be allowed any further discussion of the matter. But if B has misunderstood the question, A may address the President in explanation of the cause of his doing so.

At a "lesser assembly" alone are repeated rejoinders allowed.

XXII. Members should strive to carry on the discussion with disinterestedness and impartiality, and they should be guided by justice and unselfishness. If any of the members infringe any of the rules of debate the President will call him to order, and in the case of repeated offences the offender should, after delibe- ration, be expelled from the assembly. The President should correct any erroneous statements which may be made in the course of the debate.

XXIII. It is the etiquette of the members to remove their hats on entering the hall of assembly.

XXIV. If for any reason a member is absent on the day of meeting he may intrust to another member the discussion of any matter which he pleases, but no one member can hold two such authorisations.

XXV. No meeting will take place if six-tenths of the members are absent.

J.W.M., 1874, May 9, pp. 367-69.

2. MEMORIAL ON THE DELIBERATIVE ASSEMBLY.

(Addressed to the Daijōdaijin, June 1874.)

We humbly make the following representation, and unworthy as we are, we gratefully aoknowledge our undeserved appointment to the position of local officials. In the discharge of
the duties of this office, it has been our endeavor, in respectful
compliance with the Imperial will, to explain to the people in a
friendly way how careful the government are for their welfare,
to give their ideas a uniform bent, to cause them to attend in-
dustriously to their avocations, and to stir up a desire to co-
operate with the government in securing the national welfare.

Last year upon the return of the Ambassadors,[1] when the
question arose of sending an expedition against Korea, there was
a division of opinion among the high officers of state, and several
dismissals and appointments were the result. After that there
was the murderous attack upon the Udaijin, and the insurrection
which disturbed the western provinces. Immediately after an
expedition was suddenly taken against Formosa. Since then
there has been much confused discussion and the minds of the
people have not been at rest.

Before this the government sent out commissioners in all
directions to inform us that the creation of a Home Department[2]
had been resolved upon, which should devote its attention to
administration. We imagined that this measure would ensure
that the admonitions tending to good government would now
be effectual, and not being able to contain ourselves, we leaped
for joy, and strenuously instructed the people under our
jurisdiction.

However, upon examining the mode in which Home
Affairs are dealt with, we see that old rules are still maintained,
and that reforms have been neglected. On the contrary, since
the Home and Finance Departments have become separated,

1. The Iwakura mission to America and Europe.
2. *Supra* p. 36.

business has been embarrassed with troublesome details, and in numerous cases we receive no answers to our references and applications. After all where are the advantages which the Government led us to expect?

We have heard that the right of foreigners to travel freely in the interior will be demanded on the occasion of the revision of the Treaties. But whilst the constitutional and civil law of this country are still unsettled, and the tax regulations are unreformed, this measure if once granted would produce a multitude of evils which would be pregnant of some irremediable disaster. This, together with the matters above referred to by us, are matters of great import to the country, and are unceasing causes of extreme difficulty to the government and of anxiety to ourselves.

Fortunately by Notification No. 58 of May 2nd last,[1] an assembly was announced of the chief officials of the fu and ken. The announcement was made known to us last year, along with the regulations therefor. The date of meeting of this assembly we have looked forward to with great expectancy, and although more than a month has passed, it has not yet been announced to us. Now that important national concerns are pressing upon us, and that the people are full of apprehensions, there is no time like the present for opening the assembly. We pray that the day of meeting may be at once fixed and announced to the empire, and that the chief officials of the fu and ken may be summoned together and caused as representatives of the people to unfold their ideas, that, after referring the matter to public discussion, the powers of the Daijōkwan may be determined, and fixed rules established for the administration of fu and ken, and that we may be informed by what we ought to be guided, and what should be our policy in the future. If this is done, the apprehensions of the people will be removed, and each one will be enabled to live peaceably in his station. But if it is not done, it will

---

1. *Supra*. p. 505 ff.

be like launching a ship out into the open sea, and entrusting it to the winds, ignorant whether it be driven to the east or the west. Ought not in such a case the charge of the protection of the people which devolves upon us as local officials to send a chill to our hearts.

With fear and trembling we humbly pray you to appreciate these unconnected ideas of ours and to make them known to His Majesty.

(Signed)   Kusumoto Masatake, Kenrei of Niigata Ken.

Nakajima Nobuyuki, Kenrei of Kanagawa Ken.

Amba Yasukadzu, Kenrei of Fukushima Ken.

Morishita Kanemasa, Gon-Kenrei of Oita Ken.

Miyoshi Chikaaki,   ,,   ,, of Tottori Ken.

Iwamura Takatoshi,   ,, ,, ,, Saga Ken.

Sekiguchi Rinkichi,   ,, ,, ,, Yamagata Ken.

Mori Kiosuke, Sanji of Shidzuoka Ken.

Kata Soichi, Sanji of Akita Ken.

Ishibe Sanenaka, Sanji of Okayama Ken.

Nishino Tomoyasu, Gon-Sanji of Miōdō Ken.

Sakai Jirō, Gon-Sanji of Shimane Ken.

Uyemura Yukimasu, Gon-Sanji of Miyasaki Ken.

Kaba Sukeyuki, Temp. Official 7th rank of Ibaraki Ken.

J.W.M., 1874, Aug. 8, pp. 639-40.

3. A Second Memorial on the Deliberative Assembly.

(By the same to the same, July 1874.)

We humbly beg to make a representation. On the 17th of last month, we represented that the opening of the assembly of the local authorities is a matter of urgent national importance at the present time. We afterwards learned the decision made known by Notification No. 81 [1] of the 22nd July. With regard to this

---

1. Infra p. 520, foot note.

Notification we have now again considered what arrangements are suitable under the present circumstances, and pray that the amendments and additions set forth in the enclosed paper may be made to the constitution and rules of the deliberative assembly published in Notification No. 58 of the 2nd May last.

These amendments are proposed in the most loyal spirit, and it will occasion us intense disappointment if they are rejected. If there are any points as to which you have any doubts, we humbly pray that you will kindly question us upon them.

We humbly beg you to take this matter into your consideration, and favor us with your decision.

PROPOSED AMENDMENTS TO THE CONSTITUTION AND RULES OF THE DELIBERATIVE ASSEMBLY NOTIFIED ON THE 2ND MAY LAST.

CONSTITUTION.

I. The rule should be for the session to begin on the 1st March and last till the 30th April. This is for the reason that during the rest of the year the time is too much taken up with local administrative business, and also in order to avoid times of excessive heat and cold.

V. This Article with Articles X. and XI. provide that when the assembly has decided a matter in the affirmative or the negative, it shall be the sole prerogative of the Emperor to resolve whether or not its decision shall be carried out. In cases however where the decision of the assembly is reversed, it is essential that the assembly shall be fully informed of the grounds of such reversal, and the principles upon which it rests, so that the members of the assembly may acquiesce in it, and no feeling of dissatisfaction be left. If two-thirds of the assembly do not acquiesce in the reversal it ought to be competent for them to represent their reasons a second time to the Emperor.

VI. This Article insists on the importance of the assembly in their deliberations weighing well considerations of practical convenience in the carrying out of a measure. It is true that the members of our assembly, unlike those of civilised foreign nations, have no legislative powers, but in regard to questions of convenience or inconvenience in practice, although it will not always be possible to avoid the evil of frequent changes in the orders given by the government arising from the acceptance or rejection of our decisions, the best plan will be, when the government introduces any law, to submit it for thorough discussion, so that afterwards when it comes to be put into execution it will need no alteration. Hence all new laws should be submitted for the decision of the assembly and decided accordingly. There is no objection, as a temporary arrangement, to the question of whether or not a measure is to be put into execution being settled as provided for in Articles V., X. and XI.

IX. This Article provides that a bill is to be withdrawn by Imperial decree if its discussion proves unsuitable to the circumstances of the time.

As we have already pointed out in speaking of Article V. it is essential that the causes and principles which render the discussion unsuitable to the circumstances of the time should be fully explained to the assembly and their assent obtained.

XII. This Article says that the President will of course be appointed from among the members of the assembly, but until a good mode of appointment has been settled, the President will be appointed by the Emperor as a temporary arrangement. This matter ought certainly to be decided at the very first meeting of the assembly.

REGULATIONS OF THE DELIBERATIVE ASSEMBLY.

I. As it is sometimes the duty of the Chairman of Committee to take the place of the President, if the President is to be chosen from among the members of the assembly, the Chairman of Committees and the Chairman of the Special Committees also should be appointed from among the members.

VII. This regulation provides that the members should

continue to discharge their duties as Chiji or Kenrei. We think however that while attending the assembly in their capacitv as the representatives of the nation, they should be entirely released from all responsibility with respect to their proper offices.

XIX. This regulation provides that all memorials and petitions shall be laid before the Chairman, who will examine them and determine whether they should be laid before the assembly or not, and that if he approves of their being brought before the assembly, he will place them in the President's hands, who will bring them before the assembly, but if he does not they will be returned. We think, however, that it is the wish of persons who present memorials or petitions to the assembly ; to obtain their being submitted for public discussion by the assembly, and that the decision as to whether they should or should not be so discussed, ought not to rest with the Chairman alone, but should depend on public discussion.

PROPOSED ADDITIONS TO THE AFORESAID CONSTITUTION AND RULES.

RULES OF DEBATE.

I. When the Government refers a matter to the assembly, or a proposal is made by a member of the assembly, or a memorial is laid before it of such a kind that it might afterwards become a law, it will be impossible to avoid the evil of inconsistency in the details of its actual working afterwards, if the draft laid before the assembly only gives a general outline of the measure. For this reason such draft-bills, when laid before the assembly for discussion, should contain a distinct recital of the clauses, rules, and arrangements by which its practical working is to be carried out.

II. Not only the constitution and rules of the assembly and other new measures, but all alterations of hitherto existing regulations ought necessarily to be laid before the assembly for public discussion.

III. Whenever the course of a debate renders it desirable,

it should be allowed to ask to be produced for the inspection of the assembly, the books and records of the different Departments. Amongst other things it should be competent to question the Shō[1] and receive answers from them respecting such matters as the circumstances under which foreign treaties are concluded, and internal administrative arrangements, the receipts and disbursements of the treasury, alterations in the criminal law by the Shihōshō,[2] etc. are made.

IV. The public ought to. be freely admitted during the session except at meetings for the discussion of secret government matters.

STATUS OF MEMBERS.

I. All members of the assembly whether Chiji, Kenrei or Sanji shall be released from all responsibility in respect to the duties of their proper office during the time they act as members, and during their journeys backwards and forwards for this purpose.

II. All members shall be of equal authority whilst they are members, irrespective of their degrees of rank in their proper offices.

III. All members being relieved from the responsibility of their proper office during the session, the government will not make any appointments, dismissals or removals during the session.

IV. No member can be summoned before the Shihōshō or tried without the consent of the assembly, for any offence committed previous or during the session.

V. The desire expressed in the Imperial decree being, by the appointment of persons as representatives of the whole nation, to cause the people to take a deep interest in matters of national concern, the members of the assembly should be at liberty, with a view to inculcate this lesson, to bring with them from their jurisdictions such persons as they think fit to be appointed as representatives.

J. W. M., 1874, Aug. 8, pp. 640-41.

---

1. The Department of State.
2. The Department of Justice.

4.—POSTPONEMENT[1] OF THE MEETING OF THE DELIBERATIVE ASSEMBLY OF LOCAL GOVERNORS.

(Notif. No. 107, Aug. 17, 1874.)

It is hereby notified that His Majesty has, for reasons of expediency, decreed the postponement of the meeting fixed for the 10th proximo of the Deliberative Assembly of Local Governors, the convening of which was formerly announced.[2]

J.W.M., 1874, Aug. 22, p. 678.

5.—THE IMPERIAL SPEECH AT THE OPENING OF THE CHIHO-KWAN-KWAIGI IN 1875.

Our object in opening in person this the provincial parliament has been by its means to secure the thorough discussion of all matters affecting the interior economy of Our empire. and of securing to the provinces adequate representation. You have been convoked for this purpose, in order that your knowledge of the condition and feeling of the people of your several districts may aid you in discussing their requirements and introducing such reforms and changes as may seem to you to be most urgently demanded.

It is Our wish that your deliberations should be marked by general harmony, and that, sinking minor differences, they should tend to promote the ends in view in calling you together.

If with one mind you adhere steadily to this course your conduct will surely be conducive to the general welfare, and thus your deliberations may become the foundation of the eternal welfare of the empire.

Understand therefore Our views.

J.W.M., 1875, June 26, p. 548.

---

1. This action was taken by the Government in view of the strained relations between China and Japan over the Formosan expedition.

2. On July 22, orders were issued to the fu and ken that the local officers should arrive in Tōkyō not later than the 10th of September to attend the Local Officials Assembly.

6. THE REPLY TO THE IMPERIAL SPEECH AND THE IMPERIAL
    REJOINDER.

We cannot foretell the results of this our assembling, in
which we have no experience to guide us. But if happily inspired by Your Majesty's benevolence and justice, the results of
our deliberations, duly made known to Your Majesty, should
contribute towards the welfare of the people, then not in vain
will the Imperial will have gone forth, and the efficiency of the
Chihokwan-kwaigi will be apparent to all. Our earnest endeavors
will be directed to this end.

THE IMPERIAL REJOINDER.

It was Our intention to have convoked this assembly in
May of last year, but at that time Our foreign affairs were at-
tended with some perplexities and demanded its postponement.
We greatly rejoice that the members have assembled together.

This being your first meeting, for which our history affords
no precedent nor guiding law, Our hopes are based upon the
tenor of your reply, and We confidently trust that your efforts
will avail to bring forth from deep sources streams of lasting
happiness to the people.

J.W.M., 1875, June 26, p. 549.

7. CONSTITUTION [1] AND RULES FOR THE CHIHOKWAN-KWAIGI.

(Imp. Dec. No. 9, Mar. 15, 1878.)

CONSTITUTION.

I. A session of the assembly of local officials shall, as a
general rule, be held once in every year ; the dates of the
opening and closing of the session shall be fixed by the government, who will, at the appointed time, summon the chief local
officials from all cities and prefectures. Should any of the

---

1. A complete revision of Imp. Dec. No. 58, May 2, 1874.

latter be prevented from attending the assembly, he may be represented by his secretary.

II. The Ministers of the several administrative Departments or their representatives shall be entitled to attend at the Chamber for the purpose of discussing and explaining the bills under the consideration of the assembly, provided that they shall not be entitled to vote.

III. His Majesty the Emperor will graciously be present at the ceremonies of opening and closing each session of the assembly.

IV. All questions shall be decided by a majority of votes ; in case of the number of votes being equal the President shall have the casting vote.

V. The President shall introduce all bills for debate, and he shall subsequently submit the same, as passed by the assembly, to the Emperor for the Imperial decision.

VI. When any member wishes to introduce a bill of his own for discussion by the assembly, he shall hand a draft of his bill to the President.

VII. The President shall be appointed directly by the Emperor by special mandate ; the other officers will be appointed upon the recommendation of the President in the manner appropriate to the appointment of officers of the second grade ; and, in the case of those in and below the third grade by the President himself.

VIII. President :—His duties are to exercise authority over the assembly generally, and to enforce the " Law of the Assembly " and the " Rules of Debate."

First Official Chief of the Chamber :—His duties are to act for the President in his absence and to preside over the assembly when sitting in committee. In other respects the duties of the First Official Chief are the same as those of the other Official Chiefs of the Chamber.

Official Chiefs of the Chamber :—Their duties are to

control and transact all official business connected with the Chamber under the direction of the President.

Secretaries :—Their duties are to revise drafts of bills, to keep the official records, and generally to transact the secretarial business of the Chamber.

Chief Accountant :—His duties are to take charge of the financial business of the Chamber.

Clerks :—Their duties are to transact such miscellaneous business as shall be assigned to them respectively.

SITTINGS, DEBATES, ETC.[1]

SITTINGS.

I. Unless there is present at a sitting an absolute majority of the total number of members, no business shall be done.

II. The commencement and close of every debate shall be declared by the President.

III. The seats of members shall be fixed by means of lots as the commencement of every session.

IV. During debate, the number of the member's seat, not his name, must be mentioned.

V. The President shall have power to stop any member speaking, or to put an end to the debate.

VI. All questions arising incidentally in the course of debate, not being questions on the subject of the debate itself, shall be decided by the President himself or by the vote of the Chamber.

VII. Strangers shall be admitted to listen to the debates ; provided that they may be excluded, or their admission regulated or restricted, according to circumstances.

BILLS AND AMENDMENTS.

VIII. Bills are sent to the Chamber for consideration by the Cabinet.

---

1. These rules were originally promulgated by Imp. Dec. No. 58, 1874, and were revised in 1880 by Imp. Dec. No. 3 issued on Jan. 21.

IX. Copies of bills and reports shall be distributed among the members beforehand.

X. Amendments may be moved both on the second and third readings of a bill; provided that any amendment, not seconded on the second reading of the bill, or not supported by at least five members on the third reading, shall not be debated upon.

XI. A member wishing to move an amendment to a bill before the Chamber, may either hand his amendment in writing to the President or move it verbally in the course of the debate.

XII. Amendments which have once been rejected cannot be brought forward again at the same stage of the bill.

DEBATES.

XIII. Debates upon bills or reports shall not take place until at least one clear day after the copies of the same have been distributed among the members ; provided that where emergency is declared this rule may be disregarded.

XIV. Before the debate is opened the President shall direct the secretary to read the bill.

XV. Bills are to be read three times.

XVI. Upon the first reading the general principle of the bill shall be considered, and a decision shall be taken whether the bill shall be read a second time. If the decision be in the negative, the bill shall be considered rejected, if in the affirmative the President shall appoint a day for the purpose.

XVII. Upon the second reading the bill shall be debated clause by clause, and a decision taken as to whether the bill shall be read a third time. If the decision shall be in the negative the bill shall be considered rejected, if in the affirmative the President shall appoint a day for the purpose ; provided that if any of the clauses or paragraphs agreed to require verbal amendment, the question as to whether the bill shall be read a third time shall not be decided until a report upon such amendment has been presented by a committee appointed or the purpose.

XVIII. Upon the third reading a bill shall be finally decided, as a whole.

XIX. A bill shall not be read a third time until at least one clear day after the second reading ; provided that when emergency is declared this rule may be disregarded.

SPEECHES.

XX. A member wishing to speak in the Chamber shall rise from his seat, and, before commencing his speech, call upon the President in order to obtain his permission to speak.

XXI. If the President consider that a member is not speaking to the question he shall have power to stop him.

XXII. If a member consider that another member is not speaking to the question, he may cry " Question " and may, by permission of the President, state his grounds for so doing in a single speech. If the member whose speech has been objected to, insist upon the relevancy of his remarks, he may, by permission of the President, state his grounds in a single speech. The · President shall thereupon either decide the question himself or put it to the vote of the Chamber ; provided that when a member's speech has been thus declared irrrelevant he shall immediately cease speaking.

XXIII. If a member consider another to be out of order he may, even whilst that other or some third member be speaking, cry " Order "; and may, by permission of the President state his grounds in a single speech. If the member thus called to order do not consider himself to have been out of order, he may, by permission of the President state his grounds in a single speech. The President shall thereupon either decide the question himself or put it to the vote of the Chamber ; provided that when a member is observed to be out of order whilst another member is speaking, if his disorderly conduct has not the effect of interrupting the member speaking, attention should not be

called to such disorderly conduct, until the member speaking
has concluded his speech.

XXIV. Upon the third reading of a bill no speaker shall
be heard more than twice.

DECISIONS.

XXV. Every question shall be decided by the vote of an
absolute majority of the members present.

XXVI. All the members present must vote upon every
question put.

XXVII. The. vote shall be taken in one of the three following ways, viz.—(1) by sitting and standing ; (2) by signed voting papers ; (3) by unsigned voting papers. The method to be
adopted in each case shall be at the discretion of the President.

XXVIII. If there a difference of opinion as to the order in
which bills shall be debated, the President shall before any debate
is opened, either decide the question himself or put it to the
vote of the Chamber.

XXIX. Amendments shall be submitted for debate before
the original clauses upon which they are moved. When there
are several amendments the one differing most from the original
clause shall be taken first. If there be a difference of opinion as
to the order in which amendments are to be taken, the President,
before submitting any of them to debate, shall either decide
the question of priority himself or shall put it to the vote of the
Chamber.

XXX. If it should be proposed either by the President
himself or by two or more members to consider a portion of a
bill apart from the rest, or to consider a group of bills together,
or to consider certain clauses or paragraphs out of their order,
the President shall either decide such matter himself or put it to
the vote of the Chamber.

XXXI. If, whilst discussion is still going on, the President
considers that the subject has been fully debated, he may state
his opinion to the Chamber ; and upon a vote of the Chamber

being given in the same sense, he may proceed forthwith to take the decision of the Chamber upon the main question in debate.

XXXII. The votes shall be counted by the secretary and declared by the President.

COMMITTEE OF THE WHOLE CHAMBER.

XXXIII. Sittings in committee of the whole Chamber shall be held when it is deemed expedient to hold them for the purpose of putting questions upon bills, or upon reports of select committees, to the framers of such bills or reports, or when it is desired to hold a private consultation to decide upon the answer to be returned to questions submitted to the Chamber by the government.

XXXIV. No strangers shall be admitted to the Chamber when the committee is sitting.

XXXV. The rules herein need not be applied to the Chamber when sitting in committee, except Articles XLII., XLIII., and LXIV.

SELECT COMMITTEES.

XXXVI. If it be proposed by the President or by two or more members, to appoint a committee to examine any bill or amendment, the proposal shall be put as a motion and decided by the vote of the Chamber.

XXXVII. Committees shall be appointed from among the members of the Chamber either by the President himself or by the vote of the Chamber ; provided that every committee shall consist of an uneven number of members.

XXXVIII. Committees may in their reports recommend the adoption, rejection or revision of the whole or part of any bill or amendment referred to them. The decisions of a committee shall be taken in accordance with the votes of an absolute majority of the members. If a committee be divided in opinion into more than two sections, and an absolute majority of the whole committee cannot be obtained in favor of the opinion of any one section, the opinion of the largest section shall be adopted in the report ; but the circumstances must be reported to the President of the Chamber ; provided that notwithstanding that, in the cases contemplated in the proviso to Article XVII., the committee shall be empowered to transpose clauses or paragraphs, to make verbal amendments, or propose new clauses or paragraphs in place of those rejected, nevertheless it shall not be empowered to alter the sense of paragraphs or clauses agreed to by the Chamber.

XXXIX. The mover of an amendment may attend the sittings of a committee for the purpose of stating the grounds of his amendment ; provided that he shall not be entitled to vote upon the decision.

REPRESENTATIVES OF THE CABINET.

XL. The Cabinet shall send a representative or representatives to attend the sittings of the Chamber, or of the committee of the whole Chamber, or of select committees, for the purpose of stating the grounds of the bills sent by the Cabinet ; provided that the representatives so sent shall observe these rules, but shall not be entitled to vote upon the decision.

PRESERVATION OF ORDER IN THE CHAMBER.

XLI. The President may, when occasion arises, give such orders as he may think fit to the police officers attached to the Chamber for the purpose of preserving order in the Chamber.

XLII. In the Chamber members are not permitted in any case to extend their observations so far as to advert to the character of individuals whether in praise or blame.

XLIII. During debates members are not permitted to converse among themselves or to act in any other way calculated to interrupt the debate.

XLIV. During debates members are not permitted irregularly to leave their seats.

XLV. Members arriving late must obtain permission from the President before taking their seats.

XLVI. No person shall be admitted into the Chamber during a debate without the permission of the President.

XLVII. Any person violating the Rules in the Chamber, and not immediately desisting on the order of the President, shall be expelled from the Chamber.

SUPPLEMENTARY RULES.

XLVIII. The President may, if he thinks desirable, divide the members into groups and let each group appoint one of their number to act on their behalf in receiving and distributing among them notices and other papers.

XLIX. Any member absenting himself from a sitting shall report the cause of his absence to the President.

J.W.M., 1881, pp. 847-49.

4.—PRESS AND PUBLICATION REGULATIONS.

I. REGULATIONS GOVERNING THE PUBLICATION OF BOOKS (TOSHO-KAIHAN-NO-KITEI.)

Any book may be published, provided that the author gives notice of his intention beforehand to the local authorities. The local authorities shall thereupon apply to the government for its approval, forwarding along with the request the manuscript of the proposed book, and the name and address of the author. When the approval of the government has been given, and the book has been published, a copy of the book shall be sent to the government.

I. When it is desired to issue a new edition, or to change the size of a book or map already printed, the permission of the government is necessary. When the new edition has been printed a copy must be sent to the government.

II. The titles of books hitherto published, and the names of their authors, as well as the dates on which the approval of the government was given, shall be carefully compiled and sent in to the government by February of this year.

III. Although it was strictly forbidden by one of the recent proclamations to publish a book with the same contents as that of another, it seems to be a common practice among authors and publishers to issue under different titles books of other writers. Any one who commits such an offence must certainly be punished.

H-Z., 1869, 44.

2. BOOK AND PRESS REGULATIONS [1] (SHUPPAN-JŌREI).

I. Any book to be published shall have inscribed upon it the name and address of the author, the publisher, and the book-seller. A printed sheet of paper shall conform to the same regulations.

II. Any one who promulgates his views, accuses others falsely, publishes political secrets, or makes statements which lead others into lewd practices, shall be punished, due consideration being given to the nature of the offence. (The reference here is obviously to published statements such as were current in the so-called newspapers of the day.) [2]

III. The author of a book shall be protected by the government, so that he may be allowed to enjoy the pecuniary benefits arising from a monopoly of the sale of his book.

This protection shall, as a rule, last only during the life of the author ; however if some of his relatives desire the prolongation of the term, their request shall be entertained.

---

1. It must be borne in mind that the newspaper was in its earliest infancy in Japan when this law was issued. Printing was in all cases done by means of blocks, and the sheets sold were of the roughest description. For a short account of the history of the Japanese press see Dening, *Japanese Modern Literature*, p. 90 ff. *A. S. J. Trans.*, Vol. XLI, Part I.

2. The parenthesis is added by the editor.

IV. Before the publication of any book can be undertaken, information as to its title, the names and addresses of its author and proposed publisher, and its contents, shall be sent to the School (Shōhei), along with a request for permission to issue the book. The School shall examine the petition and affix its seal thereto and return it to the petitioner, and the document thus sealed shall constitute a certificate of permission. The date of the official permission shall be inscribed in the book.

V. Any one who requests permission to publish a book shall state in his petition that copies of the book shall be sent to the government after it is published. In case the book has not been printed after an interval of several months, he shall be required to ask for an extension of the term during which the permission holds good.

VI. After a book has been printed five copies shall be sent to the School, and shall be distributed among the libraries.

VII. In case a book has been published without permission from the Government, the blocks together with the copies of the book shall be confiscated.

Money which has been obtained by the sale of the book shall also be confiscated by the goverment.

VIII. Any one who sends in false information when asking for permission to publish a book shall be fined.

This rule shall apply even in cases where the book has not yet been published or sold.

IX. In case a book having the same contents as one by another author is published, the blocks along with copies of the book shall be confiscated, and a fine shall be imposed upon the publisher. The book-seller shall also be fined. The amount of the fine in such cases shall be determined after due consideration has been given to the loss suffered by the original author and publisher.

X. Anyone who reprints a foreign book shall be protected by a copyright. In cases where an edition of a book has been destroyed or injured permission may be granted to bring out another edition.

XI. Any original or reprinted book may be published without liability to a penalty for " pirating" provided the parties to the arrangement have agreed beforehand.

XII. Books dealing with military subjects, whether original or translated from foreign languages, may be published at any time, for it is necessary that milltary science should be kept up-to-date.

XIII. All printed matter shall have to conform to the above regulations.

XIV. Pictures, portraits, caricatures, etc. shall conform to the above regulations.

H-Z., 1869, 174.

3.—BOOK AND PRESS REGULATIONS.

(Notif. of the Department of Eduction, Jan. 13, 1872.)

I. Any book to be published shall have inscribed upon it the name and address of the author and the publisher.

A printed sheet of paper shall conform to the same regulations.

II. It is forbidden to abuse the existing laws or to accuse others falsely in a book.

III. The author of a book shall be protected by the government, so that he may be allowed 'to enjoy the pecuniary benefits arising from a monopoly of the sale of his book.

The regulations concerning copyright privileges shall be promulgated along with the general tax law.

IV. Before the publication of a book can be undertaken, information as to its title, the names and addresses of the author and proposed publisher, and its contents shall be sent to the Department of Education (Mombushō). The Department of

Education shall examine the petition and affix its seal thereto and return it to the petitioner, and the document thus sealed shall constitute a certificate of permission to publish. The date of the official permission shall be inserted in the book.

V. The same as Article V. in the Regulations of May, 1869.

VI. After a book has been printed three copies shall be sent to the Department of Education.

VII. In case a book has been published without permission from the government the blocks together with the copies of the book shall be confiscated, and a fine shall be imposed.

VIII. The same as Article VIII. of the Regulations of May, 1869.

IX. In case an author's book has been republished secretly the blocks together with the copies of the book shall be confiscated and punishment shall be inflicted after due consideration of the circumstances of the case.

X. The same as Article X. of the Regulations of May, 1869.

XI. The same as Article XI. of the Regulations of May, 1869.

XII. The same as Article XII. of the Regulations of May, 1869.

XIII. All printed matter shall conform to the above regulations.

Newspapers, pictures, portraits, and caricatures, etc. shall conform to the above regulations.

XIV. The terms to be used in referring to foreign countries are as follows :—

> Gwaikoku, to foreign countries in general.
> Eikoku, England.
> Fukkoku, France.
> Fukoku, Prussia.
> Rokoku, Russia.
> Beikoku, The United States of America.

H-Z., 1872, 1169.

4. NEWSPAPER REGULATIONS.

(Notif. No. 352, Oct. 19, 1873.)

I. Every issue of a newspaper must be marked with its proper number.

II. Supplements must be marked with the number of the issue to which they belong.

III. No supplement may be issued if a number of the paper is not issued along with it.

IV. When the official seal of authorisation has once been attached to the letter of application, it is unnecessary to submit each number of the paper for inspection.

The application should be drawn up in the same form as that for permission to publish a book.

V. Every number must have printed on it the year, month, day, and place of issue, and the names of the editor and publisher.

VI. When printed one copy must be sent to the Department of Education and one to the local government office.

VII. If they have no evil tendency the following subjects are admissble :—Extraordinary natural occurrences, fires, war, prices, produce, trade, births, deaths, and marriages, official notifications, literature, manufactures, amusements, clothing, land and houses, translations of foreign writings, miscellaneous foreign news, and other unimportant public matters.

VIII. Papers, correspondence, miscellaneous paragraphs, etc. sent to the paper may be published if they have been authenticated with the writers name.

IX. No newspaper may be established without official permission.

X. It is prohibited to attack the constitution of the government, to discuss the laws, or to cast obstacles in the way of the working of national institutions by the persistent advocacy of foreign ideas.

XI. It is forbidden to append uncalled-for remarks to the laws, etc. which are published in the papers.

XII. Moral teachings must not be introduced in such a way as to obstruct and injure the government.

XIII. It is forbidden to disturb or demoralise the minds of the people.

XIV. It is forbidden to denounce a man for crimes on the faith of groundless rumors.

XV. Editors must not take it upon themselves to publish remarks upon officials during their term of office, or their official conduct, or even anything, however trifling, which is connected with our foreign intercourse.

This prohibition does not extend to documents which have been notified publicly, or for the publication of which an official order has been made.

XVI. All errors which may have been made must be corrected.

XVII. The editor is responsible for giving explanations with regard to any matter upon which it may be necessary to question him.

XVIII. Any persons infringing the above regulations shall be punished in accordance with the law.

J.W.M., 1883, p. 881.

5. MEMORIAL CONCERNING THE PRESS LAWS.

(Addressed to the Sa-in, May 4, 1874.)

I am struck with wonder at my good fortune at living under the present reformed regime, and at a time of so great enlightenment throughout the world, and it is my intention to form a newspaper company, to publish in this newspaper the opinions of the people and to maintain their natural rights and liberties, by new arguments and striking opinions, to search for what is proper and fair, and to correct the errors of the time by honest criticism I hope thus on the one hand to promote enlightenment and on the other to advance the lustre of the blessings of peace. I fear, however, that Articles X., XI. and XII. of the Press Regulations notified in October last seem calculated not only to cramp the liberty of printing, but as a consequence to destroy the rights and the free communication of the people, to suppress intelligence and interfere with the opportunity for the increase of enlightenment.

Are not these Articles not a little in contradiction with the oath taken by the Emperor just after the Restoration, as it is clearly set forth in the beginning of the *Kempo-mi-hen ?*[1] It states that everything will be decided by public discussion, and that intelligence will be sought for throughout the empire. Now it is well known to the government that in every country liberty of discussion in the newspapers is allowed, and I therefore pray that His Majesty, in the exercise of a wise discretion, will cancel these Articles and so disperse the cloud on the minds of the people, that he will largely adopt public opinion, seek for intelligence throughout the country and so add greatness to our country.

Humbly represented,

KITADA MASAYOSHI,
Samurai of Ōsaka.

J.W.M., 1874, p. 372.

6. PETITION ON THE SUBJECT OF THE PRESS LAWS.

(Presented to the Sa-in, 1875.)

Since the new regime " newspapers " of various designations and the " *Nisshin Shinjishi* " etc. have been permitted to be established, which print matters of all kinds, from the records of the Sa-in downwards, and publish these throughout the country, so that even in the most remote parts of the realm the actions of the government, the many discussions of every place

1. Collection of Documents of the Constitution.

are known. This certainly tends in no small degree to the development of civilisation.

But there are in these newspapers what are known as anonymous communications, the authors of which either do not publish their names or write under a *nom de plume*[1] such as " the proprietor of such and such a grass-hut," and the drift of which is to find fault with and cavil at the course pursued by the government and to rail at the proceedings of the government Departments, the object (of the writers) being to make the government authority null and void.

With regard to the nature and intent of petitions[2] (presented to government) on various subjects, there is of course a difference amongst petitioners, inasmuch as some are learned and others ignorant, some wise and others foolish, but as each has a right to reflect and argue on his own honest convictions, he is perfectly justified in criticising the policy of the government, or in pointing out what (he thinks) right or wrong in the action of public Departments or prefectures. If the writers (of these anonymous communications) published their names, in the case of one (of these writers) failing to apprehend the true bearings of a question, he would be enlightened (by the government) on the point as to which he was ignorant and in error, and even if only one individual was thus converted to the right view, this might serve as an example to others and so be the first step to the advancement of civilisation.

To say evil things whilst concealing one's name is in short, if we reflect, the language of temporising fellows. Why is it that these persons who have (thanks to the government) lived in security hitherto in their country, do not acquiesce in the (recent) change of administration, a change wholly unprecedented in its magnitude ? Why is it that they seek neither to

1. It was common in Japan in the case of anonymous writings for the author to sign himself "The proprietor of the grass-hut near the Sumidagawa " or " near Asakusa," etc., etc.

2. " Petitions " here used in contradistinction to the " communications " complained of.

learn from experienced men nor to enlighten those who are ignorant, nor desire to recompense the government for the benefits they have received, but with misdirected energy give vent to obstinate and selfish ideas?

It would be well, I think, if this class of people were warned, and if the government in accordance with the Newspaper Regulations made known by Notification No. 352 of the 9th day of the 10th month of last year the 6th year of Meiji, (Oct. 9th 1873) were to prohibit the printing at the *Nisshindo*[1] of (communications) having reference either to the government or laws of the country emanating from persons other than those authorized (to publish such).

The effect of these statements[2] is that the country people living in the most remote places and distant corners of the empire not only disregard the motive, cause, and object in view (of these communications), but even accept these perverted statements for the truth, and thus the (good) intentions of the government are thwarted and frustrated, and people are led astray into false beliefs.

The opinions I have stated are narrow and the arguments I have brought forward trivial, but in saying what I have said, I have been actuated solely by a desire to make widely known the benevolent intentions of the government.

THE OPINION OF THE SA-IN.

With regard to the subject of the petition, there are already laws enacted bearing on the conduct of newspapers, and discussion is not needed on that point.

As for "people living in distant corners of the country believing in the perverted statements," etc., etc., as regards all arguments and views the deeming of them good or bad, correct in their reasoning or mistaken, their adoption or rejection, these are matters which newspaper readers can decide for themselves.

---

1. Name of a newspaper office.

2. *i.e.* those contained in the anonymous communications

The original document has been returned with this expression.

J.W.M., 1875, pp. 69-70.

7. THE NEWSPAPER PRESS LAW.

(Notification No. 101, June 28, 1875.)

I. Whenever it is desired to publish a newspaper or periodical magazine, the proprietor, or, if a company, the director, must send in a petition to the Home Department through the office of the fu or ken for permission to do so. In any case of publication without such permission a charge will be laid against the offender before the judicial authorities,[1] the publication will be put a stop to, and the proprietor or director as well as the editor and printer will be severally punished by a fine of one hundred *yen*. Any one who falsely describes himself as having obtained permission will be fined not less than one hundred and not more than two hundred *yen*, and his types and machinery will be confiscated.

II. The following particulars are to be inserted in the petition :—

1. The title of the proposed publication.
2. The time when published, whether daily, weekly, monthly, or at indefinite times.
3. The name and residence of the proprietor, or if a a company, of the director or directors, exclusive of persons having only a share in the newspaper.
4. The name and residence of the editor, or where there are several editors, of the principal editor.
5. The name and residence of the printer. If the editor and printer are the same person, this should be stated.

Any false declaration with regard to the above five particulars will be punished by the stoppage or suspension of the publication, and by a fine of from ten to one hundred *yen*.

---

1. The fu and ken authorities will act as prosecutors in the case of offences against this law.

III. In the event of the death or resignation of an editor or chief editor, the publication may be continued with a provisional editor or chief editor, but the name and residence of the new editor or chief editor must be reported by the proprietor or director to the office of the fu or ken within fifteen days at latest, counting from the day after the death or resignation. If a report is not made within this time, the publication will be suspended, and the proprietor or director will pay a fine of one hundred *yen*.

If any change should occur in any of the other particulars mentioned in Article II. the proprietor or director and editor or chief editor should report it jointly within at least fifteen days thereafter. Failure to report within the time specified renders the proprietor or director and editor or chief editor liable to a fine of one hundred *yen* each.

IV. No other persons than Japanese subjects can be proprietors or directors, editor or chief editor.

V. The proprietor or director may himself be also the editor or chief editor.

VI. When there are two or more editors one shall be selected and made chief editor.

The names of the editor and printer shall be inserted at the end of each number or volume, and where there are several editors, that of the chief editor. If the editor or chief editor is ill, a substitute should be provided, and his name published instead.

An infraction of this rule renders the editor, chief editor or substitute liable to a penalty of not less than one hundred *yen* and not more the five hundred *yen*, and the printer to a fine of one hundred *yen*.

VII. If anything contained in the number or volume infringes the prohibitions of Article XII. and the following Articles, or if an offence is committed against the law of slander, the editor will be considered the principal, and the writer an accessory, and if the proprietor or director is cognizant of it, he will be considered as if he were the responsible editor.

VIII. With the exception of the ordinary paragraphs of news, the writers of articles in newspapers or magazines (in which contributors are included) must sign their names in every case where the discussion turns upon foreign or domestic politics, finance, the feelings of the nation, the aspect of the times, learning or religion, or matters affecting the rights of officials and people.

The writer who signs a feigned name renders himself liable to imprisonment for thirty days and to a fine of ten *yen*. If he signs another man's name he renders himself liable to imprisonment for seventy days and to a fine of twenty *yen*.

Either or both of the above-named punishments may be inflicted. The same rule holds for the punishments mentioned below.

IX. When articles are translated from foreign newspapers or magazines, the translator, except in the case of ordinary paragraphs of news, must sign his name to them, and if such articles infringe the prohibitions of Article XII. and the following Articles, or if they offend against the law of slander, the responsibility of the translator is the same as that of the writer in Article VII., who is considered an accessory.

X. If the editor only is sentenced to imprisonment for an offence, the proprietor or director may appoint an acting-editor or a new editor and continue the publication, unless it has been at the same time suspended. If the publication is continued without an editor having been appointed, it will be suspended.

XI. If in any newspaper or magazine, any public office, company or private individual is mentioned by name, the newspaper or magazine must publish in their next issue after receiving it, any explanation or correction which such public office, company or person may furnish to them. An infraction of this rule renders the editor liable to a penalty of not less than ten *yen* and not exceeding one hundred *yen*.

XII. Any person who in a newspaper or magazine incites to the commission of any crime will be considered equally guilty with the person who has been caused to commit it, and if his inciting has not resulted in any offence being committed the penalty is imprisonment for not less than five days and not more than three years, and a fine of not less than ten *yen* and not exceeding five hundred *yen.*

Anyone who incites to riot a number of evil-disposed persons or who stirs them up to a violent attack upon the authorities will be considered equally guilty with the ring-leader. If his persuasions do not result in causing a crime to be committed he will be punished as above.

XIII. Anyone advocating a revolution against the government or the subversion of the state, or who attempts to stir up rebellion is liable to imprisonment for not less than one year and not more than three, and in the case of crime committed (owing to such instigation), to the same punishment as the principal offender.

XIV. Anyone who reviles existing laws, or confuses the sense of duty of the people to observe them, or who by perverted reasoning attempts to justify offences plainly contrary to the criminal law, will be punished with imprisonment for not less than one month, and not more than one year, and with a fine of not less than five *yen*, and not exceeding one hundred *yen.*

XV. It is not allowed to publish the preliminary proceedings in Criminal Courts before sentence has been publicly delivered, nor the deliberations of the judicial officers respecting the trial. Any breach of this rule is punished with imprisonment for not less than one month and not exceeding one year, and a fine of not less than one hundred *yen*, and not exceeding five hundred *yen.*

XVI. Memorials and petitions may not be published without the sanction of the *In, Shō, Shi* or *Chō*.[1] Any breach of this rule renders the offender liable to the same penalties as in the preceding Article.

ADDITIONAL REGULATIONS.

Any person who has already received authorisation to

---

1. These are names of various kinds of offices in the central and local government, *e.g.* Genro-in, Naimushō, Kaitakushi, Keishichō.

publish a newspaper or magazine before this law was notified need not send in a fresh application, but he should report to the Home Department, through his fu or ken, within ten days counting from the day following his receipt of this notification, the five items specified in Article II. If after ten days have elapsed, this report has not been sent in, the fu or ken will suspend the publication. Fresh application must follow the rule laid down in Article I.

When there have hitherto been several editors but no chief editor, a chief editor or provisional chief editor must be appointed within two days, counting from the day following the rec ipt of this notification.

If after two days, the newspaper or magazine continues to be published without the name of any chief editor, the fu or ken will suspend the publication. Fresh application should follow the course described above.

J.W.M., 1875, July 3, pp. 572-73.

8. NEWSPAPER REGULATIONS.

(Imp. Ord. No. 75, Dec. 28, 1887.)

I. Any person desiring to publish a newspaper shall, two weeks previous to the first issue thereof, send in a notice to that effect to the Department of State for Home Affairs ' through the local government authorities (in Tōkyō, through the Metropolitan Police authorities) in whose jurisdiction the said newspaper is to be published.

II. In the said notice of intention to publish a newspaper the following particulars shall be mentioned :—

    1. The name of the newspaper.

    2. The nature of the subjects to be treated.

    3. The periods of publication.

    4. The place wherein published and the place wherein printed.

    5. The names and ages of the publisher, editor, and printer.

When there are two or more editors the name of that editor shall be given who has the principal charge of the editorship. It is, however, permitted that the editing of a paper shall be divided into several sections, and that a responsible editor be placed over each one thereof.

III. When, after the foregoing notice has been given, any change is to be made in the name of the newspaper, in the nature of the topics to be treated, or of the publisher, a notice shall be sent in two weeks beforehand in accordance with the provisions of Article I.

Whenever any change has been made in the period or place of publication of any newspaper, in the place where it is printed, in its editor, or its printer, a notice to that effect shall be sent within one week, in accordance with the provisions mentioned in Article I.

IV. When the publisher of a newspaper has died or has become legally disqualified, a new publisher shall be installed and a notice thereof shall be given within one week, in accordance with the provisions of Article I. In the meanwhile the paper shall be published under the name of the " provisional publisher."

V. When there has been no issue of a newspaper after a lapse of fifty days from the day on which the notice of its intended publication has been sent in, or from the day on which its publication has been stopped, the said notice of publication shall become void.

VI. Only a Japanese male subject above twenty-five full years of age can become the publisher, editor, or printer of a newspaper.

No one who has been deprived of his public rights can become the publisher, editor, or printer of a newspaper, nor can any one do so whose public rights have been suspended, as long as they remain so suspended.

VII. Neither the editor nor the printer of a newspaper is allowed to act at one and the same time in both capacities.

VIII. Every publisher of a newspaper shall simultaneously with the giving of notice of intended publication of a newspaper, deposit with the local government authorities (in Tōkyō, with the Metropolitan Police Office), one or other of the following sums of money as security :—

1. In Tōkyō, one thousand *yen.*
2. In Kyōto, Ōsaka, Yokohama, Hyōgo, Kobe, Nagasaki, seven hundred *yen.*
3. In all other localities, three hundred *yen.*

One-half only of the above specified respective amounts shall be required of newspapers published three or fewer times per month.

The security required may be furnished in the form of public loan bonds at the current market rate, or in the form of deposit notes issued by the national banks.

Such papers as contain only matters relating to science, art, statistics, government notifications, or to reports of market-prices, shall not fall within the scope of the present Article.

IX. The security shall be returned when the publication of the newspaper has been discontinued or prohibited.

X. When the notice mentioned in Articles I., III., and IV. has not been sent in, or when a newspaper for which security is required, has been published without the deposit thereof, the Chief of the Metropolitan Police Office or the Governor of the locality, shall stop the publication of such newspaper, until the proper notice has been given, or the security has been deposited.

XI. A newspaper shall contain in every issue the names of the publisher, editor, and printer, as well as of the place of publication.

Anyone appending his signature to a newspaper or to any statement therein contained, otherwise than the publisher or printer of the newspaper, shall be held equally responsible with the editor thereof.

XII. On the issue of every number of a newspaper, two copies thereof shall be at once sent to the Department of State for Home Affairs, and one copy each to the local government authorities (in Tōkyō to the Metropolitan Police Office) and to the Public Prosecutor's Office in the Court of First Instance of the locality of publication.

XIII. Whenever a misstatement has been made in a news-paper, and the party affected thereby, or any party concerned in the matter, demands its correction, or sends for publication a communication containing correction or protest, the correction shall be made or the communication of correction or protest shall be published in full in the second or third issue after the receipt of such protest or communication. In case the number of words in the communication should exceed twice the number thereof in the original statement, the newspaper may make for the number of words in excess, a charge at the rate established for ordinary advertisements.

The correction or protest shall be published in the same type as was the original statement, and at the head of the same division of the newspaper.

When either the language or spirit of the said communica-tion of correction or protest is in conflict with the law, or when the person demanding the publication of the said communication does not give his name and address, such communication need not be published.

XIV. Whenever, with respect to items taken from the *Official Gazette* or any other newspaper, a correction has been made or a communication of correction or protest has been published in the *Official Gazette*, or in some other newspaper, every newspaper shall make the correction according to the form prescribed in the foregoing Article, in its second or third issue after the receipt of the said newspaper, even if the party affected or any party concerned in the matter has not demanded it. The charge of advertisement cannot be demanded therefor.

XV. Whenever a newspaper has had a judgement pro-nounced against it on account of some matter published in one or other of its issues, it shall publish the sentence of the Court in full in its next issue.

XVI. No matters concerning the preliminary investigation of crimes or delicts shall be published before the public trial thereof has occurred.

No matters relating to law cases tried with closed doors shall be published.

XVII. No article perversely vindicating a criminal shall be published.

No writing the object of which is to defend or sympathise with a person or persons accused of a crime, or with an offender or offenders against criminal laws, shall be published.

XVIII. No official document which has not been made public, no memorial, representation, or petition shall be published, either in full or in an abridged form, without permission of the competent government office.

No deliberation in a government office, and no deliberation in a public assembly conducted with closed doors in compliance with the law, shall be published either in full or abridged form.

XIX. When the Minister of State for Home Affairs recognises that a newspaper is prejudicial to public peace and order, or is detrimental to morals, he may either suspend or prohibit the publication of the said newspaper.

XX. When the publication of a newspaper has been either prohibited or suspended, the Minister of State for Home Affairs may prohibit the sale or distribution of the said newspaper ; he may also seize it.

XXI. When a newspaper published in a foreign country is deemed to be prejudicial to public peace and order or detrimental to morals, the Minister of State for Home Affairs may prohibit the sale or distribution of the said newspaper within the territories of this empire ; he may also seize it.

XXII. The Minister of State for War or the Minister of State for the Navy may issue a special order prohibiting the publication of matters relating to the movements of troops or war vessels or to military or naval secrets.

XXIII. When a public prosecution has been instituted against a newspaper for a statement made therein, the public prosecutor may temporarily seize the said newspaper.

The Judge may, according to the nature of the offence, confiscate the seized copies of the newspaper in question.

XXIV. Whenever a suit has been instituted against a newspaper for a statement made therein, and the plaintiff has proved that the avowed editor of the said newspaper has not in fact the principal charge of the editorial departments, but that there is besides him a chief editor, the Judge shall hold both the avowed editor and the real editor equally responsible for the statement.

XXV. Whenever a suit for libel has been brought against a newspaper for a statement made therein, and the Court recognises that the statement has been made with no malicious intention to injure the person concerned, but for the sake of public interest, the Court may permit the defendent to prove the fact, except when the statement relates to personal matters. When the proof has been established, the newspaper shall be cleared of the charge of libel. The same shall also apply when a newspaper has been sued for damages.

XXVI. When a newspaper does not pay the full amount of the expenses or the fine to which it has been condemned, or does not pay the damages pronounced against it, within a week after the conclusion of the case, the security it has deposited shall be utilised for the purpose; and when the security is insufficient, the deficiency shall be exacted according to the provisions mentioned in the Criminal Code for the collection of the expenses of justice and of civil amends.

In case the security has been utilised for the expenses of the trial, for the damages or for the fine imposed, the publisher shall make up the deficiency within a week from the receipt of the notice to that effect from the local government authorities (from the Metropolitan Police Office, in Tōkyō). Should there be any failure to pay the full amount due, the chief of the Metropolitan Police Office or the Governor of the locality shall stop the publication of the newspaper in question until the said full amount shall have been paid.

XXVII. When the notice mentioned in Articles I., III., and IV. has not been sent in, or the provisions of Articles VI., VII., and XI. (first clause), and XII. have been violated, or when a newspaper for which security is required, has been published without the deposit of the security, the publisher shall be liable to a fine of not less than five *yen* and not more than one hundred *yen*. Any one convicted of the offence of the assumption of a false signature or title shall be liable to the same punishment as the publisher.

When truth is withheld in sending in the notices required in Articles I., III., and IV., the publisher shall be liable to minor imprisonment of not less than one month and not more than six months, or to a fine of not less than five *yen* and not more than one hundred *yen*.

When a newspaper belonging to the category mentioned in the last clause of Article VIII., publishes matters that ought properly to be contained in a newspaper for which security is required, the editor shall be liable to the same punishment as is set forth in the preceding clause.

XXVIII. In the case of the violation Articles XIII., XIV., and XV. the editor shall be liable to a fine of not less than five *yen* and not more than one hundred *yen*.

XXIX. In case of violation of Articles XVI., XVII., and XVIII. the editor shall be liable to minor imprisonment of not less than one month and not more than six months, or to a fine of not less than twenty *yen* and not more than two hundred *yen*.

XXX. Any person who sells or distributes a newspaper in violation of Article XXI. shall be liable to the same punishment as is set forth in the preceding Article.

XXXI. In case of the violation of Article XXII., the publisher and editor shall be liable to minor imprisonment for not less than one month or not more than two years, or to a fine of not less than twenty *yen* and not more than three hundred *yen*.

XXXII. When in a newspaper an article has been published the object of which is to undermine the existing system of government or to disturb the constitutional laws of the empire, the publisher, editor, and printer shall be liable to minor imprisonment of not less than two months and not more than two years, with a fine of not less than fifty *yen* and not more than three hundred *yen*.

In case of the violation of this Article the apparatus used for the purpose shall be confiscated.

XXXIII. When a newspaper of obscene character has been published, the publisher and editor thereof shall be liable to minor imprisonment of not less than one month and not more than six months, or to a fine not less than twenty *yen* and not more than two hundred *yen*.

XXXIV. In the case mentioned in Article XIII., the offence connected with personalities shall be brought to a settlement by the institution of a suit by the injured person.

XXXV. The provisions mentioned in the Criminal Code for the mitigation of penalties on account of voluntary confession, for the aggravation of penalties on account of repetition of the offence, and for the concurrence of several infractions committed by the same person, shall not be applied in cases of the violation of any of the provisions of the present Regulations.

XXXVI. The term of prescription for the institution of public prosecution in connection with the present regulations shall be six months.

XXXVII. The present regulations shall apply also to such magazines as do not come within the scope of the Publication Regulations.

J.W.M., 1888, Jan. 22, pp. 56-7.

9. PUBLICATION REGULATIONS.

(Imperial Ordinance No. 76, Dec. 28, 1887.)

I. By the term "publication" shall be understood the printing, by means of machinery, by the use of chemicals, or by any other process, and the sale or distribution, of literary works or pictures or drawings of whatsoever kind. The term "author" shall mean any person who has written or compiled a literary work or who has delineated anything by drawings or paintings. The term "publisher" shall apply to those engaged in the distribution or sale of literary works or of pictures or drawings of whatsoever kind. By the term "printer" shall be implied any person engaged in the practice of printing.

II. The present regulations shall apply to the publication of every kind of literary work and of pictures and drawings, with the exception of newspapers and magazines issued at fixed intervals. Such magazines, however, as are devoted to science and arts, may be brought within the scope of the present Regulations with the permission of the Minister of State for Home Affairs.

III. When a literary work or a picture or a drawing is issued, a notice of the same shall be sent to the Department of State for Home Affairs, together with three copies of the literary work, or picture or drawing, ten days previous to the day of publication thereof, leaving out of the calculation the number of days required for transmission.

IV. When a literary work or a picture or a drawing is issued by a government office, the said government office shall, previous to the publication of the same, send three copies thereof to the Department of State for Home Affairs.

V. The notice of publication shall be sent in with the seals of the author or his heir, and that of the publisher. But in the case of a publication not intended for sale, the notice may be sent in with the seal of the author only.

When the author or his heir cannot be ascertained, notice

thereof shall be sent in by the publisher, with a statement of the attendant circumstances.

When the literary work or a picture or drawing is issued under the authorship of a school, a company, an association or of any other like body, the notice of publication shall be sent in with the joint signatures and seals of the publisher and the person repesenting the school, company, or other like body.

VI. Only those who are engaged in the sale of literary works, pictures, or drawings shall be allowed to become publishers. But an author or his heir may at one and the same time become a publisher.

VII. When any person prints a literary work or a drawing or picture, he shall put thereon the date of printing together with his name and address, irrespective of whether the literary work or picture or drawing is intended for publication or not ; and when it is intended for publication the name and address of the publisher shall also be appended.

VIII. As to the rules of a company, the rules of a boarding-school, hand-bills, programs of performances, and note paper of all kinds for which there are common forms, or the various kinds of certificates, the provisions of Articles III. and IV. need not be followed.

IX. In case of literary works and of pictures and drawings which are issued in a series of succeeding numbers, the process mentioned in Article III. shall be gone through for each and every issue of the same. In the case of magazines, however, the said process shall be omitted with the permission of the Minister of State for Home Affairs.

X. No notice of the publication of a second edition of a literary work or of a picture or drawing, for which notice of publication has already been once given, is required. When, however, the original is remodelled, enlarged or reduced in scale, or when notes, an appendix, pictures, etc., are to be added to it, the provisions of Article III. shall be observed.

XI. When the reports of speeches or lectures are collected

and made into the form of a book, the deliverer of the speeches or lectures shall be looked upon as the author of the same. When, however, such reports have been published without the consent of the speaker or lecturer, the latter shall not be held responsible for authorship.

No reports of a lecture or speech not delivered in public, can be published unless the consent of the speaker or lecturer has been first obtained. Any person violating the provisions of this clause shall be held responsible for their act, according to the Copyright Regulations.

XII. When the writings of more than one person, or when the lectures or speeches of more than one orator have been compiled into one book, the compiler shall be looked upon as the author thereof.

The provisions mentioned in the latter portion of the first clause, and those mentioned in the second clause of the preceding Article shall also apply in the case of this Article.

XIII. In the case of translations the translator shall be looked upon as the author of the work. In the term "translation" shall be included the popularisation of Chinese writings.

XIV. In the case of a literary work or of a picture or drawing issued by a school, a company, an association, or any other like body, under its own authorship, the person in whose name the notice of publication has been sent in, shall be regarded as the author.

XV. No official document that has not been made public, no memorials, representations or petitions shall be published, either in full or in abridged form, without the permission of the competent government office.

No deliberation in a government office or in a public assembly conducted behind closed doors in agreement with the requirements of law shall be published either in full or in an abridged form.

XVI. When a literary work or a picture or a drawing which is recognised to be prejudicial to public peace and order or detrimental to morals, shall have been published, the Minister of State for Home Affairs may prohibit its sale or distribution, and may seize the plates and impressions thereof.

XVII. When a literary work or picture or drawing, printed in a foreign country, is deemed to be prejudicial to public peace and order, or detrimental to morals, the Minister of State for Home Affairs may prohibit the sale or distribution of the said work or picture or drawing, within the territory of this empire, and may seize the impressions thereof.

XVIII. The publishing of a literary work or picture or drawing, touching matters relating to military or naval secrets in prohibited.

XIX. No matter relating to the preliminary investigation of a crime or delict, shall be published before the public trial thereof.

XX. To publish discourses perversely vindictating a criminal is prohibited.

To publish writings the object of which is to sympathise with a person or persons accused of crimes, or with an offence or offenders against the Criminal Law is prohibited.

XXI. Any person who has published a literary work or a picture or a drawing without giving the notice mentioned in Article III. shall be punishable with a fine of not less than five *yen* and not more than one hundred *yen.*

XXII. When a publisher has published a literary work or a picture or a drawing, wherein neither his own name and address, nor those of the printer, nor the date of publication has been mentioned, the publisher shall be liable to a fine of not less than two and not more than fifty *yen.* When these particulars are not given truthfully, the publisher shall be liable to minor imprisonment of not less than one month and not more than six months, or to a fine of not less than five and not more than fifty *yen.*

Any infraction of Article VI. shall be punishable with the same penalty as is imposed in the preceding clause.

XXIII. The printer who has not inserted his name and address in a literary work, nor upon a picture or drawing printed by him, or who has not done so truthfully, shall be liable to the same penalty as in the case of the preceding Article.

XXIV. When a literary work, the tendency of which is to undermine the existing government or to disturb the constitutional laws of the empire, has been published, the author, publisher, and printer thereof shall be regarded as co-offenders, and shall be punished with minor imprisonment of not less than two months and not more than two years, together with a fine of not less than fifty *yen* and not more than three hundred *yen*.

In the case of a picture or drawing the intent of which is the same as is mentioned in the preceding clause, the penalty shall be the same as in the preceding clause.

XXV. When a literary work or a picture or a drawing of an obscene character has been published, the author and the publisher thereof shall be regarded as co-offenders, and shall be punished with minor imprisonment of not less than one month and not more than six months, or to a fine of not less than twenty and not more than two hundred *yen*.

XXVI. When the photograph of a literary work or of a picture or drawing has been taken, and Articles XVIII., XXIV., and XXV. have been violated, the punishment shall be meted out according to the respective Articles violated.

XXVII. When a literary work or a picture or drawing, the publication of which is prohibited by the present regulations, has been published, the author and the publisher shall be regarded as co-offenders, and shall be liable to minor imprisonment of not less than one month and not more than two years, or to a fine of not less than twenty and not more than three hundred *yen*.

When a literary work or a picture or drawing, the sale or distribution of which has been prohibited, has been published, the publisher and the agent concerned in the sale and distribution thereof shall be dealt with as in the case mentioned in the previous clause. Works or pictures or drawings not yet sold shall be confiscated.

XXVIII. In the case of Articles XXIV., XXV., and XXVII., the public prosecutor may provisionally seize the plates and impressions in question. The plates and impressions that have been seized shall be returned on the conclusion of the trial, if the accused is pronounced not guilty ; but if he is pronounced guilty they shall be confiscated.

XXIX. In carrying out the seizure mentioned in the previous Article, if the articles to be seized are bound, and if the style of binding is such that the portion to be seized can be separated form the rest it shall be so separated.

XXX. When Articles XXIV. or XXV. have been violated by the publication of reports or the compilation of speeches and lectures or by that of literary works or pictures or drawings compiled from the writings or drawings of one or various authors, the lecturer, speaker, author or authors in question, shall if he or they have consented to the said publication, be liable to the same punishment as the reporter or compiler of the same.

XXXI. When, in case a suit for libel has been brought against a publisher for the publication of a work or picture or drawing, the Court recognises that the publication in question has been made with no malicious intention to injure the person concerned, but for the sake of public interest, the Court may permit the defendant to prove the facts, except when the statement relates to personal matters. When the proof is established the publisher shall be cleared of the charge of libel. The same shall apply when the publisher shall have been sued for damages.

XXXII. The provisions mentioned in the Criminal Code for the mitigation of penalties on account of voluntary confession, for the aggravation of penalties on account of repetition of the offence, and for the concurrence of several infractions committed by the same person, shall not be applied in the case of the violation of any of the provisions of these regulations.

XXXIII. The period of prescription for the prosecution of offences against the present regulations shall be two years, and shall be computed from the last time that the literary work or the picture or drawing was sold or distributed. When no copies of the work or drawing or picture have been sold or distributed, the computation shall be made from the time of the printing thereof.

XXXIV. Those literary works and pictures and drawings which, though already printed, have not been sold or distributed, shall also come within the scope of the present regulations, if they are intended for sale or distribution.

J.M.W., 1888, Jan. 21, pp. 57-58.

5.—COMMUTATION OF PENSIONS OF NOBLES AND SAMURAI.

1. SAMURAI MAY ENTER THE OCCUPATIONS OF COMMON PEOPLE.

(Notif. No. 425, Dec. 27, 1873.)

A proclamation[1] was issued in the 12th month of the 4th year of Meiji, that nobles (kwazoku), gentlemen (samurai) and foot-soldiers (sotsu), those in official employment excepted, were henceforth permitted to carry on the callings of husbandmen, artisans and merchants, but as it has come to our ears that persons with small incomes are unable to accomplish their wishes, owing probably to the want of the necessary capital, we have

---

1. The last months of the year 1871 witnessed the promulgation of a number of notifications dealing with the privileges and duties of the feudal aristocracy. Among other things permission was given to leave off wearing two swords, and to enter into gainful occupations as farmers, artisans or traders. These privileges were availed of in some localities but not in others, and as there was no compulsion to make any changes the more conservative minded of the aristocracy retained their old ways.

framed the annexed scheme [1] for their special benefit, by which the surrender to the goverment of their family incomes and good service pensions, less than 100 koku in annual amount, is allowed. Those, therefore, who wish to surrender them must make a petition to that effect to their local governments. You [2] will make this proclamation known to the samurai and former sotsu. NOTE :—Those who make a petition according to the text need not pay any tax [3] on their incomes.

I.W.M., 1874, p. 24.

2. REGULATIONS FOR THE COMMUTATION OF INCOMES, ETC.

(Notif. No. 426, Dec. 27, 1873.)

Whereas it has been proclaimed that the petitions of persons of the rank of gentlemen and sotsu, whose family incomes are less than 100 koku of annual value, to give up their incomes to the government, shall be granted, they must comply with the annexed regulations and each case shall be dealt with accordingly. This information is communicated.

REGULATIONS FOR GIVING CAPITAL TO PERSONS WHO GIVE UP THEIR INCOMES TO THE GOVERNMENT.

I. To persons whose family incomes and good service pensions do not amount to 100 koku, who henceforth petition to

---

1. The present notification offered an inducement to the samurai to m rge themselves in the ranks of the common people, by furnishing them with cash to be used as capital with which to enter business or buy land. The purpose of the government in making this offer was in part to relieve itself of the burden of the pension list and in part to abolish the samurai caste.

2. The Governors of the fu and ken to whom the present notification was addressed.

3. As a further inducement to the success of the scheme it was proposed by the government to levy taxes on all ordinary pensions, and exempt from such taxes the incomes of those samurai who surrendered their pensions to the government, and received in lieu thereof interest-bearing government bonds. The Regulations for the taxation of ordinary pensions were promulagated by Notification No. 424, on the same day as the present notification.

surrender them, the sum of six years' income is given to those who hold hereditary incomes, and the sum of four years' income is given to those who hold incomes during life, to serve as capital for trade.

II. The whole amount mentioned in the preceding Article shall be turned into money according to the market price of rice when the taxes are paid this year in each fu and ken. Half shall be paid in cash, and half in government bonds. Eight per cent shall be paid on these government bonds in the 11th month of each year by the local authorities.

NOTE :—As five classes of government bonds have been made, viz., 500, 300, 100, 50 and 25 *yen*, according to the sum, the difference between it and any of those classes must be added to or substracted from it.

III. Persons can if they wish sell or mortgage these bonds to anyone but foreigners. The mode of transaction is the same as if they had been newly issued by the government. The details of this will form another proclamation.

IV. After the third year of issue these bonds shall be exchanged into ready money at the convenience of the government during the space of seven years.

V. When "one-life" sotsu, whose names have been already entered on the register of husbandmen, and who are entitled to incomes for their life-time, request to give them up, permission shall be given in accordance with the previous Article.

VI. If persons whose incomes are limited to a certain number of years petition to give them up, the periods for which they have already been paid and have still to be paid shall be ascertained and specially referred by the local government to the Ōkurashō.

VII. Persons who have changed their domiciles shall apply to their original local government from which they have up to this time received their incomes.

VIII. The cases of those who wish to pursue the calling of husbandmen or graziers shall be dealt with according to the

Regulations for selling those portions of government forests, paddy, arable land, waste-land, etc., which are not wanted for government purposes.

Rules for Selling Waste Land and Government Forests to Provide Capitals for (those wishing to Pursue) any Calling.

I. Paddy-land, arable land, castle-grounds, the sites of old yashiki, waste-lands, hills, forests, etc., belonging to the Crown, the sale of which does not inconvenience the original villages, or associated villages or the government, shall be made over to such persons as after surrendering their family incomes and receiving capital, shall petition for the sale of the same with the object of undertaking farming or grazing, at half the fair price ; and they must send in to their local government up to the thirtieth day of the following sixth month sealed applications according to the form in the appendix.

Persons desirous of obtaining land under a local government other than their own, must apply through their original local government to the government of the district in which they desire to buy land, within the above named fixed period. Persons who apply after the expiration of that period shall purchase land by sending in tenders.

Note.—Lands which are for sale shall be sold at half the real price ; houses and trees on them shall be sold at their market value.

II. A day being fixed for opening the tenders for land which persons petition the government to sell, the petitioners assemble and after the tenders have been opened the first, second and third degrees of tenders shall be forwarded to the Ōkura-shō. When two or more persons tender the same price they shall have their tenders accepted according to the date on which they sent them in.

III. Upon permission being given to sell land the local government shall give orders for payment to be made and shall give a title-deed for the land—on the face of the deed the market value is written. After the time fixed for bringing the ground under cultivation has passed and a tax is levied the deed shall be revised.

IV. With respect to the limit to the number of tsubo sold to each person, since that depends on whether the number of petitioners be great or small, and whether the land to be sold is extensive or not, the local authorities shall exercise their judgment and report to the Ōkurashō.

NOTE.—(Allotments of) paddy and arable land, also land formerly occupied by castles or yashiki, shall be restricted to three thousand tsubos and under ; waste-land to nine thousand tsubos and under ; mountain forest land to fifteen thousand and under ; fifteen hundred tsubos of paddy and arable land and seven thousand five hundred of mountain forest land may be sold together. Moreover there is no restriction made in the case of extensive districts in Mutsu and Dewa, and in distant parts of all the provinces, but the extent shall be ascertained and reported according to the above regulation.

V. When the government considers that the price offered for the land is not the market price of it, the sale shall be prohibited.

VI. The price of land, houses, and trees shall be paid in one sum.

VII. Cultivated portions of paddy and arable land shall pay taxes as heretofore. The amount of the taxes to be paid on the land on which taxes have not been previously fixed shall be settled by comparison with that paid on neighboring land. Land with title-deeds shall pay 3% land-tax. Land subject to the old regulations shall pay the old tax of rice and money.

VIII. Land occupied formerly by castles and yashiki shall be free of taxes for ten years in order to have it worked ; waste-land for fifteen ; portions of mountain forest land for twenty years.

The amount of the tax to be paid on land where forests

and trees are left .in their original state shall be ascertained by comparison with the neighboring land.

IX. Land which is sold by the government is not trans·ferrable during the years it is under cultivation, and mortgaging it shall be strictly forbidden.

NOTE.—If the proprietor during a long illness cannot get any of his relations to help him, or if persons have unavoidable reasons (for not cultivating the ground) they may inform the local government of all the particulars and obey any orders.

X. Persons who petition the Government to sell land and lend their names to others, or those who make false statements as to the number of trees and do other wrong acts, if these things come to light after the sale, even though they are cultivating the ground and even have completed the cultivation of it, shall have the said land taken from them and the owner and his associates shall receive condign punishment. If the said land has been sold the same punishment shall be decreed.

J.W.M., 1874, pp.24-25.

3. CAPITALISATION OF INCOMES.

(Imp. Notif. No. 108, Aug. 5, 1876.)

Incomes, and augmentations of income (by way of reward) have hitherto been granted either in perpetuity, or for one generation, or for a certain term of years. These rules are now altered,[1] and such incomes will, from next year, be commuted

---

1. The alterations consisted not only in changes in the details of the regulations, but what was far more important, in the transformation of the previous permissive rules into compulsory regulations. Whereas the former law offered a privilege, this imposed upon the samurai and nobility the necessity of commuting their pensions for bonds at certain rates specifically indicated. The effect of this law was instantaneous and manifested itself in an epidemic of samurai riots and lawless demonstrations against the government. What effect it had in bringing to a head the rebellion in Satsuma is uncertain, but the safe presumpt-

and paid in government bonds according to the annexed regulations.[1]

REGULATIONS FOR THE ISSUE OF GOVERNMENT BONDS FOR INCOMES.

I. The rules relating to the payment of the incomes, or
augmentations of income, of kwazoku, shizoku, and heimin are
now altered, and such incomes will be commuted and paid in
government bonds in the following manner.

INCOMES IN PERPETUITY.

Incomes in perpetuity will be commuted according to the
following scale :—

Original assessment of income, including augmentation also, if such exist.				Number of years allowed.		
70,000 *yen* and upwards.				5 years income.		
Above 60,000 *yen* but below			70,000	$5\frac{1}{4}$	,,	,,
,,	50,000	,,	,,	60,000	$5\frac{1}{2}$	,,	,,
,,	40,000	,,	,,	50,000	$5\frac{3}{4}$	,,	,,
,,	30,000	,,	,,	40,000	6	,,	,,
,,	20,000	,,	,,	30,000	$6\frac{1}{4}$	,,	,,
,,	10,000	,,	,,	20,000	$6\frac{1}{2}$	,,	,,
,,	7,000	,,	,,	10,000	$6\frac{3}{4}$	,,	,,
,,	5,000	,,	,,	7,000	7	,,	,,
,,	2,000	,,	,,	5,000	$7\frac{1}{4}$	,,	,,
,,	1,000	,,	,,	2,000	$7\frac{1}{2}$	,,	,,

ion is that its influence on that event was not slight. On the other hand there is
no doubt but that this measure was popular with the great mass of the people, and
that it was justified in view of the financial condition of the country, for the payment of the pensions constituted the largest item in the expenditures of the
government, and was a serious drain upon the national treasury.

1. On the 11th December, 1876 further changes were made in the regulations by the following notification :—Hereditary incomes or service pensions
which, since the time of the constitution of the han have been permitted to be
sold and purchased, shall, irrespective of their amount, be exchanged by the
government for bonds for ten years' purchase of the amount of such income or
pensions.—*J. W. M.*, 1876, Dec. 23, 1160.

Interest will be paid on the above (commutation) at the rate of 5% per annum.

Above	900 *yen* but below		1,000	$7\frac{3}{4}$ years income.	
,,	800 ,,	,,	900	8	,, ,,
,,	700 ,,	,,	800	$8\frac{1}{4}$	,, ,,
,,	600 ,,	,,	700	$8\frac{1}{2}$	,, ,,
,,	500 ,,	,,	600	$8\frac{3}{4}$	,, ,,
,,	450 ,,	,,	500	9	,, ,,
,,	400 ,,	,,	450	$9\frac{1}{4}$	,, ,,
,,	350 ,,	,,	400	$9\frac{1}{2}$	,, ,,
,,	300 ,,	,,	350	$9\frac{3}{4}$	,, ,,
,,	250 ,,	,,	300	10	,, ,,
,,	200 ,,	,,	250	$10\frac{1}{4}$	,, ,.
,,	150 ,,	,,	200	$10\frac{1}{2}$	,, ,,
,,	100 ,,	,,	150	11	,, ,,

Interest will be paid on the above at the rate of 6% per annum.

Above	75 *yen* but below		100	$11\frac{1}{2}$ years income.	
,,	50 ,,	,,	75	12	,, ,,
,,	40 ,,	,,	50	$12\frac{1}{2}$	,, ,,
,,	30 ,,	,,	40	13	,, ,,
,,	25 ,,	,,	30	$13\frac{1}{2}$	,, ,,
Below	25 *yen*			14	,, ,,

Interest will be paid on the above at the rate of 7% per annum.

LIFE INCOMES.

Persons holding life incomes will receive allowances calculated at the rate of one-half of the number of years allowed for incomes in perpetuity.

NOTE—Interest on these will be the same as in the case of the incomes in perpetuity.

INCOMES FOR LIMITED TERMS.

Persons holding incomes for a certain term of years will receive as follows :—

Proportion of term allowed
for incomes in perpetuity.

For 10 years and upwards .... $\frac{2}{5}$

For from 8 to 10 years .... $\frac{7}{20}$

  ,,   ,, 6 ,, 8 ,, ... $\frac{3}{10}$

  ,,   ,, 4 ,, 6 ,, ... $\frac{1}{4}$

  ,,   ,, 3 ,, 4 ,, ... $\frac{1}{5}$

For 2 years only.................... $\frac{3}{20}$

NOTE—Interest on these will be the same as in the case of the incomes in perpetuity.

II. The interest due upon these government bonds will be paid, for the year 1877, in November of that year and May of the following year. The same rule will be followed in all subsequent years.

III. Should any difference be caused in the amount of the interest, owing to the term of years for which the original assessment of the income and augmentation of income is paid, the following rules shall be observed for issuing the government bonds, in view of such original assessment :—

Take for instance :—

A.—Total amount of income and augmentation ... 10,000 *yen*

Then, $6\frac{1}{2}$ years allowance of this .... 65,000 ,,

Interest on government bonds for same, at the

    rate of 5 per cent. per annum .... $=$ 3,250 ,,

B.—Total amount of income and augmentation ... 9,900 ,,

Then, $6\frac{3}{4}$ years allowance of this .... 66,825 ,,

Interest on government bonds for same, at the

    rate of 5 per cent. per annum .... $=$ 3,341 *yen* 25 *sen*

It will be seen, on comparison of the above, that the interest due on the sum of 9,900 *yen* would be 91 *yen* 25 *sen* in excess of the other. In such case, the rule observed shall be that the amount of interest shall not exceed the amount of that due upon the 10,000 *yen*. All other similar cases to be decided in the same manner.

IV. Although there may, on account of the rates of interest, be some difference between the government bonds, the several issues of those bonds shall always be for the following amounts ; viz.—for 5, 10, 25, 50, 100, 300, 500, 1,000, or 5,000 *yen* each.

V. At the time of the issue of the foregoing government bonds any petty sums over and above the amount of the bonds shall be paid in currency.

VI. The original sums for which these government bonds are issued shall be allowed to stand over for a period of 5 years. Commencing from the 6th year, however, they shall, according to the convenience of the Finance Department, be redeemed every year by lot. Within the space of 30 years, the whole of them will have been redeemed.

VII. In all matters relating to the procedure, etc., to be followed in respect to the issue of these government bonds, such not being mentioned in these regulations, care must be taken to act in accordance with the regulations for the Issue of Old and New Government Bonds.

J.W.M., 1876, p. 735·36.

APPENDIX.

1. DISCOURSE OF KIDO TAKAYOSHI[1] UPON HIS RETURN TO JAPAN, 1873.

I, Takayoshi, have always been filled with fear at the thought that I, an unlearned man and of inferior capacity, have presumed to take a share in the conduct of affairs, and I am sensible that I have in many ways failed to discharge aright the diplomatic duties imposed upon me by my late appointment as Envoy to the states of Europe and America. I have not succeeded in fulfilling the charge contained in the full powers given me by my government, nor, on the other hand, have I been able to satisfy the expectations of the people. For this I deserve no small blame.

In the course of my travels, however, while observing the forms of government and the civilisations of the various countries, I have noted the causes of the modifications which they have undergone, and taking into account the points of resem-

---

1. Although Kido died in 1877, it is even now impossible to write a complete record of his services to the country during and after the Restoration. He never held as conspicuous offices as some of the other members of the clan to which he belonged, and his term of service as a member of the Government was short; for these and other reasons he is not as well known to the world as many of his associates. As Saigo was the arm and sword of the Restoration, Kido was its brain and pen. He knew well that every national movement must arise out of the ideas and principles of the time, and it fell to him to formulate the philosophy of the Restoration, as it did to Saigo to lead its armed forces. Each man was preëminent in his sphere. However, Kido was not as available politically as Ito, Inouye, or Yamagata, his fellow clansmen, or Okubo or Okuma, of Satsuma and Hizen, hence, when differences of principle arose in the little group of leaders, he withdrew, in 1874, from active participation in the administration. Although he continued to serve in the capacity of Court Councillor till his death, and though opposed to the precipitate measures which gradually con-

blance and difference which are owing to likeness or unlikeness of national customs and character, I went on to mark the analogies with the condition of our country before and after the revolution and maturely to weigh the advantages and disadvantages of the measures by which these modifications have been brought about.   This inquiry has convinced me that the history of all countries, great or small, enlightened or unenlightened, proves that the inquiry into the causes of their conservation or downfall resolves itself into the question of the state of vigour or decay, and the merits or faults, of their laws and constitutions. No matter how extensive their territory may be or how numerous their subjeçts, if a due control is not exercised over them by means of the laws and constitution, one man will basely follow his own selfish ends, while another will presumptuously turn right to wrong and so the government will swarm with parasites and place-hunters.   In such a case although an outward semblance of prosperity, power, and enlightenment may be maintained, the foundations of the country have been impaired and the evil will finally become past remedy.

The Chinese saying, " We have before us the example of the Sho dynasty," may be applied to the downfall of the country of Poland, in Europe: When it was free and independent,

---

verted a popular into an odious administration, he was unable to stem the tide of change which followed so swiftly after 1873.   He resisted with all his might not only the project of invading Korea, but also the despatch of that costly and indefensible raid, the expedition against Formosa.   The spoliation of the samurai in 1876 by the enforced capitalisation of their pensions outraged his sense of justice, and it was commonly said that his indignation was deep and strong against the criminal blundering that forced on the struggle with the Saigo in 1877.

The document here printed is not only intrinsically valuable as an exposition of those liberal principles which were immediately taken up by Itagaki, Soyejima, and many others, and made the basis of an agitation which must be regarded as among the finest incidents of the period, but when compared with an earlier expression of his philosophy, contained in the address of the four Western Lords (see above pp. 29-32), a document which is commonly attributed to him, it displays the astonishing development of his views.

Poland had a wide territory and a large population. It was not that her kings were tyrants or her officials corrupt ; the tendencies of the age brought on changes which rendered it impossible for the constitution of her government to maintain its integrity. One was thoroughly convinced of his own wisdom and styled himself a sage, another, relying on himself, assumed to be a clever man, and each refused to be guided by the other. The nobles and rich, some bent on selfish gain, others turning right into wrong, by their strife and jarring reduced the country to a state bordering on anarchy. The distress to which the people were brought was too painful to describe ; what wonder that there was no one who did not look around him for some means of preventing himself from starving ! The whole country, therefore, rose in tumult and wreaked its vengeance on the rich and noble, and the disorder spread as far as the neighbouring countries of Russia, Prussia, and Austria, so that at last there was hardly one of the people who remained peaceably pursuing his own occupation. The three countries could no longer stand by unconcerned. They assembled an army, and having chastised the remaining robbers, divided the country into three parts, each uniting one to its own territory. Whom can the people of the ruined country blame for this, or whom can they hate ! The essence of independence their country never had, nor did they themselves ever enjoy any original rights as citizens. When I was travelling in a railway carriage from Prussia to Russia, one morning at dawn my dreams were suddenly broken by the melancholy notes of a flute. I got up and opened the window. I was in Poland, and the flute player was a poor native who was begging copper coins from the passengers. This incident carried my mind back to the days of Poland's greatness, and it was long before I was able to restrain my tears. Alas ! what country can escape the same fate if it does not maintain its constitution and preserve the integrity of its laws. As the turning point between prosperity and decay, between safety and destruction, is so critical, I felt compelled to note down this example so as to submit it for the opinion of my enlightened readers.

A single rod, even though a stout one, may be broken by a young child, but if ten rods, though weak ones, are made into a bundle, they cannot be broken by a full grown man. They will even maintain a weight of a thousand pounds without breaking.

In the same manner, if a country is divided among a multitude of petty rulers, each one having full authority in his own district, the lines of policy are multiplied, inasmuch as each prince will seek his own advantage and devise schemes for his own gain. Under such a system the national strength is dissipated, and although the fellow rulers may know each other's relative strength, how will they stand in comparison with foreign nations? How could they ever withstand a powerful enemy whose forces were harmoniously united? But if, on the contrary, one sovereign can exercise control over the numberless petty rulers if he maintains one national line of policy and balances the gains of one province with the losses of another,—if he thus exercises supreme control,—though his territory may not be large or his people numerous, they will be able to protect themselves against the insults of their neighbours. This is a principle founded in nature, and is nowadays a commonplace with the powerful nations of the five continents.

Not many years ago our own country passed through a revolution which was demanded by the altered tendencies of the age, and during it multitudes of the people were deprived of their occupations and fell into great distress. We have also had to lament the campaigns of Kyōto and the North, when Japan was forced, as it were, to sit in dust and ashes. I give as an example the misfortunes which befell one family. The father sacrificed his life for his country at the castle of Kyōto, while his son discharged the debt of gratitude he owed his lord by laying down his life on some battle-field in the North. Even yet, when I recall to mind those days, a cold sweat breaks out

over me. But the misfortunes of one family were mere private
griefs : the crisis in the State was a public matter and demanded
our most serious concern. It was no time for indulgence in
private sorrow. The whole nation spared neither pains nor
labour, and so it became at last possible to lay the first foundations of our constitution. It thereupon followed that in reforming the old system of rule there were none of those things which
catch the eyes and ears of the people which were not changed
from their ancient customary form. In some this engendered
suspicion, other tried to stand aloof, and it almost seemed as if
there was no one who knew whither the Imperial purpose really
tended. But how could it be supposed that these measures of
the Government proceeded from a mere idle pleasure in changing the old system of rule ? The truth was there was no change
made which had not become unavoidable, chiefly owing to the
internal condition of the country, but also, though in a less
degree, to our relations with foreign countries. The object of
them was to promote the wealth and power of the nation, to
spread enlightenment, and to secure to every one a peaceful life
in his own sphere.

Hence it was thought advisable, so early as the spring of
1868 when the northern provinces were still unsubdued, to summon together at the castle of Kyōto all the officials and nobles
of the Empire. The Emperor then prayed to the gods of
Heaven and Earth and pronounced an Oath containing five
clauses, which was thereupon published throughout the Empire,
removing all doubts as to the objects the Emperor had in view,
and guiding the ideas of the people in one fixed direction. The
heading of this Oath contains the following expression :—" By
this oath we set up as our aim the establishment of the national
weal on a broad basis and the framing of a constitution and
laws." This led at last to granting the petitions for leave to
restore the fiefs to the Emperor, which occasioned the abolition
of the daimyō and the concentration of the dissipated national
strength. Is not all this consonant with that commonplace

argument of the powerful countries of the five great continents? And if this be so, then surely we must consider those five clauses as the foundation of our constitution. Now the constitution is a thing which sets on a firm basis the weal of the entire nation, which prevents officials from taking unauthorised steps merely on their own judgment, and which by placing under one control all the business of administration, renders it necessary that all measures be conformable to it. Is there at the present day any subject of the Empire who does not gratefully acknowledge its profound and farsighted policy and admire the soundness of the Emperor's views.

But in enlightened countries, though there may be a sovereign, still he does not hold sway in an arbitrary fashion. The people of the whole country give expression to their united and harmonious wishes, and the business of the State is arranged accordingly, a department (styled the government) being charged with the execution of their judgments, and officials appointed to transact business. For this reason all who hold office are faithful to the wishes of the whole nation and serve their country under a deep sense of responsibility, so that even in extraordinary crises, they take no arbitrary step which is unauthorised by the unanimous consent of the nation. The strictness of the constitution of these governments is such as I have just described, but as an additional check upon illegal acts, the people have officers for discussion (members of parliament) whose duty is to sift everything that is done and to check arbitrary proceedings on the part of officials. In this way a very admirable form of government is produced. But if the people are still insufficiently enlightened, it becomes necessary, at least for a time, that the Sovereign should by his superior discernment anticipate their unanimous wishes and act for them in arranging the affairs of State and in entrusting to officials the execution of their wishes. By this means he will gradually lead them forward in the path of enlightenment. Such a course is consonant with natural principles, and I am inclined to believe that upon this idea was founded the thought of the Emperor when he inaugurated by an oath his energetic policy. My belief is that although Japan has not yet reached that stage where everything is submitted for the sanction of a parliament, in the weight which the Imperial command bears with it and the importance of the business transacted, our country differs not a whit from those countries of Europe and America whose government is carried on on the principle of executing the wishes of the people, and it is important that our officials should not be forgetful of their responsibility and should keep constantly before their eyes our five-clause Constitution.

The Constitution is the mind of the State ; the officials are the members.[1] If, when the mind issues its commands, the members act in a contrary direction, or without waiting for the mind's orders, the affairs of the whole country must fall into confusion and the whole nation feel ill as ease. The final results of such a state of things it would be hard to foresee. If such were to be the lot of our own country the vigorous policy inaugurated on a former day would stop short with the mere idle abolition of the former system of government, and the pains and labour of the people would have been spent to no purpose and vanish like foam on the surface of water. To talk of the affairs of the empire is easy ; to put one's ideas into practice is hard. Let us then, while it is still open to us to do so, keep strict watch over all our proceedings.

Whilst pondering on the Emperor's words on the occasion referred to, the following thoughts occurred to me. What reason could there be for making the entire empire the private possession of a single family ? The Emperor dwells in it, along with his people he defends it, and of all the parts of the administration there is not one which does not affect them. The sub-

1. *Note by the author.*—It is a common saying in Europe that " the Constitution is the the mind and the the officials the members." Another version is "the people are the mind and the officials the members." But as the Constitution proceeds from the unanimous wishes of the people, the principle of the two maxims is the same, although their language is different.

iects ought, on the other hand, each to have his full rights and bear his due share of the public burdens. During my visit to France, a learned gentleman of that nation named Brook (*sic*) said to me, "The people of France cannot compare with the people of England, and this is deeply to be lamented. The reason is that, generally speaking, there is no Englishman who does not enjoy to the full the rights given by his government, whilst not only are the French deprived of more than half their legal rights, but many of them are eager wrongfully to seize privileges never granted them. This has been the sure cause of the frequent revolutions which have kept our country in a state of weakness. This state of things is truly lamentable." These words sent a thrill through me and filled me with shame. Every citizen's object in life is to maintain all his rights and so preserve his natural liberty, and to assist in carrying on the government by bearing his part of the national burden ; and therefore they (i.e., the rights and burdens) are specified exactly in writing and men bind themselves by a solemn promise to permit no infringement of them, but to act as mutual checks on each other in maintaining them. These writings are what we call laws. The laws are the offspring of the constitution, for the constitution is the root of every part of the system of government, and there is none which does not take its rise from this. And this is the reason why every country, when the time comes for changing its constitution, bestows on it the greatest care and the ripest consideration and ascertains to the full the general wishes. No new measures are put in force lightly or hastily or if they are not imperatively called for by the circumstances. In the case of a country where the sovereign goes to meet the wishes of the people, the greatest care must be taken to conjecture them with accuracy, the internal condition of the country must be profoundly studied and a wide view taken of the national industries. Then comes the most important point of all, and that is to suit the measures to the degree of civilisation of the people.

Again, in ordering the affairs of a nation, its strength must be taken into account. If not, one good will be converted into a hundred evils. The poor man's son who tries to rival the son of the rich ;man ruins his property and his house, and in the end does not make a show equal to his rival. Those who order the affairs of a nation should remember, before taking action, to consider the due sequence of measures, and should proceed by gradual steps in nourishing its strength, for no nation ever attained to a perfect state of civilisation in a single morning.

Every country in the world has inhabitants of some sort, and, putting aside its condition as civilised or barbarous, some of the people are wise and others foolish, some are rich and other poor. Those who are wise and able and competent to conduct affairs find their way to offices of state, while the wealthy preside over industry and give employment to the poor ; all this is nothing more than the natural order of things everywhere. But as the return of one swallow does not allow us to say that spring has everywhere commenced, and it is not till the mists extend their veil and the hundred flowers are seen rivalling each other in beauty that we can praise spring's gentle warmth ; so in spite of the appearance of one or two able men or of a few opulent men, all the rest of the nation may still remain buried in poverty, ignorance and degradation. Such a country it would be premature to class with prosperous and enlightened states.

When I consider the results of the measures of the past few years with reference to the present condition of our country it appears to me that the tendencies of the period are still wanting in directness. The people's minds are perversely turned in one direction, and instead of exercising their rights, many of them mimic idly the arts of civilisation ; instead of discharging their responsibilities to the state, they are much given to ill-judged pretensions to enlightenment. The consequence is that although they are gradually acquiring more elegance in externals and the old rustic coarseness is becoming abolished by degrees, they find it hard all at once to become enlightened in their hearts.

Another evil is that the laws are promulgated without due consideration. What was thought right yesterday is condemned to-day, and before one measure comes into operation it is followed by another. The people must certainly find it hard to put up with this. The business of government is multifarious; there is no limit to progress, and the important matters of the nation must follow the advance of civilisation. The government ought not therefore to reason as if the position of affairs was now the same as it was in 1868. If those who hold the reins of government were now to guide themselves by those five clauses as the whole constitution, they would be at a loss as often as a decision had to be taken on any unusual matter, and they would probably fail to satisfy the wishes of the people. Our most urgent duty at present is to avoid future difficulties by giving effect to the August Command, adding to the five clauses others founded upon them, and establishing laws. It is also essential to nourish the people and to enable them quietly to raise themselves from their present state of degradation, having done which the day of great results for the nation may calmly be awaited. When once the condition of the people has been improved it will then be the occasion for statesmen to devote themselves to their country's service, for if they do so they will lay in a rich store of blessings for the future. But if the day of great results is not calmly awaited, if one or two clever men, seeking their own personal aggrandizement alone and regardless of the wishes of the people, should, with the hope of gaining a reputation as successful statesmen, cause a leading department to monopolise all the powers of government, and attempt to imitate the example of civilised countries in every detail of the administration, without due consideration, the progress of the country will become involved in difficulties and its position as precarious as that of a pile of eggs. I fear that in such a case I, and such as I, would feel deeply the responsibilities of another time.

I have now given my reasons for thinking that our most urgent need at present is to establish the constitution and the laws. I have been told that the ancient Romans had a saying "Wherever there is a people, there are laws." By this, it may be seen that a constitution and laws are indispensable things.

In the midst of all that I saw and experienced during my travels in Europe and America, my deep reflections on the past stirred up in my own mind apprehensions for the future. These views I have felt unable to restrain from uttering, and I therefore put them before you, my readers, that you may examine and pass judgment upon them.

J. W. M., 1873, Nov. 8, pp. 796-98.

2. THE HISTORY OF THE JAPANESE PARLIAMENT.

(By Fukuzawa Yukichi.)

The Constitution of the Japanese empire was only promulgated on 11th February, 1889, by His Majesty the Emperor. We have not yet been able to peruse calmly all the seventy-six articles of which the Constitution consists, chiefly because we have as yet barely recovered from the excitement aroused by the ceremony of its promulgation, excitement which is not surprising at all if we remember the stupendous change which has been ushered in. When we recollect that throughout the world such events have hitherto owed their origin to popular discontent and clamour, and that in too many cases Parliaments are little more than evidences of internal dissension, it is matter for the highest congratulation that our Constitution has been promulgated and a Parliament provided under the most auspicious circumstances of a tranquil and prosperous reign. Surely in this happy consummation we see portrayed the merits and virtues of our venerable and sacred court, which has become endeared to the hearts of the people. In unison with forty millions of our fellow-countrymen we pray that the Imperial House may last for ever, and that our Emperor may long occupy the throne of

his august forefathers. It is not our intention to comment upon
or criticize the Constitution at present ; we shall rather devote
ourselves to the duty of recording such incidents in the life of
the nation during the last thirty years as may serve to convey
to future generations of Japanese or to foreigners unacquainted
with the circumstances, some idea of the events which led to
this great work. Various comments have been made by
numerous politicians upon the Constitution ; some hold that its
provisions are too liberal ; others that they are too severe. To
us, however, any discussion on these points seems to be useless,
for the measure is so novel and strange that we can form
no conception of its efficiency or otherwise till we see it in actual
operation.

The government of this country, during the historic period,
has been absolute—known by different names it is true, but still
absolute all the time. Indeed, in not very ancient times the
people had not even dreamt of a constitutional system, and no
ideographs for the expression of that idea existed. Had any
one spoken of the possibility of the nation being permitted to
take part in the government of the country by means of a Parliament, and of the reins of administration being transferable
according to the views of political parties, his suggestions to the
people, imperfectly understood as they were, would have been
received with horror. For the law strictly forbade more than
three persons to meet together and talk about politics, and men
would have recoiled from the idea of combining to contest
supremacy in the councils of the empire. It is truly wonderful
that from this absolute system of government we should receive
the gift of popular representation.

In the West parliamentary institutions have been called
into being by the advancing requirements of the times. As the
people grew in knowledge, and consequently in power, despotic
government showed features alike distasteful to men's sense of
freedom and opposed to their rights, and thenceforth the admission of the important factor, public opinion, to a share in

government became a foregone conclusion. In the Japan of to-day, however, a widely different state of affairs exists. The general mass of the nation is indifferent to political power, and ignorant of its value ; people mostly occupy themselves with their own personal affairs and are well content, no matter whose hands hold the reins of rule, if only their burdens are lessened and their condition ameliorated. The rivalry which in the West leads people to compete for power, is due simply to the high value they place upon their personal rights ; in this country, owing to the peculiar customs which have for so long existed, we are not at all sensitive about our privileges and our rights. From this indifference arises the fact that, as compared with Western nations, the Japanese are not so strongly moved by sentiments of self-respect and self-assertion. It is enough that an order should issue from the government ; it is at once submissively obeyed, even though it may be inconsistent with reason. We need not say that personal rights are before political rights in importance ; that is a fact which is beyond discussion, for the former must be recognised and established on a sound and solid basis before the latter can come into existence. Nevertheless the Japanese people have not yet recognised or appreciated the value of their personal rights ; how, then, can they understand their political rights ? We, therefore, assert without fear of contradiction that the nation generally has not yet manifested any desire to take part in politics, or at any rate if such a wish has been expressed, it has not been so formulated as a result of mature deliberation on the subject.

The idea of opening a Parliament in Japan is not, strictly speaking, of recent origin. In 1874[1] Messrs. Gōtō, Itagaki, and Soejima, now Counts Gōtō, Itagaki and Soejima, and Mr., now Viscount Yuri, jointly submitted to the government their views as to the establishment of a House of Representatives. In 1878 many leading and influential men from the provinces arrived in the capital, as delegates of politicians in the different

1. *Supra* pp. 426-33.

districts, to present to the government memorials also urging that the Parliament should be inaugurated. To a superficial observer it might have seemed at that time that the movement which those delegates represented was widespread and general, but as a matter of fact their petitions did not express the views of the people in general, and the agitation of which they were the mouth-pieces was not by any means universal. The Government treated the movement with a good deal of indifference and in time it gradually subsided. The memorials were not supported by any general expression of public opinion, and were simply allowed to lie on the table. In short this display of enthusiasm was confined to a very limited circle, being merely a piece of strategy wrought by various sections of the then unemployed shizoku class. The fact indeed that many of those who were foremost in the agitation for a House of Representatives afterwards availed themselves readily of any opportunity to obtain government posts, would sufficiently indicate that their zeal in the movement was not sincere or the result of genuine conviction. From all this it will be evident that to the Japan of to-day the principles of democracy are practically unknown, and the temporary agitation on the subject which at times shows itself, is simply the handiwork of idle shizoku, who desire to annoy the goverment because they cannot obtain office. The schemes of these men do not hurt the administration, for, as they are without funds or influence, their only weapons are the tongue and the pen. The government, on the other hand, stands on a firm foundation ; wields the military power and has funds at its command ; arrayed also on its side is the police force, a highly disciplined and effective body, while the efficiency of the means of communication throughout the country vastly enhances its strength. Even in 1877 it was able with comparative ease to crush the formidable rebellion in the south-west ; while in the autumn of 1887, by the promulgation of the Peace Preservation Regulations,[1] several hundreds of

---

1. *Supra* pp. 502-04.

politicians whose presence in the capital was regarded as dangerous, were compelled to withdraw—though for our part we secretly doubted the efficacy of the measure, believing that, even though any evil intention were harboured, the plotters would be powerless to work any real harm. From the foregoing it will, we think, be clear that not only has parliamentary representation not been conceded in consequence of any general demand on the part of the people, but that it has been given voluntarily so far as concerns the great mass of the nation.

This may at first sight appear strange, but if the real conditions and circumstances existing both prior and subsequent to the establishment of the present government on a reformed and restored basis be examined, the reasons for what would otherwise, no doubt, seem unintelligible will be apparent. The arrival of the American squadron off our coasts in 1853, with its immediate results—the opening of the country and the conclusion of treaties with several Western Powers—constituted a series of events perhaps the most gravely important since the foundation of the empire, and as a necessary consquence the minds of the people were affected to an unprecedented extent. The government of feudalism, with the Tokugawa regency in the centre, and some 300 daimyō of different magnitude and influence forming the cicumference, had for more than 260 years ruled in the most profound peace and tranquillity throughout the provinces. From the most important institution down to trivial rites, all were regulated by unalterable rules ; so that alike in military, political, and financial matters and in the duties of education and the ceremonies of marriage and burial, the wheels of government rolled smoothly along in well-worn grooves. Those who during that halcyon period held the reins of administration, were not called on to govern ; they simply watched the affairs of state proceeding along a beaten track. It was only to be expected that the same causes which produced this system of rule should, as time wore on, have an influence on the minds of the people, moulding them in a fixed and uniform type, so that in the course of events the nation came imperceptibly to adapt itself to the automatic-like movement and unvarying tranquillity of the machinery of government. Neither in the ranks of those who formed the central figures of the regency, nor in the local clan governments, was there a succession of able rulers or of able councillors ; though the majority of them were, on the contrary, ignorant and narrowminded, the course of politics remained tolerably uniform. Matters were much the same whether the feudal rulers and their courts were wise and enlightened or the reverse—their wisdom or ignorance signified little. In short the great principle of the feudal system was its dependance not on men, but on institutions and customs. The word Hōken is usually rendered into English by the phrase " feudal system," chiefly for want of a suitable and expressive equivalent, and foreigners assert with a good deal of complacency and satisfaction that the feudalism of Japan was similar in character to that which existed in Europe in the middle ages. Nothing, however, could well be more misleading. The civilisation which had been developing and maturing since the foundation of the Japanese empire, attained its climax during the Tokugawa regime, not a few institutions of which might with benefit be reverted to even at the present day.

It might be supposed that, as the genius of Japanese political government during the feudal period did not call for unique personal qualities—as manners not men were its moving power—and as public life did not thus afford any opportunity for the display of high gifts or attainments, the absence of stimulus or incentive would have conduced to a dead level of mediocrity.

But the contrary was the case, for it was a noteworthy characteristic of feudalism under the Tokugawa, that the sentiment of chivalry and the taste for learning were as intense and cultured among the middle class shizoku, when Commodore Perry reached these shores, as they were at the beginning of the regency. Inheriting in a high degree the proud spirit of his fathers, but fettered in his actions by the restraint of old customs, the shizoku could only be compared to a hound confined within the bars of his kennel while the quarry gambolled in safety outside.

Such was the condition of the nation when the American ships arrived on our shores, an event which was shortly followed by the conclusion of treaties with several of the foreign Powers. Completely at a loss how to deal with the new and startling emergency, the regency had been driven for the first time since its foundation to seek the advice of the daimyō with reference to the policy which should be pursued in respect to the intruders. But this unprecedented condescension exposed the weakness of the Shōgunate. Its actions now became vacillating and uncertain. It is true that it declared neither for seclusion nor for the admission of the foreigners, but as it seemed to be virtually under foreign influence, the shizoku, fretting under their enforced term of idleness, at once sprang into action, and the people were speedily called on to say whether the "barbarians" should be admitted or excluded. To the mass of the nation this platform was a perfectly intelligible one, and they responded with alacrity and enthusiasm to the movement. But while the popular mind was thus inflamed by the thoughts that such a discussion would naturally arouse, the shizoku found themselves embarassed by the want of suitable means to carry out their plans. In the first place their feudal lords were for the most part an ignorant class of men, and in the second, the institutions and customs which for 260 years had been rooted in the country appeared to constitute an almost insuperable obstacle in the way they wished to tread. They turned then, in their dilemma, to the court, cultivated close relations with various court nobles in Kyōto, and by gaining the protection and authority of the Throne, strove to win their feudal masters to their side. Their scheme was undoubtedly known to the Shōgun's government, but harassed on one side by the foreign demands for treaty-making, and on the other by the popular outcry for the expulsion of the "barbarians," it could not check the movement. The shizoku now approached the feudal barons. They produced no Imperial authority, but they hinted vaguely at secret commands emanating from the Throne and instructions received from Princes of the Blood, and they mentioned casually the names the noblemen about the court whose assistance and sympathy they had enlisted. By this means they were sucessful in many instances in ranging the clans on the side of expulsion. And as their dependence had all along been on the court, they now saw that the next part of this program must be the overthrow of the regency. With the movement for the expulsion of the foreigner was joined the principle of loyalty to the Emperor, and ere long a spirit of actual hostility to the Shōgunate had plainly manifested itself; the loyalist party, as they now termed themselves, declared their line of policy to be first the overthrow of the Shōgunate ; secondly, the restoration of the court to its proper place as the supreme centre of government, and thirdly, the expulsion of the " barbarians." The majority of the daimyō ranged themselves on this side, the most powerful clans, such as Satsuma, Chōshū, Tosa, and others, taking the lead in opposition to the regency, the downfall of which was soon accomnplished. A new government was formed, really however on the original lines, with the Emperor as its actual head, and thus in fifteen years after the arrival of the American squadron, the practical administration of political affairs fell into the hands of middle-class shizoku, and at the same time the old feudal distinctions of caste were swept away for ever. These shizoku were, so to say, the flower of the nation, for with the indomitable spirit that they had inherited from their ancestors they combined the best education then obtainable, and to this day they are the class who have specially identified themselves with polical power.

The Tokugawa regency having now been overthrown, and the government established on a restored basis, the question arose, on whom should political rule devolve. The Emperor was of course, not merely in name but in substance, the centre of government, but the point was to whom should the work of administration be entrusted ? It was clear that this important matter should not be left to the court nobles, who, besides possessing no special aptitude or abilities for the duty, had not taken any active part in the work of the Restoration. It is true that one of the most powerful daimyo might have been selected to establish another regency and control the rest, but at that time no one feudal baron had shown himself to be so far superior to the others as to justify such a step ; moreover the real workers in this great event were the shizoku, their lords being simple puppets whose names and influence were deemed necessary to help forward the cause. And even admitting that one of those had possessed sufficient ability, another stage of bloodshed, suspension of business, and waste of money must have taken place before the supremacy of Satsuma, Chōshū, or Tosa could be asserted against their rivals and another regency established. Fortunately, however, for the nation, the daimyō of the time were all on a level of mediocrity, and, besides, their power and influence had been so skilfully balanced that no one potentate was strong or enterprising enough to attempt a supreme position single handed.

The practical political power of the state then fell into the hands of the shizoku. At the outset, while as yet the regency held sway, they were all for the expulsion of the strangers in opposition to the policy of the Shōgunate ; but when they had effected the overthrow of the latter and had the management of foreign affairs in their own hands, they soon became convinced of the folly of the course they were advocating. Their prejudices in reference to the admission of foreigners thus dispelled, they now went to the other extreme and became the leaders of progressive principles. The effect of this change was soon apparent throughout the empire, for so anxious did people become to acquaint themselves with the state of Western countries that the little pamphlet Seiyo jijyo, or "Facts about foreign lands," the only work of the kind then in existence, was in such demand that in one year 100,000 copies were sold. Having, at it were, been permitted to peep at Western civilisation, shizoku gradually increased in confidence and ventured to avail themselves of its principles. And now a strange and inexplicable theory, hitherto undreamt of by Japanese, began to gain ground among them : they proposed that public opinion should have a share in public affairs. The work of the Restoration having been accomplished, it seemed to them impolitic to invest with the administrative power either A or B or C alone ; but that the affairs of the State should be controlled by all conjointly. For this, said they, is the method followed in Western civilised countries. By a deft use of the word civilisation, then, the conflicting opinions of the shizoku of the different clans were reconciled. The public opinion then meant, however, was different from the public opinion of to-day : it in no wise comprised the views of the general mass of the nation, though there is no doubt that the method resorted to was eminently calculated to concilate the various and divergent interests of the shizoku. In the Imperial Oath of that time the following sentences occur :[1]—" A deliberative assembly shall be summoned and all measures shall be decided by public opinion." " Both the Court and the people shall unite their minds to carry on the administration prosperously." " Matters should be so arranged that not only government officials and shizoku but also the common people may be enabled to attain the objects at which they aim, in order that their minds may not become stagnant." " The uncivilised and vicious customs of former times shall be broken through, and the great principies co-existing with heaven and earth shall be taken as the basis of action." " Intellect and learning shall be sought far and wide in order to establish the foundations of the Empire." From the Imperial Oath we can gather an idea of the tendency of the so-called popular opinion at that time. By the declaration that affairs of State should be decided according to the judgment of the public

1. *Cf.* p. 8.

mind, the position to be occupied by the masses of the nation in the national life was definitely fixed. And now people began to think that surely Japan was the country of public thought, of civilisation and enlightenment, and that nothing could withstand the march of reason which had begun. The disintegration of the old institutions was commenced. In no other revolution that had taken place in the empire was there any breaking up of ancient customs and usages; change had simply involved a re-shuffling of the figures that held office and wielded power. But as these re-arrangements were invariably due to the action of some more than ordinarily enterprising spirit whose hostility was not against manners but men, and who followed up his success by adopting the methods of his predecessors and re-building up the fragments of the regime which he had supplanted, the new government could not observe any such rule. For there was no man of prominence and genius among them. The work that they did was performed by the united efforts of shizoku ; and the object that they had in view was the abolition of the old institutions, for it was necessary for the security of their own position that they should, so to speak, revolutionise the face of the country, and bring the people face to face with the new civilisation. Thus from the first attempts made to reform the system of education and to reorganize trade, to the abolition of feudalism this was the guiding feature. Japanese as well as foreigners were astounded by the ease with which the metamorphoses was accomplished, because they forgot that the leading shizoku of the clans now occupied positions in the government, and, preferring their new role to their former position under their feudal lords, their zeal for the interests of their clans was not particularly intense. Therefore they now assaulted feudalism from the outside who in former days would from within have resisted attack. The feudal barons, destitute of all ability to offer resistance and finding themselves left with none to aid them but the scum of their former retainers, had to submit. At the first glance it seems as if they had of their own accord handed back their fiefs to the Imperial court ; as a matter of fact they merely transferred their possessions to their former clansmen, the shizoku.

Although it had been clearly declared that men of ability and learning should be sought far and wide, and that the affairs of the nation should be conducted by a deliberative body, it was natural that the highest offices in the government should fall to those who had been chiefly instrumental in achieving the Restoration. The power of government therefore came into the hands of shizoku of the Satsuma, Chōshū, and Tosa clans. Ere long, however, differences arose among them ; and many who found themselves unable to agree with the views of those with whom they had hitherto been in accord, left the government, their hostility eventually culminating in the insurrections of Sàga (1874) and Satsuma (1877). These civil wars were in reality quarrels between former friends. The government, however, wielding legal and recognised rule in the empire, had this advantage ; that its opponents were rebels by the mere fact of their hostility ; and the struggle was almost as a matter of course of very short duration. While the government now became gradually more firmly established, one disadvantage which always attached to it was the want of a statesman of sufficient ability to act as head of the administration. The shizoku, who had been accustomed to render the most unquestioning obedience and submission to their superiors, found it difficult to carry on a system of government, bearing within it the germ of popular representation, with the efficiency and absence of friction which could only result from the guidance of a master spirit. Chief there was none, for though the highest post in the State might be assigned to him who had won most prestige in their common achievements, no one had the power of controlling his colleagues. The more orderly and systematic arrangements only served to accentuate this difficulty. Occupants of high office in the State could, it is true, be distinguished by being made the recipients of honours, such as official grades and decorations, or elevation to the peerage, but as the circle of those so honoured widened, the value of the distinction was lowered. It could not be said, therefore, that there was one person in the government distinguished above the others ; and the prodigality with which honours were bestowed led the people to apply to it the epithet of the "self-seeking government." No one could be held responsible for this state of things ; it was really the outcome of the circumstances under which the administration had been inaugurated.

Yet amid all the difficulties with which it was surrounded, the affairs of State were administered satisfactorily upon the whole, a result due in part to the innate spirit of sincerity and integrity which has always distinguished the Japanese shizoku, and partly to the august and sacred mediating influence of the court. But while outwardly the course of government seemed to be smooth and propitious, internally it had many troubles to contend with. The men who occupied the high offices of State were pretty much alike in respect of age and achievements, forming in fact a kind of brotherhood. But there were many occupying positions in the public service who, belonging to a later generation and being full of aspirations and ambition, were at cross purposes with their seniors. To foreigners the situation will be barely intelligible, but we may say generally that there were existing in the ranks of the government several minor political parties, a condition of affairs which could not conduce to smooth and easy administration. From among shizoku of an irresponsible kind the cry for the inauguration of Parliament was not long in spreading, and just as the *jōi* [1] agitation became general during the early part of the country's relations with foreign Powers, so the *kokkai kaisetsu* [2] movement became the fashion, and so-called *sōdai*, or delegates, were sent up to the capital from various quarters. These, however, did not by any means represent the people at large, and had the matter been

1. "Expel the barbarians."
2. Council-chamber chosen by the people.

treated by the government with indifference, the agitation would have disappeared of its own accord. The Government, however, so far from acting in this fashion, actually decided upon the inauguration of Parliament.[1] It is difficult to define the reason for the step, but it is probable that the Cabinet were wearied of the difference of opinion existing among the younger official class, who were wanting in patience and perseverance, and whose resentment in consequence of the non-realisation of their ambitions and aspirations might well have proved harassing to their superiors. It is not difficult to imagine then that the men who occupied the higher offices of State became tired of these continual bickerings, and determined to inaugurate Parliament and give the grumblers an opportunity of trying their own plans. Or it may be that, in the second place, the government while fully cognizant of the tractability of the common people, have found it desirable to conciliate and, so to speak, reward that very large class of shizoku who rendered services in the Restoration, but for whom official position has not been provided. By inaugurating Parliament these will be afforded an opportunity of showing what abilities they possess.

The third point involves a good deal of intricacy, but is worthy of some attention. As the shizoku of Satsuma and Chō-shū were chiefly instrumental in the work of the Restoration it was natural that the chief seats in the government should be occupied by them, though members of other clans shared in the administration of the national affairs. The Saichō element, however, was the principal ingredient of the compound. During the years immediately following the Restoration, the state of public affairs kept all sufficiently occupied ; but as matters became more methodical and system and order gained foothold, the various elements of the government began to exhibit their peculiar characteristics. Broadly speaking the statesmen of the present day may be divided into two classes, those who are open and straightforward, and those who are wily and diplomatic. The former

1. In 1881. *Vide* pp, 86-87.

are men who would sacrifice their lives in behalf of their country; they are rich in decision so far as they go, but they lack shrewdness and diplomacy. Their influence and power, however, are by no means insignificant. The second class are distinguished by their skill and ingenuity, and they easily adapt themselves to any circumstances, but in a society where the true samurai spirit still predominates, and where simplicity and straightforwardness are prized, they do not command much power or influence. The public have a habit of saying that the Satuma people are blunt and straightforward, and that Chōshū men excel in diplomacy and statesmanship. This distinction, however, is not necessarily correct, especially as many of the other clans are represented in the government. These two opposite parties existing then in the administration, it is easy to see how difficulties may arise. If the men destitute of real statesmanship are allowed to do as they like, mistakes must certainly be made, unnecessary time and money spent, and the smooth working of the machinery of State interfered with. And yet it is not easy to restrain such officials, particularly as the present government has been evolved from the principles of public opinion and joint deliberation, and there is no one person in whom absolute power is vested. The other class of statesmen have thus been driven to resort to the expedient of framing laws and regulations with the object of checking the actions of officials; and new measures have been promulgated in such rapid succession as to suggest the complete domination of officialdom. But these attempts to fetter human action have in many cases been productive of no good results, and the object aimed at has not been attained. The establishment of a Parliament is now resorted to with the view of removing the difficulty. Thanks to the benign influence of the Throne, both parties have agreed to this measure, and it is matter for highest congratulation that our statesmen have shown themselves such worthy descendants of Japanese samurai as to sink their differences for the national interest.

Some foreigners have expressed their apprehensions as to the future. They regard the inauguration of Parliament as an indication that the spirit of resistance and the power of the people with regard to the government has been much developed by the progress of education ; they believe that steps should be taken to prevent the nation from encroaching on the rights of the government ; they are even much concerned about the future relations between the people and the Court. But these foreigners make the mistake of applying to the state of affairs in Japan tests furnished by the history of Western countries. The circumstances which have led to the opening of the Japanese Parliament are unique and unprecedented.

We believe we may safely predict that at first the House of Representatives will represent, not the agricultural, commercial, and industrial interests, but the shizoku. This condition of affairs, however, will not last long, and, as is now the case in local assemblies, business men will be elected in increasing numbers. In course of time, if Japanese society remains under the influence of Western civilisation, the power of wealth will be shown, and intellect, that is learning and education, will be relegated to a subordinate position. The shizoku will therefore have to prepare to adapt himself to the changed circumstances of the times. We suppose his class will gradually drift into agricultural, mercantile, and industrial pursuits, becoming more highly sensible to the value of money, while at the same time the present business class will learn the advantages of education. So in course of time society will fall under the control of a new class, possessing brains, means and influence. But this change will not come in a day ; for the sake of Japan we trust it will be slow and steady. Nor is it at all likely that it will be attended by disturbance. For the Japanese are an obedient people. Long centuries of submission to the most stern and exacting rules for the regulation of all their relations, public and private, have made them so ; and to day they bow to the most inconvenient law or rule with unquestioning readiness. They are obedient to their superiors, content to live within the limits fixed by customs and laws, solicitous for the general order and safety of the State, patient and richly endowed with natural gifts. They have shown indeed that there is a limit to their patience, as when in former times farmers braved the danger of imprisonment, torture, and death, to set forth their grievances. And it has been proved that 270 years of unbroken tranquillity have not made the Japanese less of a soldier than he was in the old times. A people who so readily adapted themselves to the greatest changes their country had undergone since its foundation are not the least likely to be bewildered by the inauguration of a Parliament. Difficulties may arise at the outset ; there may be misunderstanding on the part both of the government and the people ; undesirable or rash persons may inadvertently be admitted to Parliament. But rashness is not a quality which recommends itself to the Japanese people, and such errors will soon be remedied. These difficulties need not be dreaded. If we remember that society is in this country under the final control of the sacred Throne, which sheds a benign influence all around, we shall have no cause to fear that political excitement will lead our people to stray from the path of order and duty. We may be told that the quality of obedience, though hereditary in the Japanese nation, can be affected by the influence of the ever changing times. We do not think that is probable. We cannot believe that an hereditary quality will so easily yield to external circumstances, or that even education will quickly impair it. Though the institution of Parliament is a novel and unprecedented one in this country, we firmly believe that both government and people will by virtue of their hereditary spirit of obedience faithfully observe and conform to the duties required of them.

J.W.M., 1889, April 6, pp. 336-38.

3. LOCAL GOVERNMENT UNDER THE TOKUGAWA SHŌGUNATE[1].

(From the *Chōya Shimbun*).

During the Tokugawa Regency officials called machi bu-gyo were appointed in Yedo, Kyōto, Ōsaka, and Shizuoka, others called dai-kan in each gun, and bugyo at Sakaye, Nara, Niigata, and Nagasaki. Under each of these officials a certain number of honorary officers were appointed, whose duty it was to deal with matters arising in connection with the various commercial associations (kumi-ai). In other respects the practice varied in different localities. One of the distinguishing characteristics of the administration of Yedo was that landholders were appointed to honorary offices. Of such there were three classes:—(1) itsuki-ji-nushi, or landholders who resided on their own property, (2) iyemochi-ji-nushi, or householders who either let their property to others or occupied it themselves; and (3) tsujo-ji-nushi, or ordinary landholders. The rights of these classes differed considerably. Such honorary officials as we have described were entrusted with the duty of managing general matters connected with their own streets. Then there were householders who had control over persons who leased property. The owners of property in each street elected from among their number a nanushi; the office, however, was practically hereditary. These nanushi were formed into eighteen sections and did duty by monthly turns. The promulgation of official notifications was carried into effect by an officer called ko-guchi. In Yedo there were three machi-toshi-yori (city elders) who had control of the various sections of nanushi, and the former were in their turn under the supervision of two machi-bugyo. There were thus in Yedo machi-bugyo, machi-toshi-yori, and nanushi, whose office was hereditary; in Kyōto, machi-bugyo, otoshi-ban, and machi-toshi-yori, who held office

---

1. This newspaper article is reproduced here for what it is worth, the editor not being competent to express an opinion upon its value. It is, however, a convenient *precis* of a very difficult subject. For further information see A. S. J. Transactions, Vol XIX., Part I.

for three years ; in Osaka machi-bugyo, sō-toshi-yori and machi-toshi-yori who were appointed for life, and in Nara bugyo, sō-toshi-yori, and machi-toshi-yori, appointed for three years. For Ōsaka and its three suburbs there were eleven sō-toshi-yori, who by means of four offices—one in the city and in each of the suburbs—controlled all the affairs of the communities, with the exception of purely civil and criminal matters. The office of sō-toshi-yori therefore corresponded pretty closely to the present district headman. The sō-toshi-yori appointment was hereditary ; the duties of the incumbents of the post included dealing with the estimates of expenditure, the taxes and other burdens borne by the various streets, and the appointment of machi-toshi-yori, and they had further to carry presents to Yedo at the commencement of every year. They were in receipt of no regular salary, but were exempted from several obligations and burdens, and were further permitted to receive money presents from business firms of the streets over which they had control. In each street there was an office for the transaction of the business of the toshi-yori, who were elected for life from among those families who had occupied houses, their own property for three generations in the same street, and enjoyed much respect among their neighbours. Their duty was to control under the orders of the sō-toshi-yori the business of their respective streets, but in practice their office was a sinecure, their functions being chiefly performed by the chō-dai (or street representatives) whose headquarters were in the office of the toshi-yori. Like sō-toshi-yori they received no salary, but were exempted from various responsibilities and allowed to accept money presents.

Two or three accountants were appointed for each street to perform the necessary clerical work connected with the proper administration of the locality ; and the machi-toshi-yori was represented when absent by two tsuki-gyoji, who attended to the promulgation of official notifications and other matters. The residents in each street were divided into parties of five or more (go-nin-gumi), all of whom were required to become surety for the sale or purchase of land or house property or the borrowing or lending of money by any one of this number. Subject to the sō-toshi-yori there was a salaried official known as sōdai, under whose supervision all petitions and applications to the bugyo were sent forward, his monthly salary being 10 *ryo*. The office of chōdai was hereditary and there was attached to it a salary equal to about 300 *me* per month. The appointments of the accountants and tsuki-gyo-ji were purely honorary.

Though no land tax existed, there were various duties which were divided into general and specific imposts. The former was regulated by the sō-toshi-yori and was levied generally on all streets; the latter, adjusted by the machi-toshi-yori, was levied on each street specifically, in addition to the general tax. From the general duty were defrayed wages of labourers employed on official works, of fire brigades, the cost of horse and coolie relays, the repairs of embankments, the salaries of sōdai, the maintenance of fire alarm stations, and the dredging of rivers; while the specific imposts were to meet the salaries of chōdai, the cost of street offices, and the wages of their employees, and the hakama allowance of machi toshi-yori (hakama-sure-ryo). The estimates of income from the general tax were compiled by the bugyo and transmitted to the sō-toshi-yori, who determined the amount leviable on each street and instructed the machi-toshi-yori as to its collection, the tax being payable in most cases to the bugyo. In the levying of the specific tax, the residents os each street had some voice, but practically the procedure waf the same as in the previous case.

J.W.M., 1889, Jan. 19, pp. 60-61.

4. VISCOUNT TANI'S MEMORIAL.[1]

Having, as was ordered, made various observations in

---

1. This Memorial was presented to the Cabinet toward the close of 1887, b. t its purport was disregarded, and as a consequence the memorialist, who was Minister of Agriculture and Commerce, left the Cabinet.

Europe and America, and having reflected on the state of this country, I perceive certain things which cause me uneasiness, and concerning which I cannot remain unconcerned. I have been desirous of expressing my opinions on these subjects to the members of the Cabinet, but as what I have to say could hardly be said in a day or a night, I have written down my general convictions.

Keeping on a straight path and following the best course, a land of a hundred *ri* is not at all too small to maintain its independence, and even to grow into a rich and strong country ; Sweden, Greece, and Belgium are examples of such a country. On the contrary, if a straight path is not pursued and the best course is neglected, even a land of a thousand *ri* can scarcely escape the aggression of its enemy, and also from sinking to a miserable condition. India, Holland and Turkey are appropriate examples of such a country. Those who bear the sceptre of a nation must therefore be very prudent. The ultimate success of the affairs of a country ought to be looked to, and hence great care should be exercised in fixing the national policy. There are matters which must be attended to at once, while there are things which can be done at any time. There are also matters of small interest, while there are matters of deep importance ; moreover there are affairs which though of great consequence and importance, do not require to be dealt with hastily nor demand instantaneous attention. All these points must not be neglected. There are many things in this country which I would like to discuss, but among others, I see one which is of a most momentous character and calls for my immediate attention,—one on which the welfare of the nation is staked. What is it ? It is treaty revision.

Treaty revision, notwithstanding the utmost exertions of our administrators, and the long interval of fifteen or sixteen years which has occurred since that work was first begun, remains to this day unaccomplished. Recently, however, that which had been the cherished desire of my countrymen for so many years had almost approached completion, and the fortunate era was dawning when foreigners would throw over their extra-territorial privileges and submit to our laws. Was not this really a matter for congratulation for the nation's sake? From another source, however, I hear that as it was insisted that our laws and regulations are inadequate or unsuited for the governing of foreigners, and foreigners therefore object to submit to our jurisdiction, the government intend to revise our laws and regulations so as to satisfy the demands of foreigners. If this information be true, I cannot help saying that our administrators have lost their independence. The laws of a nation have to be framed in harmony with the history, customs, manners, and religious beliefs of the people. If, therefore, anyone contemplates reforming our laws and regulations on behalf of foreigners, I cannot but think that the spirit of independence has departed from the mind of such a person.

It is of course desirable to reform our laws, if these are not perfect; even then if the government consult with foreigners who are ignorant of the history of Japan, and the customs, manners, and religious beliefs of the people, if the government revise our laws with the sole object of satisfying the foreigners, if these things be done in order to obtain the consent of the foreign powers to the proposed treaty revision, th n we authorise foreigners to interfere with our legislation, the exemption from which interference is regarded as indicating the independence of a nation. I venture to say that such concessions as these will be the source of miseries which will at last bring the country to ruin.

The laws of a country are framed for the purpose of advancing the welfare of its own people; foreigners have nothing to do with the laws of other countries than their own. Therefore, if the government admit the proposals of foreign countries one by one while conferring with the foreign representatives, and if the negociations result in giving to the foreigner the right to participate in our legislation, then the evils which will follow from such a concession will not be few, indeed. A man of

ancient times said, " Names and vessels should not be lent." If
foreigners are allowed to interfere with our legislature, it will be
accounted that the independence will not long thereafter depart.

Besides, treaty revision is the greatest event that has happened in this country since the origin of the nation. If the
treaties are once signed, there is little hope of making further
alteration. Good or bad, right or wrong, everything effected by
treaty revision will affect the reputation of our country. Suppose,
when it is accomplished, that the disgrace which we have suffered
for thirty years will be washed away; suppose, on the other
hand, that it result unfavorably to us; the evils arising from
treaty revision will not cease in our time, but will be inherited
for a hundred years; it is even doubtful whether or not the independence of the country will last so long. For example, we
can see what resulted from the treaty which the Tokugawa
government contracted with Mr. Harris, the United States
Ambassador. It does not, of course, admit of a single doubt
that Mr. Harris did all that he could on behalf of our
country, yet in spite of that fact the representatives of the
Tokugawa government conferred upon foreigners extra-territorial privileges, a concession which is even now distressing
the nation. If the past can serve as guidance for the future
we must be very prudent in revising the treaties. Some persons
may say, " When our country was first opened, the Tokugawa
government signed the present treaty, which injures the national
rights and preserves no power of governing ourselves. The
responsibility for this treaty, must be borne by the Tokugawa
government. The oppressive power exercised by the Tokugawa
government for some three hundred years had almost destroyed the interest of the people in national affairs. No one
in the days of the last Shōgun knew the condition of foreign
nations, nor was there one who comprehended what extra-
territorial privileges meant. No one in those days had inquired
as to how commerce and customs duties affected the resources
of the country. In addition to this, there were many ronin who

threatened to overthrow the Tokugawa government. Under these circumstances how could the government compel foreigners to submit to our laws? When we consider the state of affairs in those days there is little we can blame the officials of the Tokugawa government for. But now the times have changed. The condition of the world is thoroughly known. The administration of foreign affairs is wisely conducted. The evils of extra-territoriality and the effects of trade and duties have all been investigated. There are none of the daimyō who were objects of horror to the Tokugawa government, and there are no ronin insisting on the expulsion of the foreigners. Thus while the whole country is unanimously in favor of treaty revision, there is not a single foreign power which intends to preserve the old treaty, even by force. What we demand is just and what we propose is right. It might therefore have been anticipated that when we entered into negotiations with the foreign representatives, informing them of the exact condition of our country, foreign powers would have acceded to our proposals." It is true that we are exerting ourselves to the utmost to procure the revision of the treaties, and that the present time affords some opportunity to alter the old treaties. But if, under these circumstances, the government effects the revision in the form which I hear they intend to do, the censure of posterity will be much heavier upon them than that we now impose upon the officials of the Tokugawa government.

Others might assert that be the result of treaty revision what it may, we must be content; and that it is utterly impracticable to make foreigners abandon their extra-territorial privileges unless we grant some concession; and also that the desire of foreigners to reform our laws and participate in our legislation is as nothing as compared with the abolition of extra-terrritoriality. Such presumptions as these are however, erroneous. There are always two means of knowing a thing. There is the name and there is the reality. The name of a thing may be very grand without implying its genuineness. The reality may be very pure though the name may not be elegant. Consequently it is a gross mistake to pass judgement upon a thing when its name only is known. It is an undeniable thing that extra-territoriality is not only disgraceful in name but utterly objectionable in reality. As an actual fact, however, the injury extra-territoriality inflicts upon us is not so great as it nominally appears. The independence and welfare of our country are actually but slightly affected on account of foreigners possessing extra-territorial privileges. On the other hand, the revised treaty is, I hear, inadmissable both in name and reality. To abolish extra-territoriality is, indeed, a praiseworthy act; but if on that account the government lead foreigners to interfere with the internal affairs of the country, the real injury which we must sustain is unutterably large. Alas! how can those who administer the national affairs seek the name and not the reality? Such action will ruin the country, whatever its reputation, and must not be ventured upon by the members of the present Cabinet.

Another might insist that the latest exertions (of the Ministers) have brought the long-pending treaty revision negociations almost to a close, and that though the whole nation were engaged in the task, we would not be able to produce so fair a result as we are now approaching. I am, of course, unable to say how the negociations have been proceeding, for I am an outsider, as far as treaty revision is concerned; but I have conversed upon such subjects as treaty revision and inter-migration with eminent scholars and prominent men in Europe and America; and there was not a single person who was not astonished when I told him of the secret manner in which treaty revision was being negociated, and who did not denounce the evil of entrusting such a prominent matter to the Foreign Office alone. In Europe and America when any great national event occurs, the Minister of each Department is called upon to express his opinion, and after careful deliberation, the Foreign Office is authorised to act in accordance with the decision of the Cabinet.

Briefly, the Foreign Office can do nothing more than transmit
the decision of the Cabinet. If we leave the whole power of
negociating treaty revision, as we do to-day, to the Foreign
Office, no matter how experienced the officials may be, the
result must be far less satisfactory than if the negotiations
depended on the decision of the Cabinet after the subject had
been repeatedly discussed by the Cabinet. For instance, the
Department of Agriculture and Commerce, which at present is
under my control, has the greatest interest in the result of treaty
revision. The prosperity of industries depends upon whether
the customs duties are heavy or light. Home commerce has close
relations with foreign trade. Inter-migration must influence
agriculture and mining. To entrust the Foreign Office alone
with the power of negociating treaty revision, therefore, is not
sound policy. Alas! it is on treaty revision that even the
security of the country depends. It is on treaty revision that
the welfare of the whole nation hangs. Is it not then extremely
dangerous to leave such an important matter in the hands of the
officials of the Foreign Office? If a misguided step is taken,
the Cabinet of 1886 will be regarded as having been disloyal to
His Majesty, the Emperor, and unfaithful to his subjects. To
speak emphatically, the Cabinet of 1886 will be denounced as
having persuaded his Majesty to sin against his whole people, as
well as against the Imperial Ancestors. The responsibility of the
members of the Cabinet is as heavy as the reputation of the
country is great. Considering the position they occupy, how
can they act imprudently ? Having reasoned as above, it may
now be asked what shall we do with treaty revision? After
having thoroughly inquired of many able men both in Europe
and America with reference to the subject, I have now resolved
in my heart as to the most aceptable course, one very diverse
to that pursued by the Foreign Office. Let me state my
oninion.

Treaty revision will, of course, be consummated ; but to
carry it into effect at the present day is not convenient. I say it

should be effected in 1890, when the present system of government has been changed and the constitutional assembly has
been opened. Besides, we must necessarily have sufficient
courage to act decisively towards other countries when we
propose to deal with such an important question as treaty
revision. I think there will be few European nations which
will refuse to adopt the proposals we will make, and which will
threaten to maintain their privileges by force. Such countries,
if there be any, are not to be regarded. In the present condition of Europe and America, if any country showed hostility
towards us another country would proceed to form an alliance
with us. Moreover, the peoples of Europe and America are
thoroughly accustomed to the system of constitutional assembly,
and fully recognise the power of public opinion with regard to
national affairs. Therefore nothing would make a stronger impression than an expression of public opinion. Consequently in
fixing our national policy it is necessary to bear this in mind.
At the same time we must ·endeavor to cultivate friendly
relations with all foreign countries in every respect. Meanwhile,
if we continue to rely on one or two powers, the world will
despise us and we will gradually lose their respect. Many
diplomatists insist that conferences relating to foreign affairs must
be held in secret, and that when we disclose every matter to the
eyes of the world, the points of our weakness are shown, and
foreign countries learn to despise us. The only thing we can
depend on is public opinion. We will, obedient to the gracious
will of His Majesty, the Emperor, consult with the people on all
questions concerning treaty revision, and by means of public
opinion conduct the treaty revision negociations. Turkey is at
present disregarded by the neighboring countries on account of
its adopting the principle of depending upon others ; but when
we consider how Turkey has maintained its independence
among the most powerful countries of Europe, it soon becomes
evident that she has acted with unusual prudence and energy.
Though it is an undeniable fact that Turkey is only kept from

being absorbed by the protection of one or two strong countries, still we must remember that it holds a self-governing power. In a word, public opinion alone rules the minds of people in Europe and America. Now, to develope public opinion we must rely upon the press and public speech. Therefore we must encourage the press and public speech instead of discouraging these things. That is to say, we must revise and moderate the press and public meeting laws. It is, however, doubtful whether there is no European country which would object to our proposals regarding treaty revision. Therefore we must have in reserve a well equipped militia. As regards coast defence, I will refer to that some other day.

If, when the constitutional assembly has been opened, the Foreign Office will propose treaty revision, stating that such is the gracious wish of His Majesty, the Emperor, as well as the desire of the whole nation, and give the reasons for such revision in the press, both at home and abroad, it will not be at all difficult to get foreign countries to adopt our proposals. Moreover, I am certain that at the present time no European country would despatch their men-of-war for the sole purpose of preserving the present treaty. Though it may look unnecessary, therefore, to make warlike preparations, there are not a few examples of the more powerful countries of Europe subjecting less powerful countries. If we are not backed by a strong army and navy, though we may take advantage of public opinion, we have little hope of obtaining success. Warlike preparations must not be neglected even for a day. If those who govern the nation depend wholly upon the other country, and trust to fortune, the result will be such as we can see in the Port of Alexandria. The members of the Cabinet must think seriously of this.

Japan Gazette, 1888, January 8, pp. 6-8.

5. MR. ITAGAKI ON LIBERTY.

(A lecture delivered at Koshiu, 1882.)

Gentlemen:—Our Liberal Party[1] is not yet thoroughly established as a political organisation, and therefore what I am now about to say, in deference to your request, must not be considered in the light of a political exposition but of a private enunciation. I mention this, because I have good hopes for the future formation of a strong political association, and I beg you to bear this in mind. However difficult of attainment a matter may appear to be, it will be achieved by diligent application. Any one contemplating a difficult achievement must make up his mind to accomplish it, before he ventures to commence it. And at this day when the members of our party, aiding and assisting each other, are sowing the seeds of liberty expecting to reap a full harvest, they must reclaim the waste lands, uproot all obstacles, and realising that the work before them is difficult, take to their hoes and ploughes and toil with vigor. And now I will indicate what obstructions you have to encounter, in order that you may appreciate the full extent of your task.

When the country was under the feudal system in bygone days the people were overborne by the martial power of their lords, and had no voice in their own government. Not only were they prevented from participating in national affairs, but they were kept in the condition of slaves, and the result was that they were utterly devoid of patriotism, and quite without union among themselves. Even the samurai, though they had some conception of being the "people" of the country, yet regarded their *devoir* to their lords alone, and accepted no other obligation. They desired to be isolated from men of other clans, and had no care for a national unity. They knew liberty,—but only personally and egotistically—not as a public and universal benefactor. The fabric, as it were, of the country was only held together by the ties that

1. The Jiyuto, of which Itagaki was the leader.

bound baron and vassal, and if those bonds were broken the disturbances that ensued were wellnigh irreparable. Then the liberty of the samurai degenerated into extravagance and pride, and the class had no idea of extending public and national freedom by some sacrifice of private privilege. This is the first obstacle[1] that you have to remove.

Again, under the feudal regime, the people were despotically ruled and had no rights of self-government. Hence men of energetic spirit, while governing others, never thought of controlling themselves. They deemed that, unless they were actually occupied in ruling, their abilities were wasted, and so they roughly competed for positions of control, wholly ignorant of the principle which impels a man to sacrifice private advantage to public benefit. Jealousy then caused them to sneer at others' actions and to impugn others' fame. This was both a private and a public grievance, and is the second obstacle in your way.

While active men inclined to rule the people despotically, and to give them no chance of self-government, they (the people) for the most part deemed it a sacred duty to accept oppression. The lower classes hugged their dependence and had no thought of freedom ; deprived of self-government and self protection they were willing to rely upon the protection of others, and revered the persons, if not the principles of their superiors. The tyranny under which our country groaned so long rendered these abuses almost incradieable, and here you find a third obstacle.

Under the feudal system, the samurai, great in power and responsibility, were well educated and primed with knowledge, but all the other people, whose main idea of existence was to pay taxes and acquire property, had no desire to learn, and if

---

1. The lecturer apparently meant, in this and subsequent allusions to obstacles, that traces of the prejudices he deprecated still remained in the minds of those who less than twenty years before were a privileged class, and that these must be obliterated before national progress would be possible.

they were rich were ignorant. Thus intellect and money were incompatible possessions. Moreovor, since the opening of this country to foreign intercourse, civilisation has rapidly progressed, and western science and art have thrown their rays all around us. The spirit of the time is rapidly infusing itself into our youth, but is slow in making any impression on the old. As a rule the former are cultured in occidential lore, while the latter are content with the old abuses. Hence the experience of the old clashes with, instead of being united in a common fund with, the vigor of the young, for the benefit of the whole country. This is the fourth obstacle.

In the middle ages our people were divided into two classes, military and civil. The former were the controllers, the latter the controlled. Hereditary tradition creates common custom. The samurai made it their exclusive business to participate in affairs of state, and were therefore much concerned in politics ; whereas the commoners, satisfied with long subjection, cared for none of those things. Some one has said that any idea of politics is non-existent in our country. This is true of the vulgar and ignorant, but political knowledge is widely diffused in circles of well-informed people. Truly the difference in the amount of appreciation of politics existing in our lettered and unlettered communities is as wide as the expanse between heaven and earth. To maintain balance and harmony between them is most difficult, the wise adding to their wisdom and the foolish progressing in their ignorance. This is the fifth obstacle.

Two thousand five hundred and more years ago our nation was founded. Since then many changes have occurred, but as they were merely dynastic struggles between two houses of imperial lineage, or contests for military supremacy on the part of various heroes, no opportunity occurred for introducing reform into the system of government, which remained as despotic as ever through hundreds of years. Hence there was no chance for political progress. Slow indeed were the steps of our country in civilisation as compared with those of occidental nations.

Uncivilised peoples maintaining their natural dispositions are not bereft of the power of growth, and hence we may call them young, but semi-civilised nations whose innate strength has been arrested by artificial laws we must call old. Thus our countrymen seem to be not young, but very aged. This is the sixth obstacle.

Our national education is of three kinds, Shintōist, Confucian, and Buddhist. The first is a relic of the old theocratic rule, and was long of valuable assistance to the ancient sovereign administration. Buddhism is an imported creed, and almost became the state religion, but is always subservient to politics, forming a link between government and faith. Again, in Confucianism we have a mixture of politics and religion, the principles controlling either being held to emanate from the same source, government being regarded as a paternal institution whose main office is to instruct and protect the people. Thus government and religion trespassing on each other's domains have interfered, here with the private life of the people, there with the administration of public affairs, inflicting injury on one side and on the other. This is the seventh obstacle.

Such is the land which our party has to reclaim; such the obstacles to be removed. I know that the work before us is difficult. What kind of hoe and plough shall we then employ? In order to organise a constitutional government and perfect the liberty of the people, each individual must cast egotism away and assume a pure patriotism. People must work into the groove of mutual assistance. A country and government institutions are but means for the protection of personal rights by means of popular unity. Hence, if a man wishes to enjoy liberty through the protection of his government he must sacrifice a portion of his inherent and personal freedom, and must strive to acquire a national liberty. If an individual can live satisfactorily in a state of isolation without caring for the common weal, he may be as selfish and extravagant as he pleases, without sacrificing any of his personal freedom. Nevertheless, people can only enjoy life by mixing with their fellows and depending on the community, and therefore their aim should be to secure civil liberty by making mutual concessions. The extension of national liberty is an addition to the security of individual freedom ; and this should be the ambition of every community. Yet our compatriots are still enamoured of seclusion, and destitute of patriotic feeling, and cannot comprehend the meaning of sacrificing personal latitude to public benefit. This is a traditional abuse born of despotism. The only way to ameliorate it is to allow the public to participate in public affairs, by which means they will grow to understand that national and individual advantages are identical in their effects. Our party should abjure all ideas of petty insolation, and should strive for the public benefit. This is the first thing I hope from you.

The aim of our party should be to govern themselves, not to control others. The latter operation is much more easy than the former. Naturally every person prefers ease to hardship, but those who lead the public should give ease to others and keep difficulties for themselves. The accomplishment of this duty is the first wish of a great man responsible for the discharge of government functions, and anxious to write his name in deeds of merit, regardless alike of personal name and risk. In countries where the men capable of such deeds are few the lighter is the task of those who undertake it. In a country where all are eager the fewer will succeed ; and in our country there is plenty of room for as many as like to try to exercise their ability and put their knowledge to good use without endeavoring to be absolute rulers. Spencer, the learned Englishman, wishing to inculcate this principle, says that he himself is an emperor and a born legislator. And so, to discharge a difficulty duty manfully, benefiting the public and governing oneself, is to be in the goverment without occupying an official position. Our party should leave ease to others and court difficulty for themselves. It should dash jealousy aside, hold fast to uprightness, and lay the foundation on which shall be built the edifice of self-government.   This is my second desire for your welfare.

Should our party really desire to cement its union, and to vanquish its opponents, its members must most evidently be mutually friendly, and must respect the principles, rather than the persons, of their associates.   The freedom to which we so earnestly aspire is the principle which pervades heaven and earth, and not a merely selfish attribute.   A party which is merely devoted to the persons of its leaders is a private under-taking, while one concerned with the public benefit is alone a public institution.   The one is weak through depending on the power of its leaders, the other is strong in its own faith and the power of its members.   An old author says :—" All the soldiers of a great army may be captured, but the thoughts of the most vulgar person cannot be arrested."   The reason is that, in the former case, the courage of the whole force depends upon one man's reliance upon another, while in the latter, a person has full faith in himself.   So long as people revere the principles, rather than the persons of their leaders, they will preserve the existence of their party even though their leaders should die. My third desire for you is that you should follow the principles rather than the persons of your leaders.

One urgent need of our party is to accumulate the force of many individuals.   Speaking generally, the well educated are highly progressive, while the mere well-to-do are inclined to put a rein on thought, and men of experience are of even a more advanced conservatism.   Thus in the people we find many grades of opinion, but so long as their object is identical with our own, we should do our best to draw them to ourselves, car-ing nothing for minor differences of opinion.   We find such disagreement even among those whose main views for the re-form of the government are the same.   Thus one would have a unicameral, another a bicameral parliament.   Some believe in a universal franchise, while others desire a property qualification for electors.   The decision of these questions, however, can well be relegated to the time when the form of government has been reconstituted. To engage in frivolous disputes on small subjects before the time for full reform has come, disregarding the accomplishment of our main object is, in the words of an old proverb, " to be like a singing-girl who expends her voice before she leaves the green-room." In the West the strife of political parties conduces to the welfare of the public. But there the controversialists have the tradition of time and experience. And should parties without skill and knowledge, in a country entering upon a new phase of life, fall into causeless disputes upon trifling matters, they may cause us to fail in the objects of our enterprise. What I wish to indicate is that our party should not concern itself too much with particulars, but generously strive to establish a great union. This is my fourth wish for you.

The object of our union is to institute a form of government wherein the people shall have a voice in public affairs. Public opinion is the axis round which should revolve government policy. On its prosperity or decay depends the prosperity or decay of the government. For its promotion and a simultaneous inauguration of a beneficial policy we must educate the people in politics. A good administration and the felicity of the commonwealth are dependent upon public opinion, insomuch as the governed can prevent their rulers from making arbitrary use of political power. If those who are governed are wholly ignorant and unable to impose any check upon their rulers by the expression of public opinion, even a good and perfect polity may degenerate into selfishness and tyranny, and the people will be deprived of all the benefits designed for them.

Good people make good governments. Therefore while reforming the government and making it a permanent institution, we must reform the national character and make our people good. When the differences of political opinion between the lettered and unlettered classes are very great and their concord is disturbed, there is no hope of establishing a substantial public opinion. Our party should strive to bring the cultured into communion with the uncultured, to improve the ignorant, and thus to form a communion of ideas, building up public happiness and national welfare upon a sound foundation. This is my fifth desire.

Should our party desire to bring with swift steps our country, already old, in the sense I have described, to the path of civilisation, we must take decisive measures. To illustrate :— A youth who has plenty of time for study before him may pursue a regular curriculum on established rules, but an old man desiring to learn must take extraordinary measures. It is quite in the regular course of events that a man who is able to control himself and govern his family should take part in the national affairs ; but our countrymen—who are really old—must learn their lesson by an expeditious method. The enlightened systems of government obtaining in western lands have grown with the growth of the people, and are therefore in accord with the ordinary course of events. If our old country desires to overtake the occident it must take the nearest way. Some old literate may object to this proposition, asking how a man who cannot govern himself or keep his family in order can participate in national business ? Or again, while western countries have progressed in the natural order of things, how can our country be expected to reach the end of its journey by a short cut ? Such querists are of obsolete ideas. The affairs of this world are full of life, not dead. Our party must not heed such worthless and commonplace persons. They must contribute to our national progress until they have outpaced the western world. This is my sixth hope for you.

Our party desires a liberal, but not a meddling, policy. The interference of a government with the private affairs of the people is due to its ignorance of the distinction between politics and religion, public and personal matters. Government interference means the loss of independence. Our party should discriminate between politics and religion, and oppose government interference with private affairs. Propagation of liberal principles by our party is a public, not a private venture. Those who agree with us in these respects are good friends of liberty, and, although they may not be in harmony with us in our private relations, yet we can be in perfect accord with them otherwise, and on the other hand those who, no matter how intimate they may be with us privately, oppose the cause of liberty, cannot march in the same way with us. Thus in striving for public progress we must not be encumbered with private relations, and *vice versa*. What we have to do is to go steadily forward, taking a foot where we sacrifice an inch. This is my seventh hope for you.

I am well aware, as I said before, that it is not an easy task to reclaim the waste lands, and to sow the crop that shall bring in a good harvest of liberty. Yet employ the aims that I have expressed as your hoes and ploughs. Anything can be accomplished by steadfast endeavor, while no success awaits the man who dislikes and neglects his work. Take for instance the case of the late Saigo Takamori. He was a great and valiant man. At the first rising of the people of the western coast, he deemed his enterprise so difficult, so impossible, that with the priest Gessho, he threw himself into the Satsuma Sea. He was rescued and thereafter strove so earnestly that he brought about the Restoration. In more recent years, thinking that the object he then had in view was easy of attainment, he signally failed. He was no braver at first than at last; but his first success was due to his strenuous endeavors, and his last failure to his careless remissness. From all this I conclude that, in our propagation of liberal pinciples, we shall obtain success, if we strive steadily, neither contemning the work as too easy, nor turning back from it if we find it difficult. To secure liberty we need sincerity and strong endeavor, not trick and intrigue. Some inconsiderate persons, wishing for freedom, plot and scheme to attain their object. I say that they are both injudicious and imprudent. There is reason in all things. The wise man does not hesitate, the brave man does not fear. Although there are many obstacles on that waste land of liberty which we are anxious to reclaim with your aid, yet staunch toil with hoe and plough will remove them all. Sharp cold of winter and suffocating heats of summer alike must not arrest our labor, though they may injure the growth of the plant and the ripening of the fruit. I believe that ere long our party will be reaping the crop of liberty. You must, then, be diligent.

J.W.M., 1882, June 15, pp. 459-61.

6. Count Ito on the Constitution.

(A speech at Ōtsu, 1889.)

Gentlemen, it is with great satisfaction that I meet you here to-day in response to your invitation. You have asked me through Governor Nakai to address you on the subject of the Constitution, but as I did not expect to be called on to speak to you, I have not had time to prepare myself. As I do not wish to disappoint you, however, I shall make some remarks, disjointed no doubt, on the topic that has been suggested. I trust you will bear in mind that the points that I am about to bring to your notice are of the utmost importance, and should be kept constantly in view by the people. Now that the Constitution has been promulgated, it will be of interest to discuss it briefly from a historical point of view, with the object of demonstrating that this momentous event is no mere fortuitous occurrence. It will not be necessary for us to go back a distance of hundreds of years ; all that is required is that we should examine the facts connected with the grand work of the Restoration. That great achievement, resulting in the return of power and rule to the proper hands, was due to two causes ; namely, loyalty and foreign intercourse. The loyalty found its expression in a strong desire to revert to that system under which power was vested in the Emperor, while foreign intercourse operated through an earnest wish to substitute for the national policy hitherto pursued (that of seclusion) a course aiming at the extension and development of our relations with foreign peoples. It does not concern my subject to discuss in detail the connection which existed between the loyal sentiment and the Jōi principle; that point may therefore be passed over with very few remarks. It will be sufficient to say that as the result of the combination of the one with the other, public feeling ran almost unprecedently high, and the Tokugawa regency at length, finding it impossible to stem the current, had to restore the reins of government to the rightful owner. As you are no doubt aware, the affairs of the country were, in the simple days of old, administered under the personal direction of the Emperor, by means of the gun and ken systems. As time went on the military classes, however, acquired a hold on the governing power, and eventually the court became a mere ornament; though the people at large, remembering the facts of history, always entertained a hope that sooner or later the Throne should have its own again. Of the existence of this loyal feeling the actions of Kusunoki and Nitta (in the reign of the Emperor Godaigo) afford us the most notable examples. Their efforts, however, were unhappily not only defeated but in the end more firmly established the feudal system. This page of our history cannot be sufficiently regretted, but as a matter of fact the failure of the loyalists then operated beneficially by stimulating to greater enthusiasm the minds of later generations. For feudalism long presented to its enemies a firm and impregnable front; but its end was surely though slowly approaching. Towards the close of the Tokugawa regime, the regency found itself face to face with the disagreeable necessity of opening to foreigners the gates which for so long had been closed against them; and of concluding treaties with some of those whom the Japanese people had been accustomed to despise as "barbarians." The unsatisfactory course pursued by the Shogunate with regard to foreigners speedily evoked disappro-

bation, and as its policy went from bad to worse, the old loyal
sentiment, which had only been slumbering, was at last roused
into action, and the Restoration was accomplished.   But for the
happy development of this feeling in its original and true form,
simultaneous with the opening of the country to foreigners, in all
probability the historian of that era would have had to record a
repetition cf the unsuccessful attempt of the Genkō and Kemmu
periods.[1]   As matters turned out, however, the inherent feeling
of attachment matured in time to operate, in conjunction with the
action of the regency in admitting foreigners, towards effecting
the overthrow of the Shōgunate and restoring power to the Imperial court.   But when this great result was achieved, it became evident that further attempts to maintain the seclusion and
isolation of the country from the rest of the world would be
highly impolitic.   Treaties were therefore concluded with our
visitors, and intercourse with them was duly initiated.   But
those who had now been entrusted by the Emperor with the
chief share in the conduct of public affairs were not satisfied
with the restoration of power to the Throne, and the inauguration of treaty relations with foreign powers.   They set themselves
to the task of introducing Western civilisation into Japan and of
eliminating such undesirable features as became apparent by
contrast with the conditions of the West.   They saw foreign
powers actively engaged in the rivalry of cultivating their
strength and resources ; and they could not help asking themselves how Japan could hope to hold her own in the struggle, or
maintain her independence and integrity so that, in common
with other countries, she might enjoy the benefits of civilisation
and enlightenment.   It was plain to them that if the national
dignity was to be demonstrated in the face of the world the
national resources must be developed and the national power
strengthened by some uniform process of government and administration.   In short, then, they resolved to remove the chief
stone in the feudal structure, which during hundreds of years

---

1. Genkō, 1331-34 ; Kemmu, 1334-5.

had been so firmly consolidated. This was accomplished without the shedding of a drop of blood. The feudal barons, without a murmur, returned the control of their fiefs and retainers to the Throne, and thenceforward the resources of the nation were brought under a uniform system of administration. So much having been accomplished, the next question was, how should these resources be husbanded and encouraged in their development. The answer plainly was, to educate the people with a view to their becoming factors in the progress of the country. The happy results of the policy thus adopted are plainly evident at the present day. If we carefully regard the method in which public education has advanced, from the cultivation of knowledge in connection with political economy, law, and kindred branches, to commerce, trade, and industries, and compare the present state of affairs with that which existed some twenty years ago, we shall not exaggerate if we say that the country has undergone a complete metamorphosis. If we reflect upon the history of civilisation in this country it will be perceived, I think, that while several influences have been at work, still the introduction of such alien religious systems as Confucianism and Buddhism, which were largely instrumental in elevating our people, and the development of such works as have conduced to their welfare, have been due to the benevolent guidance and encouragement of the Sovereign. We may therefore say with truth that the civilisation which we now possess is a gift from the Throne. These facts, which are plainly apparent in the pages of our history, will clearly demonstrate to others the nature of our national life. I shall now proceed to discuss the subject of the participation of the people in the government of the state. It is only by the protection of the law that the happiness of the nation can be promoted and the safety of person and property secured, and to attain these ends the people may elect their representatives and empower the latter to deliberate on laws with a view to the promotion of their own happiness and the safeguarding of their rights. This, gentlemen, is enacted by the Constitution, and I think you will agree that it constitutes a concession to the people of a most invaluable right. Under an absolute system of government the Sovereign's will is his command, and the Sovereign's command at once becomes law. In a constitutional country, however, the consent of that assembly which represents the people must be obtained. It will be evident, however, that as the supreme right is one and indivisible, the legislative power remains in the hands of the Sovereign and is not bestowed on the people. While the supreme right extends to everything, and its exercise is wide and comprehensive, its legislative and executive functions are undoubtedly the most important. These are in the hands of the Sovereign ; the rights pertaining thereto cannot be held in common by the Sovereign and his subjects ; but the latter are permitted to take part in legislation according to the provisions of the Constitution. In a country which is under absolute rule the view of the Sovereign is at once law ; in a constitutional country, on the other hand, nothing being law without a concurrence of views between the Sovereign and the people, the latter elect representatives to meet at an appointed place and carry out the view of the Sovereign. In other words, law in a constitutional state is the result of a concord of ideas between the Sovereign and subject ; but there can be no law when these two are in opposition to each other. The power of the national assembly being thus of great importance, similarly the right to take part in its work of legislation is an important one and should be respected. Now as to the actions of the representative assembly. It will be seen that the opinion of the assembly must be consulted in framing a new law. The people of course must observe and obey all laws passed and enacted prior to the inauguration of the Diet, but if it should appear that such laws are enforced in a manner opposed to the object for which they were framed, the people may demand that they be properly put into practice. As the enactment of future laws, then, will depend upon the Diet, the latter may philosophically be regarded as assisting in the exercise of the right of sovereignty. Hence the term " consent" (Kyōsan), which appears in the Constitution. There may possibly be not a few members of the public who have entertained the erroneous idea that the so-termed representatives will carry on the administration of the state. To these it must be stated that the assembly is purely a body to deliberate on laws and to supervise administrative affairs, but not to administer the affairs of state. In the Constitution there are provisions setting forth clearly the duties and operations of the assembly, but on that matter I have already touched incidentally. If we trace back to its origin the principle of a representative body, we find that it first manifested itself among an ancient German people. It has been, and still is indeed, affirmed that it is a growth of the English people, but it is not so in fact, for in an old German law, that in the levying of a tax the taxpayer should be consulted, we find the germ of the popular representative principle. The system prevailing in England must be an offshoot from the seedling that appeared in Germany, and from which the principle developed largely in later times in the west of Europe, though it never gained a hold in the central and eastern divisions. Till about a century ago it was held that representative bodies should have a monopoly of the legislative right, and the theory of thus dividing the supreme right found much favour. But this conclusion has been held to be illogical by modern scholars. They say the state is like a human body. Just as one brain controls the diverse actions of the limbs and other parts, so should one supreme power superintend and control all the other members of a nation, though such members may play various parts in the whole. This view is perhaps in its turn a little antiquated, but it is sufficient to show the absurdity of the tripartite theory which maintains that the representative body should monopolise the right of legislation. If we remember that the legislative right is a part of the supreme prerogative and that the latter is the sole possession of the Emperor, it will be apparent that no such monopoly is possible. But the Sovereign may permit the representative body to take part in the process of practically applying the legislative right.   Since the tripartite theory lost favour it has come to be recognized that the supreme right must be vested in one person and be indivisible.   The representative body is not only to be permitted to participate in legislation ; it will also be allowed to take part in other equally important matters, as for example, finance.   In every country where there is a representative body, the national finances, that is the estimates of income and expenditure, are laid before that body for deliberation.   It was at one time held in Europe that the estimates were in reality a law, and although such a theory is now untenable, still it may be taken as indicating the important part that finance plays in relation to the work of legislation.   In this process the representative body is within certain limits permitted to participate.   The rights of the assembly may be divided into three sections by way of illustration ; (1) in order to its enactment every new law [must pass under the deliberation of the assembly ; (2) its decision must be obtained in reference to financial questions pertaining to the national revenue and expenditure—in other words it must be consulted as to the method and process of levying any new tax necessary to supply the needs of the treasury, or of raising a national loan, for the obligation of repayment in the latter case reverts to the treasury, or—which amounts to the same thing—is included in the burdens of the people ; (3) whenever administrative measures involve harsh or illegal treatment of the people, the assembly is entitled to demand redress.   Such demand, however, is not to be made by any individual but must come from the whole body, and the procedure to be followed is to address the views of the assembly by petition or memorial to the Emperor.   The assembly is thus practically unhampered in the exercise of the last mentioned right.   If we look back into the history of the world to the origin of the representative body, we shall find that the principle has undergone an extraordinary degree of development.   At the

Restoration the institution, then well grown in Europe, was by an enlargement and extension of the scope of our national policy adopted in Japan. Now, by carefully adapting the principle to our national characteristics, manners, and customs, and by retaining what is excellent and discarding faults, we are about to put into practice a system of constitutional politics that is without rival in the East. And this leads us not unnaturally to discuss briefly the English constitution, which in many quarters has been thought worthy of imitation. I shall, however, speak solely of the difference in the history and evolution of the two constitutions, and shall not attempt to define their relative merits. In England there is no codified constitution, and you must bear in mind how the English people obtained the so-called Great Charter. The nobles of England, as you no doubt are aware, not only form a large section of the population, but they were, and are still, powerful. The Sovereign of that day, having engaged in unnecessary warfare with a foreign country, levied heavy burdens on the people, which policy led to much discontent. But the complaints were not confined to the mass of the people ; the nobles were also angered by the monarch's actions and refused to obey his commands. Eventually they combined and required him to sign the Magna Carta ; he at first refused but was at length compelled by force to comply. You will see then that while it is quite true that the King had oppressed the people, as a matter of fact this Magna Carta pledge was extorted from him by the nobles at the point of the sword. The case of Japan is totally different. The most cordial relations prevail between the Throne and the people while our Constitution is granted. The position of our Court cannot be at all compared with that of England when the Magna Carta was granted, for we know that our Imperial House has a single aim—the welfare and happiness of the nation. Not only were there no such discontented barons in this country, but our feudal lords, great and small, joined in requesting the Crown to take back the military and political rights which for centuries they had enjoyed. Could any two things be more radically different than the origins of the English and Japanese Constitutions ? If the English people felicitate themselves on the influence exercised in promoting and developing the national welfare and interest, by a Charter given under such ominous circumstances as was theirs, how much more should we congratulate ourselves having received from our benevolent Sovereign, under the most happy and peaceful auspices, the Constitution of the Japanese empire ! Moreover, the English after dethroning the king required his successor to sign the Declaration of Rights. It will be seen, then, that to attempt imitation without heed to these historical facts would be a grave error. I can see no reason why our country, either now or in the future, should follow the example of England. These facts can be easily investigated by the merest schoolboy, and I need not dwell further on them. The course which lies now before the Japanese empire is plain. Both ruler and ruled should apply their efforts smoothly and harmoniously to preserve tranquillity ; to elevate the status of the people ; to secure the rights and promote the welfare of each individual ; and finally, by manifesting abroad the dignity and power of Japan, to secure and maintain her integrity and independence. The valuable rights that I have described to you have been bestowed by the Constitution with a view to consolidating the foundation and elevating the position of our country. To this end, while discussion on points involving national interests is allowable, nay necessary, rivalry in efforts to promote the progress of the empire should go hand in hand with public order and tranquillity. The great end that we have in view must be attained by the co-operation of Sovereign and people ; the promotion of the national welfare is impossible without a peaceful and orderly condition of society. It is not so easy as theoretically it may be imagined, to destroy that which has been existing and to satisfactorily construct something else to take its place. Rarely do destruction and construction proceed successfully together. We, who have been privileged to live in this happy and auspicious time, have the earnest hope and desire that after the Constitution is put into force, the relations between the Sovereign and the people will become more and more intimate and trustful ; that the political life of the nation will move aiong smoothly and peacefully, and that boundless peace and prosperity will be be the lot of our country.

J.W.M., 1889, May 4, pp. 431-2.

7. AGRICULTURAL DEPRESSION RESCRIPT.

(March 30, 1885.)

It is hereby notified that, as considerable apprehensions are entertained as to the success of agricultural operations this year, in view of the irregularity of the weather since the opening of spring, while the importance of the industry and its products is such as is stated in the appended notice, the undernamed Secretaries will be despatched to the various agricultural districts for the encouragement of measures of improvement, and will exert every effort towards securing the desired end.

COUNT SAIGO YORIMICHI,
Minister of Agriculture and Commerce.

(Here follow the names of nine agricultural districts, and the list of Secretaries to be dispatched to them.)

THE NOTICE.

The embarrassment of the population, arising from abuses existing for many years, seems to have now reached its highest point. As to the means and methods of relieving this state of things, a scheme has already been developed, this Department having decided to encourage any deserving industry. In addition to this, financial matters have been so far adjusted that the value of paper is about equal to that of silver. This being the case, steadiness of value only is aimed at, and measures to that end are being carried out with energy. There is therefore no room for doubt that the desired object will soon be attained.

There is, however, one thing that forms a subject of deep concern at present, and that is the irregularity of the climate this year. Since the opening of the spring, cold and heat have alternated without any order of succession, and the damage caused to crops in all districts is very great. The crop of tea has fallen five-tenths from the usual yield, and that of wheat four-tenths. A retrospect of the past shows that agricultural dearth generally occurs in this country in a cyclical period of from thirty to fifty years. This is the fiftieth year since the famine in the period of Tempō,[1] and the climate is so abnormal, that it may well be an omen of another famine.[2] Even though no great destitution should occur, this is certainly not a usual or uneventful year.

Moreover, at present, extreme depression and scarcity prevail throughout the country, and it is difficult to see how the people are to tide over the year if no provision be made to meet present wants. What steps should be taken then? There are two, and only two, ways available, and they are to increase the quantity of labor, and to establish some means by which the accumulation of wealth can be effected. By the increase of labor is meant the making up by human contrivance, for the loss caused by bad weather, e.g. the cutting of grass five or six times instead of three as heretofore. If any deficiency be still found in the annual labor, those who used to work from six in the morning till six in the evening should increase their laboring hours to from four in the morning till eight in the evening. The working classes in our country are capable of an amount of labor unsurpassed by any people in the world, but they have the fault of idly spending their time by sleeping during daylight, by useless talk, by smoking, and in other ways. The whole

---

1. Tempō, 1830-1843.

2. The Minister of Agriculture and Commerce was severely criticised, and with justice, for issuing such an alarming statement. The harvest of the year 1885 turned out to be a fair average one.

population being sunk to the depths of the distress and embarrassment of the present day, it is but reasonable to suppose that they should have no stores of wealth left. Yet what is there we cannot accomplish if we only have the spirit to do so? Let all difficulties and hardships be patiently borne; let all expenses be curtailed, even those most difficult to reduce, and of daily importance, and let the minds of the people be applied to storing and accumulating wealth. Those who have any surplus should not be prompted to make purchases only by the cheapness of commodities at present as contrasted with the time when silver rose so much in value. Even supposing that each person spends the trifling sum of twenty-five *sen* a year, the money disbursed by thirty-seven million people will amount to one million two hundred and ninety thousand *yen*. Why, then, should not sufficient care be taken for economy and accumulation?

To carry into effect the above, two measure are required; the governing and the governed must pledge themselves to unite their efforts, and apply their energy in the direction of accomplishing the desired end. Prefects should encourage officers of urban and rural divisions and individuals willing to observe the precautions described above, and these latter should encourage the people in general to practically execute them. If all act as they are recommended to do, famine will not extend its sphere of devastation. Besides these means there cannot possibly be any contrivance answering the requirements of the hour.

J.W.M., 1885, June 6, p. 528.

8. LAW OF THE CONSTITUTION OF THE COURTS OF JUSTICE.

(Law No. 6, Feb. 8, 1890.)

PART I.—THE COURTS OF JUSTICE AND PUBLIC PROCURATORS' OFFICES.

CHAPTER I.—GENERAL PROVISIONS.

I. The ordinary courts shall be the following:—

1. Local Courts.
2. District Courts.
3. Appeal Courts.
4. The Supreme Court.

II. The ordinary courts shall decide all civil and criminal matters. Those matters, however, which are determined by law to come within the competency of a special court, are excepted.

III. The District Courts, Appeal Courts, and Supreme Court shall be collegiate courts, in which all matters not otherwise specially provided for by the Codes of Procedure, or by special law, shall be heard and decided in divisions consisting of several judges.

IV. The establishment and abolition of courts and their territorial jurisdiction, as well as changes in it, shall be determined by law.

V. Each Court shall be provided with a sufficient number of judges.

VI. To each Court there shall be attached a public procurator's office. The public procurators shall in criminal matters institute prosecutions and take the steps necessary for their conduct; shall demand the proper application of the law, shall see that the sentences of the Courts are duly enforced, and they can in civil matters demand, if they find it necessary, to have the same communicated to them, and can state their opinion thereon. They shall transact the business of supervision over judicial and administrative matters, belonging to or concerning the Courts, which legally come within the scope of their authority as the representatives of public interests.

The public procurators shall transact their business independently of the Courts.

The territorial jurisdiction of a public procurator's office shall be co-extensive with that of the Court to which it is attached.

When the public procurator, if there be only one, or when all the public procurators of an office, if more than one, are prevented from attending to any particular matter, the president of the Court, or, in the case of a Local Court, the judge or superintending judge, may, if the matter admits of no delay, appoint a judge to act for the public procurator and to attend to such a matter.

VII. The public procurators' offices shall be provided with a sufficient number of public procurators.

VIII. In each Court a Court Clerks' bureau shall be established. The Court Clerks' bureau shall manage correspondence and keep accounts and records, and do any other business which is by this or any other law specially provided for.

A separate Court Clerks' bureau for the transaction of similar business in the public procurators' office attached to a court can only be established if it should be found necessary, and even then this can only be done in the offices attached to collegiate Courts.

The Minister of Justice can appoint special officials to the Courts to be entrusted by them solely with the keeping of the accounts of the Courts.

IX. In the Local Courts there shall be process servers. The process servers shall serve documents issuing from the Courts, and shall carry into execution the decisions of the Courts.

The process servers shall perform such other special duties as are provided for by this or any other law.

X. In the following cases, except those specially provided for by law, the next higher Court having jurisdiction over the respective Courts shall, when duly applied to, decide what Court is competent to decide the matter in question :—

> 1. When a Court otherwise competent is, either on the ground of law, or through particular circumstances, prevented from exercising its jurdisdiction, and the Court appointed by virtue of Article XIII. of this law to act for such Court is also prevented from exercising its jurisdiction.
>
> 2. When the competency of a Court is in doubt, owing to uncertainty as to the boundaries of its territorial jurisdiction.

3. When by virtue of law, or of two or more final judgments, two or more Courts have concurrent jurisdiction.

4. When one of two or more Courts that have declared themselves incompetent, or have been so declared, by final judgments, ought to exercise jurisdiction.

CHAPTER II.—THE LOCAL COURTS.

XI. The jurisdiction of a Local Court shall be exercised by a single judge.

In a Local Court, which has more than one judge, the business shall be distributed among them in accordance with the general principles laid down by the Minister of Justice.

Such distribution shall be decided upon annually in advance by the president of the District Court.

Any business transacted by a judge of a Local Court shall not be invalidated by the mere fact that such business, according to the arranged distribution, ought to have belonged to another judge.

In a Local Court which has more than one judge, the Minister of Justice shall appoint one of them as the superintending judge and assign to him the administrative business of the Court.

XII. When the distribution of business has once been decided upon, it shall not be changed during the judicial year except in cases of inconvenience of a permanent nature, such, for instance, as when the distributed work of a judge is excessive, or when a judge is removed, or is absent for a long time from sickness or other causes.

XIII. When the judges of a Local Court are prevented from discharging their duties, they shall act as substitutes for each other in the order fixed upon annually in advance by the president of the District Court. As to the duties of the superintending judge, they shall, however, act as his substitute in the order of their official rank.

The Local Court that shall act as substitute for another

Court, when such Court is prevented, on grounds of law or through particular circumstances, from discharging its duties, shall similarly be determined annually in advance.

XIV. In civil actions, the Local Courts, subject to the provisions of the Code of Civil Procedure with respect to counter-claims, shall have the following jurisdiction :—

1. Over claims in which the amount involved or the value of the object in dispute does not exceed 100 *yen.*

2. Over the following actions without respect to value :—

(*a*) Actions between lessors and lessees with respect to the entering into or giving up possession, or the use or occupation, or repairing of, any dwelling-house or other building or of any part of a dwelling-house or other building, or with respect to the detention of a lessee's furniture or effects by a lessor.

(*b*) Actions which concern only the fixing of boundaries of immovable property.

(*c*) Actions concerning possession only.

(*d*) Actions between employers and employees with respect to an engagement for one year or a shorter period.

(*e*) Actions between travellers and hotel or restaurant keepers, or between travellers and carriers with respect to the following matters :—

1. Payment for their board or lodging, or for the carriage of themselves or the luggage accompanying them.

2. The luggage or money, or valuables, deposited by them with such persons for safe keeping.

XV. In non-contentious matters, the Local Courts shall, within the limits and in the manner provided by law, be competent to transact the following business :—

1. To supervise the guardians or curators of minors, lunatics, idiots, absentees, and other persons prohibited, by law or any judgment, from managing their own affairs.

2. To keep registers of matters affecting titles to immovable property and ships.

3. To keep commercial registers, and registers of those patents, designs, and trade-marks which have been registered in the Patent Office.

XVI. In criminal matters the Local Courts shall have the following jurisdiction :—

1. Over contraventions.

2. Over delicts for which the nominal punishment does not exceed 1 months' imprisonment with, or without, a fine of not more than 50 *yen*, or a fine of 100 *yen* only.

3. Over delicts, except those mentioned in the Penal Code, Book II., Chapter 1, for which the nominal punishment does not exceed two years' imprisonment with, or without, a fine of not more than 200 *yen*, or a fine of 300 *yen* only, and which have been assigned to them by the public procurator's office attached to the District Court or branch division of such Court, as appearing, from the circumstances, of a nature not to require a greater punishment than that mentioned in subsection 2.

In prosecutions instituted by the abovementioned steps, the Local Court, if at any time prior to rendering judgment the offence, in case it be proved, appears to it to be of a nature which could not be adequately punished by such punishment as is mentioned in sub section 2, shall declare itself incompetent to proceed further, and the public procurator shall then take the proper steps to bring the accused for trial before the competent Court.

XVII. The competency of the Local Courts, except that mentioned in the foregoing Articles, shall in respect to the matters mentioned in this Chapter, be determined by the Codes of Procedure or by special law.

XVIII. In the public procurators' office of each Local Court, there shall be one or more public procurators.

The business of the public procurators in the public procurators' office of the Local Courts may be transacted by the members of the police force or officers of the gendarmerie or the forest officials in the locality.

The Minister of Justice may, in proper cases, authorise either the judges of the Local Courts, aspirants, or the heads of the counties, cities, towns, or villages, to act for the public procurators.

CHAPTER III.—THE DISTRICT COURTS.

XIX. The District Courts shall be Collegiate Courts of First Instance.

In each District Court there shall be one or more civil divisions and criminal divisions.

XX. In each District Court there shall be a president.

The president of a District Court shall direct the general affairs of the Court and superintend its administrative business.

In each division of a District Court there shall be a president, who shall superintend the business.

XXI. The Minister of Justice shall appoint annually one or more of the judges of each District Court to conduct preliminary examinations in criminal matters belonging to the jurisdiction of the Court.

XXII. The business of each District Court shall be distributed among the different divisions and judges of preliminary examination, in accordance with the general principles laid down by the Minister of Justice.

The disposition of the president and members of each division in each District Court, and the representation of the president of the Court and the president and members of each division in case of their being prevented from attending to duty, shall also be determined every year in advance.

The matters mentioned in the above two paragraphs shall be decided upon by the majority of votes in the meeting which is to be held by the president of the Court, presidents of divisions, and a senior judge of each division, and in which the president of the Court shall preside. In the case of a tie, the president of the meeting shall have the casting vote.

The president of the District Court shall name the division in which he intends to preside himself during the ensuing year.

XXIII. Any business which has been commenced in any division but not finished by the end of the judicial year or before the commencement of the vacation, may, if the president of the Court should consider it expedient, be brought to a conclusion by the same members of such division.

Any business which is to be transacted by the judges of

preliminary examination, and which has not been finished, may similarly be concluded.

XXIV. When the distribution of the business, and the disposition of the judges, has once been decided upon in accordance with Article XXII. it shall not, excepting during the vacation, be changed during the judicial year, unless it be on grounds of inconvenience of a permanent nature, such, for instance, as when the distributed work of a division is excessive, or when a judge is removed, or is absent for a long time from sickness or other causes.

In the event of the business of a Court being excessive for its existing divisions, a new divisions, or division, may be established, if the Minister of Justice should consider it advisable.

XXV. In the event of a judge of a District Court being prevented from attending to a particular matter, and there being no other judge of the same Court who can represent him, the president of the Court may, if such matter be found of an urgent nature, order that a judge of a Local Court within the territorial jurisdiction of the District Court, or a supernumerary judge, shall act as his substitute.

XXVI. In civil actions the District Court shall have the following jurisdiction :—

1. In first instance :

Over claims other than those which come within the competency of the Local Courts or that of the Appeal Courts provided by Article XXVIII.

2. In second istance :

(a) Over appeals from judgments of the Local Courts.
(b) Over complaints so far as the same are provided for by law against rulings and orders of the Local Courts.

XXVII. In criminal actions the District Court shall have the following jurisdiction :—

1. In first instance :

Over criminal actions which are not within the competency of the Local Courts and the special competency of the Supreme Court.

2. In second instance:

(*a*) Over appeals from judgments of the Local Courts.

(*b*) Over complaints so far as the same are provided for by law against rulings and orders of the Local Courts.

XXVIII. The District Courts shall have general jurisdiction in bankruptcy.

XXIX. The District Courts shall have jurisdiction over complaints, so far as the same are provided for by law, made against rulings and orders of the Local Courts in non-contentious matters.

XXX. The competency of the District Courts and the extent and manner in which their jurisdiction is to be exercised, shall, so far as the same are not provided for by the law, be determined by the Codes of Procedure or by special law.

XXXI. The Minister of Justice may, if he sees fit on account of the distance or difficulty of access of a District Court from some of the Local Courts within its territorial jurisdiction, order that one or more branch divisions of the District Court shall be established for the transaction of part of the civil and criminal business belonging to such Court, and shall determine the Local Court or Courts at which such branch division or divisions shall sit.

In the composition of such a branch division the judges either of the Local Court where the branch division is established, or of a neighbouring Local Court, may be employed. In this case the selection of such judges shall rest with the Minister of Justice.

The Minister of Justice shall appoint the judges of preliminary examination, as well as the public procurators, who are to serve in such branch divisions.

The Minister of Justice may appoint as judges of preliminary examination the judges of Local Courts with the territorial jurisdiction of the District Court of which the division is a branch.

The provisions of Article XXIII. with respect to representation shall also be applied to branch divisions.

XXXII. In the District Courts, the matters, which by the Codes of Procedure are to be tried and decided in Court, shall be heard and decided by :a division consisting of three judges, one of whom shall be the presiding judge, and in which under no circumstances shall more than one supernumerary judge be allowed to sit. Other matters shall be disposed of of by the judges as provided for by the Codes of Procedure or by special law.

XXXIII. In the public procurators' office of each District Court there shall be a head public procurator, who shall distribute, direct and superintend the transaction of the business of such office. With regard to the transaction of such business, the other public procurators of the office shall, however, have power to act for him in any matter whatever, without being specially authorised.

CHAPTER IV.—THE APPEAL COURTS.

XXXIV. The Appeal Courts shall be collegiate Courts of second instance.

In each Appeal Court there shall be one or more civil divisions and criminal divisions.

XXXV. In each Appeal Court there shall be a president.

The president of the Appeal Court shall direct the general affairs of the Court and superintend its administrative business.

In each division of the Appeal Court there shall be a president who shall superintend the :business of his division and determine its distribution.

XXXVI. With respect to the distribution and conclusion of business and the representation of one judge by another, Articles XXII., XXIII. and XXV shall be applied to the Appeal Courts, subject to the following modifications :—

1. That the power conferred by each of the above mentioned Articles on the presidents of the District Courts shall

be considerred as conferred on the presidents of the Appeal Courts.

2. That when a judge of an Appeal Court is prevented from attending to any particular matter, and there is no other judge of the same court who can represent him, a judge of the District Court of the place where the Appeal Court has its seat, and not a supernumerary judge, may, if such matter be found of an urgent nature, he required to act for such judge in the Appeal Court upon a notice being sent by the president of the Appeal Court to the president of the District Court to furnish him with such judge.

XXXVII. The Appeal Court shall have the following jurisdiction :—

1. Over appeals from judgments of the District Courts rendered in first instance.
2. Over appeals on ground of error in law against judgments of the District Courts rendered on appeals from judgments of the Local Courts.
3. Over complaints, so far as the same are provided for by law, against rulings and orders of the District Courts.

XXXVIII. The jurisdiction both in first and second instance over civil actions against members of the Imperial family shall belong to the Appeal Court at Tōkyō. With regard to the procedure in first instance to be followed in this case, the procedure in first instance in the District Courts shall be applied.

XXXIX. The competency of the Appeal Courts, and the extent and manner in which their jurisdiction is to be exercised, shall, so far as the same are not provided for in this law, be determinded by the Codes of Procedure, or by special law.

XL. In the Appeal Courts, the matters which by the Codes of Procedure are to be tried and decided in Court, shall be heard and decided by a division consisting of five judges, one of whom shall be the presiding judge. Other matters shall be disposed of by the judges as provided for by such Codes.

XLI. In the case provided for in Article XXXVIII. the action shall in first instance be tried and decided by a division consisting of five judges, and shall in second instance be tried and decided by a division specially composed of seven judges ; one of such five or seven judges shall be the presiding judge.

XLII. In the public procurators' office of each Appeal Court there shall be a chief public procurator.

With respect to the authority of the chief public procurator and the other public procurators Article XXXIII. shall be applied.

CHAPTER V.—THE SUPREME COURT.

XLIII. The Supreme Court shall be the highest court of justice.

In the Supreme Court there shall be one or more civil divisions and criminal divisions.

XLIV. In the Supreme Court there shall be a president.

The president of the Supreme Court shall direct the general affairs of the Court and superintend its administrative business.

In each division of the Supreme Court there shall be a president, who shall superintend the business of his division and determine its distribution.

XLV. The distribution of business in the Supreme Court, and the order of representution, shall be determined in advance by the president of the Court after consultation with the presidents of the divisions.

The president of the Supreme Court shall name the division in which he intends to preside himself during the ensuing year.

When a judge of the Supreme Court is prevented from attending to any particular matter, and there is no other judge of the same Court who can represent him, a judge of the Appeal Court of the place where the Supreme Court has its seat, may, if such matter be found of an urgent nature, be required to act for such judge in the Supreme Court upon a notice being sent by the president of the Supreme Court to the president of the Appeal Court to furnish him with such judge.

XLVI. The president, or any member, of a division may at any time be transferred to another division by the president of the Court after first obtaining the consent to such transfer of such president or member.

XLVII. When the composition of a division once decided upon is changed, Article XXIII. shall be applied to the businesss then pending.

With regard to changes in the distribution of business during the judicial year, Article XXIV. shall be applied.

XLVIII. The opinions expressed by the Supreme Court on any point of law in giving any decision shall be binding on the lower courts in all proceedings in the same action.

XLIX. When a division of the Supreme Court, after hearing an appeal on ground of error in law, is of an opinion contrary to a former decision of one or more divisions of the Court upon the same poine of law, such division shall report it to the president of the Court, who shall, upon receipt of such report, order all the civil or criminal divisions, or all the civil and criminal divisions of the Court, according to the nature of the appeal, to sit together, and re-try, and decide the appeal.

L. The Supreme Court shall have the following jurisdiction :—

1. In last instance :—

> (a) Over appeals on ground of error in law against the judgement of the Appeal Courts, other than those rendered by virtue of Article XXXVII. sub-section 2, and those rendered in first instance mentioned in Article XXXVIII.

> (b) Over complaints so far as the same are provided for by law, against rulings and orders of the Appeal Court.

2. In first and last instance :—

> Over the preliminary examination into and decision of crimes mentioned in the Penal Code, Book II., Chapters I. and II., as well as offences committed by members of the Imperial family, which render them liable to imprisonment or to a severer punishment.

LI. For the trial and decision of the matters mentioned in the preceding Article, sub-section 2, the Supreme Court may, it found necessary, hold its sittings in an Appeal Court or District Court.

In the above case, the judges of the Appeal Courts may be appointed to sit as members of a division, but they must be less than one-half in number of the division.

LII. The competency of the Supreme Court, and the extent and manner in which its jurisdiction is to be exercised, shall, so far as the same are not provided for in this law, be determined by the Codes of Procedure, or by special law.

LIII. In the Supreme Court, matters which by the Codes of Procedure are to be tried and decided in Court, shall be heard and decided by a division consisting of seven judges, one of whom shall be the presiding judge. Other matters shall be disposed of by the judges as provided for by the Codes of Procedure.

LIV. In the case provided for by Article XLIX, at least two-thirds of the judges of the combined divisions must attend.

When, in the above case, all the civil or criminal divisions or all the civil and criminal divisions combine, the judge highest in rank of all the judges in such combined division shall be appointed as the president of such division; the president of the Court, if he may see fit, shall have the right to preside himself in such division.

LV. The president of the Supreme Court shall for each particular case, which by Article L. is to be tried by the Supreme Court in first and last instance, order a judge of the Court to conduct the preliminary examination. He may, however, order, if it be convenient, the judges of any Court to conduct such preliminary examination.

LVI. In the public procurators' office of the Supreme Court there shall be the public procurator-general.

With respect to the authority of the public procurator-general and the other public procurators, Article XXXIII. shall, be applied.

PART II.—THE OFFICIALS OF THE COURTS OF JUSTICE AND
OF THE PUBLIC PROCURATORS' OFFICES.

CHAPTER I.—THE NECESSARY PREPARATION AND
QUALIFICATIONS IN ORDER TO BE CREATED
A JUDGE OR PUBLIC PROCURATOR.

LVII. With the exception of the cases mentioned in Article LXV, two competitive examinations must be passed in order to be created a judge or public procurator.

LVIII. The particulars concerning the qualifications necessary for candidates in order to enable them to compete for the examinations mentioned in the preceding Article, as well as the particulars relating to such examinations, shall be determined by the Minister of Justice in the Regulations for Examinations for Judges and Public Procurators.

Candidates who have passed the first examination, shall, before competing for the second examination, be required to go through a period of three years' practical training in the Courts and public procurators' offices as aspirants.

The particulars concerning the above-mentioned training shall also be provided for in the said Regulations for examinations.

LIX. When the Minister of Justice finds the conduct of an aspirant to merit dismissal, he may at any time dismiss him. The particulars concerning such dismissal shall also be provided for in the said Regulations for examinations.

LX. Those aspirants who have gone through the training for one year or more, may transact certain judicial business in the Local Courts if ordered to do so by the judge who has for the time being the superintendence of their training.

Judges of preliminary examination, and commissioned judges of the District Courts, can similary make use of aspirants under their charge to transact certain business for them.

LXI. Aspirants shall in no case be competent to transact the following business :—

1. To render any decision whether in contentious or non-contentious matters.

2. To take evidence, except in the cases mentioned in the second paragraph of the preceding Article.

3. To make entries in the registers.

LXII. An aspirant who has passed the second competitive examination, can be created a judge or public procurator.

LXIII. A newly created judge or public procurator shall, if there be a vacancy, be appointed to a local court or district court, or to a public procurators' office of a local court or district court as the case may be.

The Minister of Justice shall order such judge or public procurator to act, until there be a vacancy, as supernumerary public procurator, and shall employ him either in the Department of Justice, or in a local or district court, or in a public procurators' office of such a court.

LXIV. A supernumerary judge or supernumerary public procurator, employed in a local or district court, or in the public procurators' office of such a court, may, when a judge or public procurator is prevented from attending to his duties and the ordinary course of representation cannot then be followed, be authorised by the Minister of Justice to represent, subject to the restriction of Article XXXII., such judge or public procurator.

The Minister of Justice may authorise a supernumerary judge or supernumerary public procurator, to fill, within the limits of this law, any temporarily vacant position of judge or public procurator in a local or district court, or in the public procurators' office of such a court so long as such vacancy continues.

LXV. A person who has been for three years or more a professor of law in the Imperial University or an advocate, may be created a judge or public procurator, without passing the examinations mentioned in this Chapter.

Graduates in law of the Imperial University may be appointed aspirants without passing the first examination.

LXVI. The following persons cannot be created judges or public procurators :—

1. A person who has been convicted of a crime, unless such crime be of a political nature and he has been rehabilitated.
2. A person who has been convicted of a delict punishable with hard labour.
3. A person who is an undischarged bankrupt.

CHAPTER II.—THE JUDGES.

LXVII. The judges shall be created by the Emperor or by his order, and such creation shall be for life.

LXVIII. The president of the Supreme Court shall be appointed by the Emperor from among the judges created by the Emperor. The president of each Appeal Court and the presidents of divisions in the Supreme Court shall be appointed, upon the nomination of the Minister of Justice, from among the judges created by the Emperor. The appointments of other judges shall be made by the Minister of Justice.

LXIX. No person can be appointed judge of an Appeal Court, unless he has been a judge for five years or more, or created a judge after he had been a public procurator, or a professor of law of the Imperial University, or an advocate, for five years or more.

LXX. No person can be appointed judge of the Supreme Court, unless he has been a judge for ten years or more, or created a judge after he had been a public procurator, or a professor of law of the Imperial University, or an advocate, for ten years or more.

LXXI. In calculating the periods of time mentioned in Articles LXIX. and LXX., it shall not be necessary that the service should have been continuous is one only of the employments mentioned in each of the said Articles up to the time of the said appointment.

LXXII. Judges, as long as they remain on the active list of the judicial service, shall not be permitted to do the following :—

1. To publicly interest themselves in politics.

2. To become members of any political party or society or of any local, municipal, or district assembly.

3. To occupy any public office to which a salary is attached, or which has for its object pecuniary gain.

4. To carry on any commercial business or to do any other business prohibited by the administrative ordinances.

LXXIII. With the exception of the cases mentioned in Article LXXIV. and LXXV. a judge shall not, against his will, be either removed to any other official position, or be transferred from one court to another, or be supended from exercising his judicial functions, or be dismissed, or have his salary reduced unless it be by virtue of a criminal sentence or a disciplinary punishment; the cases in which a judge is ordered to be transferred from one court to another, when he is a supernumerary judge, or when there is necessity to fill up any vacant position of judge, are excepted.

The above provision shall not affect the suspension of judicial functions which may be permitted by law, either at the commencement, or while the same is pending, of a disciplinary enquiry, or a criminal prosecution.

LXXIV. A judge may, when he becomes so enfeebled in his physical constitution or mental faculties that he is not able to discharge his duties, be ordered by the Minister of Justice, under the resolution of a general meeting of an Appeal Court or the Supreme Court, to retire from the judicial service.

LXXV. In the event of a change in the organisation of a court being made by law, the Minister of Justice shall have the power, if there is no vacancy to which he can appoint a judge left without a post thereby, to place such judge temporarily on half salary to await a vacancy.

LXXVI. The regulations concerning the official rank, salary, and promotion of jndges shall be determined by Imperial Decree.

LXXVII. Judges, upon their retirement from the judicial service, shall be pensioned in accordance with the Pension Law.

LXXVIII. The salary of a judge shall continue to be paid to him in spite of his having been suspended from discharging his duties on account of a disciplinary enquiry, or criminal prosecution, having been instituted against him.

CHAPTER III.—PUBLIC PROCURATORS.

LXXIX. The public procurators shall be created by the Emperor or by his order.

Articles LXXVI. and LXXVII., shall also be applied to the public procurators.

The public procurator-general and chief public procurators shall be appointed, upon the nomination of the Minister of Justice, from among the public procurators created by the Emperor. The appointments of other public procurators shall be made by the Minister of Justice.

LXXX. The public procurators shall not against their will be dismissed, unless it be by virtue of a criminal sentence or a disciplinary punishment.

LXXXI. The public procurators cannot in any way interfere with the judges in the discharge of judicial duties, nor can they trans ct any judicial business.

LXXXII. The public procurators shall obey the orders of their official superiors.

LXXXIII. The public procurator-general, chief public procurators and head public procurators shall have the power to transact personally any business coming within the scope of the duties of a public procurator in any court within the limits of the respective districts in which they have authority to act.

They shall have the power, within the same limits, to transfer any business from the public procurator who should in the ordinary course transact it, to another public procurator.

LXXXIV. The members of the judicial police shall obey the orders issued to them officially by the the public procurators within the territorial limits of their office, as well as orders issued to them by the official superiors of such public procurators.

The Department of Justice or the public procurators' .offices, and the Department of the Interior or the local administrative authorities, shall in consultation together determine those members of the police force who shall act as judicial police within the district of each court, and shall receive and carry out the orders above mentioned.

CHAPTER IV.—COURT CLERKS.

LXXXV. The Courts shall be provided, in accordance with Article VIII, with a sufficient number of clerks.

There shall be at least one clerk for each judge in the local courts, and for each division in the collegiate courts.

LXXXVI. In the clerks' bureau of a district court, there shall be superintending clerk. In the clerks' bureau of an appeal court, and of the supreme court, there shall be a chief clerk.

In the clerks' bureau of a local court and of a public procurator's office, there shall, if there be more than one clerk, be a superintending clerk.

Superintending clerks and chief clerks shall, subject to the orders of their official superiors, direct and superintend the business in their respective bureaux.

LXXXVII. Any business transacted by a clerk, within the limits of the duties of such an official, shall not be invalidated by the mere fact that such business, according to the arranged distribution of business, ought to have belonged to another clerk.

LXXXVIII. Clerks shall be created and appointed by the Minister of Justice.

Chief clerks shall be created by the order of the Emperor.

The appointments of the chief clerks shall be made by the Minister of Justice.

LXXXIX. In order to be created a clerk, an examination must be passed as determined by Imperial Decree.

The particulars concerning the qualifications necessary for candidates in order to enable them to pass the examination, as well as the particulars relating to such examination and the practical training to be gone through after passing the same, shall be determined by the Minister of Justice in the Regulations for the examination of court clerks.

XC. A candidate who has been created a clerk, shall, if there be no vacancy, be meanwhile appointed a supernumerary clerk.

A supernumerary clerk can temporarily be ordered to act as a clerk.

XCI. Clerks shall obey the orders of their official superiors.

In the sittings of the courts they shall obey the orders of the presiding judge, or, if there be only one judge, then of such judge.

They shall similarly when employed in a public procurator's office, or when attached to any judge or public procurator for any particular business, obey the orders of such office, or judge, or public procurator, as the case may be.

If the abovementioned orders concern the taking down of any statement, or the making or alteration of any written document or record, and in their opinion such making or alteration is not justified, they can attach thereto a note stating their own views.

The duties of clerks, excepting those mentioned in the above four paragraphs, and the manner in which their business is to be conducted, shall be determined by the Minister of Justice in the Regulations concerning clerks.

XCII. The president of a collegiate court, or the judge or or superintending judge of a local court, may temporarily authorise an aspirant under training in such court to transact the business of clerks.

In such cases such aspirant shall, when he must sign his name officially, note that he does so by virtue of a special authorisation.

XCIII. In the transaction of business, supernumerary clerks shall equally be competent with clerks, except that for which restrictions are made in the regulations for clerks.

Chapter V.—Process Servers.

XCIV. Each local court shall be provided in accordance with Article IX., with a sufficient number of process servers.

XCV. Process servers shall be created and appointed by the Minister of Justice. He can delegate to the president of an appeal court the power to create and appoint process servers to serve in the courts within the territorial jurisdiction of such appeal court.

The regulations concerning the qualifications necessary for being created a process server, and the examination for process servers shall be determined by the Minister of Justice.

XCVI. Process servers shall receive fees. If such fees do not amount to a certain sum, they shall receive an allowance.

XCVII. Process servers shall perform their duties anywhere within the territorial limits of the district court that has jurisdiction over the local court to which they belong.

XCVIII. All documents issuing from the court and requiring service shall, except in those cases in which the law permits service to be made directly or through the post by a clerk, be served by process servers.

Process servers shall, in criminal matters, carry into execution the decision of the Courts, so far as this is not done by the members of the police force.

The competency of process servers, except as mentioned in the above two paragraphs, shall be determined by the Codes of Procedure, or by special law.

XCIX. Process servers shall be required to give money security for the proper discharge of their duties.

The particular regulations for the duties of process servers, as well as the regulations concerning money security, shall be determined by the Minister of Justice.

C. Process servers shall obey the orders of clerks who have received the orders of the official superiors of the Court to which they belong, as well as of clerks who have received the orders of the official superiors of the District Court having jurisdiction over that Court, and of the official superiors of any such clerks.

CHAPTER VI.—USHERS.

CI. Ushers shall be engaged and dismissed in the Supreme Court, Appeal Courts, and District Courts by the presidents of those Courts, and in the Local Courts by the presidents of the District Courts.

CII. Ushers shall be ordered to attend the sittings of the Courts and to transact such business as is laid down in the general regulations published by the Minister of Justice.

They may, in the event of the services of a process server not being procurable, be employed by a Local Court to serve documents at the place where such Court has its seat.

PART III.—THE TRANSACTION OF JUDICIAL BUSINESS.

CHAPTER I.—SITTINGS OF THE COURTS.

CIII. The sittings of the Courts shall be held at the Courts or branch divisions.

A Local Court may be ordered by the Minister of Justice, if circumstances should appear to him to require it, to perform its functions at fixed places within the territorial limits of such Court.

CIV. The presidency and the direction of proceedings shall belong, in the collegiate Courts to the presiding judge holding the sitting, and in the Local Courts to the judge holding the sitting.

The powers belonging to a presiding judge shall also be vested in any single judge when acting judicially.

CV. When a decision to suspend public trial is made by a Court, such decision with its reasons for so deciding, shall be delivered before the public is excluded, and the public shall in such cases be re-admitted when the judgment is to be delivered.

CVI. The presiding judge shall have the power, in spite

of suspension of public trial, to admit into the Court persons to whom he may see fit to give special permission.

CVII. The presiding judge can exclude from the Court women or children, as well as persons not properly dressed ; the reasons for such exclusion shall be recorded in the minutes of proceedings.

CVIII. The maintenance of order during the sitting of a Court shall rest with the presiding judge.

CIX. The presiding judge shall have the power to exclude from the Court any person who interrupts the trials, or who behaves himself improperly.

The presiding judge shall have the power, if the conduct of the above mentioned offender appears to him to require it, to order him to be taken into custody and to be detained until the end of the sitting, when the Court shall either order him to be set at liberty, or shall punish him with a fine not exceeding five *yen*, or with imprisonment not exceeding five days.

Against such punishment there shall lie no appeal except on the ground of error in law, and it shall be without prejudice to any criminal prosecution for such act, if it constitutes a delict or crime.

CX. The provisions of the preceding Article shall also be applied to parties, witnesses, and experts, subject to the following modifications :—

1. The Court may punish such an offender at once instead of at the end of the sitting.
2. The Court may, if the offender be a plaintiff, in addition to any punishment awarded, suspend the trial until he has purged himself, by apology or by obedience, of his contempt.

CXI. The presiding judge can prohibit an advocate who makes use of improper language from the exercise of his right to further address the Court in the same case. Such prohibition shall be without prejudice to any disciplinary prosecution for such conduct.

CXII. The powers conferred by Articles CIX., CX., and CXI., for the keeping of order in the sittings of the Courts, may also be exercised by a judge of preliminary examination or a commission judge or by an aspirant, when legally discharging the functions of such a judge.

In these cases a protest may be lodged with such judge or aspirant within twenty-four hours.

If the order has been made by a judge of preliminary examination or an aspirant commissioned by him, such protest shall be decided by the criminal division, or branch criminal division, of the Court to which such judge belongs, and if made by a commissioned judge, or an aspirant commissioned by him, by the Court which has commissioned such judge.

CXIII. When the powers conferred by Articles CIX., CX., CXI., and CXII. have been exercised, it shall be entered in the minutes of proceedings, as well as the reasons that necessitated it.

If in the above case the act constitutes a crime or delict, or is an act that should be punished disciplinarily, such entry shall contain full particulars, and a report shall be made by the presiding judge to the authorities competent to deal further with the matter.

CXIV. Judges, procurators, and court clerks shall, at sittings held in open court, wear the dress of office.

Advocates who take part in the proceedings in the above mentioned sittings, must also wear the dress of their profession.

CHAPTER II. THE LANGUAGE OF THE COURTS.

CXV. In the Courts the Japanese language shall be used.

When a party or witness or expert is unacquainted with the Japanese language, an interpreter shall, where the Codes of Procedure or special law so require, be employed.

CXVI. Regulations concerning the appointment and employment of interpreters and the duties to be performed by them in judicial proceedings shall be determined by the Minister of Justice.

CXVII. When the services of an interpreter cannot be procured, court clerks may, with the consent of the presiding judge, be used to interpret, if they are acquainted with such language as it is necessary to interpret.

CXVIII. When the person interested in any action to which a foreigner is a party, and the officials who take part in the trial of such action are acquainted with a particular foreign language, the presiding judge may, if he deem it expedient, permit the oral proceedings to be conducted in such foreign language; but the official record of such proceedings shall kept in the Japanese language.

CHAPTER III.—DELIBERATION AND DELIVERY OF DECISION.

CXIX. Decisions of the collegiate Courts shall be deliberated by the fixed number of judges in accordance with this law.

CXX. In criminal trials which will probably last for more than three days, the president of the Court may appoint a supplementary judge to attend the trial. Such supplementary judge shall have the power, in case a judge should during such trial be prevented by sickness or other causes from further taking part in it, to take his place and conclude the trial and decision in his stead.

CXXI. The deliberations of the judges shall not take place in public, but supernumerary judges and aspirants may be admitted to be present.

The deliberations of the judges shall be opened and regulated by the judge who has presided at the trial of the case for which such deliberations are held. With respect to what takes place at such deliberations, as well as with respect to the opinion of each judge, and the number of the majority or minority, strict secrecy must be observed.

CXXII. In the deliberations, the judges shall deliver their opinions consecutively, commencing with the judge who is lowest in rank, and concluding with the presiding judge. If two or more judges should happen to have equal rank, the one who is junior in age should deliver his opinion first, and with regard to a commissioned matter, the commissioned judge should deliver his opinion first.

CXXIII. The opinion of the absolute majority shall constitute the decision of the Court.

When, in respect to an amount of money to be determined, there are more than two different opinions, none of which obtains the absolute majority, the number of the opinions in favour of the largest amount is to be added to the number of those in favour of the next largest, and so on, until an absolute majority of opinion is obtained.

When, in respect to a criminal matter, there are more than two different opinions, none of which obtains the absolute majority, the number of opinions most unfavourable to the accused is to be added to the number of those next most unfavourable, and so on, until an absolute majority is obtained.

CXXIV. No judge can refuse to deliver his opinion on any question that has to be decided.

CHAPTER IV.—REGULATIONS FOR THE TRANSACTION OF BUSINESS IN THE COURTS AND PUBLIC PROCURATORS' OFFICES.

CXXV. The Regulations for the guidance of the courts and public procurators' offices shall be determined by the Minister of Justice.

The presidents of the Appeal Courts and chief public procurators shall, under the above mentioned Regulations, respectively issue instructions to the Courts and the public procurators' offices within their districts, for the general and as far as possible uniform transaction of business, and more particularly with regard to the hours during which the offices of the courts and the public procurators' offices should be open, and the hours and days of sittings of the courts.

The Supreme Court shall determine its own regulations for the transaction of business, but before putting the same in force shall obtain the approval thereto of the Minister of Justice.

Chapter V.—The Judicial Year and Vacation.

CXXVI. The judicial year shall commence on the 1st January and shall end on the 31st December.

CXXVII. The vacation of the courts shall commence on the 11th July and shall end on the 10th September.

CXXVIII. During the vacation civil proceedings other than the following, already begun, shall be stayed, and no fresh proceedings, other than the following, shall be commenced :—

1. Claims concerning bills of exchange, promissory notes, and other negotiable instruments.
2. Claims in *rem* against ships, freight, or cargo.
3. Seizure of any property.
4. Actions between lessors and lessees with respect to the entering into or giving up possession, or the use, or occupation, or repairing, of any dwelling-house or other building or of any part of a dwelling-house, or other building, or in respect to the detention of a lessee's furniture or effects by a lessor.
5. Claims for aliment.
6. Claims to obtain the giving of security.
7. Matters relating to continuation of the construction of a building already commenced.
8. Claims or matters other than those mentioned above which in the opinion of the judge of a Local Court, or in the opinion of the vacation division, or the president of such division as the Civil Code of Procedure may provide for, are of a sufficiently urgent nature to justify their being immediately proceeded with.

CXXIX. The vacation shall not suspend criminal proceedings, non-contentious proceedings, execution of judgments, proceedings in bankruptcy, and those proceedings which by the Civil Code of Procedure may be conducted in a summary manner.

CXXX. In the collegiate Courts one or more divisions, to be called vacation divisions, shall be constituted to transact business during the vacation.

The composition of such division or divisions shall be determined by the president of the Court before the commencement of the vacation. Article XXIII. shall also be applied to such divisions.

Chapter VI.—Judicial Co-operation.

CXXXI. The Courts shall render each other legal assistance as provided for by the Codes of Procedure or by special law.

Such legal assistance shall, except when otherwise provided for by law, be rendered by the Local Court of the place where the business in question is required to be transacted.

CXXXII. Public procurators' offices shall similarly render each other legal assistance in the transaction of business required to be done within their respective territorial jurisdiction.

CXXXIII. Court Clerks' bureaux shall also render each other legal assistance in matters coming either within their own competency, or within the competency of the process servers under their orders.

Part IV.—Judicial Administrative Duties and Power of Supervision.

CXXXIV. The presidents of the collegiate courts, judges of local courts, and the public procurator-general, chief public procurators and heads procurators shall be the officials through whom the Minister of Justice shall perform the judicial administrative duties.

CXXXV. The exercise of the judicial administrative power of supervision shall be accomplished in accordance with the following provisions :—

1. The Minister of Justice shall have supervision over every court and public procurators' office.

2. The president of the Supreme Court shall have supervision over his court.

3. The presidents of the Appeal Courts shall have supervision over their courts and the inferior courts within the respective territorial jurisdiction of their courts.

4. The presidents of the Districts Courts shall have supervision over their courts or branch divisions of the courts, and the Local Courts within the respective territorial jurisdiction of their courts.

5. The single judges, or superintending judges, of the Local Courts shall have supervision over the clerks and process servers belonging to their courts.

6. The public procurator-general shall have supervision over his office and over the inferior public procurators' offices.

7. The chief public procurators shall have supervision over their offices, and the public procurators' offices, within the respective territorial jurisdiction of the Appeal Courts to which their offices are attached.

8. The head public procurators shall have supervision over their offices, and the public procurators' offices within the respective territorial jurisdiction of the District Courts to which their offices are attached.

CXXXVI. The power of supervision mentioned in the preceding Article shall include the following matters :—

1. To draw the attention of officials to any business that has been improperly or insufficiently transacted, and to instruct them to transact it in a proper manner.

2. To warn officials for any conduct unbecoming their position, whether in the discharge of their official duties or not ; but before giving such warning the official must have had the opportunity of offering an explanation.

CXXXVII. The officials mentioned in Articles XVIII. and LXXXIV. shall be included in the officials over whom supervision is to be exercised by virtue of Article CXXXV.

CXXXVIII. When Article CXXXVI. cannot be applied to any official of the courts or public procurators' offices, who fails to properly discharge his duties, or whose conduct is unbecoming to his position, he shall be prosecuted according to the Disciplinary Law.

CXXXIX. The judicial administrative duties and power of supervision mentioned in the preceding Articles shall not be made use of to procure satisfaction from a judge or public procurator, of any claim brought against him, for anything done by him in his official or any other capacity.

CXL. Complaints made against the manner in which judicial business is transacted, and more particularly those against the manner in which any business is transacted or against delay in transacting it, or refusal to transact it, shall be dealt with under the judicial administrative duties and power of supervision mentioned in this Part.

CLXI. The courts and public procurators' offices shall, when required by the Minister of Justice, or by the judge or public procurator having the power of supervision over them, give their opinion on any matter of a legal nature, or which concerns judicial administration.

CLXII. In a civil action brought against the judicial authorities, the public procurators' office of the court in which such action is brought, shall represent such authorities.

CXLIII. The provision of the preceding Articles mentioned in this Part shall not affect or limit the judicial power of the judges when acting judicially.

J.W.M., 1890, Feb. 22, pp. 188-92.

9. Regulations for Carrying out the Law for the Constitution of the Courts of Justice.

(Law No. 22. March 18, 1890.)

I. Under the Law for the Constitution of the Courts of Justice existing Peace Courts will become Local Courts, Courts of First Instance will become District Courts, and the present Appeal Courts and the Supreme Court will continue under the same titles.

II. Public Procurators' offices of Courts of First Instance will become Public Procurators' offices of Districts Courts under the Law for the Constitution of the Courts of Justice. Public Procurators' offices of Appeal Courts and of the Supreme Court shall remain as hitherto.

III. Changes in towns and villages which are part of the territorial jurisdiction of Local Courts will affect said jurisdiction of such Courts.

IV. Civil or criminal suits which were begun before the enforcement of the Law for the Constitution of the Courts of Justice, and which have come under Local Court jurisdiction, shall be taken up by the competent Local Court, and such decisions as have already been given shall be assumed to have emanated from a Local Court.

V. Such cases as may have begun in an Appeal Court, but in accordance with the Law for the Constitution of the Courts of Justice have been transferred to the jurisdiction of a District Court, shall be decided by such Appeal Court; and appeals laid in the Supreme Court, though devolving under the Law for the Constitution of the Courts of Justice upon an Appeal Court, shall be decided by the Supreme Court.

VI. Criminal cases begun in a Court for the trial of major crimes, prior to the enforcement of the Law for the Constitution of the Courts of Justice, shall be transferred to a competent District Court, and decisions rendered in such cases shall be regarded as having been rendered in a District Court.

VII. Civil suits against heads of rural or urban districts, Kochō or chiefs of municipalities, towns or villages, begun in Courts of First Instance prior to the enforcement of the Law for the Constitution of the Courts of Justice, shall be judged by such (District) Courts even though, under the new Law they may come within the jurisdiction of Local Courts; and civil suits brought in an Appeal Court against a Department, Prefecture, City or other office prior to the enforcement of the new Law, shall be decided by such Appeal Court.

VIII. Criminal suits raised in the *Koto-Hō-in* (High Criminal Court) prior to the enforcement of the Law for the Constitution of the Courts of Justice shall be transferred to a competent Court. Cases which ought to come before the *Koto-Hō-in* and have yet been begun in an ordinary Court, shall be similarly disposed of.

IX. The Regulations as to the Summary Trial of Contraventions, promulgated by Notification No. 31, 1885, shall not undergo any change in consequence of the enforcement of the Law for the Constitution of the Courts of Justice.

X. Laws which relate to the disposal of cases coming within the scope of the Common Code of Criminal Procedure, and the Military and Naval Codes of Criminal Procedure, Notification No. 12, 1885, shall not undergo any change in consequence of the enforcement of the Law for the Constitution of the Courts of Justice.

XI. Imperial Ordinance No. 64, 1881, shall continue in force.

When a Judge becomes temporarily unfitted to discharge his duties at a detached Local Court, the Clerk of Court may take upon himself the disposal of business connected with registry.

In localities such as Hokkaido or other islands, which are distant from Local Courts, the Minister of State for Justice may direct the heads of rural or urban districts or chief men of villages to take upon themselves the disposal of business connected with registry.

XII. In the Bonin Islands and the Seven Islands of Idzu, which are within the territorial jurisdiction of the Tōkyō District Court, civil or criminal suits which by their nature should come under the cognizance of a Local Court, or noncontentions matters, shall be disposed of by the officials of such islands until a District Court is opened. The procedure of a criminal suit, however, may be regulated according to convenience.

XIII. In Okinawa Prefecture civil or criminal suits which by their nature should come under the cognizance of a Local or District Court, or non contentious matters, shall be disposed of by the officials of that Prefecture. Such cases, however, as may come within the jurisdiction of an Appeal Court shall be dealt with by the Nagasaki Appeal Court.

XIV. Notifications No. 16 and 41, 1882, Notification No. 42, 1885, which refer to the trial of prisoners in the penitentiaries of Kabato, Sorachi, and Kushiro, who commit offences of the nature of or below misdemeanours, shall continue in force.

The trials referred to in the preceding paragraph shall be regarded as having taken place at a District Court.

XV. Regulations concerning trials by Consuls in China and Korea, Imperial Ordinance No. 31, 1888, shall not undergo any change in consequence of the enforcement of the Law for the Constitution of the Courts of Justice.

XVI. Judges or Public Procurators who hold office at the date of enforcement of the Law for Constitution of the Courts of Justice, need not possess the qualifications mentioned in Part II, Chapter I of the said Law.

XVII. Clerks who hold office at the date of enforcement of the Law for the Constitution of the Courts of Justice, need not possess the qualifications mentioned in Article LXXXIX, Part II Chapter IV, of the said Law.

XVIII. During three years subsequent to the date of enforcement of the Law for the Constitution of the Courts of Justice, the Minister of State for Justice may reduce the period of service of probationers to one year and a half, and those that have been appointed probationers under the Regulations for the Examination of Judges, Ordinance of the Daijōkwan, No. 102, and the Regulations for the Examination of Civil Officers, may be appointed Judges or Public Procurators without being required to pass a second examination.

XIX. During one year after the date of enforcement of the Law for the Constitution of the Courts of Justice, the Minister of State for Justice may fill offices, irrespective of the provisions of Articles LXIX and LXX, Part II, Chapter II, of the said Law.

XX. During one year after the date of enforcement of the Law for the Constitution of the Courts of Justice, officials who have held the office of Judge or Public Procurator, of Councillor or Assistant Councillor of the Sanji-in, or have been higher officials (excepting in the Accountants' Bureau) of the Judicial Department for three years or over, may be appointed Judges or Public Procurators.

XXI. Articles LXXIV. and LXXV. Part II, Chapter II, of the Law for the Constitution of the Courts of Justice, shall be applicable to Public Procurators.

J.W.M., Mar. 29, 1890, p. 330.

10. PENSION REGULATIONS.

(Law No. 43, June 20, 1890.)

I. Officials of or above *hannin* rank have the right to receive pensions under this Law, when they retire from office.

II. Officials who have been in office above fifteen years may receive life pensions subject to the following conditions :—

1. That they are permitted to retire after attaining sixty years of age.

2. That they are permitted to retire on account of wounds or sickness.

3. That they retire from office in consequence of the abolition of such office or department, or the increase or decrease of official business, or the termination of the term of hishoku (seconded list).

III. Officials who come under any of the following conditions will receive their pensions and may be granted additional pensions up to seven-tenths of the minimum sum of such pension, though the years of service may not amount to the term provided in the last article :—

1. That they have retired from office having lost the use of more than one member of the body or sustained some other like misfortune from wounds received in the discharge of their official business.

2. That they have retired from office in consequence of the loss of the use of more than one member of the body, or sustained some similar misfortune on account of sickness contracted while in the discharge of their duty.

IV. Should any Minister of State retire from office after a

term of service of more than three years, a pension will be given without respect to the limitations of Article II.

V. The annual amount of each pension will be decided in accordance with the salary of the official at the time he retires, and with the length of his service. The amount in the case of those who retire from office after service of more than fifteen years and less than sixty years, will be sixty two-hundred-and-fortieths $(\frac{60}{240})$ of their yearly salary, to which one two-hundred-and-fortieth $(\frac{1}{240})$ will be added for each full year after fifteen years up to forty years ; pensions being reckoned at forty years for those whose service has been more than forty years, and at fifteen years for those whose service has been less than fifteen years.

The pensions of officials who retire in consequence of the expiry of the term of hishoku, will be calculated on the basis of the salary they were receiving when they were put on the hishoku list.

Additional salaries received by officials who hold additional appointments will not be taken into account in fixing the amount of their pensions.

In calculating pensions each fraction of a *yen* shall be reckoned as one *yen*.

VI. When injuries or sickness received or contracted in the public service become worse after retirement, whether the official has received a pension or not, a reasonable amount of pension will, after investigation, be granted in respect of the same, if the fact be announced to the authorities with full information within the following periods :—

1. Two years after retirement in the case of these who have lost the use of one limb, or sustained a like injury.
2. Three years after retirement in the case of those who have lost one limb, or the use of two limbs, or have become totally blind, or have lost two limbs, or have sustained like injuries.

VII. In the case of officials above *hannin* rank the term of service will be reckoned from the month in which they are appointed to the month in which they retire.

In the case of officials who were appointed prior to August, 1871, the term of service shall be reckoned from that month, but when such officials retire, a sum of money representing half the monthly salary attaching to their offices in August, 1871, will be given for each year of service prior to July, 1871.

VIII. The following periods (months and days) shall be included in reckoning an official's term of office :—

1. Months of shuts'shikwan in the case of officials above *hannin* rank.

2. Days spent in service with the colours in the case of those military officials who have been appointed to civil offices, or those military officials who, having retired from service with the colours without receiving pensions, have been appointed to civil offices.

3. Periods spent in active service.

4. Months of hishoku or kyushoku.

5. Months of service in former offices in the case of officials reappointed after retirement.

6. Months of service in offices above *hannin* rank in the Household Department by officials who have been transferred from that Department to civil offices, or who after retirement from the Imperial Household Department have been appointed to civil offices.

IX. The following periods (months and days) shall not be included in reckoning an official's term of service.

1. Months of service as a minor (under the age of 20).

2. Months of service as a probationer for a higher civil office or an office of *hannin* rank.

3. Months of service in an office the salary attaching to which is not paid by the government—except in the case of clerks of rural or urban districts ; and months of service in an office where an official may engage in trade.

4. Months of service as goyogakari, employee, togwai, shuts'shi, and kiushi.

5. Days which would be reckoned under the Law as to Soldiers' Pensions, Article VIII., 2.

6. Months of former service in the case of an official who has been reappointed after retiring for his own convenience,

or after being removed by way of correction by criminal judgment.

X. In the case of civil officials who have been on active service, the period of such service shall be reckoned additionally, in accordance with the method of computation laid down in the Law as to Soldiers' Pensions.

XI. In the case of officials who are in receipt of pensions, but who are reappointed and again retire after service of over one year, pensions will be given under the following conditions :—

1. Should the salaries attached to the former office and to the latter office differ, the two terms will be added, and a pension given on the basis of the larger salary.

2. Should the salaries be equal, the pension shall be increased in accordance with the aggregate terms of service, but in the case of those who at the outset received pensions for less than fifteen years' service, no increase will be allowed unless the aggregate term of service is over sixteen years.

XII. Should a pensioner be punished for a grave offence (juzai) or lose status as a Japanese subject, the pension shall be stopped. Pensions shall also be stopped under the following conditions :—

1. When a pensioner again becomes the recipient of a government salary by being appointed to an office above *hannin* rank. The rule shall not apply, however, should such office allow of trade being engaged in.

2. When a pensioner's public rights are suspended.

XIII. When an official retires from office for his own convenience before his sixtieth year, or is removed by way of correction or criminal judgment, he shall lose his right to a pension.

Officials who retire from office in order to become members of any assembly established by law shall not lose their right to a pension.

XIV. Officials who do not receive salaries from the government, who may carry on trade, or who are probationers for higher civil offices or offices of *hannin* rank, shall not have any right to a pension. Clerks of urban and rural districts, however, are excepted.

Officials who may engage in trade, and probationers for higher civil office, or offices of *hannin* rank (as mentioned in Article III. of this Law), may in case of injury or sickness sustained or contracted in the public service, be granted during life a pension equal to one-fourth of their salary at the time they retired or were removed or dismissed from their office.

XV. The term during which a pension is to be paid shall be reckoned from the month of retirement to the month of death.

XVI The right to a pension shall lapse if not claimed within three months after it has begun to operate.

XVII. The granting of pensions shall be decided by the Minister President of State, after due investigation by the Pension Bureau, and on certificates by the chiefs of the respective offices or departments.

Officials who think their rights have not been properly dealt with administratively, may within six months memorialize the Pension Bureau to that effect, and may within one year raise an action in the Administrative Court. On the following points, however, the decision of the Pension Bureau shall be final:—

1. Cause and extent of injuries or sickness.
2. As to an official's fitness to continue in the public service.

XVIII. A pension cannot be sold, transferred, mortgaged, or hypothecated, nor can it be seized as security for debt.

XIX. Persons who have received pensions under the Regulations relating to Pensions of Officials, promulgated in 1884, shall observe those Regulations. Any question however, as to the extinction or suspension of the right to a pension shall be decided in accordance with the present law.

XX. In the case of persons who retire from office before this law comes into force, pensions shall be given under the Regulations as to the Pensions of Officials (1884). The right to a pension shall, however, be regarded as relinquished should it not be claimed within three years from the date on which this law comes into force.

XXI. This law shall come into force on and after the 1st day of the 7th month of the 23rd year of Meiji (July 1st, 1890), when all former laws or decrees conflicting with this law shall be repealed.

J.W.M., 1890, June 28, p. 657.

11. REGULATIONS FOR THE PROMULGATION OF PUBLIC DOCUMENTS.

(Imp. Ord. No. 1, 1886.)

FORMS TO BE OBSERVED FOR PUBLIC DOCUMENTS.

I. LAWS AND ORDINANCES.

I. All laws and Imperial ordinances shall be promulgated with a sanction clause of His Imperial Majesty.

As to laws that require the previous deliberation of the Senate, the existing practice shall continue in force as in the past.

II. Every law and Imperial ordinance shall be drafted in the Cabinet, and in some cases, to be laid before the Cabinet, may also be prepared by any Minister of any of the respective Departments. But in all cases such drafts shall be submitted by the Minister President of State to His Majesty, that he may obtain thereto His Majesty's sanction.

III. Every law and Imperial ordinance shall receive His Majesty's Sign-manual and shall bear the Privy Seal; it shall also be dated and countersigned by the Minister President of State.

However, when a law or ordinance relates to some particular matter within the competence of some one or other of the Ministers of State, then the Minister President of State, together with the competent Minister shall countersign it.

IV. The Minister President of State and each Minister of the respective Departments are, by virtue of their functionary powers or by that of some powers specially delegated to them and within the limits of laws and Imperial ordinances, competent to issue Cabinet ordinances and Departmental ordinances for the purpose of regulating details connected with the enforcement of laws and Imperial ordinances, and for that of maintaining the public peace and order.

V. Cabinet ordinances shall be issued by the Minister President of State ; Departmental ordinances shall be issued by the Ministers of the respective Departments.

VI. Cabinet ordinances shall be dated and signed by the Minister President of State.

VII. Departmental ordinances shall be dated and signed by a Minister of one of the respective Departments.

VIII. All regulations applicable in common to every one of the government offices, shall be issued by the Minister President of State, and regulations for individual offices for the conduct of their business, by the competent Minister to whom control of the office belongs.

IX. Articles VI. and VII. shall apply to all instructions to be issued by the Minister President of State, or by a Minister of one of the respective Departments, to the officials under his control or to those under his supervision.

II. PROMULGATION.

X. Every law and ordinance shall be promulgated through the medium of the *Official Gazette*, and its operation shall be commenced on the seventh day after the arrival of the said *Gazette* at the Government offices of the cities and prefectures, counting from the fixed number of days allowed for such arrival.

The fixed number of days for the arrival of the *Official Gazette*, shall be in accordance with Notification No. 14 of the 2nd day of the 5th month of the 18th year of Meiji (1885).

XI. In case of the non-arrival of the *Official Gazette* within the fixed number of days, by effect of the elements or other unavoidable cause, the operation of the law or ordinance shall commence from the day following the one after the actual arrival of the *Gazette*.

XII. For the Hokkaido and Okinawa Prefecture, the number of days for the arrival of the *Gazette* has not been fixed. However, the operation of a law or ordinance shall commence from the day following the one of the actual arrival of the *Gazette* at the district office or the prefectural office.

For localities in an insular position the operation of a law or ordinance shall commence from the day following the one of the actual arival of the *Gazette* at the office of the district.

XIII. Articles X., XI., and XII. herein shall not apply to those laws and ordinances that contain special provision for their operation from the very day of their promulagtion or from a date specially named therein.

III. SEALS.

XIV. The Seal of State and the Privy Seal shall be in the custody of the Nai-dai-jin (Lord Keeper of the Seals).

The Seal of State or the Privy Seal shall be affixed by the Nai-dai-jin after His Majesty has set His Sign-manual.

XV. To laws and ordinances the Privy Seal shall be affixed after His Majesty has set His Sign-manual thereto.

XVI. To letters of credence, ratifications of treaties, letters of authorisation to functionaries sent abroad, to exequaturs and to patents of decoration above the fourth class, the seal of State shall be affixed after His Majesty has set His Sign-manual thereto.

Patents of decoration of the fourth class or under shall bear the Seal of State only.

XVII. Appointments of the *chokunin* rank shall be by letters patent bearing the Privy Seal ; as to those of the *sonin* rank, the Privy Seal shall be affixed to the official recommendations of such appointments.

J.W.M., 1886, Mar. 6, p. 231.

12. JAPANESE NOMENCLATURE.

CENTRAL GOVERNMENT

Seifu	The Government (generally).
Daijōkwan	The Council of State.
Sangi	Privy Councillors.
Naikaku (less formal)... ...	The Privy Council or Cabinet.
Daijō-Daijin	First Minister of State.
Sa-Daijin	Second „
U-Daijin	Third „

SECTIONS OF THE PRIVY COUNCIL

Hosei Bu	Legislative Section.
Kwaikei Bu	Finance „
Gunji Bu	War „
Naimu Bu	Home Affairs Section.
Shihō Bu	Justice „
Gwaimu Bu	Foreign Affairs Section.

SENATE

Genro-in	The Senate.
Gichō	President of the Senate.
Genro-in Kanji	Official Chief of the Senate.
Gikwan	Members of the Senate.

VARIOUS OFFICES

Shokun Kyoku	Decorations Bureau.
„ Chōkwan ...	President of the above.
Giteikwan	Councillors.
Kwaikei Kensain	Board of Audit.
„ Chō ...	President of the above.
„ Kanji ...	Official Chief of the above.

Kwaikei Kensakwan	Audit Commissioners.
Shiushikwan	National Record Office.
„ Sōsai	Keeper of National Records.
Henshiukwan	Recording Secretaries.
Shirikiyoku	Board of Adjudication.
Shirikiyoku I-incho	President of the above.
„ I-in	Members of the above.
., Shuji	Permanent Officer of the above.
Naikaku Shokikwan Kyoku.	Cabinet Secretariat.

ADMINISTRATIVE DEPARTMENTS

THE GWAIMUSHŌ

Gwaimu-shō	Department of Foreign Affairs.
Gwaimu-kyo	Minister of Foreign Affairs.
Gwaimu-tayu	Vice-Minister of Foreign Affairs.
Gwaimu-shoyu	Assistant Vice-Minister.
„ Dai-shokikwan ...	Chief Secretaries.
„ Gon-dai-shokikwan.	Assistant Chief Secretaries.
„ Shō-shokikwan ...	Secretaries.
„ Gon-shō-shokikwan	Assistant Secretaries.

(In the Department of Foreign Affairs and in the Kaita kushi there were no bureaux, properly so called, as in the other Departments. In those two offices the work was apportioned by the Chiefs ; the divisions so made were not publicly notified, and were therefore not of sufficient importance to call for enumeration here.)

THE NAIMUSHŌ

Naimu-shō	Department of Home Affairs.
Naimu-kyō...	Minister for Home Affairs.

(The titles for Vice-Ministers, etc. are the same in all cases.)

BUREAUX

Naikyoku	Private Secretariat.
Keiho-kyoku	Police Bureau.
Kwanno-kyoku	Agriculture Bureau.
Chiri-kyoku	Topographical Bureau.

Koseki-kyoku	Census Bureau.
Shaji-kyoku	Public Worship Bureau.
Doboku-kyoku	Engineering Bureau.
Yeisei-kyoku	Sanitary Bureau.
Tosho-kyoku	Press Bureau.
Hakubutsu-kyoku	Museum Bureau.
Shomu-kyoku	Miscellaneous Bureau.
Torishirabe-kyoku	Examiners' Bureau.
Sanrin-kyoku	Forests Bureau.
Kangoku-kyoku	Prisons Bureau.
Kwaikei-kyoku	Accountants' Bureau.
Chō (added to the name of an office)...	Director of a Bureau.

BUREAUX SEMI-IDEPENDENT OF THE NAIMUSHŌ

Keishi-chō	Board of Police.
Keishisokwan	Superintendent General of Police.
Yekitei-kyoku	General Post Office.
Yekitei-sokwan	Post-Master General.

THE ŌKURASHŌ

Ōkura-shō	Finance Department.
Ōkura-kyo ... ..., ...	Minister of Finance.

BUREAUX

Shoki-kyoku	Secretariat.
Gi-an „	Drafting Bureau.
Sozei „	Inland Revenue Bureau.
Kwanzei-kyoku	Customs Bureau.
Shomu „	Commerce Bureau.
Kokusai „	National Debt Bureau.
Suito „	Accountant General's Bureau.
Zohei „	Mint Bureau.
Insatsu „	Government Printing Bureau.
Johei „	Storage of Grain Bureau.
Kiroku „	Record Bureau.

Chosa-kyoku ... ... Auditor General's Bureau.
Ginko   „   ... ... Banking Bureau.

THE RIKUGUNSHŌ

Rikugun-shō ... ... War Department.
Rikugun-kyo ... ... Minister of War.

BUREAUX

Kyo Kwambo ... ... Minister's Secretariat.
Somu-kyoku ... ... Miscellaneous Business Bureau.
Jin-in   „   ... ... Staff   „
Hohei   „   ... ... Artillery   „
Kwaikei „   ... ... Military Accountants'   „
Konoye „   ... ... Imperial Guard   „
Gumba „   ... ... Military Stables   „
Kohei   „   ... ... Engineers   „
Sanbo Hombu ... ... Head Quarters Staff Office.
   „   „   Chō ... ... Chief of Staff.
Kangun Hombu   ... ... Inspector General's Office.
   „   „   „   ... ... Inspector General of the Army.
Gun-i Hombu   ... ... Army Medical Staff Office.
   „   „   „   ... ... Chief of the Army Medical Staff.
Rikugun Saibansho ... ... Army Court-Martial Office.

THE KAIGUNSHŌ

Kaigun-shō ... ... Navy Department.
Kaigun-kyo... ... ... Minister of the Navy.

BUREAUX.

Gunma-kyoku ... ... Staff Bureau.
Kwaikei „   ... ... Accountants' Bureau.
Shusen „   ... ... Dockyards   „
Suiro   „   ... ... Hydographical „
Imu   „   ... ... Medical   „
Heiki   „   ... ... Arsenals   „
Kaigun Saibansho ... ... Naval Court-Martial Office.

THE MOMBUSHŌ

Mombu-shō	... ...	Education Department.
Mombu-kyō	... ...	Minister of Education.

BUREAUX

Kwanritsu Gakumu Kyoku.		Government Schools and Colleges Bureau.
Chiho	„ „	Local Schools and Colleges Bureau.
Henshiu		Archives Bureau.
Hokoku	„	Reports and Statistics „
Kwaikei	„	Accountants' „

THE KOBUSHŌ

Kobu-shō ...	... ...	Public Works Department.
Kobu-kyoku	... ...	Minister of Public Works.

BUREAUX

Kozan-kyoku	... ...	Mines Bureau.
Tetsudo „	... ...	Railways „
Todai „	... ...	Lighthouse Bureau.
Denshin „	... ...	Telegraphs „
Kosaku „	... ...	Engineering and Manufactures Bureau.
Yeisen „	... ...	Buildings and Manufactures Bureau.
Kwaikei-kyoku ...	... ...	Accountants' and Manufactures Bureau.
Kensa „	... ...	Auditors' and Manufactures Bureau.
Soko „	... ...	Stores and Manufactures Bureau.
Shoki „	... ...	Secretariat and Manufactures Bureau.

THE SHIHŌSHŌ

Shihō-shō ...	... ...	Department of Justice.
Shihō-kyo ...	... ...	Minister of Justice.

BUREAUX

Giji-kyoku	Council Bureau.
Keiji ,, ...	Criminal Matters Bureau.
Minji ,, ...	Civil ,, ,,
Daishin-in	Supreme Court of Judicature.
Jōtō Saibansho	Superior Courts.
Saibansho	Courts (of first instance).
Kenji-kyoku	Offices of the Advocate General (in every Court).

THE KUNAISHŌ

Kunai-shō	Department of the Imperial Household.
Kunai-kyo	Minister of the Imperial Household.
Shikibu-shō...	Board of Ceremonies.
Shikibu-no-kami	Master ,,

THE KAITAKUSHI.

Kaitaku-shi...	Colonisation Department.
,, Chōkwan ...	Chief of the Colonisation Commission.

(For Bureaux in this department see note on the subject in connection with the Department of Foreign Affairs.)

OFFICIAL GRADES

Chokunin	First Grade, includes officers of the first three classes, appointed directly by the Emperor.
Sonin	Second Grade, includes officers of the 4th to 7th classes appointed by the First Minister.
Hannin	Third Grade, includes officers of the 8th to the 17th classes, appointed by Ministers of Departments, Governors or Prefects, or Chiefs of independent or semi-independent Boards, Bureaux, etc.

TERMS RELATING TO LOCAL ADMINISTRATION.

Fu	City.
Fu-chiji	Governor of a city.
Fu-chō...	Governor's Office.
Ken	Prefecture.
Ken-rei...	Prefect.
Ken-cho	Prefect's Office.
Daishokihwan ...	Secretaries.
Shōshokikwan ...	Assistant Secretaries.
Gun (kori)	Rural Division (in city or prefecture).
Gun-chō	Magistrate of the above.
Gun-yakusho ...	Magistrate's Office.
Ku	Urban Division (in city or prefecture).
Ku-chō...	Magistrate of the above.
Ku-yakusho... ...	Magistrate's Office.
Chō	Urban District within a Division either Urban or Rural.
Son	Rural District, within a Division either rural or urban.
Kuchō	Headman of a District rural or urban.
Kochō-yakusho ...	District Office, rural or urban.

LEGISLATIVE AND ADMINISTRATIVE NOTIFICATIONS AND DOCUMENTS.

Fukoku   Imperial Decree, a legislative enactment emanating from the Emperor, signed by the First Minister of State, and applicable to the empire at large—the vehicle of the most important laws.

Futatsu   Government Proclamation or Proclamation, an act of subsidiary legislation emanating from the Minister of a Department, from the Chief of an independent Board or Bureau, or from a Governor or Prefect, upon matters within the quasi-legislative powers delegated to him by the constitution, and applicable to the empire at large or the prefecture, etc. as the case may be, and having (within the limits thus ascertained) the force of law. Also a government advertisement in certain cases.

Tasshi — Notification, (1) Administrative Instruction emanating from administrative officers, from the Minister of State downwards, addressed to subordinate officers, and, though conveying an order or serving as an authorisation to them, not having the force of law; (2) Also an Administrative Decree or Order within the legal competency of an administrative officer to address to private persons, and having so far the force of law.

Shirei — Order, a direction endorsed by an administrative authority from the highest to the lowest upon any application, memorial or enquiry from a subordinate or private person.

Ho Jōrei — Statutes, Organic Laws, Standing Regulations, including only such laws or regulations as are issued under an Imperial Decree or Imperial Notification.

Kisoku — Rules or Regulations, including some issued by Imperial Decree as well as those issued by a Government Proclamation, and sometimes applied to the contents on an Instruction or Administrative Decree.

Kempaku — Memorials, addressed to the Government, or by an inferior to a superior.

Negai — Petitions, from an inferior office or officer to a superior one, or from a private person, in a matter requiring official sanction, authority or intervention.

Ukagai — Applications or Inquiries, between the same parties and relating to matters of the same nature as in the case of Petitions.

Todoke — Informations, lodged by an inferior officer or office with superiors, or by a private person.

Hokoku — Reports, Returns, Official Statements, etc.

J.W.M., 1881, March 26, pp. 335-37.

INDEX.

JAPAN STUDIES
Studies in Japanese Law
and Government

Joseph Ernest de Becker. ELEMENTS OF JAPANESE LAW. 1916.

John Carey Hall. JAPANESE FEUDAL LAW. 1911.

Hirobumi Ito. COMMENTARIES ON THE CONSTITUTION OF THE EMPIRE OF JAPAN. 1906.

Shinichi Fujii. THE ESSENTIALS OF JAPANESE CONSTITUTIONAL LAW. 1940.

Niichiro Matsunami. THE JAPANESE CONSTITUTION AND POLITICS. 1940.

Joseph Ernest de Becker (translator). ANNOTATED CIVIL CODE OF JAPAN (four volumes). 1909.

Joseph Ernest de Becker. THE PRINCIPLES AND PRACTICE OF THE CIVIL CODE OF JAPAN: A COMPLETE THEORETICAL AND PRACTICAL EXPOSITION OF THE MOTIFS OF THE JAPANESE CIVIL CODE (two volumes). 1921.

Japan Ministry of Labor. JAPAN LABOR CODE (two volumes). 1953.

Eric V. A. de Becker. SURVEY OF SOME JAPANESE TAX LAWS. 1931.

William Joseph Sebald (translator). A SELECTION OF JAPAN'S EMERGENCY LEGISLATION. 1937.

Japan Ministry of Finance. A GUIDE TO THE ECONOMIC LAWS OF JAPAN (two volumes). 1950.

Japan Ministry of Justice. THE CONSTITUTION OF JAPAN AND CRIMINAL STATUTES. 1957.

Arthur Hyde Lay. A BRIEF SKETCH OF THE HISTORY OF POLITICAL PARTIES IN JAPAN. 1902.
bound with
Kiyoshi Karl Kawakami. THE POLITICAL IDEAS OF MODERN JAPAN: AN INTERPRETATION. 1903.

Studies in Japanese History
and Civilization

John H. Wigmore and D. B. Simmons. NOTES ON LAND TENURE AND LOCAL INSTITUTIONS IN OLD JAPAN. 1891.

Richard A. Ponsonby-Fane. THE FORTUNES OF THE EMPERORS: STUDIES IN REVOLUTION, EXILE, ABDICATION, USURPATION, AND DEPOSITION IN ANCIENT JAPAN. 1978.

Richard A. Ponsonby-Fane. IMPERIAL CITIES: THE CAPITALS OF JAPAN FROM THE OLDEST TIMES UNTIL 1229. 1978.

E. Herbert Norman. ANDO SHOEKI AND THE ANATOMY OF JAPANESE FEUDALISM. 1949.

Bunyiu Nanjio (translator). A SHORT HISTORY OF THE TWELVE JAPANESE BUDDHIST SECTS. 1886.

Ekiken Kaibara. THE WAY OF CONTENTMENT *and* GREATER LEARNING FOR WOMEN. 1913.

Nakaba Yamada. GHENKO: THE MONGOL INVASION OF JAPAN. 1916.

Charles Ralph Boxer. A PORTUGUESE EMBASSY TO JAPAN (1644-1647) *and* THE EMBASSY OF CAPTAIN GONCALO DE SIQUEIRA DE SOUZA TO JAPAN IN 1644-7. 1938.

Charles Ralph Boxer. PAPERS ON PORTUGUESE, DUTCH, AND JESUIT INFLUENCES IN SIXTEENTH- AND SEVENTEENTH-CENTURY JAPAN. 1978.

Montague Paske-Smith (editor). JAPANESE TRADITIONS OF CHRISTIANITY: BEING SOME OLD TRANSLATIONS FROM THE JAPANESE, WITH BRITISH CONSULAR REPORTS OF THE PERSECUTIONS OF 1868-1872. 1930.

Kokei Tomita. A PEASANT SAGE OF JAPAN: THE LIFE AND WORK OF SONTOKU NINOMIYA. 1912.

Augustus Henry Mounsey. THE SATSUMA REBELLION: AN EPISODE OF MODERN JAPANESE HISTORY. 1879.

Roy Akagi. JAPAN'S FOREIGN RELATIONS, 1542-1936: A SHORT HISTORY. 1936.

Peter Pratt (editor). HISTORY OF JAPAN, COMPILED FROM THE RECORDS OF THE ENGLISH EAST INDIA COMPANY AT THE INSTANCE OF THE COURT OF DIRECTORS (two volumes). 1931.

Neil Skene Smith. MATERIALS ON JAPANESE SOCIAL AND ECONOMIC HISTORY: TOKUGAWA JAPAN. 1937.

Shinichi Fujii. TENNO SEIJI: DIRECT IMPERIAL RULE. 1944.

Alfred Stead (editor). JAPAN BY THE JAPANESE: A SURVEY BY ITS AUTHORITIES (two volumes). 1904.

Walter W. McLaren (editor). JAPANESE GOVERNMENT DOCUMENTS (OF THE MEIJI ERA) (two volumes). 1914.

Yoshi-aki Yamada and F. Warrington Eastlake. HEROIC JAPAN: A HISTORY OF THE WAR BETWEEN CHINA AND JAPAN. 1897.

Kengi Hamada. PRINCE ITO. 1936.

Arthur Morgan Young. THE SOCIALIST AND LABOUR MOVEMENT IN JAPAN. 1921.

Kindly direct all orders and inquiries to:

UNIVERSITY PUBLICATIONS OF AMERICA, INC.

5630 Connecticut Avenue

Washington, D.C. 20015

CHINA STUDIES
Studies in Chinese Government and Law

Joseph En-pao Wang (editor). SELECTED LEGAL DOCUMENTS OF THE PEOPLE'S REPUBLIC OF CHINA (two volumes). 1975 and 1979.

Sheng Hu. IMPERIALISM AND CHINESE POLITICS. 1955.

Jermyn Chi-hung Lynn. POLITICAL PARTIES IN CHINA. 1930.

Leang-li T'ang. INNER HISTORY OF THE CHINESE REVOLUTION. 1930.

Eu-yang Kwang. POLITICAL RECONSTRUCTION OF CHINA. 1922.

Mingchien Joshua Bau. MODERN DEMOCRACY IN CHINA. 1923.

Cho-min Wei. THE POLITICAL PRINCIPLES OF MENCIUS. 1916.

F. T. Cheng (translator). CHINESE SUPREME COURT DECISIONS RELATING TO GENERAL PRINCIPLES OF CIVIL LAW, OBLIGATIONS, AND COMMERCIAL LAW. 1923.

Kuo-cheng Wu. ANCIENT CHINESE POLITICAL THEORIES. 1928.

Republic of China. CONSTITUTION AND SUPPLEMENTARY LAWS AND DOCUMENTS OF THE REPUBLIC OF CHINA. 1924.

Marinus J. Meijer. INTRODUCTION OF MODERN CRIMINAL LAW IN CHINA. 1950.

William S. Hung. OUTLINES OF MODERN CHINESE LAW. 1934.

Yu-kon Chang, Ching-lin Hsia, James L. Chow (translators). CIVIL CODE OF THE REPUBLIC OF CHINA. 1931.

Republic of China. LAWS, ORDINANCES, REGULATIONS, AND RULES RELATING TO THE JUDICIAL ADMINISTRATION OF THE REPUBLIC OF CHINA. 1923.

V. A. Riasanovsky. CHINESE CIVIL LAW. 1938.

Min-chi'en T. Z. Tyau. CHINA'S NEW CONSTITUTION AND INTERNATIONAL PROBLEMS. 1918.

Studies in Chinese History and Civilization

Yu-chuan Chang. WANG SHOU-JEN AS A STATESMAN. 1940.

Dmitrii Pokotilov (translated by Rudolf Loewenthal). HISTORY OF THE EASTERN MONGOLS DURING THE MING DYNASTY FROM 1368 to 1631. 1947.

Ching-shan (translated by Jan J. L. Duyvendak). DIARY OF HIS EXCELLENCY CHING-SHAN: BEING A CHINESE ACCOUNT OF THE BOXER TROUBLE. 1924.

T. Theodore Wong. CHRONOLOGICAL TABLES OF THE CHINESE DYNASTIES. 1902.

Charles W. Allan. JESUITS AT THE COURT OF PEKING. 1935.

Tulisen (translated by George L. Staunton). NARRATIVE OF THE CHINESE EMBASSY TO THE KHAN OF THE TOURGOUTH TARTARS, 1712-1715. 1821.

Alexandra E. Grantham. MANCHU MONARCH: AN INTERPRETATION OF CHIA CH'ING. 1934.

Shutaro Tomimas. THE OPEN-DOOR POLICY AND THE TERRITORIAL INTEGRITY OF CHINA. 1919.

Wuncz King (editor and translator). V. K. WELLINGTON KOO'S FOREIGN POLICY: SOME SELECTED DOCUMENTS. 1931.

Rodney Y. Gilbert. THE UNEQUAL TREATIES: CHINA AND THE FOREIGNER. 1929.

Leang-li T'ang. NEW SOCIAL ORDER IN CHINA. 1936.

Percy Horace Kent. PASSING OF THE MANCHUS. 1912.

Ge-Zay Wood. THE SHANTUNG QUESTION: A STUDY IN DIPLOMACY AND WORLD POLITICS. 1922.

Alexander Ular. A RUSSO-CHINESE EMPIRE. 1904.

Chuan-hua Lowe. FACING LABOR ISSUES IN CHINA. 1934.

R. H. Tawney (introduction). AGRARIAN CHINA: SELECTED SOURCE MATERIALS FROM CHINESE AUTHORS. 1938.

Shu-hsi Hsu. ESSAYS ON THE MANCHURIAN PROBLEM. 1932.

Andrew Wilson. THE EVER-VICTORIOUS ARMY: A HISTORY OF THE CHINESE CAMPAIGN UNDER LT.-COL. C. G. GORDON AND OF THE SUPPRESSION OF THE T'AI P'ING REBELLION. 1868.

Robert K. Douglas. LI HUNG-CHANG. 1895.

Leang-li T'ang. CHINA IN REVOLT: HOW A CIVILIZATION BECAME A NATION. 1927.

Ching-lin Hsia. STUDIES IN CHINESE DIPLOMATIC HISTORY. 1925.

Helen Gay Pratt. CHINA AND HER UNFINISHED REVOLUTION. 1937.

Hiram P. Wilkinson. THE FAMILY IN CLASSICAL CHINA. 1926.

En-sai Tai. TREATY PORTS IN CHINA: A STUDY IN DIPLOMACY. 1918.

Lu-dzai Djung. HISTORY OF DEMOCRATIC EDUCATION IN MODERN CHINA. 1934.

Hsiao-tung Fei. PEASANT LIFE IN CHINA: A FIELD STUDY OF COUNTRY LIFE IN THE YANGTZE VALLEY. 1939.

Kindly direct all orders and inquiries to:

UNIVERSITY PUBLICATIONS OF AMERICA, INC.

5630 Connecticut Avenue

Washington, D.C. 20015